**State Estimates
of Outputs,
Employment,
and Payrolls,
1947, 1958, 1963**

Volume II of
Multiregional Input-Output Analysis

Edited by
Karen R. Polenske

This is the second volume in a series entitled *Multiregional Input-Output Analysis*, edited by Karen R. Polenske. Other volumes in the series contain a presentation of the complete input-output model and additional descriptions of the data assembly, as well as state estimates of 1947, 1958, and 1963 final demands; state estimates of technology and regional estimates of interregional trade flows for 1963; and 1970 and 1980 projections of final demands, outputs, and interregional trade.

State Estimates of Outputs, Employment, and Payrolls, 1947, 1958, 1963

John M. Rodgers
Jack Faucett Associates

Lexington Books
D.C. Heath and Company
Lexington, Massachusetts
Toronto   London

The data contained in this book are the result of federally supported research. They may be freely used with the customary crediting of the source.

Published simultaneously in Canada.

Printed in the United States of America.

International Standard Book Number: 0-669-73494-2.

Library of Congress Catalog Card Number: 72-5759

Table of Contents

List of Tables

Preface

The state output, employment, and payroll estimates described in this volume were compiled for use in the multiregional input-output model that has been formulated and implemented at the Harvard Economic Research Project for the Economic Development Administration, U.S. Department of Commerce. Tabulations of the state estimates for 1947, 1958, and 1963, which are contained in Appendix C, have been reconciled with the data given in the national input-output tables for the three respective years. Although the original estimates were completed in 1968, revisions to them could be made only after the 1963 table was published in November 1969. Three additional sets of data were used for the implementation of the multiregional model: base-year and projected final demands, interindustry flows, and interregional trade flows. In other volumes of this series, the methodology of constructing these estimates and the theoretical structure of the overall multiregional model are described.

Since this is the first time that United States data have been assembled for such a comprehensive, large-scale multiregional model, it seemed important to explain the exact procedures used to estimate the state data, thus providing a basis for analyzing, evaluating, and adjusting the figures. All published and unpublished sources used are cited, unless permission to do so was specifically withheld by the agency from which the information was obtained. To make the reading of this technical writing less tedious, only brief references to the sources are given in the text, followed by numbers in square brackets. The numbers refer to the complete bibliography listing provided at the end of the text.

Since March 1967, when the overall multiregional research project was officially begun, a major portion of the work has been done at the Harvard Economic Research Project. A substantial amount of the data assembly, however, was completed by the staff of Jack Faucett Associates under subcontracts with the Harvard Economic Research Project or under separate contracts: with the Office of Business Economics for the interregional trade flows and with the Office of Civil Defense and the Institute for Defense Analyses for the initial estimates of 1963 outputs. For the present volume, the 1963 outputs were revised from earlier studies completed for the Office of Civil Defense and the Institute for Defense Analyses. All of the other 1963 data and all of the 1947 and 1958 data presented in this volume were assembled for the contract with the Economic Development Administration.

The major portion of the funds for the compilation of the output, employment, and payroll estimates was provided to Jack Faucett Associates under a subcontract with the Harvard Economic Research Project as part of its general contract (#7-35212) with the Office of Economic Research of the Economic Development Administration. Additional government agencies that had become interested in the overall multiregional project supplied part of the funds to complete the revisions that were made during the last year of the contract. These agencies are the Office of Economics and Systems Analysis, Department of Transportation; the Bureau of Labor Statistics, Department of Labor; the Office of Emergency Preparedness, Executive Office of the President; the Office of Civil Defense, Department of Defense; and the Bureau of Mines, Department of the Interior.

Carolyn W. Anderson, Amy R. Kriger, and Mary M. Shirley, of the Harvard Economic Research Project staff, made final consistency checks of the tabulations presented in Appendix C. As far as possible, all of the material in this volume has been checked for accuracy. Some of the research, however, had been completed by staff members of Jack Faucett Associates who were no longer available to assist with the final revisions, either to the data or to the descriptions presented. John Rodgers and I therefore take full responsibility for any errors that may have escaped detection.

Karen R. Polenske

Acknowledgments

Statistics described in this study represent a synthesis of research performed by Jack Faucett Associates for two sponsors. Initially, 1963 state output statistics were prepared for the Institute for Defense Analyses. This work was later revised and expanded by Jack Faucett Associates for the Harvard Economic Research Project to include estimates of 1947, 1958, and 1963 outputs, employment, and payrolls.

During the course of research, numerous public agencies and private associations provided valuable statistical information. Three sources merit individual citation. Special tabulations of the Census of Manufactures for 1947 and 1958, frequently used in estimating 1947 and 1958 output, were obtained from the Economic Development Administration, U.S. Department of Commerce. The Office of Civil Defense, U.S. Department of the Army, permitted Jack Faucett Associates to use the results of prior research on manufacturing industry shipments in revising the initial estimates of 1963 output. Finally, the Office of Business Economics, U.S. Department of Commerce, provided a substantial amount of unpublished data, as well as answers to a multitude of questions about statistics used in constructing national input-output tables.

Members of our staff responsible for significant portions of statistical research include Dr. George Selivanoff, Dwight Wolkow, Milan Davinic, John Eden, Peter Kuhn, and Angela Copeland. Secretarial assistance was provided by Mary B. Whittaker, and Charlotte Levinson compiled the extensive bibliography.

John M. Rodgers
Jack Faucett Associates

List of Abbreviations

BLS   Bureau of Labor Statistics
CAO   Central Administrative Offices and Auxiliary Facilities
CBP   *County Business Patterns*
Census   Bureau of the Census, U.S. Department of Commerce
FCC   Federal Communications Commission
FG   Federal Government
FICA   Federal Insurance Contributions Act
GPCF   Gross Private Capital Formation
GSA   General Services Administration
HERP   Harvard Economic Research Project
MRIO   Multiregional Input-Output
NEXP   Net Foreign Exports
OBE   Office of Business Economics
PCE   Personal Consumption Expenditures
RED   Regional Economics Division, Office of Business Economics
SIC   Standard Industrial Classification
SLG   State and Local Government
SSA   Social Security Administration
USDA   U.S. Department of Agriculture
USDI   U.S. Department of the Interior

1 Introduction and Summary

This volume describes the estimation of state outputs, employment, and payrolls for 1947, 1958, and 1963. All of the estimates are definitionally consistent with the input-output (IO) industrial classifications formulated by the Office of Business Economics (OBE) and listed in the appendix, Table A-1. State outputs (valued in current dollars, 1958 dollars, and 1963 dollars), employment, and payroll statistics were constructed for 81 input-output industries: IO-1 through IO-79, IO-84, and IO-86.

Consistent state statistics on outputs, employment, and payrolls serve two purposes. First, they constitute a historical record for studying locational aspects of economic activity. Second, formal analyses of these data in combination with other information can be used to project future areal impacts of changes in the structure of the economy. At the Harvard Economic Research Project, the use of these statistics in the multiregional input-output model embodies both of these applications [77].

In preparing each measure, statistical detail was maintained for subcategories of input-output industries. The output data, for example, were assembled from the value of shipments of three-digit and selected four-digit Standard Industrial Classification (SIC) code manufacturing establishments and certain nonmanufacturing industries. For the present study, these disaggregated data were used to improve the accuracy of the deflated values of state outputs (constant 1958 and 1963 dollars), but they can also be used for other purposes. In other research for the multiregional project, they were employed for the adaptation of national industry input coefficients to state industry input coefficients by means of detailed state industry output weights.

As used in an input-output table, the value of output double-counts some economic activity. It includes the value of goods and services purchased from other industries, as well as the value added by employing primary factors of production (land, labor, and capital). In general, output is the sum of actual monetary transactions between producers and consumers and/or monetary values imputed to production not normally valued in the market place. The OBE defines most input-output industries on an establishment basis. Under this scheme, the output of an industry includes the value of all of its products—both primary and secondary. In the United States transactions tables, secondary products are therefore transferred to the industry that produces them as a principal activity. This transfer results in a double-count of secondary products. Secondary products are implicitly included in the state output estimates pre-

1

sented in this study, but they are not separately identified, and no attempt was
made to transfer secondary products to their primary industry as they were in
the national tables. The total value of state outputs for each industry, therefore,
is the value of establishment output, which differs from the OBE outputs by the
value of transferred secondary products.

Industrial employment statistics measure the labor used in producing goods
and services. Two types of employment statistics were constructed for each
state industry—the number of employees and the number of self-employed
individuals. In estimating the number of employees, no distinction was made
between full-time and part-time employees; that is, both types of employees
were given equal weight in the tabulations. Although an attempt was made to
determine total employment associated with state industry output, employment
in central administrative offices and auxiliary facilities (CAO) could not be
rationally allocated to specific state industries. Instead, 1958 and 1963 CAO
employment by state was estimated for only five major industry groups:
(1) mining, (2) manufacturing, (3) wholesale trade, (4) retail trade, and (5) service
industries. National CAO employment by two-digit SIC industries during 1958
and 1963 was also tabulated. Information was not available on CAO employment
during 1947.

Industrial payroll values provide a measure of the annual wage and salary
payments to employees—the cost of labor. These payments represent the bulk
of the personal income of employees. Since wages and salaries of the self-
employed cannot be distinguished from other elements of their income, such as
interest and profits (the remuneration to capital and entrepreneurs), no payroll
estimates were made for these employees.

State outputs were constructed from secondary-source data on the value of
production or closely related industry data, such as the value of industry
shipments. For the manufacturing industries, outputs were usually based upon
the value of manufacturing-industry shipments, while for the nonmanufacturing
industries, outputs were calculated from data on agricultural production, mining-
establishment shipments, service-establishment receipts, and other related data.
State outputs for each industry were adjusted (generally by proration) to the
national OBE value of industrial output. This adjustment allocated minor
elements of industry output (inventory change, rents and royalties, excise taxes,
etc.) for which separate state data were unavailable.

Payroll and employment reporting systems differ in their classification of
establishment activity, in the comprehensiveness of coverage, and in the level of
presentation of geographic and industrial detail. In order to avoid inconsistency,
an effort was made to tabulate employment and payroll data from the same
sources used in preparing output statistics. This procedure reduces possible
distortion of the relationship between output and factor inputs.

The remainder of this book describes the procedures and data sources used
in preparing the state statistics. In Chapter 2, the general estimation procedures

for the output estimates are described for both the manufacturing and non-manufacturing industries. The specific procedures used in preparing nonmanufacturing outputs are explained in Chapters 3 through 6. Industry employment and payroll measures are covered in Chapter 7. Tables C-1 through C-9 in the appendix contain the tabulations of output, employment, and payroll data by state and industry.

2

Procedures and Sources for Estimating Industrial Output by State

State outputs for 1947, 1958, and 1963 were constructed in current, 1958, and 1963 dollars for 81 industries of the OBE interindustry study. While there were minor variations in methods and sources between years, all manufacturing outputs were basically estimated from information of the values of manufacturing-establishment shipments prepared by the U.S. Department of Commerce, Bureau of the Census (hereafter referred to simply as Census). For nonmanufacturing industries, diverse procedures and data sources were used to estimate output. Unfortunately, it was not always possible to use the same sources for each annual measure. Estimates were developed from appropriate values of production, shipments, receipts, and other relevant statistics on nonmanufacturing industry output. The four sets of deflators used to convert output (valued in current dollars) to constant dollar values were assembled from data provided by the Harvard Economic Research Project (HERP) and the OBE, and from independent research undertaken by Jack Faucett Associates.

Estimation of Manufacturing Industry Output

Manufacturing outputs are defined on an establishment basis and, therefore, include receipts from primary and secondary activities performed by the various establishments. Manufacturers' excise taxes are contained in the value of output. Resales of goods purchased from other establishments without additional processing are treated as a trade activity and, as such, are converted to a net basis so that the contribution to output is measured only by the gross margin on these sales. Further, industry output includes receipts for services provided to foreigners, rents and royalties received, and receipts for research and development performed by auxiliaries and central administrative offices. As stated in Chapter 1, the state outputs assembled for this study do not adhere to the OBE procedure of doublecounting the value of secondary products by transferring these items to the industry which produces them as a principal activity.

Current dollar 1947, 1958, and 1963 input-output industry outputs were obtained by prorating national values established by the OBE in proportion to 1947, 1958, and 1963 state values of manufacturing-industry shipments. Since Alaska and Hawaii had not yet attained statehood, data for the two areas were excluded from the 1947 and 1958 statistics. Output values were, however, prepared for the District of Columbia. By combining special tabulations prepared at the Census [153] with information published by that agency for 1947 [121], 1958 [123], and 1963 [124], comprehensive sets of state three-digit SIC manufacturing industry shipments estimates were developed for the three years. The special tabulations provided shipments statistics that the Census does not normally publish because of extensive duplication of transactions resulting from intraindustry shipments. Estimates of selected four-digit industry shipments were also constructed where necessary to define input-output industries. All three- and four-digit manufacturing industries for which data were assembled are listed in the appendix, Table A-2. Shipments data were then grouped by input-output industry definition and aggregated. For each industry, the state-by-state percentage distribution of shipments data was multiplied by the national value of industry output to obtain state outputs. The national values of industry output are compared with the sum of state shipments for 1947, 1958, and 1963 in the appendix, Tables B-1, B-2, and B-3, respectively.

Because the value of shipments constitutes the major portion of the value of production, as defined for an input-output industry, the geographic distribution of shipments by state is considered a relatively good proxy of the pattern of state outputs. Minor items included in the definition of output, but excluded from the value of shipments, consist of work-in-process and finished goods inventory changes, excise taxes, and rents and royalties.

Procedures for assembling estimates of 1947, 1958, and 1963 input-output industry shipments differed slightly as a result of variations in the Census presentation of shipments data. The Census abandoned the industrial codes that it used for 1947 and published 1958 and 1963 statistics under a completely revised classification of industrial establishments. Also, in 1958 the Census initiated publication of information on the county location of manufacturing establishments.

1947 Shipments Estimates

In preparing 1947 estimates of input-output industry shipments, the published shipments data of the Census [121] and the special tabulations [153] first had to be supplemented to include data which had been withheld in order to prevent disclosure of individual establishment operations. These shipments were estimated by prorating a portion of national or regional four-digit industry shipments (1947 Census codes) to states, based on the number and employment of four-digit establishments in the state. Employment data and statistics on the number of establishments were gleaned from footnotes in the *Census of Manufactures, 1947* [121]. To obtain an estimate of state four-digit industry shipments, average shipments per employee were multiplied by state employment. The estimates were then integrated with four-digit industry data available from the Census and then checked for compatibility with shipments information on more inclusive (three-digit Census codes) industrial groups.

The industrial classification system used by the Census in 1947 differs from the 1957 SIC codes used to define input-output industries. In the second step of estimating 1947 input-output industry shipments, four-digit 1947 Census codes were therefore split, where necessary, among three-digit 1957 SIC codes, using conversion ratios developed by HERP [78]. Reclassified components were aggregated to three-digit 1957 SIC totals and finally to input-output industry totals.

1958 Shipments Estimates

Data from the *Census of Manufactures, 1958* [123] and a special Census tabulation [153] were compiled to obtain a complete set of three-digit SIC shipments estimates for use in establishing 1958 manufacturing industry state outputs. A list of state locations of three-digit industries was prepared from data published in the *Location of Manufacturing Plants, 1958* [148]. For a given two-digit SIC code reported by the Census, actual state shipments were recorded on a worksheet, along with the three-digit industry shipments corresponding to the relevant two-digit code. States lacking shipments values were determined by comparing the list of state industry locations with tabulated shipments data, and initial estimates of missing three-digit shipments were prepared.[1] To calculate these initial estimates, the average shipments per employee (derived from national industry shipments and employment data) was multiplied by the number of persons employed by the industry within the subject state. Employment data were generally obtained from *County Business Patterns, 1959* [140]. When state employment had to be estimated, a frequency distribution of the number of plants within the state, stratified by employment-size class of the plant, was used. This information was obtained from *Location of Manufacturing Plants, 1958.* By prorating the difference between the reported two-digit shipments value and the sum of actual and estimated three-digit components, initial three-digit shipments estimates were adjusted to be consistent with Census shipments statistics. The improved shipments estimates, along with actual reported shipments, were then used to estimate industry outputs.

1963 Shipments Estimates

Procedures used in establishing 1963 input-output industry shipments for states parallel the techniques used to develop 1958 shipments values. From the *Census of Manufactures, 1963* [124] and special Census tabulations [153], 1963 shipments were compiled only for SIC industries required to define input-output industries. Detail unavailable from the Census was estimated from average ship-

---

1. As in 1947, the Census withheld shipments statistics whenever disclosure would violate the privacy of individual establishments.

ments per employee, and state industry employment was calculated exclusively from frequency distributions of plants, stratified by employment-size class. This information was obtained from *Location of Manufacturing Plants, 1963* [149]. Current dollar state outputs were tabulated from these shipments estimates.

The initial 1963 current dollar state outputs had been prepared for a study submitted to the Institute for Defense Analyses [47]. Revisions of these initial estimates were made for the present study by expanding the 1963 shipments statistics to provide detail on all three-digit manufacturing industries. During this expansion, improved estimates were developed of state industry shipments withheld by the Census. Final shipments est'mates were made by averaging shipments values calculated,using two different procedures. Under one procedure,state industry employment obtained from *County Business Patterns, 1964* [141] was multiplied by average shipments per employee to obtain state industry shipments. Under the other procedure, shipments were estimated as the product of employment calculated from the frequency distributions of plants, stratified by employment-size class, and average shipments per employee. It has been shown by formal statistical analyses presented in "1963 Manufacturing Industry Shipments Estimates for Counties, SMSA's, and States " [46] that the average of these two estimates produces more accurate final estimates than the initial set of figures.

Estimation of Nonmanufacturing Industry Output

In general, current dollar 1947, 1958, and 1963 nonmanufacturing industry outputs were constructed in three steps. First, the values of major components of output for each industry were estimated for individual states. (Table 2-1 contains a list of these major components.) The general methods used to obtain the values are described below, and a more complete description of methods and data is given in Chapters 3 through 6. Second, the difference between the national value of major components of industry output and the OBE national value of total industry output was calculated, and the residual was prorated on the basis of the compiled state data. Finally, total state industry output was established by combining the state values of major industry components with the prorated value of the residual.

The development of 1947 estimates for IO-72, Hotels & lodging places; personal & repair services, except automobile repair, illustrates the method used to construct nonmanufacturing industry output estimates for states. First, state figures were obtained for the following components of industry output: (1) hotels, (2) motels, (3) personal services, and (4) miscellaneous repair services. The figures summed to a national value of $6497 million. Since the OBE valued total industry output at $7046 million, the unexplained residual ($549 million) was distributed to states in proportion to the contribution of each state to the national value for the major components of output.

When production data were not available, the values of output components were estimated by applying coefficients derived from national statistics to state data closely related to production. The most commonly used national coefficients were output/payroll or output/employment. When available, the former were used in preference to the latter, since wage differentials should reflect differences in regional productivity. These were applied to payroll and employment statistics published by the Census.

The estimation of output for IO-69, Wholesale & retail trade, provides an illustration of the use of other coefficients (relative margins) to derive values for output components. In this instance, the dollar values of gross margins for various types of distributors were established for states by using state sales data and national sales margins. Computation of imputed and actual state rental payments (see Chapter 6, IO-71) by using property inventories and an average rent per dollar of structure value also falls into this procedural category. Here, the precedent for using coefficients may be found in procedures employed in constructing national income accounts [186, p. 46].

Conceptual problems arose in allocating the output of production facilities which serve more than one state, especially telephone communication facilities and privately owned and government-owned electric power facilities. If meaningful data on capital equipment by company and by region had been available, both the inputs of labor and capital could have been weighted to make these regional allocations. This would have been desirable, since capital and labor inputs are substitutable over a significant range in production processes. Because such data were not available, the most practical solution appeared to be to allocate revenue statistics, collected on a company or agency basis, in proportion to the location of employment of the company or agency.

The residual or unexplained component of national industry output which was prorated to states is nonhomogeneous. For some industries, the unexplained element may reflect minor errors in estimating the value of major components of industry output. In other industries, it represents portions of output contained in the industry definition used by the OBE that are not specified in the "Industry Description Appendix to Input-Output Study, 1958" [183].

Several sources of potential error in the state nonmanufacturing output estimates occurred repeatedly throughout the development of components of output. These problems include: (1) incomplete state data on a given component of output, (2) the use of national proportions to approximate state values of components from factor input statistics, (3) the lack of data on state industry inventory changes, and (4) the use of data from different temporal periods to develop measures of 1947, 1958, and 1963 output. Whenever possible, measurement procedures subject to such sources of error were avoided.

Table 2-1
Major Components of Output, Nonmanufacturing Input-Output Industries

Input-Output Industry		Major Components of Output (Value of Receipts, Production, or Shipments)
No.	Title	
1	Livestock & livestock prdts.	Cattle, hogs, sheep, and lambs, dairy products, poultry products, other livestock and livestock products
2	Other agricultural prdts.	Food grains, feed crops, cotton, tobacco, vegetables, fruits and nuts, other agricultural products
3	Forestry & fishery prdts.	Forestry products, fishery products
4	Ag., for., & fish. services	Industry total only
5	Iron & ferro. ores mining	Iron ores (SIC 1011); ferroalloy ores (SIC 106)
6	Nonferrous metal ores mining	Copper ores (SIC 102); lead, zinc, gold, silver, bauxite and aluminum ores (SIC 103, 104, 105, and 108); miscellaneous metal ores (SIC 109)
7	Coal mining	Anthracite mining (SIC 11); bituminous coal and lignite mining (SIC 12)
8	Crude petro., natural gas	Crude petroleum and natural gas (SIC 1311); natural gas liquids (SIC 1321)
9	Stone & clay mining	Crushed and broken stone (SIC 142); sand and gravel (SIC 144); dimension stone, ceramic and refractory minerals, nonmetallic minerals (except fuel), miscellaneous minerals (except fuel) (SIC 141, 145, 148, and 149)
10	Chem. & fert. mineral mining	Industry total only
11	New construction	Private residential, private nonresidential, public non-highway, highway, oil and gas wells
12	Maint. & repair construction	Highway maintenance and repair, other maintenance
65	Transportation & warehousing	Railroads (SIC 40); water (SIC 44); trucking and warehousing (SIC 42); airlines (SIC 45); pipelines (SIC 46); intercity and local transit (SIC 41); transportation services (SIC 47)
66	Communications, exc. brdcast.	Industry total only
67	Radio & TV broadcasting	Industry total only

68	Elec., gas, water, & san. serv.	Private electric utilities, private gas utilities, other private utilities
69	Wholesale & retail trade	Wholesale trade (SIC 50); retail trade (SIC 52–59)
70	Finance & insurance	Banking (SIC 60); other credit agencies (SIC 61); insurance carriers (SIC 63); other financial and insurance activities (SIC 62, 64, 66, and 67)
71	Real estate & rental	Imputed rents of owner-occupied buildings, personal and government rent receipts, real estate firms (SIC 65, except 6541)
72	Hotels; repair serv., exc. auto	Hotels and motels (SIC 701); trailer parks and camps (SIC 703); personal services (SIC 72); miscellaneous repair services (SIC 76, except 7694 and 7699)
73	Business services	Title abstract companies (SIC 6541); miscellaneous business services (SIC 73, part); miscellaneous services (SIC 89 and 76, part); legal services (SIC 81)
74	Research & development	Industry total only
75	Automobile repair & services	Industry total only
76	Amusements	Motion pictures (SIC 78); amusements other than motion pictures (SIC 79); pari-mutuel receipts (SIC 9279)
77	Med., ed. serv., nonprof. org.	Industry total only
78	Federal govt. enterprises	Post office, post exchanges, all other government enterprises
79	State & local govt. enterprises	Transit services, utility services, liquor stores, all other government enterprises
84	Government industry	Federal, state, and local
86	Household industry	Industry total only

Adjustment of Output to Constant Dollars

Four sets of constant dollar state outputs were prepared: (1) 1947 outputs valued in 1958 dollars, (2) 1947 outputs valued in 1963 dollars, (3) 1958 outputs valued in 1963 dollars, and (4) 1963 outputs valued in 1958 dollars. Nonmanufacturing industry outputs for 1947 and 1958 valued in current dollars were converted to 1958 and 1963 dollar measures by applying deflator indices to components of output and then aggregating the resultant product to a state industry total. Since the OBE had previously estimated 1947 national output valued in 1958 dollars, the deflated 1947 state outputs were further adjusted by proration to agree with the OBE deflated outputs. Manufacturing industry outputs for 1947 and 1958 valued in current dollars were deflated to 1958 and 1963 dollars in two steps. First, three-digit and selected four-digit shipments by state were adjusted to national value of production figures, using ratios of production to shipments computed from national statistics. Shipments statistics differ from production statistics by the value of net inventory change, rents, royalty receipts, and other sundry items. Second, state output estimates for three-digit (four-digit) industries were converted to constant dollars using three-digit (four-digit) deflators reflecting national average price movements. The three- and four-digit SIC deflated components were then grouped and aggregated to input-output industries. Deflators were applied to total 1963 industry outputs valued in current dollars to obtain outputs valued in 1958 dollars.

The four sets of deflators were obtained by combining data from HERP, OBE, and Jack Faucett Associates. By consolidating HERP deflators [79] to the detailed industry classification used in this project, the first set of deflators, 1947 (1958 dollars), was obtained. The remaining three sets of deflators were constructed from OBE output deflators (1958 dollars) [180] and data on prices, quantities, and the value of shipments. Since the resources available for preparing deflators were limited, preference was generally given to procedures relying on OBE deflators as the principal input, unless the industry detail of OBE deflators was inadequate. The methods used in constructing deflators from the various data sources are described below and are summarized in Table 2–2.

During previous research, HERP had constructed 1947 output deflators (1958 dollars) for the 450 industries of the *1947 Interindustry Relations Study* of the Bureau of Labor Statistics (BLS) [218]. Most of the deflators used to adjust the 1947 output of manufacturing and nonmanufacturing industries to 1958 dollars were computed as weighted averages of the HERP indices, using gross value of output weights taken from the 1947 BLS input-output table.

The OBE provided gross product originating deflators (1958 dollars) for many output components of the 1958 input-output table. (Gross product originating represents the contribution of primary factors of production to total industry output.) Because the OBE deflators cover the period 1947 through 1963, this information was used to deflate 1963 outputs to 1958 prices and was also frequently used to derive 1947 (1963 dollars) deflators. The 1947

(1963 dollars) deflators were obtained as the product of relevant 1947 (1958 dollars) deflators and 1958 (1963 dollars) deflators. The formula used for linking is:

$$D = \left(\frac{P_{47}Q_{47}}{P_{58}Q_{47}}\right)\left(\frac{P_{58}Q_{63}}{P_{63}Q_{63}}\right)$$

where

D = deflator to express 1947 output in 1963 prices

P_t = price of output in period t

Q_t = quantity of output produced in period t

In the above formula, it is implicitly assumed that no significant change in the product weights occurred within an industry between time periods. While this assumption may be tenuous, the resource constraints of the project would not permit an extensive development of deflators by collecting and analyzing data on prices and quantities.

Reciprocals of the OBE 1963 (1958 dollars) deflators were used to approximate the 1958 (1963 dollars) deflators for many nonmanufacturing industries. This procedure assumes no change in product weights between 1958 and 1963.

When neither HERP nor OBE deflators were available, other procedures were used to construct deflators (see Table 2-2). For many of the nonmanufacturing industries, deflators were calculated using appropriate samples of information on prices and quantities of output. The following formula was employed in these calculations:

$$D = \frac{\displaystyle\sum_{i=1}^{n}\left(P_t^i Q_t^i\right)}{\displaystyle\sum_{i=1}^{n}\left(P_b^i Q_t^i\right)}$$

where

D = deflator to express output in year t in prices of year b

P_b^i = price of good i in base period b

Q_t^i = quantity of good i produced in period t

P_t^i = price of good i in time period t

Deflators used to adjust 1958 manufacturing sector output to 1963 dollars

Table 2-2
Principal Methods Used to Establish Output Deflators

	Input-Output Industry	Deflators			
No.	Title	1947 (1958$)	1947 (1963$)	1958 (1963$)	1963 (1958$)
1	Livestock & livestock prdts.	PQ	PQ	PQ	AP
2	Other agricultural prdts.	PQ	PQ	PQ	AP
3	Forestry & fishery prdts.	HERP	OBE(L)	PQ	OBE(O)
4	Ag., for., & fish. services	HERP	OBE(L)	OBE(R)	OBE(O)
5	Iron & ferro. ores mining	HERP	PQ	PQ	PQ
6	Nonferrous metal ores mining	HERP	PQ	PQ	PQ
7	Coal mining	HERP	PQ	PQ	PQ
8	Crude petro., natural gas	HERP	PQ	PQ	PQ
9	Stone & clay mining	HERP	PQ	PQ	PQ
10	Chem. & fert. mineral mining	HERP	PQ	PQ	PQ
11	New construction	PQ	PQ	PQ	BDSA
12	Maint. & repair construction	PQ	PQ	PQ	BDSA
13 – 64	Manufacturing sector[a]	HERP	LINK	VS-I	OBE(O)
65	Transportation & warehousing	HERP	OBE(L)	OBE(R)	OBE(P)
66	Communications, exc. brdcast.	HERP	OBE(L)	OBE(L)	OBE(P)
67	Radio & TV broadcasting	HERP	OBE(L)	OBE(L)	OBE(P)
68	Elec., gas, water & san. serv.	HERP	PQ	PQ	OBE(O)
69	Wholesale & retail trade	HERP	OBE(L)	OBE(R)	OBE(P)
70	Finance & insurance	HERP	OBE(L)	OBE(R)	OBE(P)
71	Real estate & rental	HERP	PQ	PQ	OBE(P)
72	Hotels; repair serv., exc. auto	HERP	OBE(L)	OBE(R)	OBE(P)
73	Business services	HERP	OBE(L)	OBE(R)	OBE(P)
74	Research & development	PQ	PQ	PQ	OBE(P)
75	Automobile repair & services	HERP	OBE(L)	OBE(R)	CPI
76	Amusements	HERP	OBE(L)	OBE(R)	OBE(P)
77	Med., ed. serv., nonprof. org.	HERP	OBE(L)	OBE(R)	OBE(P)
78	Federal govt. enterprises	PQ	PQ	PQ	PQ
79	State & local govt. enterprises	HERP	PQ	PQ	PQ

			OBE(L)	OBE(L)	OBE(R)	OBE(P)
84	Government industry		OBE(L)	OBE(L)	OBE(R)	OBE(P)
86	Household industry		OBE(L)	OBE(L)	OBE(R)	OBE(P)

[a]The same type of deflators were used for all manufacturing industries.

Key:

AP	=	United States Department of Agriculture index of agricultural prices received by farmers.
BDSA	=	Business and Defense Services Administration deflators for value of construction put in place.
CPI	=	Consumer price index.
HERP	=	Weighted HERP output deflators.
LINK	=	Linked industry output deflators (1947/1958-1958/1963).
OBE(L)	=	Linked OBE gross product originating deflators.
OBE(O)	=	OBE output deflators.
OBE(P)	=	OBE gross product originating deflators.
OBE(R)	=	Reciprocal of OBE 1963/1958 output deflators.
PQ	=	Output deflators computed from price and quantity statistics.
VS-I	=	Output deflators computed from value of shipments statistics and indices of production.

were calculated from Census data on three-digit manufacturing shipments and
indices of production. This procedure has considerable merit since shipments
comprise the bulk of industry output. An algebraic expression of the derivation
of these deflators is:

$$D = \left(\frac{Q_{58}P_{58}}{Q_{63}P_{63}}\right)\left(I_{58}\right) = \left(\frac{Q_{58}P_{58}}{Q_{58}P_{63}}\right)$$

where

D = deflator to express 1958 output in 1963 prices

I = Census index of 1963 production relative to 1958 production with
1963 price weights:

$$\left(\frac{Q_{63}P_{63}}{Q_{58}P_{63}}\right)$$

P_t = price of goods shipped during time period t

Q_t = quantity of goods shipped in time period t

Finally, deflators for 1947 manufacturing output in 1963 prices were calculated by linking the output deflators for 1947 output in 1958 prices with
deflators for 1958 output in 1963 prices. This procedure is similar to the linkage
of OBE deflators described above. Once again, the relative composition of
industry output between time periods is assumed to remain constant. This
assumption may not be completely warranted, but it is more plausible (because
of the short span of time between 1958 and 1963) than the assumption made in
linking OBE deflators. The algebraic expression used in linking the deflators is:

$$D = \left(\frac{P_{47}Q_{47}}{P_{58}Q_{47}}\right)\left(\frac{P_{58}Q_{58}}{P_{63}Q_{58}}\right)$$

where

D = deflator to measure 1947 output in 1963 prices

P_t = price of output in period t

Q_t = quantity of output in period t

All four sets of deflators constructed to convert current dollar outputs to
1958 and 1963 prices are presented in Table 2-3.

Table 2-3
Output Deflators

No.	Input-Output Industry — Title	1947 (1958$)	1947 (1963$)	1958 (1963$)	1963 (1958$)
1	Livestock & livestock products	0.92625	0.90566	0.99377	1.00627
2	Other agricultural products	0.82088	0.89317	1.09631	0.91215
3	Forestry & fishery products	1.48640	1.21004	0.95600	1.04602
4	Ag., for., & fish. services	1.51745	1.80847	1.12700	0.88731
5	Iron & ferro. ores mining	1.97278	1.87643	0.92640	1.07945
6	Nonferrous metal ores mining	1.11674	1.22556	0.98859	1.01154
7	Coal mining	1.39400	1.07066	0.91039	1.09843
8	Crude petro., natural gas	1.56823	1.52943	0.98601	1.01419
9	Stone & clay mining	1.36355	1.24196	1.02751	0.97323
10	Chem. & fert. mineral mining	1.47080	1.44325	0.98380	1.01647
11	New construction	1.46229	1.58477	1.10207	0.90738
12	Maint. & repair construction	1.44232	1.62230	1.08595	0.92086
13	Ordnance & accessories	1.61970	0.49640	0.71835	0.98610
14	Food & kindred products	1.07630	1.04731	0.96695	1.00758
15	Tobacco manufactures	1.35700	1.55406	1.13048	0.97037
16	Fabrics	0.90799	0.96866	1.03873	0.98864
17	Textile products	1.05143	1.04624	0.99542	1.01711
18	Apparel	0.92608	0.93947	1.01488	0.98443
19	Misc. textile products	0.81529	0.81288	0.99704	0.96260
20	Lumber & wood products	1.29462	1.26843	0.96010	0.98706
21	Wooden containers	1.21365	1.21229	0.99888	1.00690
22	Household furniture	1.27106	1.31375	1.03358	0.94960
23	Other furniture	1.62219	1.72395	1.07318	0.97162
24	Paper & allied products	1.40967	1.29811	0.97758	1.02127
25	Paperboard containers	1.28700	1.24638	0.96844	1.00780
26	Printing & publishing	1.57015	1.78208	1.13688	0.91386
27	Chemicals, selected products	1.20174	1.11837	0.92805	1.02451
28	Plastics & synthetics	1.10814	0.95590	0.86261	1.10950

Table 2-3, cont.

	Input-Output Industry	Deflators			
No.	Title	1947 (1958$)	1947 (1963$)	1958 (1963$)	1963 (1958$)
29	Drugs & cosmetics	0.92335	0.90130	0.94178	1.03831
30	Paint & allied products	1.23319	1.23133	0.99849	1.05060
31	Petroleum, related industries	1.30747	1.27203	0.97182	1.02707
32	Rubber, misc. plastics	1.45208	1.29809	0.88635	1.07884
33	Leather tanning & products	0.90779	0.99749	1.09965	0.92606
34	Footwear, leather products	1.16371	1.22959	1.04934	0.91273
35	Glass & glass products	1.72956	1.70750	0.98815	1.01789
36	Stone & clay products	1.51082	1.55203	1.02799	0.98199
37	Primary iron, steel manufacturing	1.86108	1.76303	0.95625	0.99451
38	Primary nonferrous manufacturing	1.50376	1.53402	1.02103	0.97260
39	Metal containers	1.71015	1.76901	1.04007	0.96672
40	Fabricated metal products	1.37785	1.31766	0.95223	1.02805
41	Screw machine products, etc.	1.60501	1.62267	1.01105	0.90987
42	Other fabricated metal products	1.65439	1.59843	0.96312	0.97040
43	Engines & turbines	1.70524	1.49037	0.87400	1.02260
44	Farm machinery & equipment	1.56515	1.59695	1.02032	0.91320
45	Construction machinery & equipment	1.81914	1.88032	1.00359	0.93150
46	Materials hand. mach. & equipment	1.72104	1.68242	1.02394	0.93150
47	Metalworking machinery & equipment	1.84722	2.12564	1.15072	0.89780
48	Special machinery & equipment	1.63785	1.76776	1.07932	0.92090
49	General machinery & equipment	1.68185	1.72833	1.02763	0.97020
50	Machine shop products	1.63851	1.60813	0.98146	0.98330
51	Office, computing machines	1.32101	1.40223	1.06148	0.97680
52	Service industry machines	1.32174	1.14862	0.86902	1.10460
53	Electric transmission equipment	1.56400	1.47691	0.94171	1.04661
54	Household appliances	1.19330	1.10132	0.92292	1.11310
55	Electric lighting equipment	1.61607	1.63568	1.01214	0.95390
56	Radio, TV, etc. equipment	1.11105	1.03017	0.91788	1.07132
57	Electronic components	1.33700	1.26135	0.94342	1.02310
58	Misc. electrical machinery	1.57474	1.53976	0.97779	0.97750

59	Motor vehicles, equipment	1.53738	1.48867	0.96832	0.99760
60	Aircraft & parts	1.78051	1.94014	1.08965	0.96760
61	Other transportation equipment	1.63341	1.63295	0.97098	0.98782
62	Professional, scientific instruments	1.20250	1.49927	1.47173	0.94863
63	Medical, photographic equipment	1.34732	1.33680	1.00528	0.94435
64	Misc. manufacturing	1.16520	1.17071	1.00505	0.98098
65	Transportation & warehousing	1.42638	1.58826	1.01526	0.98497
66	Communications, excluding broadcasting	1.33636	1.36831	1.04327	0.95853
67	Radio & TV broadcasting	1.33994	1.62006	1.22530	0.81613
68	Elec., gas, water & san. services	1.16087	1.22200	1.03312	0.96794
69	Wholesale & retail trade	1.27309	1.27497	1.04410	0.95777
70	Finance & insurance	1.58607	2.23440	1.13236	0.88311
71	Real estate & rental	1.56217	1.70265	1.11384	0.89779
72	Hotels; repair service, exc. auto	1.46603	1.56713	1.13217	0.88326
73	Business services	1.74731	2.21787	1.17240	0.85295
74	Research & development	1.70999	2.15417	1.25976	0.0
75	Automobile repair & services	1.48610	1.58656	1.06505	0.93892
76	Amusements	1.75143	1.69426	1.19628	0.83593
77	Med., ed. serv., nonprof. org.	1.37559	1.78507	1.18384	0.84471
78	Federal government enterprises	1.53093	1.88081	1.32447	0.75502
79	State & local government enterprises	1.49494	1.73000	1.08772	0.91936
80	Imports	0.0	0.0	0.0	0.0
81	Bus. travel, entertainment, gifts	0.0	0.0	0.0	0.0
82	Office supplies	0.0	0.0	0.0	0.0
83	Scrap & used goods	0.0	0.0	0.0	0.0
84	Government industry	1.73527	2.09862	1.21593	0.82241
85	Rest of the world industry	0.0	0.0	0.0	0.0
86	Household industry	1.34383	1.56814	1.16692	0.85696

3

Estimation of State Outputs for the Agricultural, Forestry, and Fishery Sector

Output measures for industries of the agricultural, forestry, and fishery sector were constructed according to the general procedure outlined in Chapter 2. Specific sources of data and procedures used in preparing output estimates for individual industries comprising this sector are described below. A general critique of methods and data concludes the chapter.

IO-1, Livestock and Livestock Products

OBE Definition. Output of this industry includes the following primary products: meat animals, hides, wool, mohair, cattle feed lot operations (pt. SIC 0729), poultry and eggs, butterfat and milk, and other livestock and products (horses, mules, bees, honey, beeswax, rabbits, and pedigree dogs). Also specifically included are animal workpower and manure.

Output includes the following secondary products and receipts: processed milk, farm-slaughtered meats, miscellaneous fur-bearing animals (including mink and silver foxes), and farm rental income.

A portion of the products of Industry 1 was transferred to Industry 81 for distribution. [183, p. 2]

Definition of Output

This industry is defined on a commodity basis. Output includes farm production for open-market sale, for farm inventory accumulation, and for farm home consumption. All interfarm shipments of livestock are defined as being a part of output. Imputations are made to incorporate the value of manure and animal workpower production not normally subject to market valuation. To maintain comparability with the national income accounts, certain secondary receipts were placed in this industry. These include a portion of the gross rental income of farm landlords, a portion of the imputed rental value of owner-occupied farm dwellings, and value added by farms in processing milk and slaughtering meat animals. Primary products of this industry produced by other industries are excluded from output totals.

Procedures for Estimating State Output

Current dollar measures of state industry output were constructed in three steps. First, state outputs were estimated for six major components of output: (1) cattle, (2) hogs, (3) sheep and lambs, (4) dairy products, (5) poultry products, and (6) all other livestock and livestock products. Next, the difference between the national total of these six items and the OBE industry total was calculated, the residual representing the value of other components of output for which state data were unavailable. This residual (2.3, 6.5, and 16.4 percent of industry output for 1947, 1958, and 1963, respectively) was distributed to individual states by prorating it on the basis of the data already compiled. Finally, total state industry output was estimated by summing the major components of output and the distributed residual. Table 3-1 lists the six components of output together with their national values, the OBE national industry output total, and the residual.

Most of the state output data were obtained directly from *Agricultural Statistics, 1948* [156], *1959* [157], *1963* [158], or *1966* [159], but special estimates had to be made for some components. For cattle, hogs, sheep and lambs, and dairy products, state outputs were tabulated from value of production figures published by the U.S. Department of Agriculture (USDA). Similarly, production or gross income statistics for chickens, broilers, turkeys, and eggs were combined to estimate poultry output.

Varying procedures were employed in estimating the output category "other livestock and livestock products." Note that in Table 3-1 the 1963 value of this component is substantially smaller than in the preceding periods. For 1963, this category contains only the values of interstate, interfarm meat animal shipments; wool sales; receipts of miscellaneous livestock sales reported in the *Census of Agriculture, 1964* [101]; and a proration of total farm rental

Table 3-1
IO-1, Livestock and Livestock Products (millions of dollars)

Component	1947		1958		1963	
	Value	Percent	Value	Percent	Value	Percent
Cattle	$ 3,557	15.9	$ 5,934	22.7	$ 6,490	24.5
Hogs	4,477	20.0	3,765	14.4	3,095	11.7
Sheep and lambs	289	1.3	304	1.2	241	0.9
Poultry products	3,370	15.0	3,520	13.5	3,356	12.7
Dairy products	4,964	22.2	5,101	19.6	5,144	19.4
Other livestock and livestock products	5,209	23.3	5,767	22.1	3,816	14.4
Other components	509	2.3	1,694	6.5	4,332	16.4
Industry total	$22,375	100.0	$26,085	100.0	$26,474	100.0

income. With the exception of farm rental income, these items were tabulated from *Agricultural Statistics, 1963* [158] or the *Census of Agriculture, 1964*. Rental income in 1963 was estimated in the same fashion as for 1958, described below.

For 1947 and 1958, estimates of other livestock and livestock products include wool and mohair sales (established from cash receipts data), interfarm animal shipments (intrastate, interfarm shipments, plus interstate, interfarm shipments), manure, hides, horses, mules, imputed animal workpower, bees, beeswax, honey, goats, rabbits, fur-bearing animals, and farm rental income. Total values of output of meat animals (cattle, hogs, and sheep and lambs) were used to distribute estimated national output values of manure, interfarm meat-animal shipments, and hides. Manure was valued as the cost of replacing plant nutrient in manure with commercial fertilizers. Interfarm meat-animal shipments were estimated as the product of the cost of in-shipments and a factor to account for intrastate, interfarm shipments. To estimate this factor, data were obtained from the *Census of Agriculture, 1959* [100], *Meat Animals—Farm Production Disposition and Income by States, 1955-1959* [167], and *Agricultural Statistics, 1948* [156] and *1959* [157]. The output of hides was calculated by applying the ratio between the 1955 value of farm-hide product and an estimate of cattle- and calf-hide production for 1955 to a calculated value of cattle- and calf-hide production for 1947 and 1958. To obtain the production of cattle and calf hides, the average price per cattle hide and calf hide was multiplied by the estimated number of hides sold (calculated as a fraction of the total farm slaughter plus the death loss for cattle and calves).

For 1958, state output estimates of horses, mules, and imputed animal workpower were made by distributing national values in proportion to the number of horses and mules on farms by state. For 1947, only the number of horses was used in making the distribution. The imputed value of animal workpower for 1947 and 1958 was supplied by the Farm Production Efficiency Unit of the USDA.

State farm rental income was obtained by estimating total farm rental income; splitting the total between IO-1, Livestock & livestock products, and IO-2, Other agricultural products; and distributing the national value to states using the gross rental value of all farm dwellings. Because these data were not available by state prior to 1949, the 1947 state distribution was made on the basis of the 1949 gross rental value of farm dwellings.

The total values of output of wool, mohair, manure, interfarm meat-animal shipments, hides, horses, mules, imputed animal workpower, and farm rental income by state were used as a base for distributing the national values of the remaining livestock products (about 2.0 percent of other livestock and livestock products). Output of bees, beeswax, honey, goats, rabbits, and fur-bearing animals was estimated from data on cash receipts, home consumption, price, and quantity as published by the USDA.

Adjustment of Output to Constant Dollars

Current dollar state outputs were converted to constant dollar measures as described in Chapter 2. In deflating the 1947 and 1958 outputs, the same component detail was maintained as is shown in Table 3-1.

IO-2, Other Agricultural Products

OBE Definition. Output of this industry includes the following primary products: food grains, feed grains (including pasture), cotton, tobacco, oil-bearing crops, vegetables, fruits, tree nuts, legume and grass seeds, sugar and syrup crops, miscellaneous crops (including hops, spearmint, peppermint, broomcorn, popcorn, velvetbeans, and other miscellaneous beans, seeds, fibers, roots, and herbs), and greenhouse and nursery products (including sod).
Output includes the following secondary products and receipts: forest products, dehydrated fruits and vegetables, sugar cane syrup, receipts for custom work, such as hay baling, plowing, harvesting, storage receipts by farmers under [resale] agreements, and farm rental income.
A portion of the products of Industry 2 was transferred to Industry 81 for distribution. [183, p. 2]

Definition of Output

This industry is defined on a commodity basis. Output includes farm production for open-market sale, for placement under loan with the Commodity Credit Corporation, for farm inventory accumulation, and for farm home consumption. Imputations are made to cover nonpurchased feed consumed on cattle farms and nonpurchased seed. To maintain comparability with the national income accounts, certain secondary receipts were placed by the OBE in this industry. These include a portion of the gross rental income of farm landlords, a portion of the imputed rental value of owner-occupied farm dwellings, and sundry receipts for other activities associated with agricultural production, such as on-the-farm processing and interfarm service sales.

Procedures for Estimating State Output

Current dollar measures of state industry output were constructed in three steps. First, state outputs were estimated for seven major components: (1) food grains, (2) feed crops, (3) cotton, (4) tobacco, (5) vegetables, (6) fruits and nuts, and (7) other agricultural products. Next, the difference between the national total of these seven components and the OBE industry total was calculated.

Because state data were unavailable for this residual, it was distributed to individual states by proration on the basis of the data already compiled.

Finally, total state industry output was estimated by summing the major components of output and the distributed residual. Table 3-2 lists the seven components of output, together with their national values, the OBE national industry output total, and the residual. The data were obtained from regularly published sources wherever possible. *Agricultural Statistics, 1948* [156], *1959* [157], *1963* [158], and *1966* [159] were the principal sources. For the 1963 estimates, slightly different procedures were used from those used for the 1947 and 1958 estimates.

1947 and 1958 Components of Output. For food grains, feed crops, cotton, tobacco, and fruits and nuts, state outputs were calculated by distributing national output values by related cash receipts data, published by state in *The Farm Income Situation* [164]. National output values of food grains, cotton, tobacco, and vegetables were measured by farm value of production figures, published in *Agricultural Statistics, 1948* and *1959.* For feed crops, the national output value was likewise measured by farm value of production figures, but included imputations for the value of sorghum, grain silage, and the value of pasture. The national output value of fruits and nuts was compiled mainly from farm value of production figures, but did include some cash receipts data for several minor commodities for which farm value of production figures were not available.

State outputs of other agricultural products were obtained by summing the component state outputs of oil-bearing crops, other crops, farm rental income, receipts for custom work, and the value of fuel wood. For oil-bearing crops and

Table 3-2
IO-2, Other Agricultural Products (millions of dollars)

Component	1947		1958		1963	
	Value	Percent	Value	Percent	Value	Percent
Food grains	$ 3,391	14.9	$ 2,789	12.1	$ 2,502	9.3
Feed crops	9,903	43.7	8,867	38.5	8,715	32.3
Cotton	2,295	10.1	2,123	9.2	2,785	10.3
Tobacco	918	4.0	1,040	4.5	1,353	5.0
Vegetables	1,805	8.0	1,627	7.1	1,910	7.1
Fruits and nuts	1,051	4.6	1,492	6.5	1,768	6.5
Other agricultural products	3,610	15.9	3,836	16.6	4,826	17.9
Other components	−288[a]	−1.2[a]	1,270	5.5	3,146	11.6
Industry total	$22,685	100.0	$23,044	100.0	$27,005	100.0

[a]Negative statistic includes correction for overestimates of components of output (specific areas of overestimation cannot be identified).

other crops, national values were distributed to states using state cash receipts data. The national output value of oil-bearing crops was measured by farm value of production, while that of other crops was measured by cash receipts data.

State farm rental income was obtained by estimating total farm rental income—splitting the total between IO-1, Livestock & livestock products, and IO-2, Other agricultural products—and distributing the national value to states using the gross rental value of all farm dwellings. Because these data were not available by state prior to 1949, the 1947 state distribution was made on the basis of the 1949 gross rental value of farm dwellings.

The total values of output of food grains, feed crops, cotton, tobacco, vegetables, fruits and nuts, oil-bearing crops, other crops, and farm rental income were used as a base for distributing the national values of receipts for custom work and the value of fuel wood (about 15.0 percent of other agricultural products). For custom work, the national values of receipts were estimated as a percentage of miscellaneous current farm operating expenditures. This percentage was established using data published in the *Agricultural Industrial Relations Study, 1955* [154]. For fuel wood, the national values were taken from *The Farm Income Situation* [164].

1963 Components of Output. Each of the first six components of output was obtained by aggregating state values of production for specific crops. Values of production were calculated by multiplying the average crop price (for the state) by the quantity of state production. In estimating the seventh component (other agricultural products) value of production data were supplemented by income data on nursery, greenhouse, and forestry products. Farm rental income, also included in the last major component, was obtained by splitting total state farm rental income [165] between IO-1, Livestock & livestock products, and IO-2, Other agricultural products.

Adjustment of Output to Constant Dollars

Current dollar state outputs were converted to constant dollars as described in Chapter 2. In deflating the 1947 and 1958 outputs, the same component detail was maintained as is shown in Table 3–2.

IO-3, Forestry and Fishery Products

OBE Definition. Output is defined on a commodity basis and includes raw furs, standing timber, Christmas trees, tree seeds and seedlings, gums, barks, and miscellaneous forest products, and products of fisheries. The output total for this industry includes a transfer from Industry 1 of farmers' receipts for fur-bearing animals and forest products.

A portion of the products of Industry 3 was transferred to Industry 81 for distribution. [183, pp. 2–3]

Definition of Output

Output as operationally defined for purposes of this study does not include any transfer of farmers' receipts for fur-bearing animals and forest products. Only the receipts of private enterprises which produce forestry and fishery products as their primary activity are included in the output of this industry.

Procedures for Estimating State Output

First, separate estimates of forest products and fishery products were prepared for each state. Next, the difference between the national total of these state estimates and the OBE industry total was calculated, and the residual was distributed to individual states by proration. In 1947, the proration was based solely on the value of forestry products, since the large negative residual observed in that year was attributed to an exclusion of standing timber sales from the OBE national total. For 1958 and 1963, proration of the residual was accomplished by using the value of both forestry and fishery product estimates. Finally, total state industry output was estimated by summing the state values of forestry products, fishery products, and the distributed residual (see Table 3–3). Slightly different procedures were used in estimating forestry products and fishery products for 1947, 1958, and 1963.

1947 Estimates of Forestry and Fishery Products. A national value of fishery products was obtained from statistics in *Fishery Statistics of the United States, 1965* [212]. For the calculation of the state estimates of fishery output, statistics on the volume and value of catch of commercial fisheries were tabulated

Table 3–3
IO-3, Forestry and Fishery Products (millions of dollars)

Component	1947 Value	Percent	1958 Value	Percent	1963 Value	Percent
Fishery products	$284	69.6	$358	38.8	$ 377	36.2
Forestry products	317	77.8	563	61.1	513	49.2
Other components	-193[a]	-47.4[a]	1	0.1	152	14.6
Industry total	$408	100.0	$922	100.0	$1,042	100.0

[a]Negative statistic represents exclusion of the value of standing timber sales which is omitted in the OBE industry total.

from data reported by fishing region in the *Fishery Statistics of the United States, 1947* [210]. State estimates of the value of catch were tabulated for (1) marine and coastal rivers, (2) lakes, and (3) the Mississippi River and tributaries.

The 1947 national value of catch was divided among these three fishing regions on the basis of statistics published by the U.S. Department of the Interior (USDI). State statistics on the value of catch for the marine and coastal rivers (composed of 1945 and 1947 data) served as a base for distributing the 1947 estimated national value of catch [210]. For the lakes, the state value of catch figures were compiled directly from 1947 data reported in the *Fishery Statistics of the United States, 1947* (with the exception of 1945 data reported for Lake Okeechobee). The Mississippi River and tributaries catch for the year 1931 by state was reported in the same publication. To obtain 1947 values, the 1931 figures were moved forward by the following procedure: An estimated volume of catch for 1947 was distributed to the states by the 1931 volume of catch. This series was then weighted by the ratio of value of catch to volume of catch for each state in 1931, and this weighted series served as a base for distributing the estimated 1947 national value of catch for the Mississippi River and tributaries. The 1947 state values of catch by commercial fisheries were summed for the three fishing regions. Because the 1958 value of catch by commercial fisheries constituted about 95 percent of fishery products value of output in the 1958 OBE input-output study, the 1947 commercial fisheries total was considered to be the total 1947 value of output of fishery products.

A 1947 national value of standing timber sales was estimated from data in the *Census of Agriculture, 1954* [99] and *The Farm Income Situation* [164]. This estimate of nonfarm, nonmanufacturing sales of standing timber was distributed to the states on the basis of 1953 commercial forest land area in private ownership, excluding farm and forest industry ownership.

1958 Estimates of Forestry and Fishery Products. National values of industry output components were taken from 1958 OBE input-output worksheets. For fishery products, state output was measured by the commercial value of catch reported in *Fishery Statistics of the United States, 1958* [211]. These state figures were used as a base for distributing outputs of other fishery products. For forestry products, state outputs were computed by distributing the national OBE value to the states on the basis of the 1958 value of stumpage in the United States [162].

1963 Estimates of Forestry and Fishery Products. State receipts of commercial fisheries were tabulated directly from *Fishery Statistics of the United States, 1965* [212]. For forestry products, few data exist on the receipts of private establishments engaged in the operation of timber tracts for the sole purpose of selling standing timber. It was expedient, therefore, to distribute a national estimate of forestry product output (composed of the value of standing timber, Christmas tree stumpage, gums, and other forest products) to states, based on an index of total state stumpage production. To obtain this index, the 1958 value of stumpage cut in each state was altered in proportion to the ratio of 1962 volume of stumpage cut to 1958 volume of stumpage cut. This series was then converted to a relative basis by dividing it by its national total.

Adjustment of Output to Constant Dollars

Current dollar state outputs were converted to constant dollar measures as described in Chapter 2. In deflating the 1947 and 1958 outputs, the same component detail was maintained as is shown in Table 3-3.

IO-4, Agricultural, Forestry, and Fishery Services

OBE Definition. Output is defined on an activity basis, and includes: (1) cotton ginning, fruit picking, crop dusting, custom work, and other agricultural services; (2) poultry hatching; (3) animal breeding [part of 0729]; (4) forestry services; (5) operation of fish hatcheries. Total output of this industry includes a transfer from Industrial Categories 1 and 2 of farmers' receipts for agricultural services. [183, p. 3]

Definition of Output

For purposes of this study, the output of agricultural services includes labor as well as rents earned on farm equipment, but excludes transfers from other industries of farmers' receipts from the sale of agricultural services. Only the receipts of private enterprises which provided these services as their primary activity are included in output. The receipts of SIC 0731, Horticultural services, are also not contained in the value of state output in 1947 and 1958.

Procedures for Estimating State Output

Current dollar measures of state industry output were constructed in three steps. First, state outputs were estimated for six major components of output: (1) cotton ginning, (2) custom work, (3) soil testing, (4) chick hatching, (5) turkey hatching, and (6) forest-fire protection. Next, the difference between the national total of these six components of the OBE industry total was calculated.[1]

---

1. In order to maintain consistency in the output definitions for the three years, the 1963 OBE output total given in Table 3-4 was adjusted to exclude the receipts of SIC 0731, Horticultural services.

Because state data were unavailable, the residual was distributed to individual
states by proration on the basis of the data already compiled. Finally, total state
industry output was estimated by summing the major components of output and
the distributed residual. Table 3-4 lists the six components of output, together
with their national values, the OBE national industry output total, and the
residual.

All of the national output components in Table 3-3 represent estimates,
except the value of forest-fire protection services. The output of cotton ginning
establishments and poultry hatcheries was calculated by multiplying average
prices and annual quantities. With the exception of turkey poultry production
during 1947, these figures were published in *Agricultural Statistics, 1948* [156],
1959 [157], and *1963* [158]. The number of turkey poults hatched during
1947 by commercial hatcheries was measured by taking the number of turkeys
raised on farms [156] plus a 12 percent adjustment for death loss. For custom
work, machine hire, fruit-picking and -grading expenditures, and other sundry
items, a 1955 national benchmark was indexed to 1947, 1958, and 1963 by the
value of miscellaneous current farm operating expenses less interest on non-real
estate rent. Benchmark data were obtained from the *Agricultural Industrial
Relations Study, 1955* [154]. The 1958 national value of soil testing services
was estimated from statistics published in an article by George H. Enfield in
Plant Food Review [36], while the 1963 statistic was calculated as the product
of average prices and number of tests performed, which were obtained from
another article by Enfield, "Soil Testing Gains Ground" [35]. As no data on soil

Table 3-4
IO-4, Agricultural, Forestry, and Fishery Services (millions of dollars)

Component	1947		1958		1963	
	Value	*Percent*	*Value*	*Percent*	*Value*	*Percent*
Cotton ginning	$ 86	12.2	$ 164	16.1	$ 243	21.3
Custom work, machine hire, fruit-picking and -grading, artificial insemination, cow testing, and seed certification	199	28.4	322	31.6	391	33.4
Soil testing	NA	–	1	0.1	2	1.6
Chick hatching	203	28.9	418	41.0	392	33.8
Turkey hatching	14	2.0	52	5.1	58	5.0
Forest-fire protection	2	0.3	2	0.2	NA	–
Other components	197	28.2	60	5.9	56	4.9
Industry total	$701	100.0	$1,019	100.0	$1,142[a]	100.0

[a]Excludes SIC 0731, Horticultural services, which was added to the definition of industry
output by the OBE in its 1963 table. The 1963 total given in the OBE table is $1222
million.

testing were available for 1947, no value for this service was estimated. Further, no data could be obtained for fish hatcheries for any of the years.

For 1958 and 1963, the national value of cotton ginning was distributed to states on the basis of the number of running bales of cotton ginned per state [157; 158]. These data were not available for 1947, and cotton lint production [156] was used as a substitute distribution series.

The national values of custom work, machine hire, fruit-picking and -grading expenditures, and other sundry items were distributed to states using miscellaneous current farm operating expenses. Expense data for 1947 were not available, so the 1947 state distribution was made on the basis of 1949 miscellaneous current farm operating expenses.

For 1947, no information on soil testing by state was available. The 1958 national estimate was distributed to the states with the value of custom work, machine hire, fruit-picking expenditures, and other miscellaneous items. State soil testing receipts in 1963 were calculated as the product of the number of tests performed and average prices.

State estimates for the value of chick production were derived by distributing the national values by the number of chicks hatched by commercial hatcheries. For 1958 and 1963, the values of turkey production were derived by distributing the national value by the number of turkey poults hatched by commercial hatcheries. Because this series was not available for 1947, the number of turkeys raised on farms was used to distribute the 1947 national value of turkey poults hatched by commercial hatcheries.

State estimates for the value of forest-fire protection were derived by distributing the national values by the number of acres of total forest land in 1963 [163].

Adjustment of Output to Constant Dollars

Current dollar state outputs were converted to constant dollars as described in Chapter 2. For this industry, separate component detail was not maintained in deflating 1947 and 1958 outputs.

Critique of Procedures and Data Used in Estimating State Outputs

State output estimates for industries contained in this sector are subject to several potential sources of error. First, state statistics were unavailable for certain major components of output. Regional data, for example, could not be obtained on the production of horses, mules, and other miscellaneous livestock, and there is a dearth of state information on the sales of standing timber and forestry services. A second source of error is associated with the use of state statistics related to, but not identical with, the value of output. In estimating state ouput for IO-2, Other agricultural products, the state distribution of cash receipts for several commodities was assumed to be similar to the state distribution of the farm value of production. Actually, the value of production includes inventory changes and an imputation for on-the-farm consumption, as well as cash receipts from crop sales. Another potential source of error is the use of historical or national proportions, average prices, or other sundry assumptions in estimating output. State values of interfarm meat-animal shipments, hides, manure, silage, pasture, farm rental income, and most agricultural, forestry, and fishery services were constructed under such assumptions for want of better data.

4

Estimation of State Outputs for the Mining Sector

Procedures used to estimate state outputs for the six industries comprising the mining sector were similar to the general methodology presented in Chapter 2. Further detail on data sources and estimation procedures is given below for each mining industry. A general critique of data and methods concludes the chapter.

IO-5, Iron and Ferroalloy Ores Mining

OBE Definition. This industry involves no modification of the SIC definitions. [183, p. 5]

Definition of Output

Industry output includes the value of production of both primary and secondary products of SIC 1011, Iron ores, and SIC 106, Ferroalloy ores, establishments. In addition, output contains receipts from the provision of services and from rents and royalties. Except in the case of a specific redefinition, primary shipments of this industry also produced by other industries are not included in the output total. The OBE treats the value of such shipments as transfers-in for distribution with the output of this industry.

Procedures for Estimating State Output

Current dollar measures of state industry output were constructed in three steps. First, state outputs were estimated for two major components of output: (1) SIC 1011, Iron ores, and (2) SIC 106, Ferroalloy ores. Next, the difference between the national total of these two components and the OBE industry total was calculated. Because the residual obtained represented the value of other components of output for which state data were unavailable, it was prorated to individual states on the basis of the data already compiled. Finally, total state industry output was estimated by summing the major components of output and the distributed residual. Table 4-1 lists the two components of output together with their national values, the OBE national industry total, and the residual.

Annual values of shipments published in the *1947 Minerals Yearbook* [214]

33

Table 4-1

IO-5, Iron and Ferroalloy Ores Mining (millions of dollars)

Component	1947		1958		1963	
	Value	Percent	Value	Percent	Value	Percent
SIC 1011 Iron ores	$321	90.9	$682	87.7	$762	87.2
SIC 106 Ferroalloy ores	13	3.6	111	14.4	91	10.4
Other components	19	5.5	−16[a]	−2.1[a]	21	2.4
Industry total	$353	100.0	$777	100.0	$874	100.0

[a]Negative statistic includes correction for inventory change.

provided a basis for calculating major components of state output for 1947. By distributing the national outputs of SIC 1011 and SIC 106 establishments to states in accordance with state distributions of mined-ore shipments, 1947 values of shipments were converted from a product to an establishment basis by including the value of secondary products. Further, the proration adjusted the measures to include receipts from the provision of services, from foreigners, and from rents and royalties, and to exclude the value of ore mined by establishments not included in the industry definition. Finally, the adjustment also served to convert values of shipments to values of production by allowing for inventory changes.

Annual values of shipments for establishments published in the *Census of Mineral Industries, 1958* [127] and *1963* [128] were employed as a basis for the determination of major components of output in 1958 and 1963, respectively. These shipments data contained the value of primary products, secondary products, and receipts from the provision of services. For 1958, state components were estimated by combining a pro rata distribution of receipts from foreigners and inventory changes (established using national statistics) with the value of establishment shipments for each state. For 1963, components were estimated in a similar fashion, except that state inventory data were available for a limited number of products. These data were used, where available, in preference to a pro rata distribution of inventory change.

Where the Census listed no shipments values for mineral-producing states, estimates had to be calculated by multiplying national average values of production per plant by the number of plants (classified by employment size) located in the state. When neither shipments data nor plant-location data were available, shipments were estimated by distributing the portion of industry shipments reported for relevant Census regions to states, based on state employment in that industry.

Adjustment of Output to Constant Dollars

Current dollar state outputs were converted to constant dollars as described in Chapter 2. In deflating the 1947 and 1958 outputs, the same component detail was maintained as is shown in Table 4-1.

IO-6, Nonferrous Metal Ores Mining

OBE Definition. This industry involves no modification of the SIC definitions. [183, p. 5]

Definition of Output

The industry output includes the value of production of both primary and secondary products of SIC 102, 103, 104, 105, and 109 establishments (copper, lead and zinc, gold and silver, bauxite and miscellaneous metal ores, respectively). In addition, industry output contains value added by resales, rental and royalty receipts, electric energy sales, and receipts of SIC 108, Metal mining service enterprises. Except in the case of a specific redefinition, primary shipments of this industry also produced by other industries are not included in the output total. The OBE treats the value of such shipments as transfers-in for distribution with the output of this industry.

Procedures for Estimating State Output

Current dollar measures of state industry output were constructed in three steps. First, state outputs were estimated for three major components of output: (1) copper ores; (2) lead, zinc, gold, silver, bauxite, and mining services; and (3) miscellaneous metal ores. Next, the difference between the national total of these three components and the OBE industry total was calculated. Because the residual obtained represented the value of other components of output for which state data were unavailable, it was prorated to individual states on the basis of the data already compiled. Finally, total state industry output was estimated by summing the major components of output and the distributed residual. Table 4-2 lists the three components of output together with their national values, the OBE national industry total, and the residual.

Annual shipments and production data published in the *1947 Minerals Yearbook* [214] provided a basis for calculating major components of state output in 1947. State estimates were obtained by distributing national values

Table 4–2
IO-6, Nonferrous Metal Ores Mining (millions of dollars)

Component	1947		1958		1963	
	Value	Percent	Value	Percent	Value	Percent
SIC 102 Copper ores	$264	50.8	$ 458	45.0	$ 670	52.3
SIC 103, 104, 105, and 108, combined Lead and zinc ores; gold and silver ores; bauxite and other aluminum ores; and metal mining services	248	47.6	219	21.6	250	19.5
SIC 109 Miscellaneous metal ores	8	1.4	365	35.9	355	27.7
Other components	1	0.2	-25[a]	-2.5[a]	7	0.5
Industry total	$521	100.0	$1,017	100.0	$1,282	100.0

[a]Negative statistic includes correction for inventory change.

(provided by HERP) to states in accordance with state distributions of mined-ore shipments. In this proration, the published data were converted from a product to an establishment basis by including the value of secondary products. Further, it adjusted the measures to include receipts from the provision of services, from foreigners, and from rents and royalties; value added by resales; and electric energy sales. These items represent 24 percent of total output in 1947. Finally, the adjustment also served to convert values of shipments to values of production by allowing for inventory changes, and it excluded the value of ore mined by establishments that had not been defined as being part of the industry. Where the *1947 Minerals Yearbook* listed no state production values for mineral industries, estimates had to be calculated by multiplying state quantity of production data by average prices. When neither production nor shipments data were available for states, the industry production was distributed to states within the relevant region in accordance with state employment.

Establishment data on annual values of shipments and receipts published in the *Census of Mineral Industries, 1958* [127] and *1963* [128] were employed to estimate major components of state output in 1958 and 1963, respectively. To obtain the estimates, the value of shipments by state was combined with a pro rata distribution (established using national statistics) of receipts from the provision of services, from foreigners, and from rents and royalties; value added by resales; electric energy sales; and inventory changes. The value of shipments was estimated as the residual of nonmetallic mining and quarrying (except fuel) shipments, less IO-5, Iron & ferroalloy ores mining, shipments. This procedure reduced inaccuracies resulting from the use of shipments values estimated from employment or plant-location data. Where the Census listed no shipments values for mineral-producing states, estimates had to be calculated by multiplying national average values of production per plant by the number of plants (classified by employment size class) located in the state. When neither shipments data nor plant-location data were available, shipments were estimated by distributing the portion of industry shipments reported for relevant Census regions to states, based on state employment in that industry.

Adjustment of Output to Constant Dollars

Current dollar state outputs were converted to constant dollars as described in Chapter 2. In deflating the 1947 and 1958 outputs, the same component detail was maintained as is shown in Table 4-2.

IO-7, Coal Mining

OBE Definition. This industry involves no modification of the SIC definitions. [183, p. 5]

Definition of Output

The industry output includes the value of production of both primary and secondary products of SIC 11, Anthracite mining, and SIC 12, Bituminous coal and lignite mining, establishments. In addition, industry output contains receipts from the provision of services, value added by resales, rental and royalty receipts, and electric energy sales. Except in the case of a specific redefinition, primary shipments of this industry also produced by other industries are not included in the output total. The OBE treats the value of such shipments as transfers-in for distribution with the output of this industry.

Procedures for Estimating State Output

Current dollar measures of state industry output were constructed in three steps. First, state outputs were estimated for two major components of output: (1) SIC 11, Anthracite mining, and (2) SIC 12, Bituminous coal and lignite mining. Next, the difference between the national total of these two components and the OBE industry total was calculated. Because the residual obtained represented the value of other components of output for which state data were unavailable, it was prorated to individual states on the basis of the data already compiled. Finally, total state industry output was estimated by summing the major components of output and the distributed residual. Table 4–3 lists the two components of output together with their national values, the OBE national industry total, and the residual.

Annual shipments and production data published in the *1947 Minerals Yearbook* [214] provided a basis for calculating major components of state output in 1947. To obtain the state estimates, national values (provided by HERP) were allocated to states in accordance with state distributions of mined-ore shipments. This proration converted the published data from a product to an establishment basis by including the value of secondary products. Further, it adjusted the measures to include receipts from the provision of services, from foreigners, and from rents and royalties, and to exclude the value of ore mined by establishments not included in the industry definition. Finally, the adjustment also served to convert values of shipments to values of production by allowing for inventory changes. Where the *1947 Minerals Yearbook* listed no state production values for mineral industries, estimates were made by multiplying state quantity-of-coal-production figures by average prices.

Annual values of shipments for establishments, published in the *Census of Mineral Industries, 1958* [127] and *1963* [128], were employed to estimate major components of state output in 1958 and 1963, respectively. These data included the value of primary products, secondary products, products purchased and resold without further processing, and receipts from the provision of

Table 4-3
IO-7, Coal Mining (millions of dollars)

Component	1947		1958		1963	
	Value	*Percent*	*Value*	*Percent*	*Value*	*Percent*
SIC 11	$ 417	13.5	$ 323	11.8	$ 235	8.9
SIC 12	2,620	85.1	2,425	88.2	2,398	91.1
Other components	41	1.4	1	—	1	—
Industry total	$3,078	100.0	$2,749	100.0	$2,634	100.0

services. To obtain the estimates, the value of establishment shipments for each
state was combined with a pro rata distribution of components of output not
contained in shipments data and inventory changes (established using national
statistics). Components not contained in shipments data but included in the
definition of output are receipts from the provision of services, from foreigners,
and from rents and royalties; value added by resales; and electric energy sales.
These items represent 0.03 percent of total output in 1958. Where the Census
lists no shipments values for mineral producing states, estimates were calculated
by multiplying the national average values of production per plant by the
number of plants (classified by employment size) located in the state. When
neither shipments data nor plant-location data were available, shipments were
estimated by distributing the portion of industry shipments reported for relevant
Census regions to states, based on state employment in that industry.

Adjustment of Output to Constant Dollars

Current dollar state outputs were converted to constant dollars as described
in Chapter 2. In deflating the 1947 and 1958 outputs, the same component
detail was maintained as is shown in Table 4-3.

IO-8, Crude Petroleum and Natural Gas

OBE Definition. Output includes estimated values for Census undercoverage of the Census subindustry 1312, Crude petroleum.
Output excludes, by redefinition, oil- and gas-well drilling which is
included in Industry 11.
The following products were technically indistinguishable from primary
products of other industries and were therefore transferred out for distribution: (1) LPG, naphtha, and finished gasoline to Industry 31; and (2)
selected types of natural gas to Industry 68. [183, p. 5]

Definition of Output

Output is defined to cover the receipts of all establishments classified in
SIC 1311, Crude petroleum & natural gas, and SIC 1321, Natural gas liquids, and
includes the value of production of both primary and secondary products of
these establishments. In addition, industry output contains receipts from the
provision of services, value added by resales, miscellaneous receipts, including
research and development, rental and royalty receipts, and electric energy sales.
Only the value added in processing natural gas liquids is included in output.
Because oil- and gas-field services are classified in IO-11, New construction, they

are excluded from this industry. Products similar to those of IO-8, Crude petroleum & natural gas, but produced by establishments classified in another industry, are not included in the value of output. The OBE transfers the value of such products into this industry.

Procedures for Estimating State Output

Current dollar measures of state industry output were constructed in three steps. First, state outputs were estimated for two major components of output: (1) SIC 1311, Crude petroleum & natural gas, and (2) SIC 1321, Natural gas liquids. Next, the difference between the national total of these two components and the OBE industry total was calculated. Because the residual obtained represented the value of other components of output for which state data were unavailable, it was prorated to individual states on the basis of the data already compiled. Finally, total state industry output was estimated by summing the major components of output and the distributed residual. Table 4–4 lists the two components of output together with their national values, the OBE national industry total, and the residual.

Annual shipments and production data published in the *1947 Minerals Yearbook* [214] provided a basis for calculating major components of state output in 1947. To obtain the state estimates, the national values (provided by HERP) were allocated to states in accordance with state distributions of petroleum and gas shipments. This proration converted the published data from a product to an establishment basis by including the value of secondary products, and it adjusted the measures to include receipts from the provision of services, from foreigners, from research and development activities, and from rents and royalties; value added by resales; and electric energy sales. The adjustment also served to convert values of shipments to values of production by allowing for inventory changes and to exclude mineral extraction by establishments not included in the industry definition. Where the *1947 Minerals Yearbook* lists no state production values for mineral industries, estimates were made by multiplying state quantity of production data and average national prices.

Annual values of shipments for establishments published in the *Census of Mineral Industries, 1958* [127] and *1963* [128] were employed to estimate major components of state output in 1958 and 1963, respectively. These data included the value of primary products, secondary products, products purchased and resold without further processing, and receipts from the provision of services. To obtain the estimates, the value of shipments by state was combined with a pro rata distribution of output components not contained in shipments data and inventory changes (established using national statistics). Components not included in shipments data but contained in the definition of output are receipts from foreigners, from performed research and development, and from

Table 4–4
IO-8, Crude Petroleum and Natural Gas (millions of dollars)

Component	1947		1958		1963	
	Value	Percent	Value	Percent	Value	Percent
SIC 1311 Crude petroleum and natural gas	$3,867	91.8	$8,642	89.4	$10,138	93.0
SIC 1312 Natural gas liquids	294	7.0	855	8.8	923	8.5
Other components	49	1.2	171	1.8	-161[a]	-1.5[a]
Industry total	$4,210	100.0	$9,668	100.0	$10,900	100.0

[a]Negative statistic includes correction for overestimates of components of output.

rents and royalties; value added by resales; and electric energy sales. Where the Census listed no shipments for mineral-producing states, estimates were made by multiplying the national average values of production per plant by the number of plants (classified by employment size) located in the state. When neither shipments data nor plant-location data were available, shipments were estimated by distributing the portion of industry shipments reported for relevant Census regions to states, based on state employment in that industry.

Adjustment of Output to Constant Dollars

Current dollar state outputs were converted to constant dollars as described in Chapter 2. In deflating the 1947 and 1958 outputs, the same component detail was maintained as is shown in Table 4-4.

IO-9, Stone and Clay Mining and Quarrying

OBE Definition. Output excludes, by redefinition, construction activity which is included in Industry 11.

The following products were technically indistinguishable from similar products prepared in Industry 36 and were therefore transferred to Industry 36 for distribution; prepared talc, feldspar, gypsum, and mica. [183, p. 5]

Definition of Output

Output includes the value of production of both primary and secondary products of establishments classified in SIC 141, 142, 144, 145, and 149 (stone, clay, sand, gravel, and miscellaneous minerals). In addition, industry output contains receipts from the provision of services, from by-products, and from rents and royalties; miscellaneous receipts, including special adjustments for secondary products; value added by resales; and electric energy sales. Receipts of nonmetallic mining services (except fuel) establishments, SIC 148, are also included in the value of output. Products similar to the primary products of this industry, but produced by establishments classified in other industries, are not included in output. The OBE transfers the value of these products into this industry.

Procedures for Estimating State Output

Current dollar measures of state industry output were constructed in three steps. First, state outputs were estimated for three major components of output:

(1) crushed and broken stone; (2) sand and gravel; and (3) dimension stone, clay, ceramic and refractory materials, miscellaneous nonmetallic minerals, and non-metallic mineral services. Next, the difference between the national total of these three components and the OBE industry total was calculated. Because the residual obtained represented the value of other components of output for which state data were unavailable, it was prorated to individual states on the basis of the data already compiled. Finally, total state industry output was estimated by summing the major components of output and the distributed residual. Table 4-5 lists the three components of output together with their national values, the OBE national industry total, and the residual.

Annual shipments and production data published in the *1947 Minerals Year-book* [214] provided a basis for calculating major components of state output in 1947. To obtain the state estimates, the national values (provided by HERP) were allocated to states in accordance with state distributions of stone and clay shipments. The proration (which was used to distribute approximately 10.0 percent of total output) converted the published data from a product to an establishment basis by including the value of secondary products, and it adjusted the measures to include the value of by-products, receipts from the provision of services, from foreigners, and from rents and royalties, and to exclude the value of production of establishments not included in the industry definition. The adjustment also served to convert the values of shipments to values of production by allowing for inventory changes. Where the *1947 Minerals Yearbook* listed no state production values for mineral industries, estimates were made by multiply-ing state quantity-of-production data by average prices. When neither production nor shipments data were available for states, production was estimated by distributing the portion of industry production values reported for relevant regions to states in accordance with state employment.

Establishment data on annual values of shipments and receipts published in the *Census of Mineral Industries, 1958* [127] and *1963* [128] were employed to estimate major components of state output in 1958 and 1963, respectively. To calculate the state estimates, the value of shipments was combined with a pro rata distribution (established using national statistics) of receipts from the provision of services, from foreigners, and from rents and royalties; value of by-products; value added by resales; electric energy sales; and inventory changes. IO-9, Stone & clay mining & quarrying, shipments were estimated as the residual of nonmetallic mining and quarrying (except fuel) less IO-10, Chemical & fertilizer mineral mining, shipments. This procedure reduces inaccuracies result-ing from the use of shipments values estimated from employment or plant-location data. Where the Census listed no shipments values for mineral producing states, estimates had to be made by multiplying the national average values of production per plant by the number of plants (classified by employment-size class) located in the state. When neither shipments data nor plant-location data were available, shipments were estimated by distributing the portion of industry

Table 4-5
IO-9, Stone and Clay Mining and Quarrying (millions of dollars)

Component	1947		1958		1963	
	Value	Percent	Value	Percent	Value	Percent
SIC 142 Crushed and broken stone	$247	40.9	$ 616	43.9	$ 787	44.6
SIC 144 Sand and gravel	181	30.1	555	39.5	672	38.0
SIC 141, 145, 148, and 149, combined Dimension stone; clay, ceramic and refractory minerals; nonmetallic minerals (except fuel) services; miscellaneous nonmetallic minerals (except fuels)	113	18.8	227	16.2	297	16.8
Other components	62	10.2	6	0.4	10	0.6
Industry total	$603	100.0	$1,404	100.0	$1,766	100.0

shipments reported for relevant Census regions to states, based on state employment in that industry.

Adjustment of Output to Constant Dollars

Current dollar state outputs were converted to constant dollars as described in Chapter 2. In deflating the 1947 and 1958 outputs, the same component detail was maintained as is shown in Table 4-5.

IO-10, Chemical and Fertilizer Mineral Mining

OBE Definition. The following products were technically indistinguishable from primary products of other industries and were therefore transferred out for distribution: (1) compounds of potassium, sodium, boron to Industry 27, and (2) prepared barite to Industry 36. [183, p. 5]

Definition of Output

Output includes the value of both primary and secondary products produced by establishments in SIC 147, Chemical & fertilizer mining. In addition, industry output contains receipts from the provision of services, from by-products, and from rents and royalties; value added by resales; and electric energy sales. Products similar to the primary products of this industry, but produced by establishments classified in other industries, are not included in output. The OBE transfers the value of these products into this industry.

Procedures for Estimating State Output

National values of industry shipments, components of output for which state detail was unavailable, and industry output are given in Table 4-6. For 1947, state output estimates were made by distributing the national output (provided by HERP) to states in proportion to state mined-ore shipments. Annual shipments and production data for 1947 are published in the *1947 Minerals Yearbook* [214]. The proration converted the published data from a product to an establishment basis by including the value of secondary products. Further, it adjusted the measures to include receipts from foreigners and from rents and royalties, and to exclude the value of ore mined by industries not

Table 4-6
IO-10, Chemical and Fertilizer Mineral Mining (millions of dollars)

Component	1947		1958		1963	
	Value	Percent	Value	Percent	Value	Percent
Industry shipments	$204	95.1	$465	99.1	$577	99.5
Other components	11	4.9	4	0.9	3	0.5
Industry total	$215	100.0	$469	100.0	$580	100.0

included in the industry definition. Finally, the adjustment also served to convert values of shipments to values of production by allowing for inventory changes. Where the *1947 Minerals Yearbook* listed no state production values for mineral industries, estimates were made by multiplying state quantity of production data by average prices. When neither production nor shipments data were available for states, production was estimated by distributing the portion of industry production values reported for relevant regions to states in accordance with state employment.

Annual values of shipments for establishments, published in the *Census of Mineral Industries, 1958* [127] and *1963* [128], were employed to prepare estimates of 1958 and 1963 state outputs, respectively. These data included the value of primary products, secondary products, products purchased and resold without further processing, and receipts from the provision of services. To obtain state outputs, the value of SIC 147 shipments for each state was combined with a pro rata distribution of the components of output not contained in shipments data and inventory changes. Components not contained in shipments data, but included in the definition of output, are the value of by-products, miscellaneous receipts, receipts from services to foreigners, receipts from rents and royalties, value added by resales, and electric energy sales.

Where the Census listed no shipments values for mineral-producing states, estimates were made by multiplying national average values of production per plant by the number of plants (classified by employment size) located in the state. When neither shipments data nor plant-location data were available, shipments were estimated by distributing the portion of industry shipments reported for relevant Census regions to states, based on state employment in that industry.

Adjustment of Output to Constant Dollars

Current dollar state outputs were converted to constant dollars as described in Chapter 2.

Critique of Procedures and Data Used in
Estimating State Outputs

There are three major weaknesses in the state mining industry outputs. First, state outputs were generally estimated by distributing national outputs to states, using the value of state industry shipments as a proxy. While the value of state shipments comprises a large portion of total industry output, it does include items such as inventory change, rents and royalties, and miscellaneous receipts. The proration procedure therefore assumes that the proportion of these items in each state's output will be the same as the proportion for the nation as a whole. This is certainly questionable. A second source of error results from the need to estimate the values of 1958 and/or 1963 shipments for some states, using data on the number of establishments, classified by employment size and national average shipments for each size of establishment. It is unlikely that the productivity of establishments is the same throughout the nation. Finally, the 1947 statistics on state mineral shipments were compiled on a commodity rather than an establishment basis. While the resulting estimates are generally similar to those which would be obtained from an establishment-based tabulation, differences do exist.

5 Estimation of State Outputs for the Construction Sector

Outputs of IO-11, New construction, and IO-12, Maintenance & repair construction, reflect the value created by erecting and maintaining structures and other facilities. These industries, unlike other industries listed in the input-output classification scheme, are defined on an activity basis. Methods used to estimate state outputs of new and maintenance construction are described in this chapter.

IO-11, New Construction

OBE Definition. Output is defined on an activity basis and measures the value put-in-place of private and public original erections, additions, and alterations which increase or alter the stock of facilities. New construction includes building and nonbuilding facilities, such as housing, schools, factories, highways, oil- and gas-well exploration and drilling, sewage and water systems, and other comparable outlays charged to capital account. It also includes the value of materials used in residential construction performed by households on a do-it-yourself basis.

Equipment that is an integral part of the facility and essential for its general use is included in the value of construction. Some examples are elevators, heating, plumbing and electrical fixtures. Equipment items that are not structurally part of the facility or are meant for a special rather than general use of the facility are not included in the construction value. For example, refrigerators, ranges, built-in ovens, and room air conditioners are personal consumption expenditures, and fixed conveyor lines in factories and steam tables in restaurants are producers' durable equipment.

As indicated, new construction is measured by the value put-in-place. Materials, payrolls, profits, overhead, architectural and engineering, excavation, and demolition costs directly associated with the construction project are part of the value put-in-place. The value put-in-place refers to work done during a given time period regardless of the starting and completion date of the entire construction project. In the case of the present study, only that part of a project that was worked on during calendar year 1958 would be included.

Construction covers the value of work of construction contractors (SIC 15, 16, and 17), operative builders (part of SIC 6561), and establishments performing oil- and gas-field services (SIC 138). By redefinition, it includes oil- and gas-field services that are performed in the mining industries, force-account construction done by government agencies, and nonconstruction firms with their own employees, and manufacturers' receipts from the installation of construction-type equipment. [183, pp. 5–6]

Definition of Output

The annual output of this industry does not correspond to a grouping of familiar product flows measured by conventional market transactions of individual firms. Instead, output corresponds to the value created by the building of original structures and by additions and alterations to structures which increase or change the existing stock of facilities. It includes not only the value created by construction firms, but also force-account construction by employees of nonconstruction firms, government and do-it-yourself construction, as well as the value of oil- and gas-field services performed in the mining industries. Value put-in-place is a measure of the amount of new construction installed or erected at any site during a stipulated time period.

Procedures for Estimating State Output

The value of new construction put-in-place is regularly estimated by the Census and published in *Construction Reports* [139]. Conceptually, this activity measure corresponds to the output of IO-11, New construction, except for the small portion (about 4.0 percent) of output originating with the performance of oil- and gas-field services. To estimate the value of new construction put-in-place, the Census uses three general procedures: (1) estimating the value put-in-place as the product of monthly value of work started and monthly progress coefficients; (2) obtaining construction expenditures estimates from cooperating organizations; and (3) using periodic progress reports compiled from actual observations of construction projects. Imputations are included for the value of materials used by individual households to alter or add to existing structures.

For the present study, the total cost for drilling and equipping oil and gas wells was obtained from *The National Income and Product Accounts of the United States, 1929–1965* [187] for 1947 and 1958, and from the *Census of Mineral Industries, 1963* [128] for 1963. The 1947 and 1958 statistics included both the operations of service enterprises and the drilling carried out by firms primarily engaged in extraction.

Because state output estimates could not be directly calculated from available information, components of the value of construction put-in-place were allocated to states using related measures. The various components were then tallied to obtain an estimate of the value of construction put-in-place for each state. Construction data were combined with allocations of oil- and gas-well

Table 5-1
IO-11, New Construction (millions of dollars)

Component	1947 Value	1947 Percent	1958 Value	1958 Percent	1963 Value	1963 Percent
Private residential (except farm)	$ 9,577	47.1	$19,789	37.8	$25,843	39.4
Private nonresidential	6,681	32.9	14,907	28.4	18,016	27.5
Public nonhighway	1,920	9.4	–	–	–	–
State and local government (nonhighway)	–	–	6,638	12.7	8,168	12.5
Federal government (nonhighway)	–	–	3,274	6.2	3,780	5.8
Highway (all governments)	1,307	6.4	5,545	10.6	6,948	10.6
Oil- and gas-well drilling	844	4.2	2,263	4.3	2,061	3.1
Other components	–	–	–	–	703	1.1
Industry total	$20,329	100.0	$52,416	100.0	$65,519	100.0

drilling costs to obtain a final measure of industry output.[1] For 1947, five separate categories were identified: (1) private residential (except farm), (2) private nonresidential, (3) public nonhighway, (4) highway, and (5) oil and gas wells. Estimates for 1958 and 1963 were prepared from data on the following six construction industry categories: (1) private residential, (2) private nonresidential, (3) state and local governments (nonhighway), (4) federal government (nonhighway), (5) highway (all governments), and (6) oil- and gas-well drilling. Table 5-1 lists the major components of output together with their national values and the OBE industry total.

1947 Output Estimates. The principal source of 1947 state construction data was the "State Distribution of Construction Activity, 1939-1947" [178]. To make these data correspond with revised national values of construction put-in-place, published by the U.S. Department of Commerce [139], a proration was made. The total cost of oil- and gas-well drilling, obtained from *The National Income and Product Accounts of the United States, 1929-1965* [187], was allocated to states in proportion to the total footage of wells drilled in each state as published in the *Oil and Gas Journal* [8], weighted by the average state cost per foot in 1953 as reported by the American Petroleum Institute [7].

1958 Output Estimates. Output for 1958 was calculated as the sum of six

1. In estimating state outputs for 1963, a small residual difference between the total value of major components and the OBE industry output had to be prorated.

major components of construction activity (see Table 5-1), each component
having been estimated separately.

For private construction, state values were estimated for private residential
and nonresidential. The national value of private residential construction
put-in-place was allocated in proportion to F.W. Dodge values of state residential
construction contract awards [33].

The national value of private nonresidential construction put-in-place was
distributed to states in proportion to the F.W. Dodge values of nonresidential
contracts (adjusted to exclude the values of state and local governmental nonhighway construction) [33]. For privately owned public utilities, a part of the
private nonresidential group, estimates were made by allocating the national
value of construction put-in-place in proportion to the F.W. Dodge state nonbuilding contracts from which the values of state and local highways had been
subtracted [33]. The two nonresidential estimates were combined to obtain a
private nonresidential group estimate for each state, which was adjusted pro rata
to include farm and all other private nonresidential construction.

For state and local government highway and nonhighway construction, the
national totals were distributed to states on the basis of state and local government capital outlays for these items. Capital outlay data were obtained from
Governmental Finances in 1958 [145] and *1959* [146] for the fiscal years
1958 and 1959 and averaged to approximate the calendar year 1958. To the
state and local government highway construction estimates were added estimates
of federal highway construction. These were obtained by distributing the total
value of federal highway construction to states in proportion to conservation and
development expenditures, since most federal highway construction occurs in
federal parks and forests.

The remaining total federal construction expenditures were estimated by
allocating national values of several categories of federal construction to the
states. For federal residential construction, the national value was allocated
proportionally to private residential construction estimates by state. Federal
nonresidential construction was divided into two groups: known General Services
Administration (GSA) contracts and other nonresidential construction. The GSA
components were compiled by state from contract data [75]; other nonresidential construction was distributed to states in proportion to the private nonresidential construction estimates described above. For military construction,
the distribution was made in proportion to the F.W. Dodge nonbuilding contracts awarded by state. Conservation and development were distributed in
proportion to data on appropriations for construction by state available from
the Army Corps of Engineers [173] and the Bureau of Reclamation [209].
"All other" federal construction was distributed in proportion to the total of
the previously estimated federal construction categories.

For oil- and gas-well drilling, the national value obtained from the national accounts was distributed in proportion to the costs of drilling and equipping wells by state, reported in the *Census of Mineral Industries, 1958* [127].

1963 Output Estimates. For state and local government construction (excluding highways), highway construction, and oil- and gas-well drilling, the 1963 state estimates were prepared in the same manner as were the 1958 estimates of these components. Estimation procedures for the other major components of 1963 output differed somewhat from those used for the 1958 outputs. Private housing building permit values, obtained from *Construction Reports—Building Permits, 1964* [147], were used to distribute the value of private residential construction put-in-place, while values of private nonresidential permits were used to allocate the value of private nonresidential construction put-in-place to states.

The 1963 national estimate of federal construction was distributed to states, using a composite series of the value of federal construction projects. For federal residential and nonresidential construction, the values of construction put-in-place were distributed to the states using 1963 GSA contract awards [76], Atomic Energy Commission data on changes in the value of its plant and equipment [98], and National Aeronautics and Space Administration statistics on construction disbursements [88]. Military construction by state was calculated from appropriations data for fiscal 1962 [197]. Finally, conservation and development construction allocations were made using data collected by the Bureau of Reclamation [208], the Corps of Engineers [172], the Tennessee Valley Authority [96], and the Bonneville Power Administration.

Adjustment of Output to Constant Dollars

Current dollar state outputs were converted to constant dollars as described in Chapter 2. In deflating the 1947 and 1958 outputs, the same component detail was maintained as is shown in Table 5-1.

IO-12, Maintenance and Repair Construction

OBE Definition. Output is defined on an activity basis and includes the upkeep and restoration of existing facilities, the costs of which are charged to current expense. It also includes an estimated value of materials used in residential maintenance performed by households on a do-it-yourself basis.

Total output includes, by redefinition, the maintenance construction activity performed by other industries; i.e., maintenance by government agencies or nonconstruction firms with their own (force-account) employees. [183, pp. 6–7]

Definition of Output

The value of maintenance and repair construction output does not correspond to familiar product flows measured by production data of individual
enterprises. Rather, output is defined on an activity basis to include the value
created by any economic sector in maintaining or restoring the existing stock of
facilities. Within the definition of the industry output are included the activities
of construction firms, nonconstruction firms, and individual households. A
substantial part of output is not reflected in market transactions, but is imputed
or reflected in bookkeeping values.

Procedures for Estimating State Output

For 1947, national values of maintenance and repair expenditures were
obtained from *Construction Volume and Costs, 1915-1964* [220]. For 1958
and 1963, national values were published by the Business and Defense Services
Administration in *Construction Review* [177]. These national values include an
imputation of materials used by households for residential maintenance as well
as those used in the maintenance construction activity performed by nonconstruction industries and by governments.
    Although state data corresponding to the output of this industry do not
exist, realistic approximations of maintenance and repair expenditures for local
areas could be constructed using a simple technique. Maintenance and repair
activities are related to the stock of facilities existing in any locale. If the facilities in any area are assumed to have an age distribution and functional composition similar to those of the national stock of structures, then an estimate of local
output may be obtained as the product of the quantity of facilities and the
national average maintenance expenditure per unit. The quantity of stock is best
measured by the market value of existing structures, which can be obtained by
state for 1956 and 1961 from the *Census of Governments, 1957* [118] and *1962*
[113]. Since the market value of property in 1947 was not available, the 1956
series was used in estimating 1947 maintenance expenditures as well as 1958
expenditures, and the 1961 values were employed in preparing 1963 estimates.
To compute the national average maintenance expenditure per unit of stock, the
national values of maintenance expenditures were divided by the total market
value of the national property inventory.
    A portion of industry output consists of highway repairs. Because replace-
ment costs, which could serve as an adequate measure of the stock of highways,
were not readily available, the highway facilities located in a state were measured
by mileage. State maintenance and repair costs were then estimated as the
product of state highway mileage and the national average maintenance expenditure per mile of road. Highway mileage statistics were obtained from *Highway
Statistics* [176].

Table 5-2
IO-12, Maintenance and Repair Construction (millions of dollars)

Component	1947 Value	1947 Percent	1958 Value	1958 Percent	1963 Value	1963 Percent
Highway maintenance and repair	$1,074	11.9	$ 2,327	13.8	$ 2,937	14.8
Other maintenance and repair	9,300	103.3	15,258	90.4	17,597	88.9
Overestimate	−1,372[a]	−15.2[a]	−710[a]	−4.2[a]	−740[a]	−3.7[a]
Industry total	$9,002	100.0	$16,875	100.0	$19,794	100.0

[a]Negative statistic includes correction for overestimates of components of output.

Table 5-2 lists the major components of output for IO-12, Maintenance & repair construction, together with their national value and the OBE industry total. Because the major components were overestimated, as indicated by the fact that the OBE total is less than the sum of the two components, state outputs were reduced by proration of the overestimate to correspond with OBE statistics.

Adjustment of Output to Constant Dollars

Current dollar state outputs were converted to constant dollars as described in Chapter 2. In deflating the 1947 and 1958 outputs, the same component detail was maintained as is shown in Table 5-2.

Critique of Procedures and Data Used in Estimating State Outputs

Except for state estimates of new construction in 1947, it was not possible to obtain data on the value of new or maintenance construction put-in-place. Although the proxy series used to distribute national output to states are closely related to the value of construction put-in-place, they differ from the desired measure in terms of both total value covered and the timing of activity. For example, the value of building permits does not include all costs associated with erecting a structure. Because the permit reflects the architect's or contractor's projected cost of a structure's shell, items such as plumbing, electrical wiring, and heating equipment are frequently excluded. Further, the elapsed time required to complete a structure for which a permit has been issued normally extends beyond one year. There are similar problems associated with the use of F.W. Dodge contract data and capital expenditures data for state and local governments.

While scattered statistics on federal government construction exist, there is no single statistical series which encompasses all federal construction. Attempts to construct such a series for use in estimating state outputs undoubtedly suffer from undercoverage. This is especially true of military construction.

Finally, errors probably have occurred in estimating 1947 maintenance and repair expenditures by state, based on 1958 estimates of real estate values. Assumptions made about the age and functional composition of state-property inventories are also open to question and could result in erroneous output estimates.

6 Estimation of State Outputs for the Service Sector

As initially formulated for the OBE 1958 input-output study [194], the service sector was composed of 17 separate input-output industries.[1] With the publication of the 1963 transactions table [184], the number of service industries was reduced to 16 by combining IO-74, Research & development, with IO-73, Business services. Several other minor alterations made to the definitions of individual input-output industries at that time are discussed in Chapter 1 of the first volume of this series [92, pp. 15–16]. For purposes of this study, however, the original service industry classifications of the 1958 table have been maintained. These industries span a wide range of activities, including transportation, communications, trade, finance, personal and business services, and government. Estimation procedures for service industry outputs parallel the general methodology described in Chapter 2.

IO-65, Transportation and Warehousing

OBE Definition. This industry is defined on a modified activity basis and includes receipts for transportation, warehousing, and allied services by all private establishments. The value of these receipts is defined to include the Federal transportation excise tax.

Activities of transportation companies which are primary functions of other industries are excluded from the output total while for-hire transportation and warehousing activities performed by mining, manufacturing, and trading companies are excluded from these other industries. Thus, for example, the pipeline departments of petroleum companies and the operation of private water carriers are covered in the industry, while the coal produced in mines owned by railway companies and the value of equipment built in railway repair shops are excluded from the industry. Transportation services [that are] self-performed and self-consumed, . . . e.g., private trucking and warehousing, business flying, and the cost of business use of passenger cars, are not included in the industry output total.

While the measure of output for this industry is generally in terms of revenues from transportation and warehousing operations, the output of the industry also includes tips received by employees, the value of scrap

---

1. This enumeration excludes artificial industries, such as IO-80, Imports, and IO-81, Business travel, entertainment, & gifts.

generated in the industry, and revenues from some secondary activities. It
does not include subsidies paid by the government to offset operating
deficits.

The principal revenues from secondary activities of the Transportation
industry are rental receipts and gross margins from the sale of merchandise.
These are transferred to the primary producing industries for distribution to
the consuming industries.

The output total for the Transportation industry also includes a transfer
of transportation revenues from government enterprises, and the value of
intermediate transportation services provided to the United States by
foreign-owned carriers. The revenues transferred from the government
enterprise industries are derived from the operation of publicly owned
transit systems, air terminal facilities, and port facilities.

A portion of the output of this industry was transferred to Industry 81
for distribution. [183, p. 16]

Definition of Output

This industry is defined on a modified activity basis. Consequently, the
for-hire transportation activities performed by mining, manufacturing, and
trading companies are included in the state outputs, while secondary receipts of
companies primarily engaged in providing transportation services are excluded.

Procedures for Estimating State Output

To construct measures of state industry output, the contributions of seven
major modes of transportation were first estimated separately by state. The seven
modes were: (1) railroads, (2) water carriers, (3) for-hire trucking and warehousing, (4) airlines, (5) pipelines, (6) intercity buses and local transit, and (7)
transportation services not elsewhere classified. State outputs of each mode of
transportation were added and then combined with an estimate of excise taxes.
Table 6-1 lists the various modes of transportation together with their contributions to national output, the value of excise taxes, and the OBE national
industry total.

Transportation carriers, the producing units of this industry, are often
engaged in operations spanning the boundaries of several states. Because multi-
state operations are common, it was not feasible to estimate activity within
states from operating data of individual firms. Instead, national output estimates
for each transportation mode were allocated to states on the basis of the value
of state transportation payrolls and employment for each respective mode.
National modal shares of output were taken from "Input-Output Transactions by
Transportation Mode, 1947 and 1958" [45] or from the OBE 1963 transactions

Table 6-1
IO-65, Transportation and Warehousing (millions of dollars)

Component	1947		1958		1963	
	Value	Percent	Value	Percent	Value	Percent
SIC 40	Railroads	$ 9,991	44.7	$11,010	33.8	$ 9,470	25.5
SIC 41	Intercity buses/local transit	3,030	13.6	3,013	9.2	3,661	9.8
SIC 42	Trucking and warehousing.	4,312	19.3	10,779	33.1	13,317	35.9
SIC 44	Water	3,138	14.1	3,189	9.8	3,946	10.6
SIC 45	Airlines	765	3.4	2,396	7.4	4,192	11.3
SIC 46	Pipelines	364	1.6	865	2.7	872	2.3
SIC 47	Transportation services, n.e.c.	191	0.9	846	2.6	1,704	4.6
Excise tax		534	2.4	471	1.4	—	—
Industry total		$22,325	100.0	$32,569	100.0	$37,162	100.0

table [184]. For 1947, first-quarter payroll data from *Business Establishments, Employment, and Taxable Payrolls, 1947* [174] were used to distribute the national output contributions of each transportation mode except railroads. State estimates of 1947 railroad output were constructed from an annual state employment series compiled by the Association of American Railroads [15]. For 1958 and 1963, first-quarter payroll data from *County Business Patterns, 1959* [140] and *1964* [141] were used to estimate state outputs for all modes except railroads and warehousing. Again, annual employment data from the Association of American Railroads [14; 16] provided a distribution base for railroad output. Warehousing estimates for 1958 and 1963 were prorated to states based upon annual warehouse receipts published in the *Census of Business, 1958* [112] and *1963* [111], respectively.

Adjustment of Output to Constant Dollars

Current dollar state outputs were converted to constant dollar measures as described in Chapter 2. In deflating the 1947 and 1958 outputs, the same component detail was maintained as is shown in Table 6-1.

IO-66, Communications, Except Radio and Television Broadcasting

OBE Definition. The value of output includes Federal excise taxes and State and Local sales taxes.

Receipts from telephone directory advertising were transferred to Industry 73 for distribution. Rents and royalties are the only other secondary receipts of this industry. [183, p. 17]

Definition of Output

Output of this industry includes receipts for the primary activities of establishments classified under SIC codes 481, 482, and 489 (telephone, telegraph, and miscellaneous communications services). In addition to operating revenues, output includes the uncollectable revenues of telephone companies, excise taxes, and the installation cost of fixed nonconstruction type of equipment. Secondary receipts in the form of rental and royalty payments are considered part of output.

Procedures for Estimating State Output

First, values of telephone company operating revenues were estimated for each state. National estimates of telegraph revenues, excise taxes, installation costs of fixed equipment, and the uncollectable revenues of telephone companies were then distributed to states in proportion to the ratios of state telephone company operating revenues to national telephone company operating revenues. Next, the difference between the national total of these components of output and the OBE industry total was calculated. Because the residual obtained represented the value of other components of output for which separate statistics were not available, it was prorated to individual states on the basis of the data already compiled. Table 6-2 lists the four major components of output, together with their national values, the OBE national industry total, and the residual value of other components.

For 1947, operating revenues of telephone companies were tabulated by state for all Class A, B, C, and D carriers required to file with the Federal Communications Commission (FCC) [58], and for Class A and B carriers not under FCC jurisdiction which reported their operations to the U.S. Independent Telephone Association [224]. If the operations of a carrier under FCC jurisdiction crossed state boundaries, operating revenue was split among the states in which it operated in proportion to the number of local and toll calls of Class A and B carriers originating within those states [58]. With the exception of those carriers which also reported to the FCC, carriers reporting to the U.S. Independent Telephone Association were considered to be intrastate carriers.

To estimate 1958 and 1963 state outputs, operating revenues of telephone companies were computed by state for all Class A carriers required to file with the FCC [56; 57]. Revenues for all other Class A carriers as well as for Class B, C, and D carriers were tabulated from annual reports of the U.S. Independent Telephone Association [221; 222].

Adjustment of Output to Constant Dollars

Current dollar state outputs were converted to constant dollars as described in Chapter 2. For this industry, the separate component detail shown in Table 6-2 was not maintained in deflating 1947 and 1958 outputs.

Table 6-2
IO-66, Communications, Except Radio and Television Broadcasting (millions of dollars)

	1947		1958		1963	
Component	Value	Percent	Value	Percent	Value	Percent
Operating revenues	$2,689	78.7	$7,931	85.3	$11,438	84.7
Excise taxes	371	10.9	636	6.9	911	6.8
Labor cost of installation of fixed non-construction type of equipment	138	4.0	361	3.9	476	3.5
Uncollectable revenues	7	0.2	29	0.3	52	0.4
Other components	213	6.2	335	3.6	618	4.6
Industry total	$3,418	100.0	$9,292	100.0	$13,495	100.0

IO-67, Radio and TV Broadcasting

OBE Definition. Receipts from the sale of time and talent, which constitute the bulk of the output of this industry, were transferred to the Advertising segment of Industry 73 for distribution. [183, p. 17]

Definition of Output

Industry output consists of the receipts of establishments classified under SIC 483, Radio & television broadcasting. Network commission payments and the value of network purchases of local broadcasting station time are excluded from output, while receipts from incidental activities are included.

Procedures for Estimating State Output

Current dollar measures of state industry output were constructed in three steps. First, values of state outputs were estimated separately for television and AM radio broadcasting. Next, the difference between the national total of these two major components and the OBE industry total was calculated. Since state data were unavailable for this residual, it was prorated to individual states on the basis of the data already compiled. Finally, total state industry output was estimated by summing the major components of output and the distributed residual. Table 6–3 lists the components of output together with their national values, the OBE national industry output total, and the residual.

AM radio broadcast revenues constituted the bulk of output in 1947. State revenue statistics for this activity were tabulated from *Financial and Operating Data Relative to Standard Broadcast Stations and Networks, 1947* [55]. Due to their limited importance the FCC did not publish 1947 revenues for FM radio and television broadcasting or network activities by state. In order to approxi-

Table 6–3
IO-67, Radio and Television Broadcasting (millions of dollars)

Component	1947		1958		1963	
	Value	Percent	Value	Percent	Value	Percent
TV broadcasting revenues	$ –	–	$ 629	40.6	$ 957	41.4
AM broadcasting revenues	268	64.6	476	30.7	630	27.3
Other components	147	35.4	444	28.7	721	31.3
Industry total	$415	100.0	$1,549	100.0	$2,308	100.0

mate state revenues for these operations, national revenues reported in *Broadcast Financial Data for Networks and AM, FM, and TV Stations, 1948* [50] were distributed to states in proportion to AM broadcast revenues. State revenues for networks were estimated by allocating the national revenue total to states in accordance with state broadcasting payrolls for metropolitan areas where network facilities existed.

For 1958, television broadcast revenues were published for major market areas in *Final TV Broadcast Financial Data, 1958* [53]. State television revenues for other than major market areas were estimated by distributing portions of total national revenue to states, based on state employment for the industry. Total AM-FM broadcasting revenues were obtained by combining revenues for selected metropolitan areas published in *Final AM-FM Broadcast Financial Data, 1958* [51], with estimates for omitted areas constructed by prorating portions of total national revenues. By allocating national revenue totals to states in accordance with state totals of industry employment for metropolitan areas with network facilities, state shares of network and FM broadcasting revenues were estimated.

Estimates of 1963 putput were calculated in a fashion similar to the 1958 estimates using the relevant 1963 sources [22; 59], except that AM-FM broadcasting revenues were available for states in *AM-FM Broadcast Financial Data, 1963* [49].

Adjustment of Output to Constant Dollars

Current dollar state outputs were converted to constant dollars as described in Chapter 2. In deflating the 1947 and 1958 outputs, the same component detail was maintained as is shown in Table 6–3.

IO-68, Electric, Gas, Water, and Sanitary Services

OBE Definition. This industry includes all revenues of privately owned establishments classified in SIC 49. Utilities which are produced and consumed in the same plant are excluded, but sales of electricity and gas by one utility plant to another are included at full value. Sales taxes on electricity and gas are added to the reported revenues in deriving output of the industry.

Receipts from the sale of utilities by government enterprises (excluding public sewer and sewage facilities), manufacturing and mining establishments, and railroads are transferred to this industry for distribution to consuming industries.

Secondary receipts of this industry include coke, chemical and petroleum products resulting from gas production and rents and royalties. These are transferred to the primary producing industries for distribution to the consuming industries. [183, p. 17]

Definition of Output

State outputs do not include the value of utility services provided as a secondary activity by manufacturing and mining establishments or railroads. Services sold by one utility to another for purposes of resale are included in the output measures at full value.

Procedures for Estimating State Output

Output measures were developed independently for (1) private electric utilities, (2) gas utilities, and (3) other private utilities by state. Final state industry outputs were calculated by reconciling these statistics with corresponding national controls developed by the OBE. In the reconciliation, the value of other output components for which state detail was not available was distributed to states. Table 6-4 lists the three major components of output together with their national values.

Revenue measures for electric utilities were estimated as the product of KWH (kilowatt hour) production and average prices (per KWH). Gas service revenues were calculated as the residual of total gas sales by state, less municipal government gas sales. By combining state water and sanitation revenues, revenues were approximated for other public utilities. State water revenues were estimated by distributing the national figure to states in accordance with earnings for waterworks during a base year for which state detail was available. Sanitation revenues, a relatively unimportant component of industry output, were estimated as prorated measures generated from a national revenue statistic and 1955 city sanitation expenditures aggregated to state detail.

1947 Components of Output. Values of electricity production by state for Class A and B privately owned electric companies were estimated as the product

Table 6-4
IO-68, Electric, Gas, Water, and Sanitary Services (millions of dollars)

Component	1947		1958		1963	
	Value	Percent	Value	Percent	Value	Percent
Private electric utilities	$3,927	68.0	$ 9,344	54.4	$12,012	48.0
Private gas utilities	1,721	29.8	7,074	41.2	10,473	41.8
Other private utilities	126	2.2	759	4.4	2,543	10.2
Industry total	$5,774	100.0	$17,177	100.0	$25,028	100.0

of KWH production and average prices. To determine prices, the financial data for power companies reported to the Federal Power Commission (FPC) [72] were used. State outputs for private electric companies were then estimated as pro rata measures, calculated from a national output statistic for the industry taken from the 1947 BLS study [219], and the values of electricity production by state for Class A and B privately owned electric companies. In the proration, an implicit adjustment was made for the earnings of non-FPC-regulated companies and output components not contained in state data.

Revenues of privately owned gas services were determined as the residual of state total gas sales reported in *Historical Statistics of the Gas Industry, 1961* [4], less municipal gas sales. By adjusting these gas revenue estimates to include components of output not included in the data, such as the value of resales, by-products, credits (transfers to electric plants of combination companies), and the value of unexplained items, the private gas company output was calculated.

Water revenues were estimated by compiling 1945 state data for privately owned waterworks establishments [12] and adjusting this series by proration to approximate 1947 revenues. Sanitation revenues for 1947, a relatively unimportant component of industry output (2.2 percent), were calculated by indexing 1955 city-level expenditures [10] aggregated to state detail to 1947 measures. For the final reconciliation, water and sanitation revenues were combined, and the revenues of private irrigation, revenues of steam companies, and components of output not included in the data were prorated over the sum to obtain output for all private utilities. The data on corporate revenues were given in *Statistics of Income* [226].

1958 and 1963 Components of Output. For 1958 and 1963, state estimates of components of output were constructed, using methods similar to those described for 1947 and the relevant 1958 and 1963 sources.[2] The only significant difference in procedures was that waterwork revenues were estimated by first tabulating 1960 earnings for privately owned establishments by state from *A Survey of Operating Data for Water Works in 1960* [13]. The 1960 data were then used to prorate national estimates of 1958 and 1963 waterworks revenue to states.

Adjustment of Output to Constant Dollars

Current dollar state outputs were converted to constant dollars as described in Chapter 2. In deflating the 1947 and 1958 outputs, the same component detail was maintained as is shown in Table 6-4.

---

2. See numbers 1, 2, 3, 4, 5, 10, 13, 71, 73, 74, 94, 125, 133, 134, and 143 in the Bibliography.

IO-69, Wholesale and Retail Trade

OBE Definition. This industry reflects a modified activity definition. Its major receipts are gross margins (operating expenses plus profits) from the reselling activities of wholesale and retail trade establishments. In addition, the output of this industry covers the commissions of merchandise agents and brokers, customs revenues from import duties, state and local sales taxes, Federal excise collected and remitted at the trade level, and tips received by employees performing a trade function.

The output of the Trade industry excludes the gross margins of Manufacturers' Sales Offices on the assumption that these margins are covered by the value of manufacturers' shipments as reported in the *Census of Manufactures.*

By redefinition, the receipts of trade establishments from service and manufacturing activities are excluded from this industry while, on the other hand, the gross margins on sales of merchandise by establishments classified in the service industries are included in the Trade industry. Trade output is further augmented by the transfer of the gross margins from sales of merchandise occurring in other than trade and service establishments. The major part of this transfer represents value added by resales of manufacturing establishments and government enterprises.

Rents and royalties are the only secondary receipts of this industry. [183, pp. 17–18]

Definition of Output

Output consists of the resale activities of wholesale and retail trade establishments having SIC codes 50 (excluding manufacturing sales offices), 52, 53, 54, 55, 56, 57, 58, and 59. Some establishments belonging to SIC 7399, Business services, also perform trade-related activities which were included in the output of IO-69, Wholesale & retail trade. Gross margins on resales by manufacturing establishments and government enterprises were excluded from the value of state outputs. The OBE transfers the value of these secondary activities into this industry. By redefinition, the gross margins on merchandise and food sales of movie theaters, hotels, and motels are included in output, while the service receipts of retail establishments are excluded.

Procedures for Estimating State Output

Current dollar measures of state industry output were constructed in three steps. First, values of state outputs were estimated separately for wholesale and retail trade. For 1947 and 1958, sales taxes, customs duties, and rent receipts were also estimated separately by state. (These items were included in the 1963 estimates of wholesale and retail trade but were not given separate treatment.) Next, the difference between the national total of major components of output

Table 6-5
IO-69, Wholesale and Retail Trade (millions of dollars)

	1947		1958		1963	
Component	*Value*	*Percent*	*Value*	*Percent*	*Value*	*Percent*
Wholesale trade	$19,422	36.4	$39,689	43.0	$ 45,263	38.9
Retail trade	34,497	64.6	47,965	52.0	71,121	61.1
Adjusted sales tax and rent receipts	3,141	5.9	7,529	8.2	–	–
Other components	-3,668[a]	-6.9[a]	-2,980[a]	-3.2[a]	–	–
Industry total	$53,392	100.0	$92,203	100.0	$116,384	100.0

[a]Negative statistic includes correction for overestimates of trade margins in certain types of trade establishments.

and the OBE industry total was calculated. Because this difference represented an overestimate of certain trade margins, it was prorated to states on the basis of the data already compiled. Finally, total state industry output was estimated by summing the major components of output and the compensatory series. Table 6-5 lists the components of output, together with their national values, the OBE national industry output, and the residual difference attributed to overestimation of gross margins.

1947 and 1958 Components of Output. An estimate of 1947 retail trade margins was compiled from 1958 corporate income data published in *Statistics of Income, 1958* [231] for the following types of establishments:

SIC 52,	Lumber, building & hardware;
SIC 53,	General merchandise stores;
SIC 54,	Food stores;
SIC 55 (except 554),	Automotive stores;
SIC 554,	Gasoline service stations;
SIC 56,	Apparel stores;
SIC 57,	Furniture & appliances;
SIC 58,	Eating & drinking places;
SIC 59 (except 591 & 592),	Other retail stores;
SIC 591,	Drug stores; and
SIC 592,	Liquor stores.

For each establishment type, the cost of goods sold was subtracted from gross sales to arrive at gross profits. The latter were then divided by gross sales to yield approximate relative margins. To estimate retail trade margins by state, the relative margins were applied to adjusted Census sales statistics by state (described below). The procedure used to construct 1958 relative margins for retail trade was the same as that used for 1947, with one exception—partnership data for 1957 [228] were used instead of corporate income statistics.

As for retail trade, gross margins for wholesale trade by state were calculated as the product of relative margins by establishment type and adjusted sales statistics. In accordance with the OBE definition of industry output, the revenues of manufacturers' sales offices were excluded from the total sales of wholesale establishments.

Retail and wholesale establishment sales were obtained from the *Census of Business, 1948* [102; 109] and *1958* [103; 110]. These statistics were altered to exclude the service receipts of trade establishments and to include the sales receipts of service establishments.

National values for state and local sales taxes, federal customs duties, and rents and royalties were obtained from the *Survey of Current Business* [192], *Census of Governments, 1962* [115], and *Statistics of Income* [226; 227; 228; 229], respectively. Sales taxes and customs duties were distributed to states in proportion to total sales taxes. Rents and royalties were allocated to states in proportion to the value of all other components of output compiled for the industry.

1963 Components of Output. Although 1963 state estimates of output were constructed using methods similar to those described for 1947 and 1958 and the relevant data sources [104; 111; 150; 230; 233], better information exists on wholesale margins. Relative margins were constructed from data published in *Measures of Value Produced in and by Merchant Wholesaling Firms, 1963* [150]. The relative margins of merchant wholesalers were assumed to reflect those of all other types of wholesalers. National estimates of sales taxes, customs duties, rents and royalties, and other sundry items were first split between wholesale and retail establishments, based on the proportion of the sales of each component to total trade establishment sales. To obtain final estimates of wholesale and retail trade output, these segments were then prorated to states and added to the gross margin estimates.

Adjustment of Output to Constant Dollars

Current dollar state outputs were converted to constant dollar measures as described in Chapter 2. In deflating the 1947 and 1958 outputs, the same component detail was maintained as is shown in Table 6-5.

IO-70, Finance and Insurance

OBE Definition. The output of the financial intermediaries includes the value of services for which monetary income is received, as well as imputed values for services furnished without explicit charge. The Federal excise tax on safe deposit boxes is included in the output of this industry.

For commercial banks and regulated investment companies, the imputed service charge to business and households is equal to an imputation of interest paid. This imputed interest expense is derived by deducting monetary interest paid from dividends and monetary interest received.

A similar imputation procedure is followed for mutual savings banks, Federal Reserve Banks, savings and loan associations, and credit unions. However, in the case of these institutions, imputed interest paid is derived by deducting profits, in addition to dividends and monetary interest paid, from dividends and monetary interest received.

The output of life insurance carriers is measured by expenses. The expenses included an imputation of interest paid which is derived in the same way as that for mutual savings banks. Life insurance output is adjusted to exclude expenses incurred by U.S. companies in connection with insurance carried by foreign consumers. Expenses of private pension funds which are self-administered are added to the life insurance output.

Nonlife insurance output is measured on a net basis, that is, premiums earned less benefits paid. For accident and health insurance held by both life and nonlife carriers, net premiums earned are adjusted to exclude direct transactions with foreigners.

Output of insurance agents and brokers, combinations of real estate, insurance, loans and law offices, and holding companies is measured by total income. The output of security and commodity brokers is augmented to include net capital gain from sales of securities for their own account. The output of security and commodity brokers includes stamp taxes on securities. The output of personal and business credit agencies is measured as receipts other than business and interest receipts since their business receipts are treated as monetary interest received. The output of Agricultural Credit Institutions is measured by their loan service fees, compensation for services under CCC programs, and income from the Federal Land Banks. Federal Land Banks, Federal Home Loan Banks, the Board of Governors of the Federal Reserve System, and self-administered private pension funds are included in this industry.

Output of this industry includes a transfer from the state and local government enterprise industry.

Rents and royalties are the only secondary receipts of this industry. [183, pp. 18–19]

Definition of Output

Output covers the activities of banks and financial intermediaries classified under SIC codes 60, 61, 62, 63, 64, 66, and 67 (banking; other credit agencies; security and commodity brokers; insurance carriers; insurance agents; combination real estate, insurance, loan, and law offices; and holding companies). The output of banks corresponds to the value of services performed. For commercial banks, these services are measured by bank receipts (interest, dividends, and service charges) less the price that banks pay for money (interest paid). Alternatively, the value of bank services is equivalent to nonfinancial expenses plus profits. The outputs of mutual banks, savings and loan associations, and Federal Reserve Banks are equal to their nonfinancial expenses. For life insurance carriers, output is measured as the sum of intermediate purchases of goods and services; wages, salaries, and supplements; depreciation; and indirect taxes solely associated with the issue of life insurance. For other types of insurance, output is equivalent to expenses (excluding benefits paid) plus profits. The outputs of all other financial institutions included in this industry are defined as business receipts plus other stipulated secondary receipts. Primary services of this industry produced by other industries are not included in the output total. The OBE transfers these values into the industry for distribution with the remainder of output.

Procedures for Estimating State Output

Current dollar measures of state industry output were constructed in three steps. First, state outputs were estimated for the four major components of output: (1) banking, (2) other credit agencies, (3) insurance carriers, and (4) miscellaneous financial institutions. For these state estimates, the national estimates of component output were generally distributed to states based upon closely related economic data series. Next, the difference between the national total of these four components and the OBE industry total was calculated. Because a negative residual was generally obtained (indicating that the estimates of one or more unspecified components of output had been overvalued), a compensatory series was prepared to correct this estimate error. Finally, total state output was estimated by summing the major components of output and the compensatory series. Table 6–6 lists the components of output together with their national values, the OBE national industry total, and the amount of component overvaluation.

The national output measure for the banking component included output measures compiled for the Federal Reserve, commercial banks, mutual banks, and other trust companies. For the Federal Reserve, output consisted of the expenditures of the Board of Governors and the total earnings less dividends paid, interest paid, and transfers to surplus of Federal Reserve Banks. The output of commercial banks was obtained by expanding the current revenues (less interest paid) of insured commercial banks to estimate the output of all commercial banks. Mutual bank output was constructed by expanding revenues less taxes, dividends paid, interest paid, and net profits of insured banks to estimate the output of all mutual banks. For the national measures of banking output, the data were obtained primarily from the *Annual Report of the Board of*

Table 6-6
IO-70, Finance and Insurance (millions of dollars)

Component	1947		1958		1963	
	Value	Percent	Value	Percent	Value	Percent
SIC 60	Banking	$ 3,163	30.1	$ 7,533	28.6	$10,459	30.3
SIC 61	Other credit agencies	209	2.0	1,207	4.6	2,275	6.6
SIC 63	Insurance carriers	4,368	41.5	9,830	37.2	13,139	38.2
SIC 62, 64, 66, and 67, combined	Securities and commodity brokers; combination real estate; holding and other investment companies; insurance agents, brokers, and services	2,782	26.4	9,145	34.6	10,611	30.8
Other components		—		-1,314[a]	-5.0[a]	-2,045[a]	-5.9[a]
Industry total		$10,522	100.0	$26,401	100.0	$34,439b	100.0

[a]Negative statistic includes correction for overestimates of components of output.
[b]Includes SIC 66, Combination real estate, insurance, loan, and law offices, which was excluded from the definition of industry output by the OBE in its 1963 table. The 1963 total given in the OBE table is $33,579 million.

Governors of the Federal Reserve System, 1947 [21], *1958* [20], and *1963*
[19] and the *Annual Report of the Federal Deposit Insurance Corporation,
1947* [60], *1958* [61], and *1963* [62]. The total banking output for both 1947
and 1958 was distributed to states in proportion to the value of state bank
deposits reported by the Federal Deposit Insurance Corporation in its annual
reports. For 1963, the state output of commercial banks was tabulated directly
from Federal Deposit Insurance Corporation data, while remaining bank output
was distributed to states based on the value of mutual bank deposits by state.

National output of SIC 61, Non-bank credit agencies, included output
measures for savings and loan associations, agricultural credit institutions, and
personal and business credit institutions. Gross operating income less interest,
income taxes, transfers to surplus, and dividends paid by savings and loan
associations was combined with the operating income less interest paid by
Federal Home Loan Banks to determine the output of SIC 612, Savings & loan
associations. For agricultural credit institutions, output was calculated by combining the loan fees received by both Federal Land Banks and Production Credit
Associations. Personal and business credit institution output was estimated
either as gross income less interest on borrowed money or the net income of
credit unions. National output of SIC 61, Non-bank credit agencies, was then
distributed to states on the basis of the total assets of savings and loan associations obtained from the *Combined Financial Statements, 1947* [63], *1958* [64],
and *1963* [65] of the Federal Home Loan Bank Board.

To estimate insurance-carrier output by state for 1947, the state value of
first-quarter payrolls for the industry was used as the allocation factor. The
national measure was compiled by combining appropriate values for life insurance carriers, liability and casualty insurance carriers, and accident and health
insurance companies. For life insurance, output was approximated by personal
consumption expenditures data given in the *Survey of Current Business* [188].
Accident and health company output was constructed by combining total
premiums earned less losses of commercial carriers with the earned income of
medical insurance plans, such as Blue Cross. The output of all other carriers,
including liability and casualty companies, was calculated as earned premiums
less claims paid. In preparing the national output measures, statistics were
obtained from *The Spectator, 1963 Health Insurance Index* [24], and the *Source
Book of Health Insurance Data, 1959* [80].

For 1958 and 1963, national insurance carrier outputs were estimated in a
fashion similar to the methods described above for 1947. State output measures
were obtained by distributing the national output of life insurance companies in
proportion to the payrolls of SIC 631, Life insurance, and the remaining insurance carrier output in proportion to the payrolls of SIC 63, Insurance carriers
(excluding SIC 631). These two measures were combined by state to obtain a
single estimate of state output for the insurance industry.

The final major component of industry output—all other finance and insurance—comprises SIC 62, Security & commodity brokers; SIC 64, Insurance agents, brokers, & services; SIC 66, Combination offices; and SIC 67, Holding & other investment companies. National output estimates were obtained by compiling corporate and noncorporate business receipts given in *Statistics of Income* [226 through 233]. These were supplemented by reported capital and non-capital gains for SIC 62, Security & commodity brokers, and rents and royalties for SIC 67, Holding & other investment companies. Fiscal-year data were averaged to approximate calendar-year measures. For each SIC group, national outputs were allocated to states on the basis of relevant payroll data taken from *Business Establishments, Employment, and Taxable Payrolls, 1947* [174] and *County Business Patterns, 1959* [140] and *1964* [141]. The state industry statistics were then combined into a single state statistic for all other finance and insurance activities.

Adjustment of Output to Constant Dollars

Current dollar state outputs were converted to constant dollars as described in Chapter 2. In deflating the 1947 and 1958 outputs, the same component detail was maintained as is shown in Table 6-6.

IO-71, Real Estate and Rental

OBE Definition. The output total for this industry covers (1) all rents paid on real property, whether paid to business, government, or persons; (2) total royalty payments; (3) the imputed rental value of owner-occupied farm and nonfarm dwellings; (4) an imputed rental payment by nonprofit institutions serving individuals; (5) receipts of real estate firms for property management; and (6) receipts of real estate firms resulting from the transfer of real property, including stamp taxes on deeds of conveyance.

Rent and royalty receipts of business (other than real estate and construction firms) and the imputed rental value of farm dwellings which are secondary receipts of other industries, are transferred to this industry for distribution to consuming industries.

The addition of government receipts of rents and royalties to the output of Industry 71 is balanced by a nontax payment to government. Government rents and royalties are treated as a nontax receipt, rather than as a government sale, since these receipts are closer to net than to gross rents. Such treatment results in the minimum distortion of aggregate GNP.

The imputed rental value of owner-occupied nonfarm homes is included in the output of this industry, and the various expenses of home ownership (maintenance, taxes, interest, depreciation) together with the residual, net rental income, are shown as inputs into this industry. Similarly nonprofit institutions serving individuals are treated as making an imputed rental pay-

ment to Industry 71. This imputation is equal to their interest and depreciation expenses. This addition to output of Industry 71 is balanced by
additions to its interest and depreciation expenses. The imputation for farm
operator-dwelling rent is treated as part of gross farm income and is not
part of the primary output of this industry.

Since trading in real property is the main function of real estate
developers, their net gains from sales of real property are included in the
output and profit measures for this industry, although, in general, capital
gains are excluded from the national account measurements.

The *construction* activity of operative builders (SIC 6561) is excluded
from Industry 71 since this activity is included in the Construction industry.
The *sales* activity of operative builders remains in Industry 71, however.
[183, pp. 19–20]

Definition of Output

In conformance with general procedures of this study, services similar to
those performed by IO-71, Real estate & rental, but rendered by other industries,
are not included in the state output. The OBE transfers these services into this
industry. When transfers are excluded, output consists of the actual rental and
royalty receipts of individuals, rents paid to government, receipts of real estate
firms, and the rental and royalty receipts of construction companies. In addition,
imputations are made for rental payments on nonfarm owner-occupied dwellings
and the rental payments of nonprofit institutions.

Procedures for Estimating State Output

National values of (1) the imputed rent of owner-occupied buildings, (2)
personal and government rent receipts, (3) receipts of real estate firms, (4) rents
and royalties of construction firms, and (5) royalties received by individuals were
compiled for 1947, 1958, and 1963. By allocating the national component values
to states in proportion to closely related economic series, state estimates of
these components of output were constructed. Differences between total
industry outputs as reported by the OBE and the sum of major components of
output were then calculated and distributed to states by proration. Finally, total
state industry output was estimated by summing the major components of
output and the distributed residual. Table 6–7 lists the five components of
output together with their national values, the OBE national industry total, and
the residual.

Imputations of the 1947, 1958, and 1963 rental values of owner-occupied
buildings were obtained from the *Survey of Current Business* [188]. For each
state, market values of owner-occupied dwellings for 1950 and 1960 were cal-

Table 6-7
IO-71, Real Estate and Rental (millions of dollars)

Component	1947 Value	1947 Percent	1958 Value	1958 Percent	1963 Value	1963 Percent
Imputed rents of owner-occupied buildings	$ 8,825	40.7	$28,072	50.8	$38,944	52.2
Personal and government rent receipts	6,763	31.2	13,560	24.6	20,859	28.0
Total receipts of real estate firms	5,062	23.3	12,386	22.4	14,569	19.5
Royalties of individuals	338	1.6	559	1.0	–	–
Rents and royalties of construction firms	33	0.2	75	0.1	224	0.3
Other components	658	3.0	622	1.1	–	–
Industry total	$21,679	100.0	$55,274	100.0	$74,596[a]	100.0

[a]Excludes SIC 6541, Title abstract companies, and SIC 66, Combinations of real estate, insurance, loan, and law offices, which were included in the definition of output used in the 1963 table. The 1963 total given in the OBE table is $75,594 million.

culated as the product of the median value of owner-occupied dwelling units and the number of units in each state, obtained from statistics published in the *Census of Housing, 1950* [119] and *1960* [120]. Imputed rent values for 1947 were then distributed to states in proportion to the 1950 values of owner-occupied dwelling units, while the 1960 values of owner-occupied dwelling units were used to prorate the 1958 and 1963 values of imputed rent to states.

Personal and government rent receipts for 1947, 1958, and 1963 were taken from *The National Income and Product Accounts of the U.S., 1929-1965* [187], and portions of these rent receipts were allocated to states by proration. For 1947 and 1958, dwelling rental payments by state were estimated as the median rent paid in each state times the number of rental housing units by state, and these estimates were then used to distribute all 1947 and 1958 personal and government rent receipts to states. For 1963, net receipts of individuals, published in *Individual Income Tax Returns, 1963* [234], provided the basis for distributing total personal and government rent receipts.

Total 1947, 1958, and 1963 receipts of real estate firms obtained from *Statistics of Income* [226 through 233] were allocated among the states in proportion to state first-quarter payroll values of SIC 65, Real estate, published in *Business Establishments, Employment, and Taxable Payrolls, 1947* [174] and *County Business Patterns, 1959* [140] and *1964* [141].

Rents and royalties of construction firms were distributed to states based on state first-quarter payroll values for general and special trade contractors (SIC industries 15, 16, and 17) [174; 140; 141]. Because of the lack of relevant data, royalties received by individuals were not separately allocated by state. Instead, they were distributed to the states, based upon the combined value of all other components of output previously calculated.

Adjustment of Output to Constant Dollars

Current dollar state outputs were converted to constant dollars as described in Chapter 2. In deflating the 1947 and 1958 outputs, the same component detail was maintained as is shown in Table 6-7.

IO-72, Hotels and Lodging Places; Personal and Repair Services, Except Automobile Repair

OBE Definition. Primary output is defined on an activity basis. The value of output includes all taxes collected directly from the customer and remitted to the tax authority. By redefinition, the output of this industry includes personal and repair services performed in trade establishments and excludes the trading activities of service establishments.

A portion of the output of this industry was transferred to Industry 81 for distribution.

Receipts for Commercial Photography were transferred to the advertising segment of Industry 73 for distribution.

Rents and royalties are the only other secondary receipts of this industry. [183, pp. 20–21]

Definition of Output

Output is composed of receipts from the provision of lodgings (SIC 70), personal services (SIC 72), and miscellaneous repair services (SIC 76, except 7694 and 7699). Service receipts of jewelry stores and other minor service receipts of trade establishments are included by redefinition, while the receipts of hotels and motels for food, beverage, and merchandise sales are excluded.

Procedures for Estimating State Output

Current dollar measures of state industry output were constructed in three steps. First, the outputs were estimated for individual states for the three major components: (1) lodgings, (2) personal services, and (3) miscellaneous repair services. Next, the difference between the national total of these components and the OBE industry total was calculated. Because state data were unavailable for this residual, it was prorated to individual states on the basis of the data already compiled. Finally, total state industry output was estimated by summing the major components of output and the distributed residual. Table 6–8 lists the components of output together with their national values, the OBE national industry output total, and the residual.

1947 Components of Output. Information on establishment annual receipts contained in the *Census of Business, 1948* [108] provided the basis for estimating state output in 1947. In general, state estimates were made by distributing national values of components of industry output given in "Notes for the 1947 Interindustry Relations Study" [219] in accordance with the 1948 state distribution of receipts. Adjustments for output redefinitions were made implicitly by the proration, except as described below.

To estimate state output of hotels, SIC 7011 (1948 SIC definition), the 1948 value of state receipts of all hotels from room rentals and the sale of meals was adjusted to exclude receipts from the sale of meals. The latter series was calculated using a national average rate of merchandise and food sales per dollar of total lodging receipts, based upon data for those hotels that reported these statistics separately. To the estimated room rental receipts were added relatively small amounts of "other receipts," also given in the *Census of Business, 1948.* The resulting 1948 tabulation of relevant hotel receipts was then used as the base to prorate the 1947 total of these receipts to states. For the estimation of the state output of tourist courts, SIC 7013 (1948 SIC definition), a procedure similar to that described for hotels was employed, except that the receipts from the sale of meals by these establishments were estimated on the basis of 1958 information, since relevant data for 1947 were not available.

State outputs of SIC 76, Miscellaneous repair establishments, included explicit state adjustments for watch repairs performed by trade establishments. These were allocated to states in proportion to sales in jewelry shops.

1958 and 1963 Components of Output. Information on establishment annual receipts contained in the *Census of Business, 1958* [106] and *1963* [107] provided the basis for estimating state output. In general, state estimates were made by tabulating the Census data for all available components and adding to them pro rata shares of national rent and royalty receipts reported in *Statistics of Income* [228 through 233]. With the following two exceptions, adjustments for output definitions were included in the proration of "other components" together with components of output for which no state data were available. State estimates of output of SIC 701, Hotels & motels, were prepared by expanding state data on rental receipts by hotels and motels that reported detailed receipts to cover receipts of all hotels and motels. Outputs of miscellaneous repair service establishments were constructed by summing Census receipts of

Table 6-8

IO-72, Hotels and Lodging Places; Personal and Repair Services, Except Automobile Services (millions of dollars)

Component		1947		1958		1963	
		Value	Percent	Value	Percent	Value	Percent
SIC 701, 702, 703, and 704	Hotels, motels, tourist and recreational camps	$ –	–	$ 2,838	23.3	$ 5,560	36.2
SIC 7011	Hotels	976	13.9	–	–	–	–
SIC 7013	Motels	159	2.2	–	–	–	–
SIC 72	Personal services	4,727	67.1	7,402	60.8	9,163	59.6
SIC 76 (part)	Miscellaneous repair services	635	9.0	1,292	10.6	1,516	9.9
Other components		549	7.8	637	5.3	–871[a]	–5.7[a]
Industry total		$7,046	100.0	$12,169	100.0	$15,368	100.0

[a]Negative statistic includes correction for overestimates of components of output.

the relevant establishments by state and adding the service receipts of jewelry stores allocated to states in proportion to their total sales.

Adjustment of Output to Constant Dollars

Current dollar state outputs were converted to constant dollar measures as described in Chapter 2. In deflating the 1947 and 1958 ouputs, the same component detail was maintained as is shown in Table 6-8.

IO-73, Business Services

OBE Definition. The bulk of the service activities included in this industry are defined on an activity basis. By redefinition, this industry includes business services performed in trade establishments and excludes trading activities of business service establishments. Receipts of construction companies from equipment rental are also redefined into this industry.

Output includes a transfer from Industry 51 of an estimated value of receipts for office and computing machine rental. No other business service operations performed by manufacturing establishments are transferred or redefined into this industry.

The definition of the advertising segment of this industry has been broadened to include activities other than those covered by SIC 731. By redefinition, the output of the industry includes talent and production costs paid for directly by advertisers. By means of a transfer it also includes the receipts of industrial categories 26, 64, 66, 67, 72, and 76 from advertising activities. These advertising activities include direct mail advertising; receipts from the sale of advertising media, such as radio, television, newspapers, and periodicals; as well as receipts for art work, materials, and printing services associated with preparing the advertising message. [183, p. 21]

Definition of Output

Following the definitions of the OBE 1958 input-output table [183], industry output consists of the receipts of title abstract services, SIC 6541; miscellaneous business services, SIC 73, except SIC 7361 and 7391; miscellaneous repair services, SIC 7694 and 7699; legal services, SIC 81; and miscellaneous services, SIC 89, except 8921. In the OBE 1963 table [184], title abstract companies were reclassified as part of IO-71, Real estate & rental, while private employment agencies, SIC 7361, were considered to belong in IO-73, Business services. Output includes the rents and royalty payments received by establishments performing business services. The value of business services rendered by other industries as secondary activities is excluded from output totals.

Procedures for Estimating State Output

Current dollar measures of state industry output were constructed in three steps. First, outputs were estimated for individual states for six major components: (1) title abstract companies, (2) miscellaneous business services, (3) selected miscellaneous repair services, (4) legal services, (5) miscellaneous services, and (6) advertising talent paid for by advertisers. Next, the difference between the national total of these components and the OBE industry total was calculated. Because this residual represented the value of other components of output for which state data were unavailable, it was prorated to individual states on the basis of the data already compiled. Finally, total state industry output was estimated by summing the major components of output and the distributed residual. Table 6-9 lists the six components of output, together with their national values, the OBE national industry total, and the residual.

Establishment annual receipts contained in the *Census of Business, 1948* [108], *1958* [106], and *1963* [107] provided the basis for estimating the major part of state output. To estimate components of output for which Census data were not available, national values for individual components given in "Notes for the 1947 Interindustry Relations Study" [219] or *Statistics of Income* [228; 229; 230] were distributed to the states. Allocations were made in proportion to state employment reported in *County Business Patterns, 1959* [140] and *1964* [141] or *Business Establishments, Employment, and Taxable Payrolls, 1947* [174]. As a rule, redefinitions were not significant and were considered a part of the unidentifiable sum of "other components." The only exception was "talent costs," which was treated separately in 1947 and 1958. Descriptions of special procedures used in estimating state values for several of the output components are given below.

State outputs for the relevant parts of SIC 73, Business services, were estimated on the basis of information published in the *Census of Business, 1948, 1958,* and *1963.* In order to exclude SIC codes 7361, 7391, and 7399, Census data for 1948 had to be disaggregated by reducing the total receipts of SIC 73 in proportion to the fraction of total receipts contributed by these services in 1958. A pro rata adjustment was also made to include rents and royalty receipts.

A national output estimate of the value of SIC 6541, Title abstract companies, was calculated as the product of corporate receipts of SIC 6541 and the ratio of total industry receipts to corporate receipts. By assuming that the location of title abstract companies closely parallels the locations of the real estate group as a whole, the national total was distributed to states on the basis of real estate industry employment. State advertising outputs embodied in talent costs paid for by advertisers were constructed as follows: the national output total was allocated to the states in proportion to total output of IO-67, Radio & TV broadcasting, in 1947, and in proportion to the relative state shares of television broadcast revenue in 1958.

Table 6-9
IO-73, Business Services (millions of dollars)

Component	1947		1958		1963	
	Value	Percent	Value	Percent	Value	Percent
SIC 6541 Title abstract companies	$ 81	1.6	$ 156	0.9	$ 256	1.0
SIC 73 (part) Miscellaneous business services	1,407	27.4	8,992	54.7	13,822	56.5
SIC 76 (part) Miscellaneous repairs	915	17.7	1,123	6.8	1,500	6.1
SIC 81 Legal services	1,583	30.8	2,873	17.5	4,815	19.7
SIC 89 Miscellaneous services	1,213	23.6	3,009	18.3	6,777	27.7
— Advertising talent paid for by advertisers	99	1.9	201	1.2	—	—
Other components	-156[a]	-3.0[a]	94	0.6	-2,691[a]	-11.0[a]
Industry total	$5,142	100.0	$16,448	100.0	$24,479b	100.0

[a]Negative statistic includes correction for overestimates of components of output.
[b]Includes SIC 6541, Title abstract companies, which was excluded from the definition of industry output by the OBE in its 1963 table, and excludes SIC 7361, Private employment agencies, and SIC 7391, Research, development, and testing laboratories, which were included in the definition of output used in the 1963 table. The 1963 total given in the OBE table is $25,531 million.

Adjustment of Output to Constant Dollars

Current dollar state outputs were converted to constant dollars as described in Chapter 2. In deflating the 1947 and 1958 outputs, the same component detail was maintained as is shown in Table 6-9.

IO-74, Research and Development

OBE Definition. Output represents all research and development performed *for sale.* Primary receipts, which represent only 10 percent of the total, include those of establishments classified in SIC 7391, Research, development, and testing laboratories. The bulk of the output of this industry is transferred from manufacturing and mining establishments, nonprofit educational and scientific research agencies, and colleges and universities.

The transfers do not include R&D performed by the Federal Government [nor] R&D financed and performed within a company, college, or other institution. The transfers from manufacturing and mining include an estimated value of receipts by auxiliaries and central administrative offices from the sale of research and development. [183, pp. 21–22]

Definition of Output

Following the classification of service-sector industries of the OBE 1958 input-output table [183], Commercial research, development, and testing laboratories, SIC 7391, was treated as a separate industry. The OBE combined these activities with other business services in its 1963 input-output table [184]. State outputs include only the value of research performed as a primary establishment activity. Research services performed by establishments as secondary activities are not included in measures of output calculated for this study.

Procedures for Estimating State Output

For 1947, national industry output was estimated from statistics on business service industry output given in "Notes for the 1947 Interindustry Relations Study" [219]. To estimate 1947 research receipts, the 1958 ratio of research and development receipts to total business service receipts was calculated and multiplied by the 1947 value of total business service receipts. State outputs for 1947 were then estimated by allocating the national value of commercial research to states in proportion to 1958 state receipts of SIC 7391. State outputs for 1958 and 1963 were obtained directly from the *Census of Business, 1958* [106] and *1963* [107]. Table 6-10 lists the national values of commercial research for 1947, 1958, and 1963.

Table 6-10
IO-74, Research and Development (millions of dollars)

	1947		1958		1963	
Component	Value	Percent	Value	Percent	Value	Percent
SIC 7391 Research, development, and testing laboratories	$77	100.0	$534	100.0	$1,043	100.0
Industry total	$77	100.0	$534	100.0	$1,043[a]	100.0

[a]This component was combined with IO-73, Business services, in the 1963 OBE table.

Adjustment of Output to Constant Dollars

Current dollar state outputs were converted to constant dollars as described in Chapter 2.

IO-75, Automobile Repair and Services

OBE Definition. This industry is defined on a modified activity basis. The value of output includes all taxes on auto repairs and services collected directly from the customer and remitted to the tax authority. By redefinition, the output of this industry includes receipts of trade establishments from automobile repairs and services and excludes receipts of establishments in SIC 75 from merchandise sales which involve no repair activities. Automobile repair operations of manufacturing and mining establishments are left in their respective industries.

The output total for Industry 75 includes parking receipts transferred from Industry 79. [183, p. 22]

Definition of Output

This industry is defined on an activity basis. Output consists of revenues obtained from the repair and servicing of motor vehicles by garages, car dealers, automotive accessory dealers, and gasoline stations. Parking receipts are not included in the output measures constructed by this study.

Procedures for Estimating State Output

Current dollar measures of state industry output were constructed in three steps. First, the values of major components of output were estimated for

individual states. For 1947 and 1958, these components consisted of (1) automobile repair and service establishments, (2) car dealers, (3) accessory dealers,
and (4) gasoline stations. In estimating 1963 output, the service activities of
trade establishments were combined. Next, the difference between the national
total of these components and the OBE industry total was calculated. Because
no state data were available for the residual, it was prorated to individual states
on the basis of the data already compiled. Finally, total state industry output
was estimated by summing the major components of output and the distributed
residual. Table 6-11 lists the components of output together with their national
values, the OBE national industry total, and the residual.

Information on establishment annual receipts contained in the *Census of
Business, 1948* [108], *1958* [106], and *1963* [107] provided the basis for
estimating components of output by state. The receipts of SIC 75, Auto repair
shops, were compiled by state from these publications. For 1947, auto repair
service receipts reported in "Notes for the 1947 Interindustry Relations Study"
[219] were prorated to states using the 1948 receipts data. To estimate state
values of auto service provided by trade establishments, the national revenues of
these activities reported by the OBE were allocated to states in proportion to
trade sales receipts reported in the *Census of Business, 1948, 1958,* and *1963.*

Adjustment of Output to Constant Dollars

Current dollar state outputs were converted to constant dollars as described
in Chapter 2. For this industry, separate detail was not maintained in deflating
1947 and 1958 outputs.

IO-76, Amusements

OBE Definition. This industry is defined on an activity basis and
includes the value of amusement services wherever commercially produced.
The value of output includes Federal, state, and local admissions taxes.

A portion of the products of Industry 76 was transferred to Industry 81
for distribution. [183, p. 22]

Definition of Output

The output of this industry consists of the value of services provided by
establishments classified in SIC 78, Motion pictures, and SIC 79, Amusements &
recreation services other than motion pictures. Merchandise sales of motion
picture theaters, basically popcorn and soda pop, are redefined into IO-69,

Table 6-11
IO-75, Automobile Repair and Services (millions of dollars)

Component	1947 Value	1947 Percent	1958 Value	1958 Percent	1963 Value	1963 Percent
SIC 75						
— Automobile repair and services	$1,257	31.6	$3,892	49.3	$ 5,444	50.8
— Car dealers	2,287	57.6	3,280	41.6	4,946	46.1
— Tire, battery, and accessory dealers	101	2.6	121	1.5		
Gasoline service stations	307	7.7	567	7.2		
Other components	22	0.5	32	0.4	327	3.1
Industry total	$3,974	100.0	$7,892	100.0	$10,717	100.0

Wholesale & retail trade. Pari-mutuel tax receipts of state governments are included in the output of this industry, as are rent and royalty receipts.

Procedures for Estimating State Output

Current dollar measures of state industry output were constructed in three steps. First, the state outputs were estimated for the three major components: (1) SIC 78, Motion pictures, (2) SIC 79, Amusements & recreation services other than motion pictures, and (3) SIC 9279, Pari-mutuel receipts of state governments. Next, the difference between the national total of these three components and the OBE industry total was calculated. This residual, representing the net value of overvaluations and omissions of component activities, was prorated to individual states on the basis of the estimates already calculated. Finally, total state industry output was estimated by summing the major components of output and the distributed residual. Table 6–12 lists the three components of output together with their national values, the OBE national industry output total, and the residual.

Receipts for amusement and recreation services, other than motion pictures, were tabulated by state from the *Census of Business, 1948* [108], *1958* [106], and *1963* [107]. To estimate 1947 state outputs for this component, national receipt values reported in "Notes for the 1947 Interindustry Relations Study" [219] were distributed to states, based on the value of 1948 receipts by state. Because of differences in the form in which relevant data were presented in the Census publications for the three years, estimating procedures employed for movie theater admission and taxes differed between subject years. In the 1948 publication, receipts from admission and taxes collected were set out separately by state. Consequently, 1947 state estimates were obtained by distributing national controls given in "Notes for the 1947 Interindustry Relations Study" in proportion to these receipts. Although in the *Census of Business, 1958* and *1963* only total receipts of motion picture theaters including merchandise sales are listed, a sample breakdown of total receipts was provided. Estimates for 1958 and 1963 were therefore constructed by adjusting Census state totals to exclude merchandise sales on the basis of the proportion of relevant sales receipts to total sales given by the sample.

Estimating procedures for the costs of motion picture production and receipts of distributors varied between 1947, 1958, and 1963 because of the differences in the availability of data. In 1947, production of motion pictures was treated as a manufacturing activity, and the cost of production was reported in the *Census of Manufactures, 1947* [121]. Based on that data, the BLS estimated the national value of motion picture production [219]. Their estimate was distributed to states in proportion to the employment in motion picture production reported in the *Census of Manufactures, 1947*. On the

Table 6-12
IO-76, Amusements (millions of dollars)

Components	1947 Value	1947 Percent	1958 Value	1958 Percent	1963 Value	1963 Percent
SIC 78 Motion pictures	$2,740	71.2	$2,721	48.4	$2,725	35.5
SIC 79 Amusements other than motion pictures	1,015	26.3	2,687	47.8	3,990	52.0
SIC 9279 Pari-mutuel receipts of state governments	111	2.9	235	4.2	319	4.1
Other components	-17[a]	-0.4[a]	-23[a]	-0.4[a]	646	8.4
Industry total	$3,849	100.0	$5,620	100.0	$7,680	100.0

[a]Negative statistic includes correction for overestimates of components of output.

assumption that earnings of distributors parallel the activities of the industry as a whole, receipts of distributors, given in "Notes for the 1947 Interindustry Relations Study" were allocated to states in proportion to total employment in the amusement industry. Employment data were obtained from *Business Establishments, Employment, and Taxable Payrolls, 1947* [174]. In the *Census of Business, 1958* and *1963,* the combined receipts of producers and distributors were reported by state. Separate Census data on receipts and costs, obtained from sample surveys of (1) production other than television and (2) production for television, were used to estimate costs of motion picture production for 1958 and 1963. By subtracting the receipts of producers from the combined receipts of distributors and producers, state estimates were obtained. The costs of motion picture production were then added to the residual to estimate state values of this component of output.

Pari-mutuel receipts were tabulated by state from the *Compendium of State Government Finances, 1947* [135], *1958* [137], and *1963* [138].

Adjustment of Output to Constant Dollars

Current dollar state outputs were converted to constant dollar measures as described in Chapter 2. In deflating 1947 and 1958 outputs, the same component detail was maintained as is shown in Table 6-12.

IO-77, Medical, Educational Services, and Nonprofit Organizations

OBE Definition. This industry is defined on a modified activity basis and includes the total value of the covered services wherever they occur. An estimated value of research and development activity was transferred to Industry 74 for distribution.

A portion of the products of Industry 77 was transferred to Industry 81 for distribution. [183, p. 22]

Definition of Output

Output includes the activities of establishments having SIC 0722, Veterinarians; SIC 7361, Employment agencies; SIC 80, Health services; SIC 82, Educational services; SIC 84, Museums; SIC 86, Nonprofit organizations; and SIC 8291, Nonprofit research organizations. Rental and royalty receipts are also included in the value of output. In its 1963 table [184], the OBE included employment agencies in the output of IO-73, Business services.

Procedures for Estimating State Output

Current dollar measures of state industry output were constructed in three steps. First, state outputs were estimated for six major components: (1) SIC 0722, Veterinarians; (2) SIC 7361, Private employment agencies; (3) SIC 80, Medical services; (4) SIC 82, Educational services; (5) SIC 86, Nonprofit membership organizations; and (6) rental and royalty receipts. Next, the difference between the national total of these six major components and the OBE industry total was calculated. Because the residual obtained reflected components of output for which state data were unavailable, it was prorated to individual states on the basis of the data already compiled. Finally, total state industry output was estimated by summing the major components of output and the distributed residual. Table 6-13 lists the six components of output together with their national values, the OBE national industry output total, and the residual.

State estimates of output components were prepared by prorating national values of service receipts to states using several related proxy series. National receipts values were obtained from "Notes for the 1947 Interindustry Relations Study" [219], the *Census of Business, 1958* [106] and *1963* [107], *The National Income and Product Accounts of the United States, 1929-1965* [187], and *Statistics of Income* [226 through 233].

The receipts of veterinarians and nonprofit membership organizations were distributed to states on the basis of state employment and payroll data, respectively. State receipts of private employment agencies were obtained from the *Census of Business, 1948, 1958,* and *1963*. For 1947 and 1958, national estimates of medical service receipts were prorated to states based on the income of physicians and dentists reported in *Statistics of Income,* plus state receipts of hospitals estimated using data obtained from the American Hospital Association [6]. National estimates of medical services in 1963 were allocated to states using SIC 80 payrolls reported in *County Business Patterns, 1964* [141].

For 1947 and 1958, receipts of vocational and correspondence schools were allocated to states in proportion to the value of SIC 824 payrolls, while receipts of private elementary and secondary schools, as well as private colleges, were prorated to states on the basis of operating expenses. Educational outputs for 1963 were prorated to states in proportion to the state distribution of SIC 82 payrolls given in *County Business Patterns, 1964.*

Rents and royalties for 1958 and 1963 were distributed to states using the combined values of other state components.

Adjustment of Output to Constant Dollars

Current dollar state outputs were converted to constant dollar measures as described in Chapter 2. In deflating 1947 and 1958 outputs, the same component detail was maintained as is shown in Table 6-13.

Table 6-13
IO-77, Medical, Educational Services, and Nonprofit Organizations (millions of dollars)

Component	1947 Value	1947 Percent	1958 Value	1958 Percent	1963 Value	1963 Percent
SIC 0722 Veterinarians	$ 91	1.0	$ 92	0.4	$ 112	0.3
SIC 7361 Private employment agencies	27	0.3	101	0.4	145	0.4
SIC 80 Medical services:						
Physicians	3,744	43.1	4,574	20.1	18,040	54.2
Dentists			1,876	8.3		
Other professional services			832	3.7		
Hospitals	1,344	15.4	4,202	18.5		
SIC 82 Educational services:						
Elementary, secondary, and higher education	1,093	12.6	3,241	14.3	8,117	24.4
Vocational and correspondence schools	313	3.6	852	3.8		
SIC 86 Nonprofit membership organizations:						
Associations	1,821	21.0	931	4.1	5,277	15.8
Religious welfare and others			4,178	18.4		
Rents and royalties	–	–	9	–	29	0.1
Other components	259	3.0	1,815	8.0	1,585	4.8
Industry total	$8,692	100.0	$22,703	100.0	$33,305[a]	100.0

[a]Includes SIC 7361, Private employment agencies, which was excluded from the definition of industry output by the OBE in its 1963 table. The 1963 total given in the OBE table is $33,160 million.

IO-78, Federal Government Enterprises

OBE Definition. This industry covers the activities of those Federal Government agencies, with separate accounting records, that cover over half of their current operating cost by the sale of goods and services to the general public.

Output of Federal enterprises that are comparable to those of private establishments are transferred to the appropriate private industries for distribution. Outputs for which there are no private counterparts are distributed directly to consuming industries. [183, p. 23]

Definition of Output

Outputs of federal government enterprises are defined in the same fashion as the outputs of counterpart privately owned enterprises. Revenue is accepted as the measure of value. The net effect of the Commodity Credit Corporation on total industry output is nil, since crop subsidies reported as a purchase from farms are offset by a reduction in value added.

Procedures for Estimating State Output

State outputs of federal government enterprises were estimated in three steps. First, outputs were estimated for individual states for the three major components: (1) post office services, (2) the receipts of post exchanges, and (3) the value of services provided by other government enterprises. Next, the national sum of state components plus overseas operations of federal government enterprises (for example, revenues of the Panama Canal Company) was subtracted from the OBE industry total. The residual represented minor overestimates of the value of state output components. Because state data were unavailable for this residual, it was distributed to states by proration on the basis of major output components already compiled. Table 6-14 lists the three major components of output, the value of overseas activity, the OBE national industry total, and the amount of overvaluation of individual output components.

1947 Output Estimates. To estimate the 1947 value of output for individual enterprises composing IO-78, Federal government enterprises, an index was used to convert the 1958 output values of these activities to a 1947 level. The index, termed the "Enterprise Output Index," reflected the growth of output expressed in current dollars between 1947 and 1958. To construct the 1947 Enterprise Output Index, the 1947 value of major enterprise output components was expressed as a percentage of the 1958 value of the same items.

Table 6-14

IO-78, Federal Government Enterprises (millions of dollars)

Component	1947		1958		1963	
	Value	Percent	Value	Percent	Value	Percent
Post office	$1,333	75.0	$2,777	67.6	$4,001	68.2
Post exchanges	205	11.5	575	14.0	1,018	17.4
All other government enterprises	259	14.6	657	16.0	890	15.2
Output outside U.S.	51	3.0	96	2.4	121	2.0
Other components	−71[a]	−4.1[a]	−	−	−166[a]	−2.8[a]
Industry total	$1,777	100.0	$4,105	100.0	$5,864	100.0

[a]Negative statistic includes correction for overestimates of certain government enterprise outputs.

Because several government enterprises included in the 1958 definition of the industry output either did not exist in 1947 or only performed functions of a general government nature, their output was estimated as zero in 1947. These enterprises were the Alaska Railroad, the Housing and Home Finance Agency, the St. Lawrence Seaway, and the Southeastern Power Administration. State estimates of output were constructed by allocating national enterprise output values to states using the distribution series listed in Table 6-15 and summing state outputs to the required level of component detail.

1958 Output Estimates. National values of output were taken from worksheet data compiled by the OBE for use in its 1958 input-output table [194]. To construct state estimates, enterprise output values first were allocated to states using the distribution series given in Table 6-15, and then the state outputs were summed to the required level of detail.

1963 Output Estimates. Procedures for estimating 1963 output parallel the methods used to estimate 1947 state outputs.

Adjustment of Output to Constant Dollars

Current dollar state outputs were converted to constant dollars as described in Chapter 2. In deflating the 1947 and 1958 outputs, the same component detail was maintained as is shown in Table 6-14.

IO-79, State and Local Government Enterprises

OBE Definition. This industry covers the activities of the state and local government agencies, with separate accounting records, that cover over half of their current operating costs by the sale of goods and services to the general public. State and local government enterprises include: (1) gas and electric utilities, (2) water supply facilities, (3) transit facilities, (4) liquor stores, (5) water transportation and terminals, (6) air transportation facilities, (7) highway toll facilities, and such activities as (8) sewers and sewage disposal, (9) low-cost housing and urban renewal, and (10) some miscellaneous activities such as offstreet parking and city markets. The outputs of most state and local government enterprises are transferred to private industries in which the comparable activity is performed. Outputs for which there are no private counterparts were distributed directly to consuming industries. [183, p. 24]

Definition of Output

The output of state or municipally owned enterprises is defined in the same fashion as the output of counterpart privately owned firms.

Procedures for Estimating State Output

Current dollar estimates of state industry output were constructed in three steps. First, state outputs were estimated for four major components: (1) transit services, (2) other utility services (gas, electricity, and water), (3) government-operated liquor stores, and (4) other government enterprises. Next, the difference between the national total of these four components and the OBE industry total was calculated. The residual obtained represented the net effect of overvaluation of some enterprise outputs and minor omissions of other components for which state data were unavailable; consequently, it was prorated to individual states on the basis of the data already compiled. Finally, total state industry output was estimated by summing the major components of output and the distributed residual. Table 6-16 lists the four components of output together with their national values, the OBE industry total, and the residual.

1947 Output Estimates. Revenue data for fiscal years 1947 and 1948 given in the *Compendium of State Government Finances, 1947* [135] and *1948* [136] and the *Compendium of City Government Finances, 1947* [131] and *1948* [132] were used to estimate 1947 state output. To estimate calendar-year revenues, the average of earnings in fiscal years 1947 and 1948 were obtained for each of the following government activities: water supply, electricity, transit, gas, port facilities, airports, ferries, toll tunnels, and toll bridges. Margins on government liquor sales were also determined by averaging fiscal-year revenues. These enterprises were then combined into the four major components of industry outputs enumerated above.

Table 6-15
State Distribution Series Used to Allocate Federal Government Enterprise Outputs

Federal Government Enterprise	1947	1958	1963
Alaska Railroad	—	Allocated to Alaska	Allocated to Alaska
Army-Air Force Post Exchanges and Civilian Post Restaurants, Marine Post Exchanges, Naval Ships Stores, Naval Exchanges, Officers' and Enlisted Men's Clubs	Military personnel by state in 1950	Military personnel by state in 1960	Military personnel by state in 1960
Armed Forces Motion Picture Service	—	1958 Department of Defense motion picture receipts	1963 Department of Defense motion picture receipts
Direct Loan Program of the Veterans Administration	—	Amount of loans fully disbursed during 1958	Amount of loans fully disbursed during 1963
Federal Deposit Insurance Corporation	Agency employment by state in 1947	Agency employment by state in 1958	Agency employment by state in 1963
Federal Farm Mortgage Corporation	Total number of mortgage loans outstanding in 1947 by state	—	—
Federal Home Loan Bank Board	Agency employment by state in 1958	Agency employment by state in 1958	Agency employment by state in 1963
Federal Housing Administration	Value of family home mortgages insured in 1947 by state	Total new construction in 1958 under FHA insured home mortgages	Total new construction in 1963 under FHA insured home mortgages
Federal Intermediate Credit Banks	Loans and discounts during 1947 by state	Output by state in 1963	Output of branches tabulated from operating data
Federal National Mortgage Association	Output by state in 1963	Output by state in 1963	Agency employment by state in 1963
Federal Savings and Loan Insurance Corporation	Agency employment by state in 1963	Agency employment by state in 1963	Agency employment by state in 1963

Housing and Home Finance Agency	—	Allocated to Washington, D.C.	Allocated to Washington, D.C.
Post Office	Agency employment by state in 1947	Agency employment by state in 1958	Agency employment by state in 1963
Power Administrations	Installed kilowatt capacity by state	Installed kilowatt capacity by state	Installed kilowatt capacity by state
Tennessee Valley Authority	Agency employment by state in 1947	Agency employment by state in 1958	Agency employment by state in 1963
St. Lawrence Seaway	—	—	Agency employment by state in 1963

Table 6-16
IO-79, State and Local Government Enterprises (millions of dollars)

Component	1947		1958		1963	
	Value	Percent	Value	Percent	Value	Percent
Transit services	$ 236	13.8	$ 584	12.2	$ 437	6.1
Other utility services (gas, water, and electricity)	555	32.5	2,592	54.2	4,534	62.7
Government-operated liquor stores	194	11.3	308	6.4	148	2.0
Other government enterprises	42	2.5	1,466	30.7	2,890	39.9
Other components	681	39.9	−166[a]	−3.5[a]	−773[a]	−10.7[a]
Industry total	$1,708	100.0	$4,784	100.0	$7,236	100.0

[a]Negative statistic includes correction for overestimates of certain government enterprise outputs.

1958 Output Estimates. For 1958, statistics published in the *Compendium of State Government Finances, 1958* [137] and *Governmental Finances in 1958* [145] and *1959* [146] were employed to estimate state output. Earnings of government utilities by state were estimated as the average of fiscal-year receipts for 1958 and 1959. State liquor store margins were calculated as the product of national margins (expressed as a percent of total sales) and state liquor store sales. For the remaining enterprises (sewers and sewage disposal, housing, non-highway transportation, toll highways, etc.), state revenues were estimated by distributing national revenue totals for each enterprise in proportion to the state enterprise earnings in fiscal year 1957. All enterprise revenue estimates were combined by state to calculate values of the four major components of industry output.

1963 Output Estimates. Fiscal 1962 revenues of local governments from the provision of utility, sewerage, sanitation, housing, and transportation services and the sale of liquor were reported in *Census of Governments, 1962* [117]. These statistics were accepted as approximations of 1963 local government enterprise outputs by state. Enterprise revenues were combined to estimate values of the major components of output.

Adjustment of Output to Constant Dollars

Current dollar state outputs were converted to constant dollars as described in Chapter 2. In deflating the 1947 and 1958 outputs, the same component detail was maintained as is shown in Table 6-16.

IO-84, Government Industry

OBE Definition. This industry measures income and product originating in Federal, state, and local government. On the product side (or row total), it reflects purchases by general government of the services of its civilian and military employees. Represented on the income side (or column total), is employee compensations (wages and salaries in cash and in-kind, and employee supplements). [183, p. 25]

Definition of Output

The output of IO-84, Government industry, consists of the value of general government activities as measured by the wages and salaries paid to civilian and military employees. General government activities exclude the operations of government enterprises that perform services similar to those provided by private industry.

Procedures for Estimating State Output

In estimating state outputs, separate detail was maintained for (1) federal government services, and (2) state and local government activities. Wages and salaries paid to federal civilian and military employees and state and local government personnel were reported by state in *Personal Income by State Since 1929* [190] and in the *Survey of Current Business* [189; 191]. Because these statistics included the compensation of government enterprise personnel, estimates of government enterprise wage payments had to be deducted from the data. *The National Income and Products Accounts of the United States, 1929–1965* [187], provided national values of wage and salary disbursements made by federal government enterprises and state and local government enterprises. These controls were distributed to the states on the basis of estimated employee compensation of federal government enterprises and state and local government enterprises. With the exception of those enterprises where compensation could be directly allocated to specific states, estimates of personnel compensation were tabulated for individual federal government enterprises from data in *The Budget of the United States Government, Fiscal Year 1947* [38], *1958* [39], and *1963* [40] and distributed to states on the basis of federal enterprise paid civilian employment. Total personnel compensation expenditures of federal government enterprises by state were then reconciled with the national income account controls.

Estimates of state and local government enterprise payrolls were calculated for 1947 and 1958 from data in the *Census of Governments, 1957* [116] and

for 1963 from data in the *Census of Governments, 1962* [113] . Payrolls as of
April 1957 for state and local government enterprises were used to distribute the 1958 national value of wage and salary disbursements made by
local government enterprises. Because earlier payroll data were not available in
sufficient detail, this series was also used to distribute 1947 wage and salary
disbursements. The 1963 national value of wage and salary disbursements made
by state and local government enterprises was prorated to states based on 1962
enterprise payrolls.

After excluding the compensation of government enterprise employees, the
state estimates of (1) federal government, and (2) state and local government
output were summed to a national total, and the difference between this sum
and the OBE industry total was calculated. The residual obtained represented
the net effect of overvaluation of some components of output and minor
omissions of other components. Because state data on the residual were unavailable, it was distributed to individual states by prorating it on the basis of the
data already compiled. Finally, total state industry output was estimated by
summing the major components of output and the distributed residual. Table
6-17 lists the components of output together with their national values, the
OBE national industry output total, and the residual.

Adjustment of Output to Constant Dollars

Current dollar state outputs were converted to constant dollars as described
in Chapter 2. In deflating the 1947 and 1958 outputs, the same component detail
was maintained as is shown in Table 6-17.

Table 6-17
IO-84, Government Industry (millions of dollars)

	1947		1958		1963	
Component	Value	Percent	Value	Percent	Value	Percent
General federal government wage and salary disbursements	$ 6,916	44.6	$16,105	41.2	$20,782	37.8
Overseas military	1,556	10.1	3,030	7.8	2,456	4.4
General state and local government wage and salary disbursements	7,015	45.3	19,908	51.0	30,137	54.8
Other components	243	–	–14[a]	–	1,654	3.0
Industry total	$15,730	100.0	$39,029	100.0	$55,029	100.0

[a]Negative statistic includes correction for overvaluation of component industry outputs.

IO-86, Household Industry

OBE Definition. This industry measures income and product originating in households. The product side (or row total) reflects purchases by households of the services of domestics. (In accordance with new GNP concepts, this industry no longer includes interest payments to nonpersonal lenders.) Represented on the income side (or column total) is the employee compensation (wages and salaries in cash and in-kind and supplements) of domestic servants. [183, p. 26]

Procedures for Estimating State Output

Estimates of wage and salary payments to household domestics by state were obtained from worksheet data of the Regional Economics Division of the OBE [196]. These statistics covered annual payments in 1947, 1958, and 1963. The value of wage and salary payments by state was adjusted by proration to agree with national industry totals reported by the OBE (see Table 6-18).

Adjustment of Output to Constant Dollars

Current dollar state outputs were converted to constant dollars as described in Chapter 2. For this industry, separate component detail was not maintained in deflating 1947 and 1958 outputs.

Critique of Procedures and Data Used in Estimating State Outputs

The most serious shortcoming of service-sector output estimates is a lack of adequate state data. When information on state service receipts was unavailable

Table 6-18
IO-86, Household Industry (millions of dollars)

Component	1947 Value	1947 Percent	1958 Value	1958 Percent	1963 Value	1963 Percent
Wages and salaries	$2,361	100.5	$3,477	99.3	$3,784	99.0
Other components	−13[a]	−0.5[a]	26	0.7	40	1.0
Industry total	$2,348	100.0	$3,503	100.0	$3,824	100.0

[a]Negative statistic includes correction for overestimates of components of output.

for a specific year, it was necessary to prorate national control estimates to states either in proportion to receipts for some other year or in proportion to factor input measures such as employment or payrolls. These techniques assume that either the historical pattern of activity has not changed or that labor is always equally productive. A conceptual problem was also encountered in allocating the output of a single facility located in several states. This was particularly troublesome in estimating outputs associated with telephone communications and gas, electricity, and water utilities. The most practical solution was to allocate facility revenues to states in proportion to labor inputs. If data on capital equipment had been available, it would have been more appropriate to distribute output on the basis of the weighted inputs of labor and capital.

7

Estimation of Industrial Employment and Annual Payrolls by State

For the calculation of employment-to-output ratios or direct labor requirements coefficients by state, industry employment and annual payrolls were prepared for the years 1947, 1958, and 1963. Separate employment estimates were compiled for employees and self-employed workers. State payroll statistics represent current dollar wage and salary payments made only to employees. Because wages and salaries represent only a portion of the income which the self-employed obtain from their employment, a corresponding measure of payments to the self-employed was not developed.

Payroll and employment measures were constructed for 81 input-output industries. Wherever possible, comparability was maintained between the state output estimates described in previous chapters and state labor input estimates, but certain minor elements of output had no corresponding labor input. It was not feasible to estimate labor inputs associated with either insignificant redefinitions of establishment activity or output values determined by imputation rather than market transactions.

Redefinitions split the output of certain establishments into two or more separate activities. These activities are then assigned to appropriate input-output industries. As an example, the receipts of hotels (SIC 701) are divided into room rentals and receipts for the sale of meals and other goods. Room rental receipts are assigned to IO-72, Hotels & lodging places; personal & repair services, except automobile repair, while retail margins on the sale of meals and other goods form a portion of the output of IO-69, Wholesale & retail trade. Since the small portion of total hotel employment associated with the preparation and sale of foods could not be determined, all hotel employment and payrolls were grouped with IO-72. Similarly, the labor expended by homeowners in maintaining owner-occupied dwellings could not be determined. This factor input is conceptually associated with the imputed rent of owner-occupied housing in IO-71, Real estate & rental. Also, the imputation of force account construction contained in IO-11, New construction, output was not paralleled by the inclusion of force account construction workers in IO-11 employment and payroll statistics.

Further, the employment and payrolls of central administrative offices and auxiliary facilities could not be associated with the specific industry output of each state. To partially offset this gap in state employment and payroll statistics, separate tabulations of national CAO employment and payrolls for two-digit manufacturing SIC codes and state CAO employment and payrolls were prepared

101

for five major industry groups: mining, manufacturing, wholesale trade, retail trade, and service industries. In general, however, these differences are not considered serious impediments to future use of the state labor input statistics.

Unlike data on output, numerous sources of information exist on employment and annual payrolls. More or less comprehensive state employment and earnings information can be obtained from the Census, BLS, and the Social Security Administration (SSA). In addition, the Regional Economics Division (RED) of the OBE compiles state data on payrolls. Data available from each of these sources are gathered under reporting systems which vary slightly in their classification of reporting establishments, in the extent of worker and establishment coverage, and in the industrial and geographic detail of collection and presentation. In Table 7-1, the magnitude of difference associated with 1958 national employment statistics reported by three agencies—Census, BLS, and SSA—can be seen and compared with the average number of employees engaged in production reported by the OBE in the National Income and Product Accounts. Summaries of employment statistics presented in this study are also included.

When it was not possible to tabulate employee statistics and payroll data from the same sources of information used to establish output, data were tabulated from whatever substitute sources best fulfilled the requirements for comprehensive industry and geographic detail. The use of substitute sources was limited and was primarily associated with nonmanufacturing industry statistics. *County Business Patterns* (*CBP*), based on SSA data and published by the Census, was the most frequently used alternate. First-quarter payroll values reported in this publication were adjusted to an annual value by calculating the ratio of wages and salaries reported in the National Income and Product Accounts to the national value of first-quarter payrolls and then multiplying individual state first-quarter payroll statistics by this ratio to estimate annual payrolls. Similarly, first-quarter employment statistics were adjusted to remove seasonal variation before being incorporated into industry employment figures.

Obtaining industry employment data from different sources may result in some overlap or gaps in total employment coverage, because different sources have slight variations in industrial classification, especially of multiplant firms and central and administrative offices. Some inconsistencies result, and data based on a mixture of sources cannot be reconciled precisely with aggregate U.S. totals from a single source unless all state statistics are uniformly scaled. The effect of these differences at major industry levels can be seen in Table 7-1.

Estimates of self-employment were prepared in two steps. First, the national ratio of self-employed persons to employees was calculated for each industry. These ratios were then used to scale individual state estimates of employment by industry to estimates of self-employment by industry.

The remainder of this chapter presents, first, a brief description of data sources used to compile payroll and employment statistics. Since characteristics of these information sources are also applicable to the data used in preparing output measures, this description supplements the discussions contained in Chapters 2 through 6. After the description of data sources, the procedures used in preparing employment and payroll measures are outlined for the manufacturing and nonmanufacturing industries, respectively.

Principal Data Sources Used in Compiling Measures of Industry Employment and Annual Payrolls by State

Data used in this project were obtained from secondary source materials prepared by the federal government. The descriptions below cover the scope and presentation of material contained in recent editions of each source and provide brief explanations of the techniques used by the compiling agencies.

Census of Mineral Industries [128].—This publication covers all private mineral industry establishments with production expenses of $500 or more, as well as certain selected noncommercial operations. Employment statistics are computed as the average of four selected pay periods. For highly seasonal industries, the annual statistics are determined as the average of twelve monthly pay periods. The payroll statistics represent an annual measure and cover only employee earnings subject to federal withholding tax. When suitable primary source information was not available, estimates were made by the Census from historical data. Statistical information on payrolls and employment presented in this source is classified by SIC code and state.

Census of Business [104; 107; 111].—Data on public warehousing, wholesale and retail trade, and selected service establishments are contained in this publication. Information is collected from firms subject to taxation under the Federal Insurance Contributions Act according to the active records of the Internal Revenue Service. Although state employment statistics are for the number of employees during the workweek ending nearest November 15, payroll statistics, which include the salaries of corporate officers, are an annual measure. Statistics on payrolls and employment presented in this source are classified by SIC code and state.

Census of Manufactures [124].—This publication contains data covering all manufacturing establishments. Information is collected from firms subject to taxation under the Federal Insurance Contributions Act according to the active records of the Internal Revenue Service. State employment statistics are an average of the number of full- and part-time workers employed during the pay periods nearest the fifteenth day of four separate months: March, May, August, and November. For highly seasonal industries, employment is determined as the average of twelve monthly pay periods. (In 1947 twelve periods were used for all industries.) Payrolls cover only employee earnings subject to federal withholding

Table 7-1
Comparison of 1958 National Employment Statistics (thousands of employees)

Industry	Bureau of Labor Statistics	Social Security Administration	Source Agency Bureau of the Census	Office of Business Economics	Total of State Estimates from this Project
Agriculture, forestry, and fisheries	NA	NA	NA	1,989	2,125
Mining	751	705	749	752	615[a]
Construction	2,778	2,498	NA	2,794	3,238[b]
Manufacturing	15,945	16,207	15,996	15,908	15,287
Transportation	2,595	1,545[c]	NA	2,532	2,687
Communications	860	833	NA	858	811
Electricity, gas, and sanitation services	610	565	NA	615	541
Trade	10,750	10,835	10,708	10,783	10,708
Finance, insurance, and real estate	2,159	2,505	NA	2,552	2,548
Services:	NA	NA	NA	9,093	9,083
Hotels and lodgings	527	509	502	524	d
Personal services	877	867	919	890	d
Miscellaneous business services	639	639	616	637	d
Automobile repairs	NA	239	256	234	254
Miscellaneous repairs	NA	132	134	124	d
Motion pictures	199	189	196	199	d
Amusements	NA	286	285	306	d
Medical services	1,465	1,383	NA	1,455	d
Legal services	134	139	NA	141	d
Educational services	685	372	NA	663	d
Nonprofit organizations	NA	685	NA	1,017	d
Miscellaneous professional services	317	321	NA	353	d
Household services	NA	NA	NA	2,550	2,550

Government enterprises	7,839	{ NA	NA	996	951
General government		{ NA	NA	9,832	8,379e

aExcludes oil and gas drilling services employment (SIC 138).
bIncludes oil and gas drilling services employment (SIC 138) and a portion of operative builders employment (SIC 6561).
cExcludes railroad employment (SIC 40).
dData are not comparable since input-output definitions do not match the SIC groupings reflected by other data.
eExcludes overseas employment.
NA. Not available.

Sources: Column 1: *Employment and Earnings Statistics for States and Areas, 1939–1965* [216]; Column 2: *County Business Patterns, 1959* [140] – employment on March 15, 1959; Column 3: *Census of Manufactures, 1958* [123], *Census of Mineral Industries, 1958* [127], and *Census of Business, 1958* [106]; Column 4: *The National Income and Product Accounts of the United States, 1929–1965* [187] – average number of full-time and part-time employees.

tax. In this source, statistics on payrolls and employment are categorized by SIC code and state.

Census of Governments [113].—Two methods were used to gather information on government activity: (1) a mail canvass of all state and local governments, and (2) reports filed by individual federal government agencies with the Civil Service Commission. Employment and payroll data cover only one month and are identified by industry or activity description and state.

County Business Patterns (Social Security Administration data published by the Census) [141].—Statistics from this publication include all private, nonfarm establishments and nonprofit organizations subject to payment of social security taxes under the Federal Insurance Contributions Act (FICA). Although employment represents the number of employees during the pay period ending nearest March 15, payrolls represent wage and salary payments made during the first calendar quarter which were subject to taxation under FICA. Estimates are frequently made for small establishments which fail to properly report employment and payroll data. Statistical information is categorized by SIC codes and state.

Business Establishments, Employment, and Taxable Payrolls, 1947 [174].— This publication is the predecessor of *County Business Patterns,* and information contained in it is similar to that described above, except that less industry detail is available from this earlier source.

Employment and Earnings Statistics for States and Areas, 1939–1965 [216].—Data presented in this source are based on a monthly sample of all employers reporting under state unemployment insurance acts. Annual estimates of the number of employees are calculated as the average of monthly sample statistics supplemented by data on small firms obtained from the SSA, and the sample estimates are periodically adjusted to total levels indicated by social insurance statistics. This source has no annual payroll data corresponding to the employment data presented. Since information is gathered by state government agencies operating under separate insurance laws, establishment coverage varies by state. Employment data are presented for large SIC classifications by state.

Procedures Used to Estimate State Manufacturing Industry Employment and Payrolls

The *Census of Manufactures, 1947* [122], *1958* [123], and *1963* [124] provided the majority of all data used to establish state estimates of industry employment and the value of annual payrolls. Employment and payroll measures were compiled simultaneously. First, comprehensive sets of state three-digit and selected four-digit SIC manufacturing industry employee and payroll statistics were prepared. When the Census withheld information to avoid disclosing individual manufacturing establishment data, special estimates were made. Employee and payroll data were then grouped and aggregated by input-output industry definition.

Self-employment estimates for input-output industries were derived as the product of ratios of self-employed persons to employees by input-output industry (established at the national level) and state statistics on industry employment. National ratios used for this estimation were obtained from industry employment data contained in Census data. For 1947, self-employment data were estimated using ratios taken from the *Census of Population, 1950* [129] and for 1958 and 1963, from the *Census of Population, 1960* [130].

State tabulations of 1958 and 1963 CAO employment and payrolls for manufacturing were made from *Enterprise Statistics, 1963*, published by the Bureau of the Census [144].

1947 Employment and Payroll Estimates

As mentioned in Chapter 2, the industrial classification system employed in the *Census of Manufactures, 1947* [122] differs from the SIC coding system used in defining input-output industries. Therefore, as in estimating 1947 shipments, three-digit and selected four-digit SIC employee and payroll statistics were estimated in two steps. First, a complete set of estimates, organized according to the 1947 Census coding scheme, was constructed; second, these estimates were converted to 1957 SIC classifications, employing the same procedures and HERP conversion percentages that were used in compiling shipments estimates.

Procedures used to estimate data withheld by the Census were similar to those used in developing 1947 shipments. Where necessary, regional and/or national employee data were prorated to states on the basis of the number of four-digit establishments. Payroll estimates were calculated as the product of national and/or regional average industry earnings per employee and state employment.

1958 and 1963 Employment and Payroll Estimates

Data collected for the *Census of Manufactures, 1958* [123] and *1963* [124] were used to establish employee and payroll estimates for all three-digit industries and for four-digit industries required to define input-output industries. Estimates were prepared for industries where the Census withheld data to avoid disclosures of information on individual establishments. To estimate the number of employees, frequency distributions of plants classified by employee size were multiplied by national average employment per plant classified by plant size for the subject industry. Frequency distributions were obtained from either the *Location of Manufacturing Plants, 1958* [148] and *1963* [149] or footnotes in the *Census of Manufactures, 1958* and *1963*. In some cases, the accuracy of these estimates was increased by the proration of residual regional industry employment to individual states. Once employee estimates were established for all states, payroll estimates were calculated as the product of average national and/or regional earnings per employee and state industry employment.

Procedures Used to Estimate State Nonmanufacturing Industry Employment and Payrolls

Payroll and employment estimates for nonmanufacturing industries were prepared in the same component detail used in constructing output estimates, with one major exception—only total industry statistics were prepared for IO-1 through IO-4. As stated earlier, data used in measuring employment and payrolls were taken from the same source materials used in calculating outputs, whenever possible. Summaries of the sources used are given in Tables 7-2 and 7-3.

Table 7-2

Principal Data Sources Used in Compiling State Estimates of Nonmanufacturing Input-Output Industry Payrolls

Input-Output Industry		Year		
No.	*Title*	*1947*	*1958*	*1963*
1	Livestock & livestock prdts.	*AS*	*AS*	*AS*
2	Other agricultural prdts.	*AS*	*AS*	*AS*
3	Forestry & fishery prdts.	a	a	a
4	Ag., for., & fish. services	a	a	a
5	Iron & ferro. ores mining	b	*CMI*	*CMI*
6	Nonferrous metal ores mining	b	*CMI*	*CMI*
7	Coal mining	*BEEP*	*CMI*	*CMI*
8	Crude petro., natural gas	b	*CMI*	*CMI*
9	Stone & clay mining	b	*CMI*	*CMI*
10	Chem. & fert. mineral mining	b	*CMI*	*CMI*
11	New construction	RED	RED	RED
12	Maint. & repair construction	RED	RED	RED
65	Transportation & warehousing	*BEEP* and RED	*CBP* and RED	*CBP* and RED
66	Communications, exc. brdcast.	*BEEP*	*CBP*	*CBP*
67	Radio & TV broadcasting	b	*CBP*	*CBP*
68	Elec., gas, water & san. serv.	b	*CBP*	*CBP*
69	Wholesale & retail trade	*CB*	*CB*	*CB*
70	Finance & insurance	*BEEP* and RED	*CBP* and RED	*CBP* and RED

Table 7-2 cont.

Input-Output Industry		Year		
No.	Title	1947	1958	1963
71	Real estate & rental	BEEP and RED	CBP and RED	CBP and RED
72	Hotels; repair serv., exc. auto	BEEP and CB	CBP and CB	CBP and CB
73	Business services	BEEP and CB	CBP and CB	CBP and CB
74	Research & development	b	CB	CB
75	Automobile repair & services	CB	CB	CB
76	Amusements	BEEP	CB	CB
77	Med., ed. serv., nonprof. org.	BEEP and CB	CBP and CB	CBP and CB
78	Federal govt. enterprises	CB, RED, & CSC	CB, RED, & CSC	CB, RED, & CSC
79	State & local govt. enterprises	b	CG	CG
84	Government industry	EE	EE	EE
86	Household industry	CP	CP	CP

[a]Computed using national payroll/output ratios.
[b]Computed using state payroll/output ratios and reconciled to National Income and Product Account totals.

Key: AS   = *Agricultural Statistics*, USDA.
       BEEP = *Business Establishments, Employment, and Taxable Payrolls*, Census.
       CB   = *Census of Business*, Census.
       CBP   = *County Business Patterns*, Census.
       CG   = *Census of Government*, Census.
       CSC   = Unpublished Civil Service Commission data.
       CMI   = *Census of Mineral Industries*, Census.
       CP   = *Census of Population*, Census.
       EE   = *Employment and Earnings*, BLS.
       RED   = Unpublished Regional Economics Division (OBE) data.

When *County Business Patterns* first-quarter payroll information was used, it was expanded to an annual value by multiplying state statistics by the national ratio of National Income and Product Account annual wage and salary statistics to *CBP* first-quarter payrolls. *CBP* employment statistics were adjusted to remove seasonal variation by one of two methods. For the construction, transportation, finance, and real estate sectors, the employment data were altered using state correction factors developed from OBE Regional Economics Division state wage data. In all other cases, the employment was adjusted using national coefficients prepared from National Income and Product Account statistics.

For certain industries, state employment and payroll data were not available

Table 7-3
Principal Data Sources Used in Compiling State Estimates of Nonmanufacturing
Input-Output Industry Employment

Input-Output Industry		Year		
No.	Title	1947	1958	1963
1	Livestock & livestock prdts.	AS	AS	AS
2	Other agricultural prdts.	AS	AS	AS
3	Forestry & fishery prdts.	a	a	a
4	Ag., for., & fish. services	a	a	a
5	Iron & ferro. ores mining	b	CMI	CMI
6	Nonferrous metal ores mining	b	CMI	CMI
7	Coal mining	BEEP	CMI	CMI
8	Crude petro., natural gas	b	CMI	CMI
9	Stone & clay mining	b	CMI	CMI
10	Chem. & fert. mineral mining	b	CMI	CMI
11	New construction	BEEP	CBP	CBP
12	Maint. & repair construction	BEEP	CBP	CBP
65	Transportation & warehousing	BEEP	CBP	CBP
66	Communications, exc. brdcast.	BEEP	CBP	CBP
67	Radio & TV broadcasting	b	CBP	CBP
68	Elec., gas, water & san. serv.	b	CBP	CBP
69	Wholesale & retail trade	CB	CB	CB
70	Finance & insurance	BEEP	CBP	CBP
71	Real estate & rental	BEEP	CBP	CBP
72	Hotels; repair serv., exc. auto	BEEP and CB	CBP and CB	CBP and CB
73	Business services	BEEP and CB	CBP and CB	CBP and CB
74	Research & development	b	CB	CB
75	Automobile repair & services	CB	CB	CB
76	Amusements	BEEP	CB	CB
77	Med., ed. serv., nonprof. org.	BEEP and CB	CBP and CB	CBP and CB
78	Federal govt. enterprises	CB, RED, & CSC	CB, RED, & CSC	CB, RED, & CSC
79	State & local govt. enterprises	b	CG	CG
84	Government industry	EE	EE	EE
86	Household industry	CP	CP	CP

aComputed using national employment/output ratios.

bComputed using state employment/output ratios and reconciled to National Income and Product Account totals.

Key: AS   = *Agricultural Statistics*, USDA.
      BEEP = *Business Establishments, Employment, and Taxable Payrolls*, Census.
      CB   = *Census of Business*, Census.
      CBP = *County Business Patterns*, Census.
      CG   = *Census of Government*, Census
      CSG = Unpublished Civil Service Commission data.
      CMI = *Census of Mineral Industries*, Census.
      CP   = *Census of Population*, Census.
      EE   = *Employment and Earnings*, BLS.
      RED = Unpublished Regional Economics Division (OBE) data.

for all three time periods considered by this project. Information did not exist for IO-3, Forestry & fishery products, and IO-4, Agricultural, forestry, & fishery services, for any of the subject years. Also, for most of the mining industries, broadcasting, electric and gas utilities and state and local government enterprises, 1947 data were incomplete. These information gaps were filled by making estimates. Statistics for IO-3 and IO-4 were generated using employment or payroll to output ratios established from national statistics. For the remaining 1947 industries, estimates were made from 1958 state employment or payroll to output ratios and 1947 industry output. The resulting products were then adjusted by proration to coincide with 1947 National Income and Product Account measures for the nation as a whole.

Self-employment figures were prepared in precisely the same manner for the nonmanufacturing industries as for the manufacturing industries (see page 107). From the *Enterprise Statistics, 1963*, published by the Census [144], state tabulations were made of 1958 and 1963 CAO employment and payrolls for mining, retail trade, wholesale trade, and selected service industries.

Conclusion

To assure comparability among the output, employment, and payroll estimates, the three sets of data were investigated for inconsistencies, and adjustments were made before the final tabulations were completed. The adjusted data are presented in Appendix C.

Appendix A:
Classification Tables

Table A-1
Input-Output Industry Numbers, Titles, and Related SIC Codes

Industry Number	Industry Title	Related SIC Codes (1957 edition)[a]
1	Livestock & livestock products	013, pt. 014, 0193, pt. 02, pt. 0729
2	Other agricultural products	011, 012, pt. 014, 0192, 0199, pt. 02
3	Forestry & fishery products	074, 081, 082, 084, 086, 091
4	Agricultural, forestry, & fishery services	071, 0723, 0729, 085, 098
5	Iron & ferroalloy ores mining	1011, 106
6	Nonferrous metal ores mining	102, 103, 104, 105, 108, 109
7	Coal mining	11, 12
8	Crude petroleum & natural gas	1311, 1321
9	Stone & clay mining & quarrying	141, 142, 144, 145, 148, 149
10	Chemical & fertilizer mineral mining	147
11	New construction	138, pt. 15, pt. 16, pt. 17, pt. 6561
12	Maintenance & repair construction	pt. 15, pt. 16, pt. 17
13	Ordnance & accessories	19
14	Food & kindred products	20
15	Tobacco manufactures	21
16	Broad & narrow fabrics, yarn & thread mills	221, 222, 223, 224, 226, 228
17	Miscellaneous textile goods & floor coverings	227, 229
18	Apparel	225, 23 (excluding 239), 3992
19	Miscellaneous fabricated textile products	239
20	Lumber & wood products, except containers	24 (excluding 244)
21	Wooden containers	244
22	Household furniture	251
23	Other furniture & fixtures	25 (excluding 251)
24	Paper & allied products, except containers & boxes	26 (excluding 265)
25	Paperboard containers & boxes	265

No.	Description	Codes
26	Printing & publishing	27
27	Chemicals & selected chemical products	281 (excluding alumina pt. of 2819), 286, 287, 289
28	Plastics & synthetic materials	282
29	Drugs, cleaning, & toilet preparations	283, 284
30	Paints & allied products	285
31	Petroleum refining & related industries	29
32	Rubber & miscellaneous plastics products	30
33	Leather tanning & industrial leather products	311, 312
34	Footwear & other leather products	31 (excluding 311, 312)
35	Glass & glass products	321, 322, 323
36	Stone & clay products	324, 325, 326, 327, 328, 329
37	Primary iron & steel manufacturing	331, 332, 3391, 3399
38	Primary nonferrous metals manufacturing	2819 (alumina only), 333, 334, 335, 336, 3392
39	Metal containers	3411, 3491
40	Heating, plumbing, & fabricated structural metal products	343, 344
41	Screw machine products, bolts, nuts, etc., & metal stampings	345, 346
42	Other fabricated metal products	342, 347, 348, 349 (excluding 3491)
43	Engines & turbines	351
44	Farm machinery & equipment	352
45	Construction, mining, oil field machinery & equipment	3531, 3532, 3533
46	Materials handling machinery & equipment	3534, 3535, 3536, 3537
47	Metalworking machinery & equipment	354
48	Special industry machinery & equipment	355
49	General industrial machinery & equipment	356
50	Machine shop products	359
51	Office, computing, & accounting machines	357
52	Service industry machines	358
53	Electric transmission & distribution equipment, & electrical industrial apparatus	361, 362
54	Household appliances	363
55	Electric lighting & wiring equipment	364
56	Radio, TV, & communication equipment	365, 366

Table A-1, cont.

Industry Number	Industry Title	Related SIC Codes (1957 edition)[a]
57	Electronic components & accessories	367
58	Miscellaneous electrical machinery, equipment, & supplies	369
59	Motor vehicles & equipment	371
60	Aircraft & parts	372
61	Other transportation equipment	373, 374, 375, 379
62	Professional, scientific, & controlling instruments & supplies	381, 382, 384, 387
63	Optical, ophthalmic, & photographic equipment & supplies	383, 385, 386
64	Miscellaneous manufacturing	39 (excluding 3992)
65	Transportation & warehousing	40, 41, 42, 44, 45, 46, 47
66	Communications, except radio & TV broadcasting	481, 482, 489
67	Radio & TV broadcasting	483
68	Electric, gas, water, & sanitary services	49
69	Wholesale & retail trade	50 (excluding manufacturers sales offices), 52, 53, 54, 55, 56, 57, 58, 59, pt. 7399
70	Finance & insurance	60, 61, 62, 63, 64, 66, 67
71	Real estate & rental	65 (excluding 6541 and pt. 6561)
72	Hotels & lodging places; personal & repair services, except automobile repair	70, 72, 76 (excluding 7694 and 7699)
73	Business services	6541, 73 (excluding 7361, 7391, and pt. 7399), 7694, 7699, 81, 89 (excluding 8921)
74	Research & development	(eliminated in 1963 study)
75	Automobile repair & services	75
76	Amusements	78, 79
77	Medical, educational services, & nonprofit organizations	0722, 7361, 80, 82, 84, 86, 8921

78	Federal government enterprises	. . . .
79	State & local government enterprises	. . . .
80a	Directly allocated imports of goods & services	. . . .
80b	Transferred imports of goods & services	. . . .
81	Business travel, entertainment, & gifts	. . . .
82	Office supplies	. . . .
83	Scrap, used, & secondhand goods	. . . .
84	Government industry	. . . .
85	Rest of the world industry	. . . .
86	Household industry	. . . .
87	Inventory valuation adjustment	. . . .
88	Personal consumption expenditures	
89	Gross private fixed capital formation	
90	Net inventory change	
91	Net exports	
92	Federal government purchases	
93	State & local government net purchases	

[a]These are the SIC codes assigned to industries in the 1958 input-output study. They differ slightly from those assigned in the 1963 study.

Table A-2

Manufacturing Input-Output Industries Defined by Three- and Four-Digit SIC Codes

IO-13 Ordnance & accessories
      191 Guns, howitzers, mortars, and related equipment
      192 Ammunition, except for small arms
      193 Tanks and tank components
      194 Sighting and fire control equipment
      195 Small arms
      196 Small arms ammunition
      199 Ordnance and accessories, n.e.c.

IO-14 Food & kindred products
      201 Meat products
      202 Dairy products
      203 Canning and preserving fruits, vegetables, and sea foods
      204 Grain mill products
      205 Bakery products
      206 Sugar
      207 Confectionery and related products
      208 Beverage industries
      209 Miscellaneous food preparations and kindred products

IO-15 Tobacco manufactures
      211 Cigarettes
      212 Cigars
      213 Tobacco (chewing and smoking) and snuff
      214 Tobacco stemming and redrying

IO-16 Broad & narrow fabrics, yarn & thread mills
      221 Broad woven fabric mills, cotton
      222 Broad woven fabric mills, man-made fiber and silk
      223 Broad woven fabric mills, wool: including dyeing and finishing
      224 Narrow fabrics and other smallwares mills: cotton, wool, silk, and
           man-made fiber
      226 Dyeing and finishing textiles, except wool fabrics and knit goods
      228 Yarn and thread mills

IO-17 Miscellaneous textile goods & floor coverings
      227 Floor covering mills
      229 Miscellaneous textile goods

IO-18 Apparel
      225 Knitting mills
      231 Men's, youths', and boys' suits, coats, and overcoats
      232 Men's, youths', and boys' furnishings, work clothing, and allied
           garments
      233 Women's, misses', and juniors' outerwear
      234 Women's, misses', children's, and infants' undergarments
      235 Hats, caps, and millinery
      236 Girls', children's, and infants' outerwear
      237 Fur goods
      238 Miscellaneous apparel and accessories
    3992 Furs, dressed and dyed

Table A-2 cont.

IO-19 Miscellaneous fabricated textile products
    239 Miscellaneous fabricated textile products

IO-20 Lumber & wood products, except containers
    241 Logging camps and logging contractors
    242 Sawmills and planing mills
    243 Millwork, veneer, plywood, and prefabricated structural wood products
    249 Miscellaneous wood products

IO-21 Wooden containers
    244 Wooden containers

IO-22 Household furniture
    251 Household furniture

IO-23 Other furniture & fixtures
    252 Office furniture
    253 Public building and related furniture
    254 Partitions, shelving, lockers, and office and store fixtures
    259 Miscellaneous furniture and fixtures

IO-24 Paper & allied products, except containers & boxes
    261 Pulp mills
    262 Paper mills, except building paper mills
    263 Paperboard mills
    264 Converted paper and paperboard products, except containers and boxes
    266 Building paper and building board mills

IO-25 Paperboard containers & boxes
    265 Paperboard containers and boxes

IO-26 Printing & publishing
    271 Newspapers: publishing, publishing and printing
    272 Periodicals: publishing, publishing and printing
    273 Books
    274 Miscellaneous publishing
    275 Commercial printing
    276 Manifold business forms manufacturing
    277 Greeting card manufacturing
    278 Bookbinding and related industries
    279 Service industries for the printing trade

IO-27 Chemicals & selected chemical products
    281 (exc. 28195) Industrial inorganic and organic chemicals
    286 Gum and wood chemicals
    287 Agricultural chemicals
    289 Miscellaneous chemical products

IO-28 Plastics & synthetic materials
    282 Plastics materials and synthetic resins, synthetic rubber, synthetic and other man-made fibers, except glass

Table A–2 cont.

IO-29 Drugs, cleaning, & toilet preparations
    283 Drugs
    284 Soap, detergents and cleaning preparations, perfumes, cosmetics, and other toilet preparations

IO-30 Paints & allied products
    285 Paints, varnishes, lacquers, enamels, and allied products

IO-31 Petroleum refining & related industries
    291 Petroleum refining
    295 Paving and roofing materials
    299 Miscellaneous products of petroleum and coal

IO-32 Rubber & miscellaneous plastics products
    301 Tires and inner tubes
    302 Rubber footwear
    303 Reclaimed rubber
    306 Fabricated rubber products, n.e.c.
    307 Miscellaneous plastics products

IO-33 Leather tanning & industrial leather products
    311 Leather tanning and finishing
    312 Industrial leather belting and packing

IO-34 Footwear & other leather products
    313 Boot and shoe cut stock and findings
    314 Footwear, except rubber
    315 Leather gloves and mittens
    316 Luggage
    317 Handbags and other personal leather goods
    319 Leather goods, n.e.c.

IO-35 Glass & glass products
    321 Flat glass
    322 Glass and glassware, pressed or blown
    323 Glass products, made of purchased glass

IO-36 Stone & clay products
    324 Cement, hydraulic
    325 Structural clay products
    326 Pottery and related products
    327 Concrete, gypsum, and plaster products
    328 Cut stone and stone products
    329 Abrasive, asbestos, and miscellaneous nonmetallic mineral products

IO-37 Primary iron & steel manufacturing
    331 Blast furnaces, steel works, and rolling and finishing mills
    332 Iron and steel foundries
   3391 Iron and steel forgings
   3399 Primary metal industries, n.e.c.

IO-38 Primary nonferrous metals manufacturing
    333 Primary smelting and refining of nonferrous metals
    334 Secondary smelting and refining of nonferrous metals and alloys
    335 Rolling, drawing, and extruding of nonferrous metals

Table A-2 cont.

336 Nonferrous foundries
3392 Nonferrous forgings
28195 Industrial inorganic chemicals, n.e.c.

IO-39 Metal containers
3411 Metal cans
3491 Metal shipping barrels, drums, kegs, and pails

IO-40 Heating, plumbing & fabricated structural metal products
343 Heating apparatus (except electric) and plumbing fixtures
344 Fabricated structural metal products

IO-41 Screw machine products, bolts, nuts, etc., & metal stampings
345 Screw machine products, and bolts, nuts, screws, rivets and washers
346 Metal stampings

IO-42 Other fabricated metal products
342 Cutlery, hand tools, and general hardware
347 Coating, engraving, and allied services
348 Miscellaneous fabricated wire products
349 (exc. 3491) Miscellaneous fabricated metal products

IO-43 Engines & turbines
351 Engines and turbines

IO-44 Farm machinery and equipment
352 Farm machinery and equipment

IO-45 Construction, mining, oil field machinery & equipment
3531 Construction machinery and equipment
3532 Mining machinery and equipment, except oil field machinery and equipment
3533 Oil field machinery and equipment

IO-46 Materials handling machinery & equipment
3534 Elevators and moving stairways
3535 Conveyors and conveying equipment
3536 Hoists, industrial cranes, and monorail systems
3537 Industrial trucks, tractors, trailers, and stackers

IO-47 Metalworking machinery & equipment
354 Metalworking machinery and equipment

IO-48 Special industry machinery & equipment
355 Special industry machinery, except metalworking machinery

IO-49 General industrial machinery & equipment
356 General industrial machinery and equipment

IO-50 Machine shop products
359 Miscellaneous machinery, except electrical

IO-51 Office, computing, & accounting machines
357 Office, computing, and accounting machines

Table A–2 cont.

IO-52 Service industry machines
 358 Service industry machines

IO-53 Electric transmission & distribution equipment, and electrical industrial apparatus
 361 Electric transmission and distribution equipment
 363 Electrical industrial apparatus

IO-54 Household appliances
 363 Household appliances

IO-55 Electric lighting & wiring equipment
 364 Electric lighting and wiring equipment

IO-56 Radio, television, & communication equipment
 365 Radio and television receiving sets, except communication types
 366 Communication equipment

IO-57 Electronic components & accessories
 367 Electronic components and accessories

IO-58 Miscellaneous electrical machinery, equipment, & supplies
 369 Miscellaneous electrical machinery, equipment, and supplies

IO-59 Motor vehicles & equipment
 371 Motor vehicles and motor vehicle equipment

IO-60 Aircraft & parts
 372 Aircraft and parts

IO-61 Other transportation equipment
 373 Ship and boat building and repairing
 374 Railroad equipment
 375 Motorcycles, bicycles, and parts
 379 Miscellaneous transportation equipment

IO-62 Professional, scientific, & controlling instruments & supplies
 381 Engineering, laboratory, and scientific and research instruments and associated equipment
 382 Instruments for measuring, controlling, and indicating physical characteristics
 384 Surgical, medical, and dental instruments and supplies
 387 Watches, clocks, clockwork operated devices, and parts

IO-63 Optical, ophthalmic, & photographic equipment & supplies
 383 Optical instruments and lenses
 385 Ophthalmic goods
 386 Photographic equipment and supplies

IO-64 Miscellaneous manufacturing
 391 Jewelry, silverware, and plated ware
 393 Musical instruments and parts
 394 Toys, amusement, sporting and athletic goods
 395 Pens, pencils, and other office and artists' materials
 396 Costume jewelry, costume novelties, buttons, and miscellaneous notions, except precious metal
 398 Miscellaneous manufacturing industries
 399 (exc. 3992) Miscellaneous manufacturing industries

Appendix B:
Values of Manufacturing
Sector Shipments and Output:
1947, 1958, 1963

Table B-1

Values of Manufacturing Sector Shipments and Output: 1947 (millions of dollars)

Input-Output Industry		Value of Shipmentsa	Value of Outputb	Value of Shipments as a Percent of Output
No.	Title			
13	Ordnance & accessories	$ 158	$ 149	106
14	Food & kindred prdts.	37,073	43,523	85
15	Tobacco manufactures	2,515	3,970	63
16	Fabrics	7,517	10,315	73
17	Textile prdts.	1,604	1,832	88
18	Apparel	10,689	11,019	97
19	Misc. textile prdts.	1,485	1,082	137
20	Lumber & wood prdts.	4,263	5,284	81
21	Wooden containers	510	523	98
22	Household furniture	1,824	1,839	99
23	Other furniture	675	695	97
24	Paper & allied prdts.	5,323	4,742	112
25	Paperboard containers	1,731	1,597	108
26	Printing & publishing	6,391	6,464	99
27	Chemicals, selected prdts.	4,345	4,492	97
28	Plastics & synthetics	1,423	1,428	100
29	Drugs & cosmetics	3,002	3,043	99
30	Paints & allied prdts.	1,271	1,298	98
31	Petroleum, related inds.	7,284	7,880	92
32	Rubber, misc. plastics	3,238	3,471	93
33	Leather tanning prdts.	1,127	1,132	100
34	Footwear, leather prdts.	2,550	2,607	98
35	Glass & glass prdts.	1,098	1,123	98
36	Stone & clay prdts.	2,531	2,921	87
37	Primary iron, steel mfr.	13,319	11,023	121
38	Primary nonferrous mfr.	4,534	5,515	82
39	Metal containers	853	862	99
40	Fabricated metal prdts.	3,361	3,674	91
41	Screw mach. prdts., etc.	1,906	1,943	98
42	Other metal prdts.	2,930	2,568	114
43	Engines & turbines	894	831	108
44	Farm mach. & equip.	1,702	1,420	120
45	Construction mach. & equip.	1,425	1,585	90
46	Materials hand. mach. & equip.	375	566	66
47	Metalworking mach. & equip.	1,713	1,697	101
48	Special mach. & equip.	1,799	1,815	99
49	General mach. & equip.	1,756	1,800	98
50	Machine shop prdts.	423	390	108

Table B-1 cont.

Input-Output Industry		Value of Shipments[a]	Value of Output[b]	Value of Shipments as a Percent of Output
No.	Title			
51	Office, computing machines	$ 585	$ 648	90
52	Service industry machines	1,057	1,167	91
53	Elect. transmission equip.	2,282	2,432	94
54	Household appliances	2,330	2,148	108
55	Electric lighting equip.	1,074	1,100	98
56	Radio, TV, etc. equip.	2,083	2,078	100
57	Electronic components	425	570	74
58	Misc. electrical mach.	848	890	95
59	Motor vehicles, equip.	11,655	12,189	96
60	Aircraft & parts	1,520	1,446	105
61	Other transport. equip.	2,348	2,412	97
62	Professional, scien. instru.	1,325	1,293	102
63	Medical, photo. equip.	609	648	94
64	Misc. manufacturing	3,206	3,202	100

[a]The value of shipments represents the sum of state estimates produced by this project. These estimates are not fully reconciled to national totals for the industries published by the Census.

[b]The value of output for each industry differs from the OBE published output figures by the value of secondary products transferred into the industry.

Table B-2

Values of Manufacturing Sector Shipments and Output: 1958 (millions of dollars)

Input-Output Industry		Value of Shipments[a]	Value of Output[b]	Value of Shipments as a Percent of Output
No.	Title			
13	Ordnance & accessories	$ 4,221	$ 4,149	102
14	Food & kindred prdts.	59,326	62,347	95
15	Tobacco manufactures	3,961	5,918	67
16	Fabrics	7,797	10,481	74
17	Textile prdts.	2,098	2,028	103
18	Apparel	14,191	14,201	100
19	Misc. textile prdts.	1,928	1,856	104
20	Lumber & wood prdts.	7,152	7,644	94
21	Wooden containers	428	408	105
22	Household furniture	3,261	3,177	103
23	Other furniture	1,405	1,351	104
24	Paper & allied prdts.	9,302	9,297	100

Table B–2 cont.

Input-Output Industry		Value of Shipments[a]	Value of Output[b]	Value of Shipments as a Percent of Output
No.	Title			
25	Paperboard containers	$ 3,582	$ 3,559	101
26	Printing & publishing	12,545	12,450	101
27	Chemicals, selected prdts.	11,274	10,304	109
28	Plastics & synthetics	3,737	3,766	99
29	Drugs & cosmetics	6,381	6,220	103
30	Paints & allied prdts.	1,884	1,815	104
31	Petroleum, related inds.	15,473	16,870	92
32	Rubber, misc. plastics	6,506	6,541	99
33	Leather tanning prdts.	807	874	92
34	Footwear, leather prdts.	3,073	3,048	101
35	Glass & glass prdts.	2,169	2,123	102
36	Stone & clay prdts.	7,536	7,298	103
37	Primary iron, steel mfr.	18,895	18,784	101
38	Primary nonferrous mfr.	8,667	8,889	98
39	Metal containers	1,997	2,060	97
40	Fabricated metal prdts.	7,981	7,371	108
41	Screw mach. prdts., etc.	3,407	3,316	103
42	Other metal prdts.	6,020	5,509	109
43	Engines & turbines	1,993	1,954	102
44	Farm mach. & equip.	2,383	2,313	103
45	Construction mach. & equip.	3,037	2,865	106
46	Materials hand. mach. & equip.	1,025	906	113
47	Metalworking mach. & equip.	3,166	3,081	103
48	Special mach. & equip.	2,422	2,254	107
49	General mach. & equip.	3,422	3,254	105
50	Machine shop prdts.	1,453	1,473	99
51	Office, computing machines	1,764	2,132	83
52	Service industry machines	2,066	1,943	106
53	Elect. transmission equip.	4,668	4,679	100
54	Household appliances	3,324	3,421	97
55	Electric lighting equip.	2,147	2,152	100
56	Radio, TV, etc. equip.	5,602	5,635	99
57	Electronic components	2,277	2,393	95
58	Misc. electrical mach.	1,469	1,377	107
59	Motor vehicles, equip.	20,835	22,559	92
60	Aircraft & parts	13,628	11,950	114
61	Other transport. equip.	3,542	3,602	98
62	Professional, scien. instru.	3,046	3,066	99
63	Medical, photo. equip.	1,542	1,462	105
64	Misc. manufacturing	4,930	5,032	98

[a]The value of shipments represents the sum of state estimates produced by this project. These estimates are not fully reconciled to national totals for the industries published by the Census.

[b]The value of output for each industry differs from the OBE published output figures by the value of secondary products transferred into the industry.

Table B–3

Values of Manufacturing Sector Shipments and Output: 1963 (millions of dollars)

Input-Output Industry		Value of Shipments[a]	Value of Output[b]	Value of Shipments as a Percent of Output
No.	Title			
13	Ordnance & accessories	$ –	$ 4,713	–
14	Food & kindred prdts.	68,594	71,774	96
15	Tobacco manufactures	4,527	7,333	62
16	Fabrics	9,600	12,538	77
17	Textile prdts.	2,868	2,949	97
18	Apparel	18,066	17,907	101
19	Misc. textile prdts.	2,557	2,493	103
20	Lumber & wood prdts.	8,789	9,555	92
21	Wooden containers	400	379	106
22	Household furniture	4,014	3,965	101
23	Other furniture	1,857	1,789	104
24	Paper & allied prdts.	11,609	11,629	100
25	Paperboard containers	4,642	4,597	101
26	Printing & publishing	16,256	16,083	101
27	Chemicals, selected prdts.	15,313	14,316	107
28	Plastics & synthetics	5,272	5,501	96
29	Drugs & cosmetics	8,573	8,440	102
30	Paints & allied prdts.	2,463	2,369	104
31	Petroleum, related inds.	17,911	20,459	88
32	Rubber, misc. plastics	9,268	9,126	102
33	Leather tanning prdts.	831	898	93
34	Footwear, leather prdts.	3,344	3,352	100
35	Glass & glass prdts.	2,674	2,798	96
36	Stone & clay prdts.	9,472	9,165	103
37	Primary iron, steel mfr.	23,534	23,354	101
38	Primary nonferrous mfr.	11,947	12,742	94
39	Metal containers	2,337	2,369	99
40	Fabricated metal prdts.	8,688	8,218	106
41	Screw mach. prdts., etc.	4,493	4,420	102
42	Other metal prdts.	7,850	7,406	106
43	Engines & turbines	2,037	2,064	99
44	Farm mach. & equip.	2,844	2,813	101
45	Construction mach. & equip.	3,827	3,673	104
46	Materials hand. mach. & equip.	1,478	1,377	107
47	Metalworking mach. & equip.	4,504	4,439	101
48	Special mach. & equip.	3,308	3,241	102
49	General mach. & equip.	4,713	4,616	102
50	Machine shop prdts.	2,167	2,091	104
51	Office, computing machines	2,600	3,689	70
52	Service industry machines	2,837	2,780	102
53	Elect. transmission equip.	5,714	5,786	99
54	Household appliances	4,129	4,178	99
55	Electric lighting equip.	2,832	2,798	101
56	Radio, TV, etc. equip.	11,389	11,574	98
57	Electronic components	3,821	3,846	99
58	Misc. electrical mach.	1,936	1,939	100

Table B-3 cont.

	Input-Output Industry	Value of Shipments[a]	Value of Output[b]	Value of Shipments as a Percent of Output
No.	Title			
59	Motor vehicles, equip.	$35,734	$39,320	91
60	Aircraft & parts	13,603	13,630	100
61	Other transport. equip.	4,199	4,667	90
62	Professional, scien. instru.	3,822	3,684	104
63	Medical, photo. equip.	2,310	2,287	101
64	Misc. manufacturing	6,500	6,418	101

[a]The value of shipments represents the sum of state estimates produced by this project. These estimates are not fully reconciled to national totals for the industries published by the Census.

[b]The value of output for each industry differs from the OBE published output figures by the value of secondary products transferred into the industry.

Appendix C:
1947, 1958, and 1963 State Estimates
of Outputs, Employment, and Payrolls
(MRIO Data Set 2)

This data set provides state estimates of output, employment, and payrolls for the three base years, 1947, 1958, and 1963, for 87 industries. The data for each year were constructed on a basis consistent with the industry definitions of the national input-output tables prepared by the Office of Business Economics (OBE). The procedures used to estimate the state values are described earlier in this volume.

The state output estimates sum to a figure that is exactly equal to the national output values of the primary matrix (column sums of that table) in the OBE input-output tables listed below:

1.   1947: OBE computer listing of the table (dated September 1967). As of the fall of 1971, this table, which was revised by the OBE from the original 1947 Bureau of Labor Statistics (BLS) table, had not been officially published.
2.   1958: *Survey of Current Business*, September 1965 [194, pp. 34–39].
3.   1963: *Survey of Current Business*, November 1969 [184, pp. 30–35].

For the published national table, a secondary product matrix is added to the primary matrix to obtain a balanced table of total transactions, which double-counts secondary products. The national control used for the multiregional input-output (MRIO) calculations can be obtained by taking the value listed in the row marked "Total" in the OBE table and subtracting from it the respective value in the row marked "Transfers." The result represents the total value of goods and services produced by domestic establishments of the establishment's "own" product plus the value of its secondary products. It therefore excludes transferred imports (and the transportation, trade, and insurance margins on those imports) and the double-counting of secondary products that are included in the national input-output table. For the multiregional calculations, these values that are called "transfers" were estimated at the 44-region level and added as row 81 (imports) and row and column 83 (secondary products) of the regional tables. (The transportation, trade, and insurance margins on the imports were added to the entries in rows 65, 69, and 70, respectively.) Transferred imports could only be estimated at the 44-region level and are not included until that stage of the calculations.

**Notes About the State Estimates of Outputs,
Employment, and Payrolls**

1. Throughout the estimation process, an attempt was made to construct the
    state figures on a basis comparable with the national input-output tables.
    Whenever an unreconcilable discrepancy occurred between the state figures
    and the national controls, the discrepancy was allocated to the states in
    proportion to the original entries in the state tables.
    a. The rows are the 87 industries listed in the OBE tables plus a row 88 of
        state totals.
    b. The columns are the 51 regions (50 states plus the District of Columbia),
        arranged in alphabetical order, plus a column 52 of residuals and a
        column 53 of industry totals. Only the first 49 of the 51 regional
        columns contain values for 1947 and 1958 (columns 50 and 51 are
        zero) because Alaska and Hawaii did not become states until 1958. For
        1963, all 51 regional columns contain values.
    c. Column 52 contains values for data that were not allocated to the states.
        These represent figures for which purchases or payments were made
        outside the 51 regions (such as purchases for the Panama Canal, wage
        payments to overseas military employees, etc.).

2. The data for the three years are given in thousands of current dollars and
    are in producer prices.
    a. Deflators. For comparisons of the data for the three years, the output
        and payroll figures must be deflated to constant dollars. The national
        output deflators were used for deflation of the outputs in the multi-
        regional calculations. (National value added deflators could be used
        as an approximation for the payrolls.) The output deflators are listed in
        Table 2-3 (pp. 17-19).
    b. Significant digits. The final adjustments to the three sets of data were
        made in double precision on the IBM 360/65 at Harvard.
    c. Producer prices. It is customary for the input-output data to be given
        in producer prices. The margins on the goods (the differences between
        the producer prices and the purchaser prices) are then recorded as
        parts of IO-65, Transportation & warehousing; IO-69, Wholesale &
        retail trade; and IO-70, Finance & insurance.

3. IO-11, New construction. All purchases of new construction are recorded
    in the final demand sector of the input-output table, that is, no purchases
    from this industry are considered to be intermediate purchases. Because
    the output of new construction is assumed to be used in the region in
    which it is produced, the total output must equal the total consumption in
    each state. The total output of the industry, given state-by-state in row
    11 of Tables C-1, C-2, and C-3, should be consistent with the respective

state elements obtained by adding the figures in row 11 of the state final
demand tables for gross private capital formation, net foreign exports,
state and local government net purchases of goods and services, and
federal government purchases. For 1947, however, a discrepancy exists
between the two sets of data, and no immediate way of reconciling the
differences could be found.

4. IO-74, Research & development. For 1947 and 1958, values of research
   and development were estimated for each state because the industry
   was given in the national input-output table. For 1963, this industry was
   eliminated in the national input-output table, and the values were included
   as part of the industries where the research and development was actually
   performed, and SIC 7391, Research, development, and testing laboratories,
   was added to IO-73, Business services; therefore, no separate state estimates
   were made for IO-74 in the 1963 output, employment, or payroll tables
   given in this appendix. To use the 1947 and 1958 state data for the
   multiregional calculations, the values given in the appendix tables for
   IO-74 (the SIC 7391 portion) must be added to the values for IO-73 for
   the respective year.

5. IO-78, Federal government enterprises. For this industry, a value appears
   in the residual column 52 of the output matrices only. This value represents
   output of federal government enterprises that are located outside the
   states, such as the Panama Canal or the Alaska Railroad in 1947 and 1958
   (before Alaska became a state). In the payroll and employment matrices,
   the entry in column 52 is zero, and the total for industry 78 excludes
   these values because of lack of information, although these enterprises had
   employees.

6. IO-80, Imports. No state values were estimated for this industry. For the
   multiregional input-output calculations, imports were constructed at
   the 44-region level.

7. IO-81, Business travel, entertainment, & gifts, and IO-82, Office supplies.
   These two industries are especially constructed for the national input-output
   tables, and the values appear in the transfer (secondary) matrix; therefore,
   no state estimates were made for these industries.

8. IO-83, Scrap, used & secondhand goods. The values for this industry are
   given in the transfer (secondary) matrix of the national input-output
   table; therefore, no state output, employment, or payroll estimates were
   made for this industry.

9. Value added in final demand: IO-84, Government industry, IO-85, Rest of
   the world industry, and IO-86, Household industry. For these industries,

figures appear only in the value added portion of the final demand sector of the input-output table and represent payments to government employees; purchases by foreigners and foreign interest payments and receipts; and payments to household employees, respectively. The following balances exist between the final demand values given in MRIO DATA SET 1 and the payroll and output values given in MRIO DATA SET 2:[1]

$$IO\text{-}84 \text{ PAYROLLS} = IO\text{-}84 \text{ OUTPUT} = IO\text{-}84 \, SLG + IO\text{-}84 \, FG$$
$$IO\text{-}85 \text{ OUTPUT} = IO\text{-}85 \, PCE + IO\text{-}85 \, NEXP + IO\text{-}85 \, FG$$
$$IO\text{-}86 \text{ PAYROLLS} = IO\text{-}86 \text{ OUTPUT} = IO\text{-}86 \, PCE$$

Part of the value of IO-84 represents wages paid to government military employees overseas. This value appears in column 52 of the payrolls, outputs, and federal government final demand tables.

10. IO-87, Inventory valuation adjustment. No state estimates were made for this industry. The total value appears in columns 52 and 53 of the output tables. Because the item represents an adjustment of the total of net inventory change for the differences in the value of the goods when they are placed in inventory compared with their value when they are withdrawn from inventory, no figure is given in either the employment or payrolls tables.

11. Row 88 is the state total for either outputs, employment, or payrolls, obtained by summing all elements in each column.

12. Column 52 contains values for data that were not allocated to the states (explained above under 1).

13. Column 53 contains the industry total for the particular table of outputs, employment, or payrolls. As explained under 1 above, this total was forced to equal the respective national figure for the industry.

14. For certain regional analyses, an additional adjustment would have to be made to the state outputs. To balance the data in the interregional trade matrices with the regional input-output tables, the inventory depletion component of net inventory change must be subtracted from the final demands and added as a row in the regional input-output tables. (These tables are described in the first volume of this series.) This adjustment is

---

1. For a detailed description of the methodology of constructing the state final demands given in MRIO DATA SET 1, refer to the first volume of this series, *State Estimates of the Gross National Product, 1947, 1958, 1963* [92].

required to account for all shipments of a given commodity, regardless of the year in which it was produced, and essentially augments each of the output figures presented in the accompanying tables by the value of commodities that are withdrawn from inventories in the given year.

The nine tables of state outputs, employment, and payrolls follow.

MRIO Data Set 2
1947, 1958, and 1963 State Estimates of
Outputs, Employment, and Payrolls (88 x 53)
(in thousands of current dollars)

Table No.	Table Title
C-1	1947 Outputs
C-2	1958 Outputs
C-3	1963 Outputs
C-4	1947 Employment
C-5	1958 Employment
C-6	1963 Employment
C-7	1947 Payrolls
C-8	1958 Payrolls
C-9	1963 Payrolls

TABLE C-1

STATE ESTIMATES OF 1947 OUTPUTS
(THOUSANDS OF CURRENT DOLLARS)

INDUSTRY TITLE	1 ALABAMA	2 ARIZONA	3 ARKANSAS	4 CALIFORNIA	5 COLORADO	6 CONNECTICUT	7 DELAWARE	8 DISTRICT OF COLUMBIA	9 FLORIDA
1 LIVESTOCK, PRDTS.	261036	90916	279002	817610	300806	110529	81008	0	135579
2 OTHER AGRICULTURE PRDTS.	349392	168958	423447	1786568	378706	66449	28648	0	225991
3 FORESTRY, FISHERIES	10673	73	6301	64221	587	3112	5627	0	24860
4 AGRI.,FORES.,FISH. SERV.	15946	6961	21607	51237	6780	7327	8199	0	6787
5 IRON, FERRO. ORES MINING	24802	24	48	1929	101		0	0	0
6 NONFERROUS ORES MINING	0	134679	8658	20561	16151	0	0	0	3033
7 COAL MINING	105851	0	12650	0	29193	0	0	0	0
8 CRUDE PETRO.,NATURAL GAS	614	0	61968	696853	30840	0	0	0	403
9 STONE, CLAY MINING	7927	1769	2299	49177	3556	3628	525	0	9998
10 CHEM.,FERT. MIN. MINING	0	233	2565	4668	1020	0	0	0	35316
11 NEW CONSTRUCTION	257487	133105	220612	2714831	194841	236075	36753	108490	653791
12 MAINT., REPAIR CONSTR.	102972	53558	76089	1033384	120533	126938	23944	43596	239652
13 ORDNANCE, ACCESSORIES	16	2378	93	283	5383	149	4607	123	38
14 FOOD, KINDRED PRDTS.	6687606	971423	139666	112749	1280804	292121	1452489	48689	6
15 TOBACCO MANUFACTURES	1938	10340	2137	1972	207511	6504	210585	783	0
16 FABRICS	882183	114208	9750	6073	518805	31775	36126	21291	5179
17 TEXTILE PRDTS.	83466	8276	119	1076	84524	1190	19801	710	8
18 APPAREL	236962	29873	206	23036	919216	71237	90464	2471	5
19 MISC. TEXTILE PRDTS.	12036	4620	0	583	51673	2947	98265	678	492
20 LUMBER, WOOD PRDTS.	731972	2360	1850	877	167011	3662	471911	494	306
21 WOODEN CONTAINERS	2558	739	0	0	11656	416	9141	54	0
22 HOUSEHOLD FURNITURE	7574	4908	1178	507	65629	253	114928	400	0
23 OTHER FURNITURE	690	1571	73	24	14812	901	22142	1	255
24 PAPER, ALLIED PRDTS.	72858	54218	869	194	533193	3232	143953	5514	577
25 PAPERBOARD CONTAINERS	33763	0	0	0	36504	0	33802	0	0
26 PRINTING, PUBLISHING	224536	905	20205	28138	382868	36146	471925	752	1569
27 CHEMICALS,SELECT. PRDTS.	866820	285	17	2156	56997	5492	137370	2675	9501
28 PLASTICS, SYNTHETICS	0	4895	366	4708	63157	6254	34504	18502	391
29 DRUGS, COSMETICS	3119	2215	1056	113479	64561	28693	36721	1245	1174
30 PAINT, ALLIED PRDTS.	3093	730	332	121947	4696	7906	342	664	3431
31 PETROLEUM, RELATED INDS.	8907	3261	56507	1105168	12991	2622	4941	14	4827
32 RUBBER, MISC. PLASTICS	85018	60	3859	223528	6885	170217	15788	273	6729
33 LEATHER TANNING, PRDTS.	0	0	0	16901	181	5655	23198	0	3626
34 FOOTWEAR, LEATHER PRDTS.	2304	342	5975	32923	9002	9051	0	0	1434
35 GLASS, GLASS PRDTS.	377	80	10120	50144	3944	13129	0	0	332
36 STONE, CLAY PRDTS.	61247	6414	11740	216566	15900	39649	2005	1285	25781
37 PRIMARY IRON, STEEL MFR.	485945	3038	557	200705	60778	98111	12996	5	353
38 PRIMARY NONFERROUS MFR.	93066	90440	69144	213989	29136	434725	787	0	8668

#	Industry	C1	C2	C3	C4	C5	C6	C7	C8	C9
39	METAL CONTAINERS	2929	0	2987	117610	2192	1427	1001	0	20959
40	FABRICATED METAL PRDTS.	75627	8907	3857	279543	18991	67795	6631	3118	15793
41	SCREW MACH. PRDTS., ETC.	8260	636	99	53339	309	99011	7506	0	268
42	OTHER FAB. METAL PRDTS.	17436	1	2814	128078	5277	203450	2547	813	5056
43	ENGINES, TURBINES	46	0	0	36565	357	6779	0	0	46
44	FARM MACH., EQUIP.	7145	133	5668	32852	4937	2634	151	0	2024
45	CONSTRUC. MACH., EQUIP.	4470	0	2217	93466	20389	12908	0	0	2659
46	MATERIAL HANDLING MACH.	1907	166	2162	13429	4633	5654	0	0	392
47	METALWORKING MACHINERY	530	399	10	22821	338	110976	7021	13	177
48	SPECIAL MACH., EQUIP.	4516	0	1260	68209	6101	60647	15366	50	4315
49	GENERAL MACH., EQUIP.	7772	268	981	86930	4957	165310	1140	827	4943
50	MACHINE SHOP PRDTS.	948	0	251	25194	1370	9924	783	64	783
51	OFFICE, COMPUT. MACHINES	80	0	0	33419	630	113411	0	80	113
52	SERVICE IND. MACHINES	1451	1680	796	74101	661	17632	443	0	43
53	ELECT. TRANSMISS. EQUIP.	2652	1382	0	76969	1812	47715	160	0	976
54	HOUSEHOLD APPLIANCES	5756	117	595	43740	297	134787	469	0	372
55	ELECTRIC LIGHTING EQUIP.	3503	261	142	42837	942	76408	5	13	627
56	RADIO, TV, ETC. EQUIP.	4782	86	0	10593	2890	52717	0	1205	638
57	ELECTRONIC COMPONENTS	1572	0	0	31769	86	12953	0	377	209
58	MISC. ELECTRICAL MACH.	604	0	0		1151	14133	0	607	4359
59	MOTOR VEHICLES, EQUIP.	8387	6032	1227	506562	4346	48520	4918	206	11606
60	AIRCRAFT, PARTS	0	165	0	491212	332	189731	515	7	515
61	OTHER TRANSPORT. EQUIP.	42904	2098	1715	151014	12017	16287	10586	0	37913
62	PROFESS., SCIEN. INSTRU.	1032	734	543	51270	1349	81217	1021	1861	1265
63	MEDICAL, PHOTO. EQUIP.		1	7	12077	2021	5346	0	106	279
64	MISC. MANUFACTURING	3558	706	5199	97465	11634	215376	10927	1267	6848
65	TRANSPORT., WAREHOUSING	282209	90155	139474	1831202	184107	155814	86651	89356	293865
66	COMMUNICA., EXC. BRDCAST.	29078	10190	11593	311839	23351	128378	8209	43708	37179
67	RADIO, TV BROADCASTING	4575	2536	2332	42846	3429	3978	582	14234	6830
68	ELEC.,GAS,WATER,SAN.SER.	72819	21019	38728	439247	19093	110279	12456	42284	67356
69	WHOLESALE, RETAIL TRADE	606542	236828	385382	4423170	489862	701666	115051	398041	882542
70	FINANCE, INSURANCE	111052	31496	42965	874674	73270	292189	61122	95550	157171
71	REAL ESTATE, RENTAL	238487	102527	141876	2108198	198019	323827	46347	224303	471134
72	HOTELS, PERSONAL SERV.	76323	38421	49864	637109	67488	99349	13796	90675	174533
73	BUSINESS SERVICES	34953	15595	17316	538319	34627	53561	8990	80890	82695
74	RESEARCH, DEVELOPMENT	1205	77	62	24065	206	1096	616	696	1040
75	AUTO. REPAIR, SERVICES	55102	19704	35410	380906	45120	57010	10082	28981	77042
76	AMUSEMENTS	27735	14162	20119	919228	26791	40600	9982	30280	88058
77	MED.,EDUC. SERVICES	71860	29595	46536	885175	75447	149986	16732	150501	105857
78	FEDERAL GOVT. ENTERPRISE	36687	6607	15455	138596	15635	19194	2560	26772	26167
79	STATE, LOCAL GOVT. ENT.	29026	6191	2460	230548	12182	4764	2068	6360	35416
80	IMPORTS	0	0	0	0	0	0	0	0	0
81	BUS.TRAVEL, ENT., GIFTS.	0	0	0	0	0	0	0	0	0
82	OFFICE SUPPLIES	0	0	0	0	0	0	0	0	0
83	SCRAP, USED GOODS	0	0	0	0	0	0	0	0	0
84	GOVERNMENT INDUSTRY	192850	82978	87318	1651514	164426	139833	21093	532746	341895
85	REST OF WORLD INDUSTRY	-5412	-6248	-3354	-93911	-5734	-8136	-1288	-6951	-15741
86	HOUSEHOLD INDUSTRY	57455	11501	19527	197836	14325	43508	10065	38124	84713
87	INVENTORY VALUATION ADJ.	0	0	0	0	0	0	0	0	0
88	STATE TOTAL	5499834	1562532	2999222	3237068	3320794	6706975	1051665	2252645	5252375

TABLE C-1

STATE ESTIMATES OF 1947 OUTPUTS
(THOUSANDS OF CURRENT DOLLARS)

INDUSTRY TITLE	10 GEORGIA	11 IDAHO	12 ILLINOIS	13 INDIANA	14 IOWA	15 KANSAS	16 KENTUCKY	17 LOUISIANA	18 MAINE
1 LIVESTOCK, PRDTS.	317018	2055/1	1392456	989660	2350507	715004	474095	195051	89511
2 OTHER AGRICULTURE PRDTS.	450113	306542	2240532	722062	1552732	957499	433701	259976	123216
3 FORESTRY, FISHERIES	3450	589	1949	1236	908	522	5384	30630	20288
4 AGRI.,FORES.,FISH. SERV.	22000	4894	34542	27285	34360	15969	6930	10583	3684
5 IRON, FERRO. ORES MINING	735	91	0	0	0	0	0	0	0
6 NONFERROUS ORES MINING	487	34607	1133	0	0	6178	102	0	0
7 COAL MINING	238	0	216468	83062	6520	9293	374708	0	0
8 CRUDE PETRO.,NATURAL GAS			152302	13074		221544	36654	371876	
9 STONE, CLAY MINING	28417	2181	35860	20346	12880	8218	10373	2974	2267
10 CHEM.,FERT. MIN. MINING	680	4375	6596	0	0	6135	2911	31567	0
11 NEW CONSTRUCTION	322687	79582	1081646	446254	357298	331815	245883	359815	62297
12 MAINT., REPAIR CONSTR.	125124	52024	584810	258351	210359	156175	110235	125065	35669
13 ORDNANCE, ACCESSORIES	478	1981	2	17062	4423	98	1083	813	1402
14 FOOD, KINDRED PRDTS.	294264	112949	65513	3827633	2472881	99637	143245	277258	57363
15 TOBACCO MANUFACTURES	11954	2159	0	504857	258027	21078	22853	44987	13531
16 FABRICS	24643	39551	2533	1114862	360409	54870	27532	68209	35955
17 TEXTILE PRDTS.	587	975		210773	143074	7359	1174	6943	4093
18 APPAREL	9941	60354	3383	1422239	252443	342842	157963	54442	32915
19 MISC. TEXTILE PRDTS.	2938	1524	344	106647	64856	7123	694	6277	1221
20 LUMBER, WOOD PRDTS.	779	8307	0	477342	217293	9442	3008	8633	865
21 WOODEN CONTAINERS	216	706	0	20551	38355	3244	738	330	
22 HOUSEHOLD FURNITURE	317	3611	0	319998	122289	66863	13867	7083	400
23 OTHER FURNITURE	236	1771	40	186318	46615	3347	593	4909	15
24 PAPER, ALLIED PRDTS.	58425	21664	0	164106	309073	19536	32415	20477	71068
25 PAPERBOARD CONTAINERS	0	0	0	290546	43706	15492	0	8147	8147
26 PRINTING, PUBLISHING	25367	2000	8686	972001	302462	44437	11816	16512	726
27 CHEMICALS+SELECT. PRDTS.	2164	10694	123	715454	196512	66480	19135	6559	495
28 PLASTICS, SYNTHETICS	4254	6023	0	92919	36605	7788	2397	3639	3229
29 DRUGS, COSMETICS	19756	3366	182649	333397	27246	71330	4938	8136	5872
30 PAINT, ALLIED PRDTS.	10275	10	190623	27346	15579	1008	35500	7072	866
31 PETROLEUM, RELATED INDS.	11505	2765	559960	375485	2415	296695	58359	546560	1323
32 RUBBER, MISC. PLASTICS	10769	0	103597	104969	40755	17882	33206	406	1291
33 LEATHER TANNING, PRDTS.	5009	0	89135	7924	0	0	6286		7751
34 FOOTWEAR, LEATHER PRDTS.	15694	195	190884	16654	5642	964	25042	2285	101793
35 GLASS, GLASS PRDTS.	215	0	116552	88572	987	46	1277	6800	790
36 STONE, CLAY PRDTS.	54600	4272	195945	99288	51951	35463	26494	18501	5109
37 PRIMARY IRON, STEEL MFR.	25037	145	946124	1080782	12746	2317	87786	1226	494
38 PRIMARY NONFERROUS MFR.	14908	34004	542555	254796	7625	15807	67957	20766	3564

136

#	Industry	(1)	(2)	(3)	(4)	(5)	(6)	(7)	(8)	(9)
39	METAL CONTAINERS	1095	0	188253	18894		0	736	15897	2869
40	FABRICATED METAL PRDTS.	20219	1750	285968	152947	2965	37956	82832	21979	8182
41	SCREW MACH. PRDTS., ETC.	5693	25	272971	71253	47764	1056	3808	2003	374
42	OTHER FAB. METAL PRDTS.	3530	0	391685	80873	2625	1683	15948	8983	4117
43	ENGINES, TURBINES	0	0	81345	83917	1338	462	0	0	315
44	FARM MACH., EQUIP.	8550	1407	507624	71858	104720	12725	12353	1860	1751
45	CONSTRUC. MACH., EQUIP.	12378	662	217270	49811	75952	18136	4987	5749	376
46	MATERIAL HANDLING MACH.	5293	50	83970	10548	9822	3556	6583	324	416
47	METALWORKING MACHINERY	574	6	221546	40513	11464	1136	3782	291	46875
48	SPECIAL MACH., EQUIP.	18121	4	161895	41439	16072	7545	4419	3436	83
49	GENERAL MACH., EQUIP.	2564	579	179411	109108	11982	1168	10561	2054	260
50	MACHINE SHOP PRDTS.	243	102	35122	34498	3517	2756	2559	977	60
51	OFFICE, COMPUT. MACHINES	160	0	77041	1972	155	0	729	0	250
52	SERVICE IND. MACHINES	3833	0	97679	171778	5713	2732	4246	785	
53	ELECT. TRANSMISS. EQUIP.	6239	0	149170	133846	12318	2093	2356		
54	HOUSEHOLD APPLIANCES	4235	0	375290	143419	78416	16264	8307	469	518
55	ELECTRIC LIGHTING EQUIP.	553	0	163801	57657	1633	2812	7355		
56	RADIO, TV, ETC., EQUIP.	7413	0	676228	166229	14074	646	336	59	
57	ELECTRONIC COMPONENTS	1572	0	105661	61627	3653	195	10762		
58	MISC. ELECTRICAL MACH.	12358	0	67804	141279	13524	3459	3836	645	176
59	MOTOR VEHICLES, EQUIP.	45187	181	318220	942018	11651	49787	4171	1764	117
60	AIRCRAFT, PARTS	5	0	14419	78667	8867	37232	9		1
61	OTHER TRANSPORT. EQUIP.	10885	891	376417	138709	10689	14063	9383	48184	18506
62	PROFESS., SCIEN. INSTRU.	2153	22	171171	27921	2011	1718	2077	665	1559
63	MEDICAL, PHOTO. EQUIP.	6	304	77778	2521	2332	13	8	97	602
64	MISC. MANUFACTURING	10404	1022	268838	73822	37693	5160	9253	4897	21123
65	TRANSPORT., WAREHOUSING	347341	76610	1678322	564248	310303	495405	314848	409951	90576
66	COMMUNICA., EXC. BRDCAST.	40975	14587	286186	144458	39503	22462	28101	41334	20478
67	RADIO, TV BROADCASTING	10476	1571	27296	5938	6820	3168	4140	5530	1825
68	ELEC.,GAS,WATER,SAN.SER.	75248	16371	403801	181020	100413	86052	66309	91416	26386
69	WHOLESALE, RETAIL TRADE	809184	178926	3872452	1277060	895853	636377	618921	748633	246984
70	FINANCE, INSURANCE	179473	17641	820961	197478	125591	76074	93449	116779	36296
71	REAL ESTATE, RENTAL	301470	65213	1759581	483963	306793	217151	255972	269737	91579
72	HOTELS, PERSONAL SERV.	110547	21103	549126	158381	88051	64957	84704	74935	31653
73	BUSINESS SERVICES	56673	10534	475303	67453	51116	43119	29310	63340	11791
74	RESEARCH, DEVELOPMENT	203	146	9805	308	165	143	112	411	440
75	AUTO. REPAIR, SERVICES	72380	18692	246093	109887	77995	63204	53145	52014	22474
76	AMUSEMENTS	35878	10324	237987	62319	39389	26717	35026	38304	11069
77	MED.,EDUC. SERVICES	104627	23517	715401	203733	131659	82294	86188	100887	38573
78	FEDERAL GOVT. ENTERPRISE	33648	4942	119380	32636	24820	22845	26103	17666	10024
79	STATE, LOCAL GOVT. ENT.	11207	4856	44288	17474	21629	2660	8696	11517	10130
80	IMPORTS	0	0	0	0	0	0	0	0	0
81	BUS.TRAVEL, ENT., GIFTS.	0	0	0	0	0	0	0	0	0
82	OFFICE SUPPLIES	0	0	0	0	0	0	0	0	0
83	SCRAP, USED GOODS	0	0	0	0	0	0	0	0	0
84	GOVERNMENT INDUSTRY	256486	47726	726715	257145	152630	159222	173175	191614	69810
85	REST OF WORLD INDUSTRY	-6671	-4183	-48419	-13777	-9140	-5726	-6790	-7725	-4074
86	HOUSEHOLD INDUSTRY	76212	4194	100426	37690	24135	18796	28180	51941	12688
87	INVENTORY VALUATION ADJ.	0	0	0	0	0	0	0	0	0
88	STATE TOTAL	6638432	1545139	34196551	13676939	9840329	6545025	5713297	6512707	2127023

TABLE C-1

STATE ESTIMATES OF 1947 OUTPUTS
(THOUSANDS OF CURRENT DOLLARS)

INDUSTRY TITLE	19 MARYLAND	20 MASSA-CHUSETTS	21 MICHIGAN	22 MINNESOTA	23 MISSISSIPPI	24 MISSOURI	25 MONTANA	26 NEBRASKA	27 NEVADA
1 LIVESTOCK, PRDTS.	199369	137550	596123	1245219	251348	1120188	268946	859596	55796
2 OTHER AGRICULTURE PRDTS.	142118	76547	422097	959540	440902	429988	321128	1051823	17705
3 FORESTRY, FISHERIES	9666	41242	10685	3096	6953	4457	1339	609	50
4 AGRI.,FORES.,FISH. SERV.	13316	6704	13743	26120	24091	31445	3721	14230	583
5 IRON, FERRO. ORES MINING			49511	219133		616	4437		3128
6 NONFERROUS ORES MINING						3079	33683		23366
7 COAL MINING	9979		7706			13695	6604		0
8 CRUDE PETRO.,NATURAL GAS		2704	712			540	19230	431	0
9 STONE, CLAY MINING	8495		47593	8112	64872	16807	2323	2824	5014
10 CHEM.,FERT. MIN. MINING		10132	27331		1435	2580	1685	511	511
11 NEW CONSTRUCTION	308838	523787	915388	367907	194325	391052	91238	165775	48687
12 MAINT., REPAIR CONSTR.	136423	207824	393692	173940	68139	222794	60016	113107	25132
13 ORDNANCE, ACCESSORIES	143	1916	12458	11108	540	358	3731	16	133
14 FOOD, KINDRED PRDTS.	15329	682660	820673	3077982	224460	33174	518095	187321	41312
15 TOBACCO MANUFACTURES	2214	60099	81391	30259	13739	773	44155	3635	3430
16 FABRICS	12254	165124	303606	1152769	126067	4924	233955	3967	20104
17 TEXTILE PRDTS.	509	1212	70984	249700	16219	511	31406	4509	1325
18 APPAREL	6896	40434	81322	578848	212432	11643	107868	4	20603
19 MISC. TEXTILE PRDTS.	49	5597	44676	79094	5204	1535	11918	164	1110
20 LUMBER, WOOD PRDTS.	504	12748	234203	398837	79284	298	69245	0	4013
21 WOODEN CONTAINERS		1769	25023	20798	12782	0	21477	290	886
22 HOUSEHOLD FURNITURE	442	9615	38110	185887	40688	0	44905	1	2867
23 OTHER FURNITURE		13192	40603	12475	8460	491	7523	207	2926
24 PAPER, ALLIED PRDTS.	27683	184159	108108	815767	26494	24161	90813	0	1952
25 PAPERBOARD CONTAINERS		8147	179256	18577	19943	8147	19943	94	0
26 PRINTING, PUBLISHING	1467	32945	351749	511676	44273	24247	68072	59	19943
27 CHEMICALS,SELECT. PRDTS.	3566	22193	220974	182082	9020	337	37582	263	14166
28 PLASTICS, SYNTHETICS	32054	29811	95024	16954	20796	3048	40092	29427	7339
29 DRUGS, COSMETICS	60107	135972	49423	61634	28173	41438	26823	294	7136
30 PAINT, ALLIED PRDTS.	15019	31046	96321	4642	141	49216	0	8539	3021
31 PETROLEUM, RELATED INDS.	78773	61974	109226	71214	4769	43299	33496	7127	0
32 RUBBER, MISC. PLASTICS	58693	312484	297490	74009	29203	28518	0	2682	9
33 LEATHER TANNING, PRDTS.	4282	314441	36589	5331	322	4686	0	1646	4
34 FOOTWEAR, LEATHER PRDTS.	19528	476790	13467	10151	17	338343	71	22	0
35 GLASS, GLASS PRDTS.	13469	11746	16866	8622	3230	18135	36	46	5872
36 STONE, CLAY PRDTS.	43108	101573	149585	26525	8478	100723	6972	11158	0
37 PRIMARY IRON, STEEL MFR.	317975	151608	532965	47593	327	70107	10224	994	10
38 PRIMARY NONFERROUS MFR.	87450	111992	298734	29887	704	90249	88075	14424	14231

#	Industry	(1)	(2)	(3)	(4)	(5)	(6)	(7)	(8)	(9)
39	METAL CONTAINERS	65850	11449	2522	7505	756	28229	0	2855	0
40	FABRICATED METAL PRDTS.	55628	77085	238105	60188	3030	102166	2732	14011	925
41	SCREW MACH. PRDTS., ETC.	46722	63539	282674	17991	0	18245	0	3346	0
42	OTHER FAB. METAL PRDTS.	12811	160508	321721	14571	2588	59466	496	359	0
43	ENGINES, TURBINES	109	35395	137802	9859	693	12398	2	10227	0
44	FARM MACH., EQUIP.	9652	2718	108064	59375	2126	11266	171	2829	65
45	CONSTRUC. MACH., EQUIP.	6088	3815	83472	44229	124	11282	662	403	0
46	MATERIAL HANDLING MACH.	2445	15674	63709	9904	14	2990	1739	821	35
47	METALWORKING MACHINERY	9608	94986	292869	14088	3698	13556	15	353	0
48	SPECIAL MACH., EQUIP.	21717	230273	79894	19118	2582	26249	47	1867	0
49	GENERAL MACH., EQUIP.	9417	75159	133060	8754	140	20050	6	199	4
50	MACHINE SHOP PRDTS.	9133	11101	61001	4288	0	16735	102	0	0
51	OFFICE, COMPUT. MACHINES	60	11729	53825	250	0	1636	0	3392	205
52	SERVICE IND. MACHINES	8745	55877	150350	45211	0	36083	149	2852	0
53	ELECT. TRANSMISS. EQUIP.	8540	226716	91893	71048	364	89247	0	3362	0
54	HOUSEHOLD APPLIANCES	11276	44695	218007	47719	0	52664	340	1227	0
55	ELECTRIC LIGHTING EQUIP.	3621	95918	23605	1169	2951	36621	7	11040	0
56	RADIO, TV, ETC., EQUIP.	53792	79794	42714	32492	0	979	0	1044	0
57	ELECTRONIC COMPONENTS	9044	44758	12424	1510	0	6206	0	1227	0
58	MISC. ELECTRICAL MACH.	4199	25128	24893	13829	0	8682	0	6584	0
59	MOTOR VEHICLES, EQUIP.	61692	86323	6217653	41454	7390	542428	371	0	190
60	AIRCRAFT, PARTS	93095	40933	13108	7850	0	7728	13	2223	0
61	OTHER TRANSPORT. EQUIP.	86267	62739	82287	21612	18989	55177	104	1443	0
62	PROFESS., SCIEN. INSTRU.	7768	61022	44829	13791	219	16750	349	1280	0
63	MEDICAL, PHOTO. EQUIP.	528	48993	11297	3512	106	5741	0	6812	0
64	MISC. MANUFACTURING	27445	259925	101317	33918	2805	59208	1231	217552	645
65	TRANSPORT., WAREHOUSING	334498	472468	588485	436634	11772	679924	126007	36393	44230
66	COMMUNICA., EXC. BRDCAST.	54671	148091	124243	54079	16837	56010	8155	3943	7301
67	RADIO, TV BROADCASTING	4777	20920	23114	6630	1903	10777	1608	20863	455
68	ELEC., GAS, WATER, SAN. SER.	92864	240861	265232	88583	31675	121248	29010	499550	4931
69	WHOLESALE, RETAIL TRADE	732397	1824797	2216634	1217400	375839	1599989	200272	87591	66485
70	FINANCE, INSURANCE	149134	494001	308320	191138	40374	262808	21749	149774	6063
71	REAL ESTATE, RENTAL	284700	738047	932396	413779	145898	568086	71163	51086	29979
72	HOTELS, PERSONAL SERV.	98451	239326	284817	114027	45882	185269	24697	27292	23799
73	BUSINESS SERVICES	63114	180616	223380	23631		115757	9770	44822	5747
74	RESEARCH, DEVELOPMENT	2257	3709	823	1047	174		22	20585	118
75	AUTO. REPAIR, SERVICES	53747	108427	199254	87401	34269	111729	20014	67140	7376
76	AMUSEMENTS	56783	123120	129083	48960	14389	72030	8944	15332	32242
77	MED., EDUC. SERVICES	138853	402694	319426	174128	42070	223692	28315	1679	6604
78	FEDERAL GOVT. ENTERPRISE	22373	62328	53226	25969	14838	58219	5479	0	1757
79	STATE, LOCAL GOVT. ENT.	14509	79614	115374	11352	1333	27393	588	0	35
80	IMPORTS	0	0	0	0	0	0	0	0	0
81	BUS. TRAVEL, ENT., GIFTS.	0	0	0	0	0	0	0	0	0
82	OFFICE SUPPLIES	0	0	0	0	0	0	0	0	0
83	SCRAP, USED GOODS	0	0	0	0	0	0	0	0	0
84	GOVERNMENT INDUSTRY	370410	431444	480222	227160	122703	260915	56548	112524	22590
85	REST OF WORLD INDUSTRY	-9727	-22448	-38714	-19754	-2974	-15788	-5728	-5292	-3309
86	HOUSEHOLD INDUSTRY	56251	76411	66751	23589	30913	41912	4029	11178	1985
87	INVENTORY VALUATION ADJ.	0	0	0	0	0	0	0	0	0
88	STATE TOTAL	6055699	14242830	22014097	9741688	2888621	11348496	1758787	4888930	494005

TABLE C-1

STATE ESTIMATES OF 1947 OUTPUTS
(THOUSANDS OF CURRENT DOLLARS)

INDUSTRY TITLE	28 NEW HAMPSHIRE	29 NEW JERSEY	30 NEW MEXICO	31 NEW YORK	32 NORTH CAROLINA	33 NORTH DAKOTA	34 OHIO	35 OKLAHOMA	36 OREGON
1 LIVESTOCK, PRDTS.	60928	196303	126986	733470	325681	309878	977679	468294	244100
2 OTHER AGRICULTURE PRDTS.	21449	144244	100840	379872	709373	878939	588735	443616	314239
3 FORESTRY, FISHERIES	2319	11300	230	19798	6753	69	5115	2254	11443
4 AGRI.,FORES.,FISH. SERV.	6027	9047	4328	15791	18786	6265	21157	15531	6593
5 IRON, FERRO. ORES MINING	0	3905	464	14262	801	0	0	0	0
6 NONFERROUS ORES MINING	0	8634	25869	6153	464	0	0	8711	771
7 COAL MINING	0	0	6611	0	0	5371	133207	15292	0
8 CRUDE PETRO.,NATURAL GAS	0	0	82881	21479	0	14	24796	316179	0
9 STONE, CLAY MINING	546	21230	1167	34230	14304	628	46002	6291	9827
10 CHEM.,FERT. MIN. MINING	0	0	18632	7535	0	0	0	0	0
11 NEW CONSTRUCTION	47695	654068	120685	1315549	372241	76611	1047451	391146	272779
12 MAINT., REPAIR CONSTR.	29933	272329	51160	751333	160556	64146	508153	121188	105773
13 ORDNANCE, ACCESSORIES	68	517	12394	94	24533	1616	11	9964	193
14 FOOD, KINDRED PRDTS.	21018	231322	2211816	85418	2848954	56006	421	5002259	195602
15 TOBACCO MANUFACTURES	0	1130	298033	2495	204565	566	182	748719	6319
16 FABRICS	1299	12708	340207	1341	819835	36623	1704	1119106	62213
17 TEXTILE PRDTS.	0	0	70572	0	120653	1729	3	212617	2214
18 APPAREL	294	19729	370142	219	475457	25639	616	1420705	444454
19 MISC. TEXTILE PRDTS.	0	666	90657	2	120890	986	70	172395	5106
20 LUMBER, WOOD PRDTS.	2	5193	164999	0	867030	1874	5689	839200	2862
21 WOODEN CONTAINERS	0	541	22318	0	58277	208	0	131556	177
22 HOUSEHOLD FURNITURE	0	150	70271	0	105506	977	0	350355	1793
23 OTHER FURNITURE	0	56	109666	1	95888	3043	1	39599	57
24 PAPER, ALLIED PRDTS.	23	1771	335297	460	448330	5176	546	387117	2805
25 PAPERBOARD CONTAINERS	0	0	0	0	102255	0	0	544702	8147
26 PRINTING, PUBLISHING	193	16129	348840	628	1561070	14625	697	198221	24241
27 CHEMICALS,SELECT. PRDTS.	10	8149	207940	682	854101	243	85	24751	9007
28 PLASTICS, SYNTHETICS	0	18044	123488	166	235108	7160	269	179096	2031
29 DRUGS, COSMETICS	1309	315436	146178	265667	316532	2230	193459	94956	3748
30 PAINT, ALLIED PRDTS.	295	173027	0	15248	5245	730	139760	3039	6637
31 PETROLEUM, RELATED INDS.	159	673463	14268	203837	615	900	323739	307474	8787
32 RUBBER, MISC. PLASTICS	7660	193811	0	180682	11092	0	916257	32623	2261
33 LEATHER TANNING, PRDTS.	17961	58481	0	148359	20475	0	47608	0	535
34 FOOTWEAR, LEATHER PRDTS.	161298	52808	553	544245	2915	0	110090	1397	2464
35 GLASS, GLASS PRDTS.	0	79686	0	83276	3749	46	161187	29659	485
36 STONE, CLAY PRDTS.	6913	162707	2156	295270	33550	1273	322706	18603	12397
37 PRIMARY IRON, STEEL MFR.	1249	179473	124	658149	2652	39	2170637	14178	46232
38 PRIMARY NONFERROUS MFR.	6684	710741	29286	661906	16981	0	294958	79785	25001

		C1	C2	C3	C4	C5	C6	C7	C8	C9
39	METAL CONTAINERS	0	72644	0	49596	0	0	77482	2987	2551
40	FABRICATED METAL PRDTS.	3786	118030	3458	301074	21961	1293	451005	41547	28903
41	SCREW MACH. PRDTS., ETC.	4310	42422	7	158760	446	35	354581	1389	824
42	OTHER FAB. METAL PRDTS.	3028	163536	1	213912	6121	327	282983	5218	5303
43	ENGINES, TURBINES	42	26896	126	63011	28	2	91838	356	0
44	FARM MACH., EQUIP.	118	10262	0	68941	5177	543	103111	3066	2045
45	CONSTRUC. MACH., EQUIP.	6098	37402	230	24927	2659	0	278809	37441	6811
46	MATERIAL HANDLING MACH.	468	48884	572	58560	2669	14	102387	1079	19783
47	METALWORKING MACHINERY	8413	72087	4	114260	754	1	364095	729	1483
48	SPECIAL MACH., EQUIP.	28955	110128	0	214447	15257	118	219119	1091	8132
49	GENERAL MACH., EQUIP.	1120	152512	0	203373	1659	6	290020	8590	2785
50	MACHINE SHOP PRDTS.	633	21555	0	27747	1839	0	32382	783	4272
51	OFFICE, COMPUT. MACHINES	0	21160	0	184084	60	5166	142293	160	0
52	SERVICE IND. MACHINES	219	24869	0	96932	1394	0	224646	1213	987
53	ELECT. TRANSMISS. EQUIP.	7573	132223	3	232127	725	0	429795	1618	4196
54	HOUSEHOLD APPLIANCES	176	82413	0	123737	1146	7	410893	2103	5167
55	ELECTRIC LIGHTING EQUIP.	335	108524	0	172346	484	0	144481	344	250
56	RADIO, TV, ETC., EQUIP.	0	335047	0	285761	14333	0	75182	0	522
57	ELECTRONIC COMPONENTS	1811	76309	0	97885	2369	604	19346	0	172
58	MISC. ELECTRICAL MACH.	113	78205	0	98388	8932	0	186645	1208	3459
59	MOTOR VEHICLES, EQUIP.	1	397724	3793	677807	4	0	1095160	6742	5795
60	AIRCRAFT, PARTS	81	79843	0	102954	2765	72	116644	1203	0
61	OTHER TRANSPORT. EQUIP.	3067	123839	0	269653	1113	0	122775	2253	13963
62	PROFESS., SCIEN. INSTRU.	581	130409	22	305328	85	1	68012	4316	1442
63	MEDICAL, PHOTO. EQUIP.	15679	34244	0	387696	4984	492	14460	336	938
64	MISC. MANUFACTURING	38647	287058	2071	795867	196924	66901	226928	5670	8696
65	TRANSPORT., WAREHOUSING	13138	507655	92070	3088762	39874	7001	1240960	597658	215279
66	COMMUNICA.,EXC. BRDCAST.	1120	137517	3401	472642	7656	1482	181438	28900	37182
67	RADIO, TV BROADCASTING	22063	3287	1721	60804	62103	13329	27847	4604	4640
68	ELEC.,GAS,WATER,SAN.SER.	143242	246155	29636	795834	859021	203716	399170	75594	44333
69	WHOLESALE, RETAIL TRADE	29858	1612955	168320	8266947	132557	20924	2932592	628266	623045
70	FINANCE, INSURANCE	60886	432182	14699	2363468	315354	59158	465238	76124	78162
71	REAL ESTATE, RENTAL	26536	802146	73316	3510785	121609	16251	1238501	229313	223884
72	HOTELS, PERSONAL SERV.	7381	289617	26099	1079607	43845	7559	359029	79283	76484
73	BUSINESS SERVICES	166	139092	12385	1355792	103	1025	225663	61437	46452
74	RESEARCH, DEVELOPMENT	13045	3395	409	9828	72345	18751	1908	771	123
75	AUTO. REPAIR, SERVICES	16443	124527	16433	360167	38094	7290	219221	63880	58627
76	AMUSEMENTS	33080	130794	9597	642108	104882	22293	161536	31376	29071
77	MED.,EDUC. SERVICES	5276	297296	18593	1387324	27713	6837	448053	75007	88864
78	FEDERAL GOVT. ENTERPRISE	6598	44246	6490	226521	15471	291	79492	23066	13203
79	STATE, LOCAL GOVT. ENT.	0	25565	986	342874	0	0	131636	8313	24303
80	IMPORTS	0	0	0	0	0	0	0	0	0
81	BUS.TRAVEL, ENT., GIFTS.	0	0	0	0	0	0	0	0	0
82	OFFICE SUPPLIES	0	0	0	0	0	0	0	0	0
83	SCRAP, USED GOODS	0	0	0	0	0	0	0	0	0
84	GOVERNMENT INDUSTRY	45173	432574	7011	1517543	281387	44127	602355	176799	133473
85	REST OF WORLD INDUSTRY	-3672	-25340	-3625	-157074	-5762	-4149	-34335	-5737	-6619
86	HOUSEHOLD INDUSTRY	6624	95593	6034	357779	67217	3578	93418	22719	17700
87	INVENTORY VALUATION ADJ.	0	0	0	0	0	0	0	0	0
88	STATE TOTAL	1379999	16445740	1220402	51429607	9594101	2013879	2664318	5173349	4228057

TABLE C-1

STATE ESTIMATES OF 1947 OUTPUTS
(THOUSANDS OF CURRENT DOLLARS)

INDUSTRY TITLE	37 PENNSYL-VANIA	38 RHODE ISLAND	39 SOUTH CAROLINA	40 SOUTH DAKOTA	41 TENNESSEE	42 TEXAS	43 UTAH	44 VERMONT	45 VIRGINIA
1 LIVESTOCK, PRDTS.	720766	18388	157010	542259	403168	1151754	138992	114771	378437
2 OTHER AGRICULTURE PRDTS.	351093	7370	329853	701992	362371	1689988	86298	35256	293415
3 FORESTRY, FISHERIES	7957	2806	2575	94	3983	8198	42	1295	23972
4 AGRI.,FORES.,FISH. SERV.	20771	775	11641	8737	12770	77336	2869	1893	12785
5 IRON, FERRO. ORES MINING	13477	0	0	0	3426	1040	3092	535	77
6 NONFERROUS ORES MINING	58	0	0	13935	7087	34	119053	0	2866
7 COAL MINING	1052626	0	0	336	30261	61	29594	0	98752
8 CRUDE PETRO.,NATURAL GAS	76994	0	0	0	17	1838967	381	0	100
9 STONE, CLAY MINING	53591	446	6371	7389	17850	18097	2044	9801	20081
10 CHEM.,FERT. MIN. MINING	0	0	0	0	8652	74933	132	0	0
11 NEW CONSTRUCTION	1089588	84805	170156	84654	313402	1751394	92855	31534	407727
12 MAINT., REPAIR CONSTR.	447230	30653	62740	63464	119059	658247	47153	17650	172805
13 ORDNANCE, ACCESSORIES	228	20601	69	747	9	657	1206	142	966
14 FOOD, KINDRED PRDTS.	132564	5408800	252115	21230	385	327373	362367	252338	11637
15 TOBACCO MANUFACTURES	4741	587028	29388	0	2014	43325	50958	2368	1514
16 FABRICS	41273	1259592	61587	5811	3025	84055	153363	10521	6169
17 TEXTILE PRDTS.	781	205073	6298	0	194	2256	13042	196	6247
18 APPAREL	52175	843236	13977	22	1918	51021	1573928	19788	6409
19 MISC. TEXTILE PRDTS.	1656	104693	1483	1403	68	4089	9494	2	126
20 LUMBER, WOOD PRDTS.	3311	332613	4029	1150	332	7945	14356	1738	33411
21 WOODEN CONTAINERS	523	101551	203	6	209	868	1139	0	0
22 HOUSEHOLD FURNITURE	4406	137012	1622	0	266	17730	11420	153	874
23 OTHER FURNITURE	150	62811	3460	4	0	1281	1118	58	445
24 PAPER, ALLIED PRDTS.	24145	246007	17226	6546	66	26732	111260	45	306
25 PAPERBOARD CONTAINERS	0	0	0	0	0	0	0	0	0
26 PRINTING, PUBLISHING	5644	374621	62878	209	2066	38182	30641	11833	3556
27 CHEMICALS,SELECT. PRDTS.	2190	272921	127165	7183	26	22956	6308	210	16204
28 PLASTICS, SYNTHETICS	7384	246698	4109	2742	267	9527	19237	548	1849
29 DRUGS, COSMETICS	84980	83403	39424	1105	6422	42153	13412	6367	5129
30 PAINT, ALLIED PRDTS.	95303	5640	953	0	8543	28966	808	320	5444
31 PETROLEUM, RELATED INDS.	717045	16995	3728	550	12498	1927086	38406	3207	5172
32 RUBBER, MISC. PLASTICS	257074	48850	3789	0	82594	18854	110	10257	12501
33 LEATHER TANNING, PRDTS.	141925	3671	238	0	7614	4040	0	1309	15422
34 FOOTWEAR, LEATHER PRDTS.	181937	3596	313	0	90333	10073	142	1816	24474
35 GLASS, GLASS PRDTS.	217575	2518	431	0	10290	11926	80	790	8553
36 STONE, CLAY PRDTS.	366395	2041	14293	3544	50808	89536	10466	22051	31464
37 PRIMARY IRON, STEEL MFR.	3036718	44128	6149	36	69637	77660	81510	738	21932
38 PRIMARY NONFERROUS MFR.	393570	68822	404	0	83875	127473	72750	558	9506

142

#	Industry									
39	METAL CONTAINERS	63671	0	0	0	4445	49206	4400	0	2016
40	FABRICATED METAL PRDTS.	488494	10920	3299	4176	82248	104874	7331	4843	36421
41	SCREW MACH. PRDTS., ETC.	276254	19714	455	388	6543	3548	37	97	101
42	OTHER FAB. METAL PRDTS.	272427	31166	12		8076	27940	490	2596	8920
43	ENGINES, TURBINES	87809		307	1403	91	807	1	4014	399
44	FARM MACH., EQUIP.	65664	309		124	7186	14225	268	103	1616
45	CONSTRUC. MACH., EQUIP.	138757		525		6643	128203	6226		2659
46	MATERIAL HANDLING MACH.	48380	373	103	195	6391	1905	2166		2046
47	METALWORKING MACHINERY	140861	43861	8824	460	585	1969	251	22908	150
48	SPECIAL MACH., EQUIP.	178252	33942	1935	114	6879	19399	556	6906	6577
49	GENERAL MACH., EQUIP.	176124	2494	64	31	6879	15971		211	1333
50	MACHINE SHOP PRDTS.	45847	7850			2388	5193	103	582	825
51	OFFICE, COMPUT. MACHINES	1951	60		302	80	120	320	8692	60
52	SERVICE IND. MACHINES	118118	2888		594	6666	11271	464	92	233
53	ELECT. TRANSMISS. EQUIP.	525875	1329		312	2826	5041	180		5098
54	HOUSEHOLD APPLIANCES	160686	1902			20793	13394	247	1025	3499
55	ELECTRIC LIGHTING EQUIP.	98843	18480			3447	5498	277	356	438
56	RADIO, TV, ETC., EQUIP.	150633	1867			2908	950	0	1867	4900
57	ELECTRONIC COMPONENTS	84736	613				219	0	613	1572
58	MISC. ELECTRICAL MACH.	60217	17617	36		6509	16369	371	50	1296
59	MOTOR VEHICLES, EQUIP.	425693	1757	2068	172	68331	39232		95	11741
60	AIRCRAFT, PARTS	30182				179	79237	1192		2
61	OTHER TRANSPORT. EQUIP.	380050	733	4213	64	10358	33739	336	199	104056
62	PROFESS., SCIEN. INSTRU.	177825	6100	220	164	14334	3870	1	1135	1152
63	MEDICAL, PHOTO. EQUIP.	12285	8533	172	1206	112	1961	2743	7	6994
64	MISC. MANUFACTURING	268288	162307	6049	887	18588	21592	105715	5050	9890
65	TRANSPORT., WAREHOUSING	1756610	44972	98498	54913	277391	1890970	7640	35663	378883
66	COMMUNICA.,EXC. BRDCAST.	229373	21710	15251	6752	54736	158426	2516	8669	54027
67	RADIO, TV BROADCASTING	18900	2057	3241	1514	8662	19103	18723	494	5765
68	ELEC.,GAS,WATER,SAN.SER.	512850	41304	35157	13202	9600	293170	226373	17940	89696
69	WHOLESALE, RETAIL TRADE	3451503	275918	415155	203253	978429	2557597	32646	101463	786580
70	FINANCE, INSURANCE	727183	58898	71730	20405	135799	345946	90056	18299	142505
71	REAL ESTATE, RENTAL	1252636	103478	145240	63021	298786	812596	30076	36415	373523
72	HOTELS, PERSONAL SERV.	446147	38683	53803	18356	110611	329798	11923	13466	117776
73	BUSINESS SERVICES	278575	20365	19038	8853	40557	268057	38	3483	39637
74	RESEARCH, DEVELOPMENT	2286	107	436	55	804	2636	1853	38	1154
75	AUTO. REPAIR, SERVICES	252739	19257	38560	18698	69706	228378	13677	10307	68745
76	AMUSEMENTS	203246	29534	16055	8645	36585	113467	29365	5012	44646
77	MED.,EDUC. SERVICES	708754	50430	48514	23713	112650	255937	5972	22014	121330
78	FEDERAL GOVT. ENTERPRISE	82100	9622	13534	7837	64625	76442	9547	4673	79588
79	STATE, LOCAL GOVT. ENT.	109091	6124	3958	898	72014	72999		1714	50949
80	IMPORTS	0	0	0	0	0	0	0	0	0
81	BUS.TRAVEL, ENT., GIFTS	0	0	0	0	0	0	0	0	0
82	OFFICE SUPPLIES	0	0	0	0	0	0	0	0	0
83	SCRAP, USED GOODS	0	0	0	0	0	0	0	0	0
84	GOVERNMENT INDUSTRY	819149	99948	171675	50917	178517	668294	95808	24857	646517
85	REST OF WORLD INDUSTRY	-40244	-3432	-2791	-2415	-7954	-35567	-2456	-1918	-8277
86	HOUSEHOLD INDUSTRY	155760	11757	42820	4339	50966	132116	4011	6670	55894
87	INVENTORY VALUATION ADJ.	0	0	0	0	0	0	0	0	0
88	STATE TOTAL	31099191	2531606	4058713	2252740	6293117	21339921	1691391	904934	7465906

TABLE C-1

STATE ESTIMATES OF 1947 OUTPUTS
(THOUSANDS OF CURRENT DOLLARS)

INDUSTRY TITLE	46 WASHINGTON	47 WEST VIRGINIA	48 WISCONSIN	49 WYOMING	50 ALASKA	51 HAWAII	52 NO STATE ALLOCATION	53 NATIONAL TOTAL
1 LIVESTOCK, PRDTS.	260152	171960	1172854	161676	0	0	0	22375000
2 OTHER AGRICULTURE PRDTS.	472048	52283	319137	66155	0	0	0	22685000
3 FORESTRY, FISHERIES	27823	5133	6252	82	0	0	0	408000
4 AGRI.,FORES.,FISH. SERV.	8731	2870	15680	1573	0	0	0	701000
5 IRON, FERRO. ORES MINING	8	0	5550	2343	0	0	0	353000
6 NONFERROUS ORES MINING	4741	0	1615	51	0	0	0	521000
7 COAL MINING	6788	799923	0	27501	0	0	0	3078000
8 CRUDE PETRO.,NATURAL GAS	0	47336	0	82062	0	0	0	4210000
9 STONE, CLAY MINING	10664	13056	21654	2863	0	0	0	603000
10 CHEM.,FERT. MIN. MINING	194	194	0	312	0	0	0	215000
11 NEW CONSTRUCTION	481191	220680	390031	63399	0	0	0	20329000
12 MAINT., REPAIR CONSTR.	148076	70708	193418	26681	0	0	0	9002000
13 ORDNANCE, ACCESSORIES	484	850	798	2040	0	0	0	149000
14 FOOD, KINDRED PRDTS.	200555	301699	539741	122081	0	0	0	43523000
15 TOBACCO MANUFACTURES	3314	12575	15130	122329	0	0	0	3970000
16 FABRICS	58113	40700	93616	327413	0	0	0	10315000
17 TEXTILE PRDTS.	3596	2123	2259	236025	0	0	0	1832000
18 APPAREL	12808	64899	119377	728256	0	0	0	11019000
19 MISC. TEXTILE PRDTS.	792	1935	310	53322	0	0	0	1082000
20 LUMBER, WOOD PRDTS.	486	3072	286	90158	0	0	0	5284000
21 WOODEN CONTAINERS	1798	373	505	31313	0	0	0	523000
22 HOUSEHOLD FURNITURE	2983	7748	1831	71288	0	0	0	1839000
23 OTHER FURNITURE	1092	1067	2288	2968	0	0	0	695000
24 PAPER, ALLIED PRDTS.	139580	85140	9558	103108	0	0	0	4742000
25 PAPERBOARD CONTAINERS	0	0	0	197833	0	0	0	1597000
26 PRINTING, PUBLISHING	38634	2146	1208	128000	0	0	0	6464000
27 CHEMICALS,SELECT. PRDTS.	12011	8101	4028	102648	0	0	0	4492000
28 PLASTICS, SYNTHETICS	4210	6395	4664	20201	0	0	0	1428000
29 DRUGS, COSMETICS	8703	7869	29450	30097	0	0	0	3043000
30 PAINT, ALLIED PRDTS.	4803	707	33056	376	0	0	0	1298000
31 PETROLEUM, RELATED INDS.	9289	39974	28567	78637	0	0	0	7880000
32 RUBBER, MISC. PLASTICS	736	3235	55704	34	0	0	0	3471000
33 LEATHER TANNING, PRDTS.	205	22854	106898	0	0	0	0	1132000
34 FOOTWEAR, LEATHER PRDTS.	3226	3319	131713	71	0	0	0	2607000
35 GLASS, GLASS PRDTS.	4554	139071	3610	0	0	0	0	1123000
36 STONE, CLAY PRDTS.	28590	70822	46190	3021	0	0	0	2921000
37 PRIMARY IRON, STEEL MFR.	30745	282388	147673	9	0	0	0	11023000
38 PRIMARY NONFERROUS MFR.	143433	41540	110013	34	0	0	0	5515000

#	Industry								
39	METAL CONTAINERS	10572	17511	5936	0	0	0	0	862000
40	FABRICATED METAL PRDTS.	25083	41564	199203	755	0	0	0	3674000
41	SCREW MACH. PRDTS., ETC.	1397	26436	88290	0	0	0	0	1943000
42	OTHER FAB. METAL PRDTS.	7077	11009	51935	0	0	0	0	2560000
43	ENGINES, TURBINES	723	0	148193	0	0	0	0	831000
44	FARM MACH., EQUIP.	3381	2160	149533	268	0	0	0	1420000
45	CONSTRUC. MACH., EQUIP.	18629	17822	194366	114	0	0	0	1585000
46	MATERIAL HANDLING MACH.	4208	970	19483	0	0	0	0	566000
47	METALWORKING MACHINERY	3413	366	73251	4	0	0	0	1697000
48	SPECIAL MACH., EQUIP.	9229	2448	101804	3	0	0	0	1815000
49	GENERAL MACH., EQUIP.	3256	521	89703	3	0	0	0	1800000
50	MACHINE SHOP PRDTS.	3255	1008	11147	57	0	0	0	390000
51	OFFICE, COMPUT. MACHINES	117	0	1720	0	0	0	0	648000
52	SERVICE IND. MACHINES	1045	254	27170	120	0	0	0	1167000
53	ELECT. TRANSMISS. EQUIP.	2852	1441	154224	364	0	0	0	2432000
54	HOUSEHOLD APPLIANCES	9086	2147	83605	124	0	0	0	2148000
55	ELECTRIC LIGHTING EQUIP.	1614	7208	12598	0	0	0	0	1100000
56	RADIO, TV, ETC., EQUIP.	3152	0	4249	0	0	0	0	2078000
57	ELECTRONIC COMPONENTS	172	3207	1340	0	0	0	0	570000
58	MISC. ELECTRICAL MACH.	3415	497	37643	0	0	0	0	890000
59	MOTOR VEHICLES, EQUIP.	20522	11720	445209	0	0	0	0	12189000
60	AIRCRAFT, PARTS	46040	166	4975	165	0	0	0	1446000
61	OTHER TRANSPORT. EQUIP.	43669	12597	54066	3	0	0	0	2412000
62	PROFESS., SCIEN. INSTRU.	1740	424	76231	0	0	0	0	1293000
63	MEDICAL, PHOTO. EQUIP.	344	397	2686	0	0	0	0	648001
64	MISC. MANUFACTURING	8974	9581	61892	216	0	0	0	3202000
65	TRANSPORT., WAREHOUSING	433451	255051	324744	165216	0	0	0	22325000
66	COMMUNICA.,EXC. BRDCAST.	68898	23395	98646	1995	0	0	0	3418000
67	RADIO, TV BROADCASTING	6814	4101	5896	543	0	0	0	415000
68	ELEC.,GAS,WATER,SAN.SER.	62265	94347	121931	100034	0	0	0	5774000
69	WHOLESALE, RETAIL TRADE	956184	480985	1163247	100372	0	0	0	53392000
70	FINANCE, INSURANCE	153198	52173	177195	8402	0	0	0	10522000
71	REAL ESTATE, RENTAL	379608	162436	472222	35641	0	0	0	21679000
72	HOTELS, PERSONAL SERV.	111857	56139	130756	15648	0	0	0	7046000
73	BUSINESS SERVICES	62630	23381	68562	7347	0	0	0	5142000
74	RESEARCH, DEVELOPMENT	583	581	630	168	0	0	0	77121
75	AUTO. REPAIR, SERVICES	74367	35746	88509	10859	0	0	0	3974000
76	AMUSEMENTS	46872	28491	51299	5058	0	0	0	3849000
77	MED.,EDUC. SERVICES	160529	69223	183001	9658	0	0	0	8692000
78	FEDERAL GOVT. ENTERPRISE	56316	12543	37114	3877	0	51226	0	1777570
79	STATE, LOCAL GOVT. ENT.	75784	21313	13014	1209	0	0	0	1708000
80	IMPORTS	0	0	0	0	0	0	0	0
81	BUS.TRAVEL, ENT., GIFTS.	0	0	0	0	0	0	0	0
82	OFFICE SUPPLIES	0	0	0	0	0	0	0	0
83	SCRAP, USED GOODS	0	0	0	0	0	0	0	0
84	GOVERNMENT INDUSTRY	396134	110343	234451	33295	0	1556000	0	15730000
85	REST OF WORLD INDUSTRY	-16138	-4543	-17120	-1820	0	1592000*	0	823998*
86	HOUSEHOLD INDUSTRY	22121	17736	26662	2151	0		0	2348000*
87	INVENTORY VALUATION ADJ.	0	0	0	0	0	-763965	0	-763965
88	STATE, TOTAL	6571291	4186686	11041233	980616	0	2435261	0	443313725

*These figures exclude the value of secondary production. They therefore differ from those obtained by adding the corresponding values of final demand given in Appendix C of Volume I of this series. (See page 152)

145

TABLE C-2

STATE ESTIMATES OF 1958 OUTPUTS
(THOUSANDS OF CURRENT DOLLARS)

INDUSTRY TITLE	1 ALABAMA	2 ARIZONA	3 ARKANSAS	4 CALIFORNIA	5 COLORADO	6 CONNECTICUT	7 DELAWARE	8 DISTRICT OF COLUMBIA	9 FLORIDA
1 LIVESTOCK, PRDTS.	439590	142353	329719	1220290	419318	129759	98808		281067
2 OTHER AGRICULTURE PRDTS.	261262	363739	443536	2339777	345540	61286	55387		544676
3 FORESTRY, FISHERIES	24063	2430	16042	130756	904	1214	6845		44024
4 AGRI.,FORES.,FISH. SERV.	35070	17631	46099	90587	7855	11176	15974		12149
5 IRON,FERRO. ORES MINING	73419	7891	1711	29042	26246	0	0		0
6 NONFERROUS ORES MINING	2331	229971	18023	7787	112145	428	0		7391
7 COAL MINING	89591	51	3089	0	19718	0	0		0
8 CRUDE PETRO.,NATURAL GAS	16560	54	91385	1165224	170351	0	0		1035
9 STONE, CLAY MINING	15426	4826	13985	126161	13936	13091	1090		40821
10 CHEM.,FERT. MIN. MINING	0	458	2019	55970	5139	0	291		105199
11 NEW CONSTRUCTION	758078	632967	399123	6223625	716830	833604	176361	250707	2005218
12 MAINT., REPAIR CONSTR.	200900	103415	159175	1899336	228461	232324	44069	78754	449855
13 ORDNANCE, ACCESSORIES	50902	37358	7835	10622	350786	8119	91990	7507	1543
14 FOOD, KINDRED PRDTS.	865305	2399505	575508	256862	2449153	455348	1315550	101097	
15 TOBACCO MANUFACTURES	10381	38303	648	8605	714714	13446	48260	28605	358
16 FABRICS	237019	127812	19392	25419	850543	41621	396881	18110	5531
17 TEXTILE PRDTS.	19540	17802	393	3181	106740	7222	38232	6077	
18 APPAREL	428915	40781	5289	13572	594895	76582	311200	29323	164
19 MISC. TEXTILE PRDTS.	22054	3417	316	3140	120592	5246	147860	455	
20 LUMBER, WOOD PRDTS.	172473	19657	39220	11585	652307	26740	225107	4973	1270
21 WOODEN CONTAINERS	967	309	62	3322	17372	1443	10357		90
22 HOUSEHOLD FURNITURE	27389	467	0	9545	170795	531	126953	1136	
23 OTHER FURNITURE	476	5568	2617	2233	100062	326	37863	195	234
24 PAPER, ALLIED PRDTS.	70092	38500	6308	2854	686101	6532	137822	68111	100
25 PAPERBOARD CONTAINERS	86977	0	3762	0	132255	0	22417		
26 PRINTING, PUBLISHING	87423	2325	18277	25042	741324	34650	678116	13527	3027
27 CHEMICALS,SELECT. PRDTS.	639830	18166	4962	50077	471417	43534	456941	7774	2924
28 PLASTICS, SYNTHETICS	322168	7192	5579	16470	137864	5579	82348	31190	673
29 DRUGS, COSMETICS	12963	7749	3719	462122	83199	101863	44468	2920	10338
30 PAINT, ALLIED PRDTS.	6661	2717	2874	202307	7707	6766	2596	589	17284
31 PETROLEUM, RELATED INDS.	32144	6144	122907	2271499	67975	12845	61585		19712
32 RUBBER, MISC. PLASTICS	209608	5411	26024	465872	104996	264016	28101	915	8181
33 LEATHER TANNING, PRDTS.	0	0	0	20252	87	4050	27748		784
34 FOOTWEAR, LEATHER PRDTS.	7490	1099	35644	49117	24084	33005	2069		7225
35 GLASS, GLASS PRDTS.	8127	285	18166	120606	1039	9218	188	119	11906
36 STONE, CLAY PRDTS.	130966	44911	32809	725633	72148	82406	13552	17069	210723
37 PRIMARY IRON, STEEL MFR.	906968	7150	2330	694957	172861	118809	41749		7594
38 PRIMARY NONFERROUS MFR.	215523	192827	86409	443247	34050	480025	9973		69656

146

No.	Category	Col1	Col2	Col3	Col4	Col5	Col6	Col7	Col8	Col9
39	METAL CONTAINERS	73362	0	1412	190	8304	362434	3577	0	7928
40	FABRICATED METAL PRDTS.	165895	6905	25818	76251	47553	694627	18093	25660	135172
41	SCREW MACH. PRDTS., ETC.	5623	129	6466	157136	3129	206818	3097	217	28780
42	OTHER FAB. METAL PRDTS.	28009	843	12418	301390	21920	451235	19398	2089	48826
43	ENGINES, TURBINES	799	0	0	14446		68921		577	0
44	FARM MACH., EQUIP.	4920	0	818	1180	5947	47797	865	376	9575
45	CONSTRUC. MACH., EQUIP.	1764	0	156	1788	39773	129613	108	42	3461
46	MATERIAL HANDLING MACH.	707	0	0	3034	6308	64228	5977	47	8801
47	METALWORKING MACHINERY	5925	101	4178	182157	1034	111147	1951	4041	1687
48	SPECIAL MACH., EQUIP.	6711	0	14639	63958	2562	124437	604	168	13569
49	GENERAL MACH., EQUIP.	6631	1545	806	262350	9308	213969	5571	560	6063
50	MACHINE SHOP PRDTS.	15150	135	1490	52475	16622	218421	3686	6329	8150
51	OFFICE, COMPUT. MACHINES	1602	141	0	165141	198	145547	2127	5066	157
52	SERVICE IND. MACHINES	4423	538	2736	19471	1210	97004	25968	22123	5729
53	ELECT. TRANSMISS. EQUIP.	12392	0	118	111424	22653	372588	10368	474	7903
54	HOUSEHOLD APPLIANCES	2557	281	1234	137892	576	185511	8742	0	507
55	ELECTRIC LIGHTING EQUIP.	3967	194	965	118856	1106	169755	6314	954	19035
56	RADIO, TV, ETC. EQUIP.	17069	1646	191	75018	447	379037	476	20800	0
57	ELECTRONIC COMPONENTS	12659	131	0	50411	609	250955	233	5714	24018
58	MISC. ELECTRICAL MACH.	18125	0		16537	3727	47685	5371	540	
59	MOTOR VEHICLES, EQUIP.	7975	303	222948	51435	12510	1415746	75698	2819	38610
60	AIRCRAFT, PARTS	24480	123	5299	1104980	20658	3016610	1047		104803
61	OTHER TRANSPORT. EQUIP.	74391	853	2484	163590	7400	243122	2379		55179
62	PROFESS., SCIEN. INSTRU.	3895	117	5761	149350	4734	264215	92		936
63	MEDICAL, PHOTO. EQUIP.	3143	1954		19806	2479	48440	20516		82
64	MISC. MANUFACTURING	32233		10202	220952	20678	263941	212297	5813	9448
65	TRANSPORT., WAREHOUSING	783335	177122	96115	270907	349634	3020384	38716	142666	317221
66	COMMUNICA.,EXC. BRDCAST.	185744	77742	27532	31136	44043	1036715	7928	23785	99543
67	RADIO, TV BROADCASTING	33770	30788	3536	13337	15100	225674	148981	9324	13541
68	ELEC.,GAS,WATER,SAN.SER.	308585	74683	42581	271962	164469	1571326	565831	121624	213982
69	WHOLESALE, RETAIL TRADE	2416440	565884	268220	1208689	927442	8999704	117292	544038	1092252
70	FINANCE, INSURANCE	585004	223102	87041	552083	265677	2661028	288979	127390	249728
71	REAL ESTATE, RENTAL	1849482	451816	157227	907303	574792	6171118	80066	414003	618181
72	HOTELS, PERSONAL SERV.	497737	133839	27310	163192	132679	1285581	36711	101269	131599
73	BUSINESS SERVICES	348464	242470	19940	173546	122890	1890511	267	73548	94946
74	RESEARCH, DEVELOPMENT	6019	3103	7618	5661	2570	141101	61648	716	5342
75	AUTO. REPAIR, SERVICES	252173	51633	22689	115417	101296	884444	22150	68470	105749
76	AMUSEMENTS	183297	47993	18128	42194	84942	1026862	101986	27461	27822
77	MED.,EDUC. SERVICES	466342	343442	61305	404044	226279	2324697	36692	108697	204460
78	FEDERAL GOVT. ENTERPRISE	100264	68312	8626	46684	42101	368338	24352	26008	117469
79	STATE, LOCAL GOVT. ENT.	147337	12640	19404	42091	53539	489777		43297	84246
80	IMPORTS	0	0	0	0	0	0	0	0	0
81	BUS.TRAVEL, ENT., GIFTS.	0	0	0	0	0	0	0	0	0
82	OFFICE SUPPLIES	0	0	0	0	0	0	0	0	0
83	SCRAP, USED GOODS	0	0	0	0	0	0	0	0	0
84	GOVERNMENT INDUSTRY	1004931	798802	104858	400313	504465	4413723	224938	336200	636080
85	REST OF WORLD INDUSTRY	-39019	-13523	-2693	-14096	-11786	-194382	-6221	-14357	-11593
86	HOUSEHOLD INDUSTRY	162266	47779	13481	62988	24096	307555	36181	21052	95071
87	INVENTORY VALUATION ADJ.	0	0	0	0	0	0	0	0	0
88	STATE TOTAL	16180649	4083700	2381122	12573348	7511376	77196515	5107664	4562659	10280191

TABLE C-2

STATE ESTIMATES OF 1958 OUTPUTS
(THOUSANDS OF CURRENT DOLLARS)

INDUSTRY TITLE	10 GEORGIA	11 IDAHO	12 ILLINOIS	13 INDIANA	14 IOWA	15 KANSAS	16 KENTUCKY	17 LOUISIANA	18 MAINE
1 LIVESTOCK, PRDTS.	597087	267832	1655270	1059438	2648758	716074	493258	257002	145140
2 OTHER AGRICULTURE PRDTS.	422842	287897	1740665	685850	1215080	1144776	352128	229381	107924
3 FORESTRY, FISHERIES	41533	7176	3801	2353	1402	146	5541	37844	26702
4 AGRI.,FORES.,FISH. SERV.	71115	6522	25342	28971	35867	14145	9830	12557	14286
5 IRON, FERRO. ORES MINING	1404	7964	3693	0	0	0	0	0	0
6 NONFERROUS ORES MINING	151	32973		0	0	443	0	0	28
7 COAL MINING	53	3	186964	61199	4969	3357	366764	0	0
8 CRUDE PETRO.,NATURAL GAS	77	23	256783	32973	0	414309	75302	1472545	0
9 STONE, CLAY MINING	50528	5698	98220	38953	39696	19976	28647	15003	2903
10 CHEM.,FERT. MIN. MINING	6476	4907	9718	0	0	4492	3409	67804	0
11 NEW CONSTRUCTION	955492	234559	2639793	1064012	612442	795550	730432	1569160	221924
12 MAINT.,* REPAIR CONSTR.	242243	103147	1072560	485999	395981	301503	212463	236666	67201
13 ORDNANCE, ACCESSORIES	9318	9537	2417	474495	194161	726	107842	32322	70984
14 FOOD, KINDRED PRDTS.	123479	124651	209820	4830317	5421496	357200	59392	519715	415436
15 TOBACCO MANUFACTURES	87941	22887			200188	89014	69387	161719	78882
16 FABRICS	132172	77028	7138	867156	420648	81258	44599	68983	49813
17 TEXTILE PRDTS.	7874	3002	5434	1147251	97693	32458	4760	26939	10483
18 APPAREL	26740	115209	3632	263761	352300	587007	116775	37050	29374
19 MISC. TEXTILE PRDTS.	3737	6788	873	188075	103898	5433	9950	18142	1523
20 LUMBER, WOOD PRDTS.	27724	79403		623991	257173	34101	55641	197122	10908
21 WOODEN CONTAINERS	323	113		25500	24132	1139	104	1417	28
22 HOUSEHOLD FURNITURE	2355	209	712	472831	179549	134128	1580	296680	563
23 OTHER FURNITURE	3422	1648		272032	99900	12828	688	15004	106
24 PAPER, ALLIED PRDTS.	27020	200476	11166	420244	571056	13803	117590	80873	22112
25 PAPERBOARD CONTAINERS	3501	0	8335	422788	89590	0	0	279167	14135
26 PRINTING, PUBLISHING	36245	38070		1058942	349292	55742	31743	15327	12210
27 CHEMICALS,SELECT. PRDTS.	37551	147606		884304	181621	154539	9451	33155	17557
28 PLASTICS, SYNTHETICS	31256	75020		296779	140828	23526	9142	23124	33075
29 DRUGS, COSMETICS	69957	2805	690502	424257	58915	167696	16867	12573	6133
30 PAINT, ALLIED PRDTS.	30723	247	297357	23922	23582	4436	5313	10449	50
31 PETROLEUM, RELATED INDS.	25357	588	1120686	786601	6040	527337	175839	1451888	4558
32 RUBBER, MISC. PLASTICS	27043	142	331362	280014	105012	47664	15402	3770	14069
33 LEATHER TANNING, PRDTS.	5715	87	63225	5408	0	1226	4110	663	19516
34 FOOTWEAR, LEATHER PRDTS.	30843	459	166043	24848	1667	3863	22129	1306	179162
35 GLASS, GLASS PRDTS.	12904	106	243757	123800	244	128517	13059	15813	16918
36 STONE, CLAY PRDTS.	107629	15287	487584	303025	132673	8675	64625	118025	507
37 PRIMARY IRON, STEEL MFR.	29281	669	1550028	1983656	63647	27988	185390	25181	2416
38 PRIMARY NONFERROUS MFR.	30113	72024	657686	465005	108039		43133	128669	

148

39 METAL CONTAINERS	10655	54266	11628	4670	272	38409	359400	0	6953
40 FABRICATED METAL PRDTS.	13701	61718	108072	77547	101035	298596	573349	8715	77155
41 SCREW MACH. PRDTS., ETC.	0	2221	19602	3034	14831	159485	534655	609	22781
42 OTHER FAB. METAL PRDTS.	9523	24923	67206	20599	54746	217091	772046	577	10013
43 ENGINES, TURBINES	0	1025	0	0	36350	104878	186339	0	0
44 FARM MACH., EQUIP.	1076	5167	5167	41941	366195	96484	597180	3550	23225
45 CONSTRUC. MACH., EQUIP.	6536	13351	10642	25556	103469	78645	892884	621	21055
46 MATERIAL HANDLING MACH.	0	1297	1803	6511	16456	10746	117443	127	13959
47 METALWORKING MACHINERY	1310	792	7837	4055	16000	87956	375893	264	5538
48 SPECIAL MACH., EQUIP.	21155	6155	6328	11876	19201	40241	209971	139	32209
49 GENERAL MACH., EQUIP.	333	2703	32190	17654	9640	184349	333705	6444	12044
50 MACHINE SHOP PRDTS.	3270	11256	27730	18215	5630	83590	115846	944	6965
51 OFFICE, COMPUT. MACHINES	0	0	136572	209	190	3378	137854		1626
52 SERVICE IND. MACHINES		2588	47595	30674	9340	82011	161253	194	9325
53 ELECT. TRANSMISS. EQUIP.	929	266	32244	25749	23439	227231	372461	0	59632
54 HOUSEHOLD APPLIANCES	4274	611	758	1717	145686	195021	513573	0	227
55 ELECTRIC LIGHTING EQUIP.	2090	81	668	668	937	94161	290779	0	8131
56 RADIO, TV, ETC., EQUIP.	1997	734	13648	312	93213	412548	1420726	0	203
57 ELECTRONIC COMPONENTS	644	275	28614	6003	25021	134027	214391	0	1525
58 MISC. ELECTRICAL MACH.	1471	531	1647	15292	10983	204336	79986	0	15529
59 MOTOR VEHICLES, EQUIP.	27057	9436	252703	183051	23707	1328163	670907	2296	580679
60 AIRCRAFT, PARTS	60180		3542	832411	29317	457744	393871	0	255987
61 OTHER TRANSPORT. EQUIP.	834	74860	24467	18198	16093	237054	287788	1512	17736
62 PROFESS., SCIEN. INSTRU.	1673	1189	2513	1368	15209	39712	320766	2565	9905
63 MEDICAL, PHOTO. EQUIP.	16070	2609	174	610	3339	6704	149082	66	354
64 MISC. MANUFACTURING	160357	19026	20114	8768	52542	117586	490948	5119	57581
65 TRANSPORT., WAREHOUSING	39393	609716	452447	455195	365275	798669	2775677	107413	552049
66 COMMUNICA., EXC. BROCAST.	6413	157225	96094	67094	103726	385802	717462	45410	138560
67 RADIO, TV BROADCASTING	61785	16653	12846	9544	17566	22766	112613	4088	22344
68 ELEC.,GAS,WATER,SAN.SER.	401499	328487	159871	237951	262951	655946	1404287	62579	257904
69 WHOLESALE, RETAIL TRADE	83841	1430639	1047800	913686	1358413	2040890	6538669	295405	1741146
70 FINANCE, INSURANCE	203560	284741	199831	192589	278291	516425	1864027	5557	427371
71 REAL ESTATE, RENTAL	58244	754625	587386	526248	675860	1190670	4163872	160948	792525
72 HOTELS, PERSONAL SERV.	28574	162880	145369	114419	136396	258955	866424	39350	210564
73 BUSINESS SERVICES	1259	184372	86694	80850	107579	184134	1650714	21974	154126
74 RESEARCH, DEVELOPMENT	43587	113272	793	620	802	1726	61817	34287	875
75 AUTO. REPAIR, SERVICES	13559	62802	102760	105192	123834	194161	456030	9527	153587
76 AMUSEMENTS	99886	247488	46394	32877	42960	75188	320197	54069	57687
77 MED.,EDUC. SERVICES	23454	44962	236132	216090	285895	521943	1738899	13426	297341
78 FEDERAL GOVT. ENTERPRISE	19559	72946	70017	54477	45433	68049	231328	11169	91721
79 STATE, LOCAL GOVT. ENT.			49792	58180	58937	109225	278368		69911
80 IMPORTS	0	0	0	0	0	0	0	0	0
81 BUS.TRAVEL, ENT., GIFTS.	0	0	0	0	0	0	0	0	0
82 OFFICE SUPPLIES	0	0	0	0	0	0	0	0	0
83 SCRAP, USED GOODS	0	0	0	0	0	0	0	0	0
84 GOVERNMENT INDUSTRY	182604	558480	569086	534679	361691	636046	1642824	113731	977744
85 REST OF WORLD INDUSTRY	-9033	-13769	-12717	-10372	-13564	-22730	-74976	-7192	-14269
86 HOUSEHOLD INDUSTRY	17989	99282	43620	31316	35605	59194	144407	8318	132510
87 INVENTORY VALUATION ADJ.	0	0	0	0	0	0	0	0	0
88 STATE TOTAL	3554844	13382242	1025589	10530108	14103728	23681014	58563096	2678822	1446118

TABLE C-2

STATE ESTIMATES OF 1958 OUTPUTS
(THOUSANDS OF CURRENT DOLLARS)

INDUSTRY TITLE	19 MARYLAND	20 MASSA-CHUSETTS	21 MICHIGAN	22 MINNESOTA	23 MISSISSIPPI	24 MISSOURI	25 MONTANA	26 NEBRASKA	27 NEVADA
1 LIVESTOCK, PRODTS.	236742	128746	544706	1401335	399696	1117323	364930	1008570	68949
2 OTHER AGRICULTURE PRODTS.	138242	63756	476006	855465	346300	593491	312656	1132348	16392
3 FORESTRY, FISHERIES	15586	44204	9564	5987	21179	4960	3373	129	113
4 AGRI.,FORES.,FISH. SERV.	20769	7299	16666	33192	37667	35092	5079	14324	830
5 IRON,FERRO. ORES MINING	242	0	78903	383866	0	3745	20337	0	8337
6 NONFERROUS ORES MINING	35	0	3116	1342		23489	56510	27	61255
7 COAL MINING	8454	0				11951	1580		23
8 CRUDE PETRO.,NATURAL GAS	906	0	28851		138801	373	83482	66504	
9 STONE, CLAY MINING	24576	14247	60517	27017	11542	34891	6919	16190	14939
10 CHEM.,FERT. MIN. MINING			9677		0	5029	5301	0	847
11 NEW CONSTRUCTION	915977	1232527	1826682	947991	372083	1167733	266835	385958	155074
12 MAINT., REPAIR CONSTR.	250647	380367	729238	335022	13200	410053	122015	219190	62709
13 ORDNANCE, ACCESSORIES	407	83925	259506	138639	165300	18701	70042	685	3031
14 FOOD, KINDRED PRODTS.	6207	2175152	788437	3244041	221868	22914	589503	631882	196633
15 TOBACCO MANUFACTURES	12267	209668	6725	146331	8418	311	156651	290	18758
16 FABRICS	17009	115254	376947	942758	116991	30739	225026	5136	45173
17 TEXTILE PRODTS.	703	9164	110488	173900	19586	57	19642	14	2040
18 APPAREL	43521	123659	576970	1317514	247188	31003	163140	1128	41897
19 MISC. TEXTILE PRODTS.	188	11531	73073	129273	17104	829	16384	0	8173
20 LUMBER, WOOD PRODTS.	2064	64524	395755	589628	219898	8134	294328	550	4453
21 WOODEN CONTAINERS	0	2915	4107	12635	8464	61	15227		45
22 HOUSEHOLD FURNITURE	856	27734	23598	231565	91633	23087	37707		4514
23 OTHER FURNITURE	1405	25763	83667	20677	8385	5522	13293	10	6130
24 PAPER, ALLIED PRODTS.	17999	147603	110104	2605354	72324	38039	462015	304	309841
25 PAPERBOARD CONTAINERS			239193	30987		0	0		
26 PRINTING, PUBLISHING	14361	47754	1071768	411358	406296	11244	128185	2113	28470
27 CHEMICALS,SELECT. PRODTS.	22009	36175	543579	413281	83469	25696	147200	4478	46930
28 PLASTICS, SYNTHETICS	28235	76227	293417	36703	58887	8403	96998	673	14047
29 DRUGS, COSMETICS	185759	272191	84453	152358	41001	198660	21063	15493	2757
30 PAINT, ALLIED PRODTS.	33847	45826	122093	19900	1797	74575	646	2197	0
31 PETROLEUM, RELATED INDS.	124375	105463	274213	118618	26078	179027	124481	13843	294
32 RUBBER, MISC. PLASTICS	147979	537959	317272	27277	37794	47605		15841	142
33 LEATHER TANNING, PRDTS.	3933	216551	27638	8114	219	5812	109	0	0
34 FOOTWEAR, LEATHER PRDTS.	18208	527869	13753	11925	16286	342325	62	963	
35 GLASS, GLASS PRDTS.	44228	3757	59992	6697	18786	33810	370	499	158
36 STONE, CLAY PRDTS.	121459	165200	304026	179760	44237	216333	9396	41704	25126
37 PRIMARY IRON, STEEL MFR.	759639	205817	1263292	83789	168242	168242	4904	3735	0
38 PRIMARY NONFERROUS MFR.	180416	192995	384508	20718	10248	103594	211512	72910	32240

Industry	(1)	(2)	(3)	(4)	(5)	(6)	(7)	(8)	(9)
39 METAL CONTAINERS	124888	16558	2777	47312	137	96336	0	15111	0
40 FABRICATED METAL PRDTS.	98516	135129	341690	96129	31237	209652	7278	54736	1542
41 SCREW MACH. PRDTS., ETC.	41462	113902	394043	27794	1153	38117	0	2048	0
42 OTHER FAB. METAL PRDTS.	52594	294101	557416	54381	9886	102060	95	10005	1028
43 ENGINES, TURBINES	0	151627	233626	21579	0	8353	0	0	0
44 FARM MACH., EQUIP.	4736	1269	195640	99302	8496	52700	855	31045	0
45 CONSTRUC. MACH., EQUIP.	3803	7854	120416	51541	5819	14321	90	3313	0
46 MATERIAL HANDLING MACH.	3940	17712	121522	17995	5035	8411	37	354	0
47 METALWORKING MACHINERY	39784	167188	599732	28429	480	28630	0	759	0
48 SPECIAL MACH., EQUIP.	40757	220133	122162	22105	6388	24769	0	753	837
49 GENERAL MACH., EQUIP.	20459	129655	229371	30349	1470	29070	872	14501	0
50 MACHINE SHOP PRDTS.	13849	43095	159218	26885	5466	63523	0	2450	86
51 OFFICE, COMPUT. MACHINES	10047	36663	143186	112939	0	1214	0	135	158
52 SERVICE IND. MACHINES	29932	88995	228931	84315	1499	116183	0	1967	0
53 ELECT. TRANSMISS. EQUIP.	24224	235006	137441	55367	2840	176227	0	271	0
54 HOUSEHOLD APPLIANCES	30124	25632	251518	99529	25076	40957	0	0	3269
55 ELECTRIC LIGHTING EQUIP.	5232	123825	23374	2916	27969	63933	0	35111	119
56 RADIO, TV, ETC., EQUIP.	262015	342930	61199	33357	1660	9085	0	14942	0
57 ELECTRONIC COMPONENTS	5235	293107	55272	25882	2513	7896	119	1078	403
58 MISC. ELECTRICAL MACH.	13060	33196	86270	8811	67	19547	0	16640	152
59 MOTOR VEHICLES, EQUIP.	196197	140784	8420042	189992	41296	1317997	497	20800	0
60 AIRCRAFT, PARTS	510119	138858	149999	34690	8623	463554	0	4630	0
61 OTHER TRANSPORT. EQUIP.	193530	164471	190945	30064	10896	59428	599	615	0
62 PROFESS., SCIEN. INSTRU.	26400	165906	129100	136100	308	39727	285	16307	0
63 MEDICAL, PHOTO. EQUIP.	3377	143304	28818	39084	241	10156	0		1820
64 MISC. MANUFACTURING	42264	337761	178100	70405	9582	87535	3709		71920
65 TRANSPORT., WAREHOUSING	596993	745283	1029545	705384	154220	1130975	157188		21807
66 COMMUNICA., EXC. BRDCAST.	159235	327433	399874	159397	53537	141684	14327	296171	4786
67 RADIO, TV BROADCASTING	14764	35275	62663	21633	7528	40451	4986	64840	33466
68 ELEC.,GAS,WATER,SAN.SER.	252251	519444	820550	287315	120964	393519	64898	11042	150767
69 WHOLESALE, RETAIL TRADE	1375574	2916960	3940640	1878706	582780	2515418	326986	58631	28732
70 FINANCE, INSURANCE	327449	1150823	814061	460699	105242	613676	60122	766850	117240
71 REAL ESTATE, RENTAL	978211	1732605	2307389	1061415	329675	1352215	177997	227642	113313
72 HOTELS, PERSONAL SERV.	174815	362883	464791	195907	83788	309838	39903	352553	22382
73 BUSINESS SERVICES	201333	523205	843504	261601	44936	359657	23128	80645	0
74 RESEARCH, DEVELOPMENT	10024	19474	5846	7599	460	4928	156	75195	379
75 AUTO. REPAIR, SERVICES	155868	202667	348191	144097	55598	215998	33040	656	18225
76 AMUSEMENTS	89372	139907	188939	61880	16102	91792	10171	30591	147408
77 MED.,EDUC. SERVICES	366528	994636	974024	434080	98164	569659	63641	159352	23851
78 FEDERAL GOVT. ENTERPRISE	56784	124289	114020	70603	31951	119404	16438	31214	6954
79 STATE, LOCAL GOVT. ENT.	57274	145921	209979	74502	31209	73807	12302	120643	7867
80 IMPORTS	0	0	0	0	0	0	0	0	0
81 BUS.TRAVEL, ENT., GIFTS.	0	0	0	0	0	0	0	0	0
82 OFFICE SUPPLIES	0	0	0	0	0	0	0	0	0
83 SCRAP, USED GOODS	0	0	0	0	0	0	0	0	0
84 GOVERNMENT INDUSTRY	893113	1062862	1235594	512162	328302	711785	142306	285879	105825
85 REST OF WORLD INDUSTRY	-18804	-34761	-78334	-38601	-5506	-26923	-9788	-8440	-10679
86 HOUSEHOLD INDUSTRY	71787	83583	110989	48651	63845	64359	9015	19955	4452
87 INVENTORY VALUATION ADJ.	0	0	0	0	0	0	0	0	0
88 STATE TOTAL	12869087	23417448	38247667	15816737	5152798	20350499	3071194	7523845	1394697

TABLE C-2

STATE ESTIMATES OF 1958 OUTPUTS
(THOUSANDS OF CURRENT DOLLARS)

INDUSTRY TITLE	28 NEW HAMPSHIRE	29 NEW JERSEY	30 NEW MEXICO	31 NEW YORK	32 NORTH CAROLINA	33 NORTH DAKOTA	34 OHIO	35 OKLAHOMA	36 OREGON
1 LIVESTOCK, PRDTS.	64304	228563	189073	767721	519760	338496	901806	475098	279246
2 OTHER AGRICULTURE PRDTS.	16148	151434	127754	335636	882115	710269	635415	447946	291400
3 FORESTRY, FISHERIES	2291	10669	1244	15440	36698	207	6517	1978	143856
4 AGRI.,FORES.,FISH. SERV.	4495	9982	7277	17209	38982	6750	22836	14290	10303
5 IRON,FERRO. ORES MINING	0	9065	3816	34894	3024	0	0	0	1706
6 NONFERROUS ORES MINING	0	808	111802	10683	1379	272	252	2273	4961
7 COAL MINING	0	0	784	0	0	6918	167575	12572	0
8 CRUDE PETRO.,NATURAL GAS	0	0	406217	8128	0	46873	24783	703994	1
9 STONE, CLAY MINING	2807	38723	7727	82575	46850	2906	84114	14596	13387
10 CHEM.,FERT. MIN. MINING	58	0	76870	7504	1543	0	0	217	29
11 NEW CONSTRUCTION	182164	1701927	577544	4626994	762662	331669	3043851	969831	592934
12 MAINT., REPAIR CONSTR.	56437	496504	102569	1375313	308612	122832	930500	232496	206357
13 ORDNANCE, ACCESSORIES	5411	23488	368711	1707	493346	26376	289	312497	2394
14 FOOD, KINDRED PRDTS.	87146	73635	2313893	24989	3481561	103090	173	8127124	138402
15 TOBACCO MANUFACTURES	0	3011	398520	2225	394764	9441	229	655188	14144
16 FABRICS	1144	13313	463413	5991	807010	66572	4006	1184439	87696
17 TEXTILE PRDTS.	487	270	87925	112	174885	2978	20	181288	7800
18 APPAREL	0	113992	578505	2875	782237	125897	8989	1673877	114240
19 MISC. TEXTILE PRDTS.	0	7799	142137	213	191537	2697	0	265929	14957
20 LUMBER, WOOD PRDTS.	651	34473	382023	3191	1067554	60387	663	640660	16740
21 WOODEN CONTAINERS	26	766	15843	0	72775	5816	0	90220	690
22 HOUSEHOLD FURNITURE	0	120	67822	0	121236	21913	0	722230	906
23 OTHER FURNITURE	335	4918	145305	402	202644	17560	26	71698	3418
24 PAPER, ALLIED PRDTS.	132	239	380755	611	559390	22229	788	1048147	10177
25 PAPERBOARD CONTAINERS	0	0	4598	0	474232	0	0	313551	2038
26 PRINTING, PUBLISHING	568	12590	914996	10983	3848844	49428	9834	351437	40831
27 CHEMICALS,SELECT. PRDTS.	986	57233	626852	822	2738377	21459	415	556452	11625
28 PLASTICS, SYNTHETICS	0	29979	224785	2085	514639	29625	673	337046	8403
29 DRUGS, COSMETICS	5350	942199	45866	651909	211367	5194	489426	52926	13574
30 PAINT, ALLIED PRDTS.	257	237239	59	119618	14181	308	171333	2784	6597
31 PETROLEUM, RELATED INDS.	1221	1022121	54379	219835	5849	28095	793968	694205	14100
32 RUBBER, MISC. PLASTICS	18264	366444	0	395354	37247	243	1589273	59201	6055
33 LEATHER TANNING, PRDTS.	29920	58903	0	97852	6995	0	31301	0	1007
34 FOOTWEAR, LEATHER PRDTS.	176400	88614	791	563502	10678	61	84881	4042	1696
35 GLASS, GLASS PRDTS.	114	173315	238	130676	13981	0	344602	49360	3952
36 STONE, CLAY PRDTS.	20385	338739	17808	540365	83860	8396	641300	60153	48482
37 PRIMARY IRON, STEEL MFR.	11477	238642	0	810038	14258	244	3114254	14195	63783
38 PRIMARY NONFERROUS MFK.	23770	791776	9030	740896	33747	0	654504	44720	56450

152

#	Industry									
39	METAL CONTAINERS	0	193634	0	106758	245	0	74275	1113	28293
40	FABRICATED METAL PRDTS.	7622	280070	9170	572030	60738	5711	789041	115134	59185
41	SCREW MACH. PRDTS., ETC.	4510	153606	434	259967	12450	70	488296	3288	2250
42	OTHER FAB. METAL PRDTS.	5640	341481	0	402903	24483	0	622658	24781	16431
43	ENGINES, TURBINES	0	3658	0	248115	813	6669	92042	201	0
44	FARM MACH., EQUIP.	155	4575	124	67282	11926	166	113228	3007	4691
45	CONSTRUC. MACH., EQUIP.	10902	42917	2133	15954	2367	165	310603	96911	6479
46	MATERIAL HANDLING MACH.	0	102947	540	54227	2630	701	126978	1348	17346
47	METALWORKING MACHINERY	6767	89443	378	204132	2059	0	587710	1820	1644
48	SPECIAL MACH., EQUIP.	43369	156810	3584	248701	62165	741	216687	8359	20851
49	GENERAL MACH., EQUIP.	13837	252196	820	339847	4785	0	471843	26539	3788
50	MACHINE SHOP PRDTS.	1924	61174	159	109982	11148	136	116779	13224	13319
51	OFFICE, COMPUT. MACHINES	2270	54692	135	715438	7247	0	347728	145	378
52	SERVICE IND. MACHINES	700	91822	1060	273939	7602	140	158678	5093	2411
53	ELECT. TRANSMISS. EQUIP.	34478	264887	3542	548031	71371	0	639254	5117	36289
54	HOUSEHOLD APPLIANCES	131	73666	181	131682	23801	2618	784462	984	4912
55	ELECTRIC LIGHTING EQUIP.	218	184163	1812	271874	16388	0	240164	206	1316
56	RADIO, TV, ETC., EQUIP.	23691	764473	2011	963860	130606	143	115770	14752	1404
57	ELECTRONIC COMPONENTS	24431	275087	3252	314271	26857	0	102132	6505	3138
58	MISC. ELECTRICAL MACH.	0	54111		142564	38109	3389	231286	2687	3737
59	MOTOR VEHICLES, EQUIP.	258	942922		1206020	21073		2783160	14487	25644
60	AIRCRAFT, PARTS	0	351064		702371	1912		104936	69623	12299
61	OTHER TRANSPORT. EQUIP.	822	184863		226691	8411		132190	16017	31145
62	PROFESS., SCIEN. INSTRU.	1033	392040		648315	18548		129208	6897	2704
63	MEDICAL, PHOTO. EQUIP.	1798	68618		850368	17813		7190	92	5963
64	MISC. MANUFACTURING	24815	323178		1294549			309405	12279	14751
65	TRANSPORT., WAREHOUSING	49714	1337559	131266	3774183	498667	97470	1846048	348360	401726
66	COMMUNICA.,EXC. BROCAST.	24434	394034	17915	1107453	150457	19138	423574	81944	114482
67	RADIO, TV BROADCASTING	2576	8857	6009	343556	20110	3034	62260	18449	13785
68	ELEC.,GAS,WATER,SAN.SER.	76094	619330	109922	1762413	245315	28288	1190905	216237	110364
69	WHOLESALE, RETAIL TRADE	243601	3192876	355512	13398103	1691166	307650	4882207	992905	967968
70	FINANCE, INSURANCE	79325	877536	67030	6186160	326272	57986	1068443	228712	201067
71	REAL ESTATE, RENTAL	148699	2205945	252688	7970873	801964	138910	3128847	563983	499306
72	HOTELS, PERSONAL SERV.	38827	452856	59753	1677682	218184	25777	598588	136914	114525
73	BUSINESS SERVICES	20218	461670	50687	4533046	115463	15721	762258	125431	127741
74	RESEARCH, DEVELOPMENT	1317	19235	11222	58748	532	2303	11336	3397	602
75	AUTO. REPAIR, SERVICES	28596	261270	44526	685611	160525	27034	431218	111219	95066
76	AMUSEMENTS	17598	167404	15692	1426345	52224	6844	240231	38130	33801
77	MED.,EDUC. SERVICES	85408	774431	66071	3407509	314138	50175	1276637	213558	212703
78	FEDERAL GOVT. ENTERPRISE	11805	102179	22883	433975	71638	14015	167045	53117	48589
79	STATE, LOCAL GOVT. ENT.	12907	124972	16297	604184	88860	20357	293067	49142	51932
80	IMPORTS	0	0	0	0	0	0	0	0	0
81	BUS.TRAVEL, ENT., GIFTS	0	0	0	0	0	0	0	0	0
82	OFFICE SUPPLIES	0	0	0	0	0	0	0	0	0
83	SCRAP, USED GOODS	0	0	0	0	0	0	0	0	0
84	GOVERNMENT INDUSTRY	171005	1104783	338724	3169294	880519	106151	1439665	598372	314236
85	REST OF WORLD INDUSTRY	-7517	-39568	-8594	-329286	-13145	-6721	-56373	-10782	-10423
86	HOUSEHOLD INDUSTRY	10194	102495	12671	426124	110247	7943	140449	34219	25573
87	INVENTORY VALUATION ADJ.	0	0	0	0	0	0	0	0	0
88	STATE TOTAL	2434144	31646445	3520699	91641720	17871360	2705375	48946261	8785377	7818554

TABLE C-2

STATE ESTIMATES OF 1958 OUTPUTS
(THOUSANDS OF CURRENT DOLLARS)

INDUSTRY TITLE	37 PENNSYLVANIA	38 RHODE ISLAND	39 SOUTH CAROLINA	40 SOUTH DAKOTA	41 TENNESSEE	42 TEXAS	43 UTAH	44 VERMONT	45 VIRGINIA
1 LIVESTOCK, PRDTS.	773209	18729	185251	713902	453390	1359721	164593	123559	424299
2 OTHER AGRICULTURE PRDTS.	303740	7390	273838	429086	291072	2456900	49305	21018	280204
3 FORESTRY, FISHERIES	5847	4529	23402	500	9274	48104	310	2486	45964
4 AGRI.,FORES.,FISH. SERV.	25957	763	13051	8934	20676	120740	3876	1584	26450
5 IRON, FERRO. ORES MINING	20028	0			19927	4574	24368	0	1790
6 NONFERROUS ORES MINING	2253	0	391	25320	5909	2268	205482	35	2696
7 COAL MINING	773635	0		223	29986	3638	49790	0	155712
8 CRUDE PETRO.,NATURAL GAS	52157	0	20291	3	135	3951792	79604	0	925
9 STONE, CLAY MINING	88241		0	8614	34550	64445	19111	8960	40020
10 CHEM.,FERT. MIN. MINING	3004	1631	554	0	16133	60311	3486	0	1443
11 NEW CONSTRUCTION	2277212	157022	495846	248430	604056	3603421	444817	117068	1029925
12 MAINT., REPAIR CONSTR.	826682	56098	125519	125034	229267	1228864	92462	33825	322618
13 ORDNANCE, ACCESSORIES	1987	411737	4943	18223	3718	15335	9687	22658	1752
14 FOOD, KINDRED PRDTS.	278154	1646536	439182	29548	356	721239	1646254	1000195	17884
15 TOBACCO MANUFACTURES	37382	555521	5759		7484	82871	200505	8565	124
16 FABRICS	51106	1092388	57129	25149	3498	125924	250212	37435	6201
17 TEXTILE PRDTS.	3097	325160	11845	45	139	6681	58546		55
18 APPAREL	78993	1112685	89481	53192	1832	92594	479158	79951	55610
19 MISC. TEXTILE PRDTS.	2135	178004	7510	1225	92	4632	33130	304	890
20 LUMBER, WOOD PRDTS.	48114	807810	16616	5304	18	30632	177168	7709	18700
21 WOODEN CONTAINERS	207	31235	260	0	146	6081	543	26	0
22 HOUSEHOLD FURNITURE	4522	91673		15354	0	100190	9800	0	
23 OTHER FURNITURE	667	108773	4800		9152	21474	12505	551	1486
24 PAPER, ALLIED PRDTS.	16178	429996	8030	1534	870	33740	203099	2288	1249
25 PAPERBOARD CONTAINERS	0	3736	0	1782	1412	712354	3318		
26 PRINTING, PUBLISHING	35813	755570	480247	13232	30894	75009	198170	10062	13973
27 CHEMICALS,SELECT. PRDTS.	17764	548842	592847	13930	10649	146639	59865	3904	5543
28 PLASTICS, SYNTHETICS	13645	480764	6855	16470	44440	65139	26888	5579	3965
29 DRUGS, COSMETICS	163808	75780	24011	4101	132770	103155	19737	5430	22202
30 PAINT, ALLIED PRDTS.	130113	5849	2267		15042	66945	1101	838	8650
31 PETROLEUM, RELATED INDS.	1263701	12995	14827	1304	129204	4458370	143358	2124	41012
32 RUBBER, MISC. PLASTICS	401159	114911	0	219	45060	125017	6165	13017	29794
33 LEATHER TANNING, PRDTS.	82740	155	15563	72	108696	2057	87	4340	11049
34 FOOTWEAR, LEATHER PRDTS.	249195	18965	972		89449	19755	403	5321	30740
35 GLASS, GLASS PRDTS.	329222	19350	97	8578	221947	29793	178	3257	11360
36 STONE, CLAY PRDTS.	645559	9936	29265	121		378418	51710	38169	127006
37 PRIMARY IRON, STEEL MFR.	4597507	29304	46990			312651	237389	911	48925
38 PRIMARY NONFERROUS MFR.	553836	165896	4359			349755	161154	7616	81228

	C1	C2	C3	C4	C5	C6	C7	C8	C9
39 METAL CONTAINERS	154376	0	0	0	5163	107302	4304	0	0
40 FABRICATED METAL PRODTS.	951731	16288	31825	9326	152995	311937	51130	5014	85493
41 SCREW MACH. PRDTS., ETC.	353633	24285	779	545	9916	14724	1165	89	235
42 OTHER FAB. METAL PRDTS.	479279	52449	2273	531	48869	155277	1356	3001	27486
43 ENGINES, TURBINES	414623	145		1061		2612			
44 FARM MACH., EQUIP.	92029	134	111		38023	19570	924	1392	4226
45 CONSTRUC. MACH., EQUIP.	166417	164	83	943	9217	348929	29395	3578	2456
46 MATERIAL HANDLING MACH.	106059	43355	973		9982	9803	413		3049
47 METALWORKING MACHINERY	269202	25695	254	1560	3261	11377		38203	1730
48 SPECIAL MACH., EQUIP.	184683	13326	32118	222	10905	48737	1280	5579	8368
49 GENERAL MACH., EQUIP.	315835	3663	2173	246	8219	58783	540	1580	3516
50 MACHINE SHOP PRDTS.	80024	116	4595	2200	18620	47898	2376	1027	5414
51 OFFICE, COMPUT. MACHINES	65837	7218	108	310		608	292	13824	12512
52 SERVICE IND. MACHINES	116093	5361	1538	554	12802	86018	3484	1538	16659
53 ELECT. TRANSMISS. EQUIP.	718873		127		37010	26147	1157	6187	10597
54 HOUSEHOLD APPLIANCES	99572		16677		108823	10644			3921
55 ELECTRIC LIGHTING EQUIP.	260274	24407		191	16209	9978	174	5381	446
56 RADIO, TV, ETC., EQUIP.	190692	268	7428		92098	62489	6045		44051
57 ELECTRONIC COMPONENTS	326059	3246	9907		7428	40196	1216	5761	46055
58 MISC. ELECTRICAL MACH.	76863	12917		403	11713	24955	1991	2491	5170
59 MOTOR VEHICLES, EQUIP.	622538	7512	3696		84859	380209	18159	403	74195
60 AIRCRAFT, PARTS	248299	2256		4242	1938	855026	3103	1136	3921
61 OTHER TRANSPORT. EQUIP.	371926	3689	2752	182	41510	125775	215	588	203454
62 PROFESS., SCIEN. INSTRU.	322058	13657	4631		33915	61427	75	6762	5959
63 MEDICAL, PHOTO. EQUIP.	21909	8142	445	1227	496	8528		75	14517
64 MISC. MANUFACTURING	336120	240947	10918	64768	61609	43308	6057	4159	50068
65 TRANSPORT., WAREHOUSING	2329003	92253	152038	20831	473705	1896026	205129	42707	751034
66 COMMUNICA.,EXC. BRDCAST.	537084	52647	57496	3485	154958	558059	24910	14555	165043
67 RADIO, TV BROADCASTING	95877	5583	10308	31307	26382	58415	6122	2102	21383
68 ELEC.,GAS,WATER,SAN.SER.	1376785	78086	115811	298578	59746	997032	82514	44907	328363
69 WHOLESALE, RETAIL TRADE	5596877	406934	708726	51344	1489998	4716197	403154	152919	1444396
70 FINANCE, INSURANCE	1541025	135079	156201	143345	307297	1157520	87921	41183	331100
71 REAL ESTATE, RENTAL	3042161	245277	356984	30847	696250	2229305	252968	79691	1030153
72 HOTELS, PERSONAL SERV.	675455	51226	95071	16184	187643	628716	52035	22292	226006
73 BUSINESS SERVICES	836259	43779	51907	751	138109	607712	46873	8807	141128
74 RESEARCH, DEVELOPMENT	11348	676	2705	28627	25795	12400	351	216	67703
75 AUTO. REPAIR, SERVICES	503239	31964	75373	12348	130930	484109	41389	17768	143178
76 AMUSEMENTS	200504	27123	20100	56301	45266	150888	19477	5742	47491
77 MED.,EDUC. SERVICES	1666666	135344	127359	14356	289130	993522	82841	56155	280016
78 FEDERAL GOVT. ENTERPRISE	200308	20001	42255	17021	230685	203398	16485	8865	124436
79 STATE, LOCAL GOVT. ENT.	247298	11072	32326		171969	250529	24312	7509	96684
80 IMPORTS	0	0	0	0	0	0	0	0	0
81 BUS.TRAVEL, ENT., GIFTS.	0	0	0	0	0	0	0	0	0
82 OFFICE SUPPLIES	0	0	0	0	0	0	0	0	0
83 SCRAP, USED GOODS									
84 GOVERNMENT INDUSTRY	1684320	179111	560597	141753	513668	2279378	239456	59127	1308059
85 REST OF WORLD INDUSTRY	-63243	-4703	-6594	-3673	-17545	-70071	-4326	-4059	-17215
86 HOUSEHOLD INDUSTRY	196240	12451	68255	9959	81617	225883	7088	9496	88359
87 INVENTORY VALUATION ADJ.	0	0	0	0	0	0	0	0	0
88 STATE TOTAL	50873375	3402079	7529038	2939901	12064120	44647786	3878318	1384862	14299553

TABLE C-2

STATE ESTIMATES OF 1958 OUTPUTS
(THOUSANDS OF CURRENT DOLLARS)

INDUSTRY TITLE	46 WASHINGTON	47 WEST VIRGINIA	48 WISCONSIN	49 WYOMING	50 ALASKA	51 HAWAII	52 NO STATE ALLOCATION	53 NATIONAL TOTAL
1 LIVESTOCK, PRDTS.	292606	149075	1280861	209978	0	0	0	26085000
2 OTHER AGRICULTURE PRDTS.	466117	39148	244686	46465	0	0	0	23044000
3 FORESTRY, FISHERIES	92203	3418	8740	452	0	0	0	922000
4 AGRI.,FORES.,FISH. SERV.	11375	4206	21114	2056	0	0	0	1019000
5 IRON, FERRO. ORES MINING	66	35	7277	3288	0	0	0	77000
6 NONFERROUS ORES MINING	13886	0	2253	32924	0	0	0	1017000
7 COAL MINING	2538	780062	0	7824	0	0	0	2749000
8 CRUDE PETRO.,NATURAL GAS	6	57931	0	319890	0	0	0	9668000
9 STONE, CLAY MINING	16477	20193	35278	12706	0	0	0	1404000
10 CHEM.,FERT. MIN. MINING	29	0	0	11083	0	0	0	469000
11 NEW CONSTRUCTION	925063	420995	994075	217947	0	0	0	52415990
12 MAINT., REPAIR CONSTR.	277874	133224	366299	70321	0	0	0	16875000
13 ORDNANCE, ACCESSORIES	38289	23277	4640	62835	0	0	0	4149000
14 FOOD, KINDRED PRDTS.	228118	1284152	1627708	741291	0	0	0	62347000
15 TOBACCO MANUFACTURES	7460	52064	46869	305539	0	0	0	5918000
16 FABRICS	76753	69841	67451	349093	0	0	0	10481000
17 TEXTILE PRDTS.	3340	1264	12098	168288	0	0	0	2028000
18 APPAREL	28070	66288	89596	1024757	0	0	0	14201000
19 MISC. TEXTILE PRDTS.	1982	5603	1793	92572	0	0	0	1856000
20 LUMBER, WOOD PRDTS.	36602	26413	10810	230346	0	0	0	7644000
21 WOODEN CONTAINERS	1644	613	2968	48062	0	0	0	408000
22 HOUSEHOLD FURNITURE	3610	5611	1240	149881	0	0	0	3177000
23 OTHER FURNITURE	8090	1352	13449	11550	0	0	0	1351000
24 PAPER, ALLIED PRDTS.	76788	115681	11745	443633	0	0	0	9297000
25 PAPERBOARD CONTAINERS	0	0	0	410560	0	0	0	3559000
26 PRINTING, PUBLISHING	69214	38050	6812	171206	0	0	0	12450000
27 CHEMICALS,SELECT. PRDTS.	134931	36564	33777	201740	0	0	0	10304000
28 PLASTICS, SYNTHETICS	19561	28772	4905	89404	0	0	0	3766000
29 DRUGS, COSMETICS	11884	18549	132888	36969	0	0	0	6220000
30 PAINT, ALLIED PRDTS.	11266	1429	31054	0	0	0	0	1815000
31 PETROLEUM, RELATED INDS.	158904	34720	38940	161738	0	0	0	16870000
32 RUBBER, MISC. PLASTICS	7060	7589	144955	142	0	0	0	6541000
33 LEATHER TANNING, PRDTS.	385	10116	106836	0	0	0	0	874000
34 FOOTWEAR, LEATHER PRDTS.	4478	4116	136179	0	0	0	0	3048000
35 GLASS, GLASS PRDTS.	6943	178187	2653	0	0	0	0	2123000
36 STONE, CLAY PRDTS.	93296	65482	123198	9133	0	0	0	7298000
37 PRIMARY IRON, STEEL MFR.	78436	494360	325619	0	0	0	0	18784000
38 PRIMARY NONFERROUS MFR.	411581	202611	98026	172	0	0	0	8889000

156

#	Industry	(1)	(2)	(3)	(4)	(5)	(6)	(7)	(8)	(9)	Total
39	METAL CONTAINERS	33751	5962	98244		0	0	0	0	0	2060000
40	FABRICATED METAL PRDTS.	73272	52500	237341	1673	0	0	0	0	0	7371000
41	SCREW MACH. PRDTS., ETC.	10306	22617	175207		0	0	0	0	0	3316000
42	OTHER FAB. METAL PRDTS.	17561	44378	93334	98	0	0	0	0	0	5509000
43	ENGINES, TURBINES	160	0	334111		0	0	0	0	0	1954000
44	FARM MACH., EQUIP.	5288	4940	328092		0	0	0	0	0	2313000
45	CONSTRUC. MACH., EQUIP.	12408	21476	245582	272	0	0	0	0	0	2865000
46	MATERIAL HANDLING MACH.	8937	2376	25245		0	0	0	0	0	906000
47	METALWORKING MACHINERY	4987	16626	105448	87	0	0	0	0	0	3081000
48	SPECIAL MACH., EQUIP.	19490	1030	161146		0	0	0	0	0	2254000
49	GENERAL MACH., EQUIP.	9941	3182	164252		0	0	0	0	0	3254000
50	MACHINE SHOP PRDTS.	27671	7814	25270	1044	0	0	0	0	0	1473000
51	OFFICE, COMPUT. MACHINES	808		7296		0	0	0	0	0	2132000
52	SERVICE IND. MACHINES	2747	3478	100916	406	0	0	0	0	0	1943000
53	ELECT. TRANSMISS. EQUIP.	8022	18671	351450	158	0	0	0	0	0	4679000
54	HOUSEHOLD APPLIANCES	6095	1347	162795		0	0	0	0	0	3421000
55	ELECTRIC LIGHTING EQUIP.	6025	70556	19986	158	0	0	0	0	0	2152000
56	RADIO, TV, ETC., EQUIP.	1372	208	29417		0	0	0	0	0	5635000
57	ELECTRONIC COMPONENTS	1044	5015	22854		0	0	0	0	0	2393000
58	MISC. ELECTRICAL MACH.	1796	288	188960		0	0	0	0	0	1377000
59	MOTOR VEHICLES, EQUIP.	41738	17489	1192291		0	0	0	0	0	22559000
60	AIRCRAFT, PARTS	943293	1257	27620	1136	0	0	0	0	0	11950000
61	OTHER TRANSPORT. EQUIP.	99396	11858	73579	263	0	0	0	0	0	3602000
62	PROFESS., SCIEN. INSTRU.	7472	2594	69538		0	0	0	0	0	3066000
63	MEDICAL, PHOTO. EQUIP.	3195	591	5706		0	0	0	0	0	1462000
64	MISC. MANUFACTURING	25392	12045	114984	757	0	0	0	0	0	5032000
65	TRANSPORT., WAREHOUSING	529039	352063	547839	114281	0	0	0	0	0	32569000
66	COMMUNICA.,EXC. BRDCAST.	194496	67815	165709	7110	0	0	0	0	0	9292000
67	RADIO, TV BROADCASTING	20140	12023	25086	2499	0	0	0	0	0	1549000
68	ELEC.,GAS,WATER,SAN.SER.	117770	264076	365243	55500	0	0	0	0	0	17177000
69	WHOLESALE, RETAIL TRADE	1535970	627260	1841264	137011	0	0	0	0	0	92203000
70	FINANCE, INSURANCE	366736	105282	442678	26620	0	0	0	0	0	26401000
71	REAL ESTATE, RENTAL	981787	341903	1170583	94483	0	0	0	0	0	55274000
72	HOTELS, PERSONAL SERV.	185674	61308	208702	30365	0	0	0	0	0	12169000
73	BUSINESS SERVICES	181599	3499	227711	13399	0	0	0	0	0	16448000
74	RESEARCH, DEVELOPMENT	3515	58304	3932	505	0	0	0	0	0	534262
75	AUTO. REPAIR, SERVICES	131998	32906	150354	16178	0	0	0	0	0	7892000
76	AMUSEMENTS	63082	139771	64728	5874	0	0	0	0	0	5620000
77	MED.,EDUC. SERVICES	344439	24012	480705	26321	0	0	0	0	0	22703000
78	FEDERAL GOVT. ENTERPRISE	101282	25113	61671	6936	0	0	0	96087	0	4105041
79	STATE, LOCAL GOVT. ENT.	193492		59432	7251	0	0	0	0	0	4784000
80	IMPORTS	0	0	0		0	0	0	0	0	0
81	BUS.TRAVEL, ENT., GIFTS.	0	0	0		0	0	0	0	0	0
82	OFFICE SUPPLIES	0	0	0		0	0	0	0	0	0
83	SCRAP, USED GOODS	0	0	0		0	0	0	0	0	0
84	GOVERNMENT INDUSTRY	870250	175494	512591	73528	0	0	0	0	3030000	39029101
85	REST OF WORLD INDUSTRY	-33966	-7016	-24191	-2661	0	0	0	0	3489800*	2029999*
86	HOUSEHOLD INDUSTRY	42743	21020	42026	4802	0	0	0	0	0	3503000
87	INVENTORY VALUATION ADJ.	0	0	0		0	0	0	0	-311000	-311000
88	STATE TOTAL	12745175	6481792	19140543	1791284	0	0	0	0	6304887	822573403

*These figures exclude the value of secondary production. They therefore differ from those obtained by adding the corresponding values of final demand given in Appendix C of Volume I of this series. (See page 152)

TABLE C-3

STATE ESTIMATES OF 1963 OUTPUTS
(THOUSANDS OF CURRENT DOLLARS)

INDUSTRY TITLE	1 ALABAMA	2 ARIZONA	3 ARKANSAS	4 CALIFORNIA	5 COLORADO	6 CONNECTICUT	7 DELAWARE	8 DISTRICT OF COLUMBIA	9 FLORIDA
1 LIVESTOCK, PRODS.	456804	242880	396533	1722698	597555	117709	103163	0	298879
2 OTHER AGRICULTURE PRODS.	388933	375885	654064	2487742	315355	80805	48670	0	884690
3 FORESTRY, FISHERIES	25017	3003	17529	12838	961	2420	1986	0	48590
4 AGRI.,FORES.,FISH. SERV.	46562	24822	69387	132170	7242	6627	6199	0	37354
5 IRON, FERRO. ORES MINING	15489	639	544	34480	66734	0	0	0	0
6 NONFERROUS ORES MINING	968	374775	20624	7205	77289	418	0	0	8466
7 COAL MINING	97061	297	2671	70	25890	0	0	0	0
8 CRUDE PETRO.,NATURAL GAS	20973	422	72550	1047255	128289	0	0	0	2139
9 STONE, CLAY MINING	27299	12142	33650	181862	17335	14521	1037	0	51481
10 CHEM.,FERT. MIN. MINING	0	0	2880	74603	1439	0	206	0	107723
11 NEW CONSTRUCTION	840568	769136	448501	12453446	848791	1086300	201559	385666	2628530
12 MAINT., REPAIR CONSTR.	228615	183255	183867	2501539	265475	267749	42874	79517	604653
13 ORDNANCE, ACCESSORIES	75367	87384	93	2612751	35906	124682	0	0	221502
14 FOOD, KINDRED PRODTS.	798799	255877	810444	7529935	1018950	441650	206255	126317	1526051
15 TOBACCO MANUFACTURES	27690	0	0	971	0	14315	0	0	123489
16 FABRICS	601713	206	18158	28029	364	209783	56758	0	9920
17 TEXTILE PRODS.	77020	208	24888	142317	864	67017	14183	0	2250
18 APPAREL	335467	23540	78250	812045	15355	188159	48717	0	106222
19 MISC. TEXTILE PRDTS.	32229	3459	583	169487	7377	26533	3696	0	13468
20 LUMBER, WOOD PRODS.	241042	51573	273486	1192175	32265	28862	12070	900	161476
21 WOODEN CONTAINERS	7044	1464	13500	64609	1982	3439	548	1262	17543
22 HOUSEHOLD FURNITURE	38599	9114	90983	406707	14332	37153	316	0	71995
23 OTHER FURNITURE	9846	4193	17573	173667	5386	27416	1501	0	17281
24 PAPER, ALLIED PRODS.	347291	12038	185407	451098	12930	112751	10123	0	363868
25 PAPERBOARD CONTAINERS	19947	4846	41511	442428	18326	75098	9658	0	72865
26 PRINTING, PUBLISHING	82324	62783	49999	1235683	111740	277607	24268	247671	245587
27 CHEMICALS,SELECT. PRDTS.	278844	27909	36615	530706	39625	229212	75289	1945	313950
28 PLASTICS, SYNTHETICS	111299	0	874	172405	437	81190	186639	0	136677
29 DRUGS, COSMETICS	2756	4235	321	506017	9480	243281	14258	0	19549
30 PAINT, ALLIED PRODS.	7287	2759	3545	278741	9345	7748	687	0	38652
31 PETROLEUM, RELATED INDS.	55212	4562	145457	2474775	82033	17883	163659	0	34330
32 RUBBER, MISC. PLASTICS	219250	5976	45505	686778	126515	303628	64070	0	23717
33 LEATHER TANNING, PRDTS.	0	0	0	21695	410	2424	24702	0	1642
34 FOOTWEAR, LEATHER PRDTS.	9024	455	69793	53190	38664	24174	5959	0	19749
35 GLASS, GLASS PRDTS.	6885	655	13547	175135	1477	13256	615	0	16304
36 STONE, CLAY PRDTS.	162560	69941	50800	968349	96480	125660	19364	20774	252964
37 PRIMARY IRON, STEEL MFR.	955755	8860	2762	778374	165887	225582	154362	0	29513
38 PRIMARY NONFERROUS MFR.	251373	485814	138436	623123	10567	657594	15020	0	53943

39 METAL CONTAINERS	8426	0	8772	378985	20240	3104	0	0	74506
40 FABRICATED METAL PRDTS.	162973	31665	38849	776596	45530	89839	21608	4416	180028
41 SCREW MACH. PRDTS., ETC.	27894	845	9038	239693	1679	203120	7772	0	11590
42 OTHER FAB. METAL PRDTS.	82224	9045	24533	662818	35928	259569	9912	0	38022
43 ENGINES, TURBINES	0	0	0	76350	4112	54822	0	0	1713
44 FARM MACH., EQUIP.	19901	5213	5072	69387	8407	2216	770	0	9888
45 CONSTRUC. MACH., EQUIP.	9249	129	510	118631	79103	1361	283	0	2031
46 MATERIAL HANDLING MACH.	5732	129	8460	73390	3380	4756	0	0	3541
47 METALWORKING MACHINERY	4684	2919	6354	183900	1623	257081	4604	0	12369
48 SPECIAL MACH., EQUIP.	17314	812	2645	154398	6858	87539	16879	0	20172
49 GENERAL MACH., EQUIP.	10065	2096	9579	377532	18127	356511	602	0	10005
50 MACHINE SHOP PRDTS.	11143	13194	4469	292341	15215	65663	2638	1675	19697
51 OFFICE, COMPUT. MACHINES	139	110453	8346	551261	1769	207280	0	0	42446
52 SERVICE IND. MACHINES	15727	28223	16012	125110	1940	25334	3462	0	9877
53 ELECT. TRANSMISS. EQUIP.	19761	1653	51439	443643	41906	142515	132	0	7686
54 HOUSEHOLD APPLIANCES	199	162	128617	204283	432	197991	4496	0	2373
55 ELECTRIC LIGHTING EQUIP.	29920	663	22138	178746	3523	144551	2696	0	6674
56 RADIO, TV, ETC., EQUIP.	8233	79129	96287	1859128	1990	117783	109	0	177719
57 ELECTRONIC COMPONENTS	15620	68350	137	656291	1639	140088	637	0	25656
58 MISC. ELECTRICAL MACH.	12916	492	199	82170	6914	34143	5852	0	26889
59 MOTOR VEHICLES, EQUIP.	67109	7900	13993	2452638	22131	226849	447089	0	14713
60 AIRCRAFT, PARTS	539385	127900	1133	3362601	128269	1367052	7283	0	157740
61 OTHER TRANSPORT. EQUIP.	102671	4503	29779	393936	6616	75368	2054	0	117925
62 PROFESS., SCIEN. INSTRU.	1842	29755	35775	288420	12233	231764	6649	0	19974
63 MEDICAL, PHOTO. EQUIP.	0	975	97	127304	4720	41327	0	0	17680
64 MISC. MANUFACTURING	21542	7956	40919	456804	23349	342773	1468	2073	37179
65 TRANSPORT., WAREHOUSING	389201	178258	217339	3782908	429242	336561	86162	344897	1009424
66 COMMUNICA.,EXC. BRDCAST.	201786	90878	87045	1538712	144861	209037	34929	111711	418738
67 RADIO, TV BROADCASTING	19161	14158	9244	342161	19094	19772	4163	51476	53742
68 ELEC.,GAS,WATER,SAN.SER.	474277	267713	205627	2126719	307689	322354	69033	72853	567611
69 WHOLESALE, RETAIL TRADE	1346014	817693	752941	12471528	1207187	1651902	333165	737657	3179648
70 FINANCE, INSURANCE	372864	213918	182470	3600634	335529	736076	88421	244483	870057
71 REAL ESTATE, RENTAL	780741	667181	369841	8784924	797871	1143737	195852	1001649	2936320
72 HOTELS, PERSONAL SERV.	159105	156335	99217	1779235	177808	210906	31984	172012	653524
73 BUSINESS SERVICES	177668	157180	66182	3456055	214988	303262	46711	353634	657264
74 RESEARCH, DEVELOPMENT	0	0	0	0	0	0	0	0	0
75 AUTO. REPAIR, SERVICES	147191	102337	86098	1355570	136867	161941	27399	88493	343398
76 AMUSEMENTS	34684	42623	32522	1550866	70703	57325	23418	54657	249580
77 MED.,EDUC. SERVICES	198624	157090	88887	3082363	288006	760758	69211	1180420	561842
78 FEDERAL GOVT. ENTERPRISE	159389	39463	49509	599248	61060	63191	12946	145649	164099
79 STATE, LOCAL GOVT. ENT.	143014	64778	31589	736925	65777	67417	13216	17944	236554
80 IMPORTS	0	0	0	0	0	0	0	0	0
81 BUS.TRAVEL, ENT., GIFTS.	0	0	0	0	0	0	0	0	0
82 OFFICE SUPPLIES	0	0	0	0	0	0	0	0	0
83 SCRAP, USED GOODS	0	0	0	0	0	0	0	0	0
84 GOVERNMENT INDUSTRY	841379	489433	333848	6857313	754904	554375	133629	1185957	1461282
85 REST OF WORLD INDUSTRY	-20450	-27203	-10042	-306954	-21689	-18468	-3526	-96118	-53483
86 HOUSEHOLD INDUSTRY	99704	27229	40748	376514	27732	67637	14727	51286	189220
87 INVENTORY VALUATION ADJ.	0	0	0	0	0	0	0	0	0
88 STATE TOTAL	13621933	7108338	7221547	110018175	9724316	16471027	3247044	6590875	23113927

TABLE C-3

STATE ESTIMATES OF 1963 OUTPUTS
(THOUSANDS OF CURRENT DOLLARS)

INDUSTRY TITLE	10 GEORGIA	11 IDAHO	12 ILLINOIS	13 INDIANA	14 IOWA	15 KANSAS	16 KENTUCKY	17 LOUISIANA	18 MAINE
1 LIVESTOCK, PRDTS.	594546	271066	1432787	904317	2474083	1025238	487122	225929	163971
2 OTHER AGRICULTURE PRDTS.	582017	397221	1856639	1022318	1640015	730680	640608	451206	123107
3 FORESTRY, FISHERIES	39269	6846	3366	2164	923	194	5200	55842	32035
4 AGRI.,FORES.,FISH. SERV.	69115	7688	45405	25182	36892	17479	7780	21186	10452
5 IRON, FERR. ORES MINING	1707	493	0	0	0	0	0	0	
6 NONFERROUS ORES MINING	256	39559	14576	0	0	102	0	0	
7 COAL MINING	146	0	209343	58148	4461	8087	354026	0	89
8 CRUDE PETRO.,NATURAL GAS	0	0	0	32552	0	426899	82090	2400160	0
9 STONE, CLAY MINING	102287	6884	227363	47884	40797	22887	47241	19919	1947
10 CHEM.,FERT. MIN. MINING	2489	5694	90020	0	0	1272	5314	81916	0
11 NEW CONSTRUCTION	1184579	177637	2996040	1139772	614663	665160	783277	1535151	161994
12 MAINT., REPAIR CONSTR.	299710	97889	1150130	497800	385352	348587	249175	263346	74507
13 ORDNANCE, ACCESSORIES	2355	3463	91903	112980	65945		0	70940	10648
14 FOOD, KINDRED PRDTS.	1552488	372843	6023676	2062038	3291882	1266261	1264053	1356659	309745
15 TOBACCO MANUFACTURES	17348	0	20827	16490	0	0	1319600	8737	0
16 FABRICS	1421902	0	47878	12357	3963	206	29542	0	250783
17 TEXTILE PRDTS.	682463	0	98712		240	208	2865	7640	13089
18 APPAREL	591386	723	407621	131994	27794	30919	221872	55634	38535
19 MISC. TEXTILE PRDTS.	113326	648	140674	27397	7333	9462	19781	23047	8951
20 LUMBER, WOOD PRDTS.	267620	241853	169728	196599	50539	10553	87841	182613	186560
21 WOODEN CONTAINERS	23696	908	12995	3982	2272	831	18223	7570	1929
22 HOUSEHOLD FURNITURE	92563	2034	217641	277660	20639	13904	65228	14479	5767
23 OTHER FURNITURE	12617	718	185329	61522	19170	11671	10207	3200	3804
24 PAPER, ALLIED PRDTS.	492391	31918	404503	152110	38678	20389	39234	394027	474701
25 PAPERBOARD CONTAINERS	153602	3155	442796	145269	53056	58615	46675	61555	7626
26 PRINTING, PUBLISHING	162158	17145	1805092	332370	218125	107748	123558	80485	28537
27 CHEMICALS,SELECT. PRDTS.	263029	29539	793975	240558	45462	89337	246175	627767	17493
28 PLASTICS, SYNTHETICS	57577	0	101875	40473	86744	17398	221871	181270	437
29 DRUGS, COSMETICS	96401	229	977479	574288	48689	125237	2127	10354	427
30 PAINT, ALLIED PRDTS.	53467	371	357477	40617	34166	7004	75430	10489	458
31 PETROLEUM, RELATED INDS.	46324	221	1321704	895711	9919	628509	163548	1690405	3319
32 RUBBER, MISC. PLASTICS	66207	0	563864	456490	204918	93479	57208	4523	29405
33 LEATHER TANNING, PRDTS.	9110	630	58365	2469	0	0	5608	540	48539
34 FOOTWEAR, LEATHER PRDTS.	43658	0	147251	33436	6425	1572	29445	65	231303
35 GLASS, GLASS PRDTS.	23827	0	232163	145467	165	862	24046	24741	1174
36 STONE, CLAY PRDTS.	171282	17809	567054	332863	156960	172283	94339	135442	18118
37 PRIMARY IRON, STEEL MFR.	160795	1179	1949936	2543663	61000	21607	241305	22410	1126
38 PRIMARY NONFERROUS MFR.	66090	112312	911115	788311	106931	23177	89208	122613	6143

160

Industry	1	2	3	4	5	6	7	8	9
39 METAL CONTAINERS	15147	52584	4305	6264	400	41476	381917	34530	1448
40 FABRICATED METAL PRDTS.	13968	85398	103411	85524	104720	361793	560429	132161	9705
41 SCREW MACH. PRDTS., ETC.	648	4703	32299	4431	16641	204158	684424	39312	0
42 OTHER FAB. METAL PRDTS.	3828	48947	134215	24886	71381	303614	1008648	44492	585
43 ENGINES, TURBINES	0	598	0	37957	37934	71279	210830	203	0
44 FARM MACH. EQUIP.	902	11187	66575	26355	554255	114743	600416	35247	5958
45 CONSTRUC. MACH. EQUIP.	10959	21167	1595	11602	151811	90615	1190597	27332	1183
46 MATERIAL HANDLING MACH.	0	1716	21322	7921	12365	11835	163264	11818	719
47 METALWORKING MACHINERY	2214	899	10612	17753	27708	119933	539241	6482	183
48 SPECIAL MACH., EQUIP.	7333	11558	16661	23316	25876	55046	279951	48737	761
49 GENERAL MACH., EQUIP.	3010	2849	53524	27807	33447	316540	436620	10619	0
50 MACHINE SHOP PRDTS.	2656	14669	28971	282	7889	117988	165557	9302	1723
51 OFFICE, COMPUT. MACHINES	2855	729	57373	24729	129	2754	229318	3340	0
52 SERVICE IND. MACHINES	2299	6033	67583	2894	45558	110432	227763	16327	698
53 ELECT. TRANSMISS. EQUIP.	234	1839	62103	369	21351	269025	466316	95986	0
54 HOUSEHOLD APPLIANCES	6614	786	296855	1544	156801	324720	645883	4058	0
55 ELECTRIC LIGHTING EQUIP.	3314	857	53501	5449	870	143432	317617	22406	0
56 RADIO, TV, ETC., EQUIP.	17622	337	12981	13862	89144	795258	1732506	1381	0
57 ELECTRONIC COMPONENTS	2802	387	26852	17027	47301	161710	300826	2467	476
58 MISC. ELECTRICAL MACH.	709	1815	8002	240141	14335	435626	138075	21986	0
59 MOTOR VEHICLES, EQUIP.	17093	16718	246498	690988	33041	2000681	997276	798478	1986
60 AIRCRAFT, PARTS	78956	112573	1133	53930	6339	445968	117313	213077	2765
61 OTHER TRANSPORT. EQUIP.	666	157066	19012	3547	25527	34141	406330	65045	14002
62 PROFESS., SCIEN. INSTRU.	81	4565	16152	781	49789	100428	541792	22617	165
63 MEDICAL, PHOTO. EQUIP.	15821	1800	1252	7909	2103	30610	201403	414	0
64 MISC. MANUFACTURING	126352	16746	27040	27040	82988	150746	569802	66960	2911
65 TRANSPORT., WAREHOUSING	48568	788875	444883	483415	386620	809628	2966923	743368	115476
66 COMMUNICA., EXC. BROCAST.	7346	277900	174780	136425	157997	340051	692073	293385	42032
67 RADIO, TV BROADCASTING	79975	26383	22180	25519	25253	35698	158161	31846	5528
68 ELEC.,GAS,WATER,SAN.SER.	468863	466977	380586	336602	399323	814738	1754134	472985	98738
69 WHOLESALE, RETAIL TRADE	105102	1570695	1298178	1152859	1634078	2683332	8098984	2313609	364923
70 FINANCE, INSURANCE	214963	431140	307286	276694	377700	691020	2266344	625152	69708
71 REAL ESTATE, RENTAL	74314	941941	648023	647772	798934	1494857	5650980	1100306	199175
72 HOTELS, PERSONAL SERV.	41804	173860	179038	134529	182794	328264	992013	261300	47567
73 BUSINESS SERVICES									
74 RESEARCH, DEVELOPMENT		271667	139933	121565	170689	291356	2273543	301324	52434
75 AUTO. REPAIR, SERVICES	50800	149067	134572	132784	154299	247831	601256	219477	45592
76 AMUSEMENTS	17993	72531	66234	43297	56446	91101	415753	70834	13613
77 MED.,EDUC. SERVICES	122578	342893	292683	178727	337617	642673	2474468	400176	46814
78 FEDERAL GOVT. ENTERPRISE	30488	66145	105568	66309	60641	96783	305250	141079	16310
79 STATE, LOCAL GOVT. ENT.	40543	80270	61969	78833	102838	128403	395619	106731	27015
80 IMPORTS	0	0	0	0	0	0	0	0	0
81 BUS.,TRAVEL, ENT., GIFTS	0	0	0	0	0	0	0	0	0
82 OFFICE SUPPLIES	0	0	0	0	0	0	0	0	0
83 SCRAP, USED GOODS	0	0	0	0	0	0	0	0	0
84 GOVERNMENT INDUSTRY	257847	791726	768868	696498	536242	961739	2479015	1365581	171852
85 REST OF WORLD INDUSTRY	-10719	-19455	-17775	-14235	-17857	-9934	-96343	-24565	-10023
86 HOUSEHOLD INDUSTRY	18016	101618	46393	33022	39229	62554	145791	149186	8663
87 INVENTORY VALUATION ADJ.									
88 STATE TOTAL	4171280	17264621	13584159	11825705	16781347	30189166	70773861	19826351	3209364

TABLE C-3

STATE ESTIMATES OF 1963 OUTPUTS
(THOUSANDS OF CURRENT DOLLARS)

INDUSTRY TITLE	19 MARYLAND	20 MASSA-CHUSETTS	21 MICHIGAN	22 MINNESOTA	23 MISSISSIPPI	24 MISSOURI	25 MONTANA	26 NEBRASKA	27 NEVADA
1 LIVESTOCK, PRDTS.	266299	125106	558535	1345468	395593	986507	298180	1124560	51099
2 OTHER AGRICULTURE PRDTS.	156039	87887	646356	1067824	670875	834324	344351	828892	25686
3 FORESTRY, FISHERIES	16783	49878	9323	6142	24366	5392	4241	164	16
4 AGRI.,FORES.,FISH. SERV.	20993	3227	14790	35068	62324	36918	4636	15883	777
5 IRON, FERRO. ORES MINING	740	0	119183	475886	0	14454	1881	0	4529
6 NONFERROUS ORES MINING	0	0	35880	3299	0	16782	80799	33	50492
7 COAL MINING	5065	0	0	0	0	13138	2228	0	0
8 CRUDE PETRO.,NATURAL GAS	417	0	62109	0	198584	560	77523	60886	153
9 STONE, CLAY MINING	39179	22425	71472	24086	11167	55823	5671	17078	14075
10 CHEM.,FERT. MIN. MINING	0	0	6328	0	0	6219	9333	0	1307
11 NEW CONSTRUCTION	1522868	1845402	2302047	997444	392207	1167957	215578	386080	614917
12 MAINT., REPAIR CONSTR.	306326	459707	730024	419101	168240	478527	142350	244689	79482
13 ORDNANCE, ACCESSORIES	15408	86013	84874	107973	0	127716	949	949	0
14 FOOD, KINDRED PRDTS.	1232033	1460361	2020935	2659989	530193	2388027	189069	1600127	34404
15 TOBACCO MANUFACTURES	5109	3183	15697	0	0	20843	0	0	0
16 FABRICS	52387	548886	5967	16772	31107	22453	0	388	0
17 TEXTILE PRDTS.	1529	231229	70876	15875	43001	28184	0	0	0
18 APPAREL	303543	705732	70811	90714	271303	336665	0	12324	245
19 MISC. TEXTILE PRDTS.	29764	114024	359023	25643	15725	55009	140	1613	382
20 LUMBER, WOOD PRDTS.	60703	75749	189272	128286	251396	81275	194375	19040	8960
21 WOODEN CONTAINERS	7472	7533	5922	4035	22317	8333	0	651	0
22 HOUSEHOLD FURNITURE	36232	132254	120015	24216	92083	43183	616	11283	1016
23 OTHER FURNITURE	31386	34072	202931	21233	5453	37122	546	9283	280
24 PAPER, ALLIED PRDTS.	85792	544490	580772	314751	80104	118281	4797	9526	118
25 PAPERBOARD CONTAINERS	117677	208043	251392	73488	12829	138402	0	15100	0
26 PRINTING, PUBLISHING	223721	637568	477627	304077	26366	425234	18262	76882	17208
27 CHEMICALS,SELECT. PRDTS.	203185	171676	613532	117469	63679	347646	6599	24445	25985
28 PLASTICS, SYNTHETICS	53515	214840	113140	13788	4325	3625	0	0	0
29 DRUGS, COSMETICS	241825	173526	359657	134244	29219	316614	328	39998	2071
30 PAINT, ALLIED PRDTS.	41930	58468	169794	18557	687	101517	0	1494	229
31 PETROLEUM, RELATED INDS.	112321	76782	364542	162586	84721	181120	142287	12329	1214
32 RUBBER, MISC. PLASTICS	199401	655628	422628	65491	62196	106839	221	45965	0
33 LEATHER TANNING, PRDTS.	3984	191031	27004	9035	0	7736	0	1754	0
34 FOOTWEAR, LEATHER PRDTS.	18534	488982	28869	14268	20889	337026	65	575	0
35 GLASS, GLASS PRDTS.	46325	3832	138738	15989	12035	59085	0	165	0
36 STONE, CLAY PRDTS.	150485	235882	368301	185542	77693	237715	23100	54034	48095
37 PRIMARY IRON, STEEL MFR.	485301	190444	2161805	176659	7885	174336	1289	3852	548
38 PRIMARY NONFERROUS MFR.	338817	267599	687128	27018	13871	137633	222157	79830	75693

Code	Industry	(1)	(2)	(3)	(4)	(5)	(6)	(7)	(8)	(9)
39	METAL CONTAINERS	115610	22946	11257	53751	200	96696	0	13220	0
40	FABRICATED METAL PRDTS.	111995	162857	393820	89949	50184	213644	6359	74910	5614
41	SCREW MACH. PRDTS., ETC.	39265	139235	624264	51717	20254	51999	0	2173	129
42	OTHER FAB. METAL PRDTS.	77747	299333	739801	79424	18470	171611	434	9056	546
43	ENGINES, TURBINES	0	186880	437144	19209	0	10948	0	0	0
44	FARM MACH., EQUIP.	770	1334	235414	132582	28510	59064	902	35892	283
45	CONSTRUC. MACH., EQUIP.	4006	4402	135839	86935	13108	33689	142	3973	0
46	MATERIAL HANDLING MACH.	9464	32789	201395	21376	12499	13700	127	1058	0
47	METALWORKING MACHINERY	62648	210521	924691	30620	179	48187	0	1280	121
48	SPECIAL MACH., EQUIP.	64986	332638	188813	32260	10760	43021	0	790	127
49	GENERAL MACH., EQUIP.	16451	155709	304691	50405	2304	48334	1506	21561	1026
50	MACHINE SHOP PRDTS.	30608	65237	226825	40980	7560	91158	0	2539	698
51	OFFICE, COMPUT. MACHINES	9051	9051	296691	325180	0	21460	0	139	580
52	SERVICE IND. MACHINES	35500	86414	281388	129546	10989	142337	0	1699	0
53	ELECT. TRANSMISS. EQUIP.	33379	226284	181646	84316	11725	159487	0	673	3790
54	HOUSEHOLD APPLIANCES	9428	32294	264352	131136	21181	48584	0	1276	161
55	ELECTRIC LIGHTING EQUIP.	3855	176020	44602	18436	45059	95815	0	0	120
56	RADIO, TV, ETC., EQUIP.	447206	890685	71496	110329	8718	109912	0	97129	429
57	ELECTRONIC COMPONENTS	16103	346620	59905	46457	7086	8185	0	19741	121
58	MISC. ELECTRICAL MACH.	26548	55653	20782	20175	2692	31164	447	3103	63
59	MOTOR VEHICLES, EQUIP.	678266	303722	15325597	286277	50256	2521989	0	54343	0
60	AIRCRAFT, PARTS	220273	200563	161617	39680	0	344085	1078	121	3244
61	OTHER TRANSPORT. EQUIP.	251684	106174	249836	21741	7089	98356	1827	32293	95084
62	PROFESS., SCIEN. INSTRU.	22342	291604	247778	50845	6035	39495	0	24033	15637
63	MEDICAL, PHOTO. EQUIP.	7064	226150	12485	24597	97	16338	3112	398	4819
64	MISC. MANUFACTURING	47097	405337	241424	86239	35891	86241	136507	16668	75819
65	TRANSPORT., WAREHOUSING	617721	901760	1105429	649460	179818	1156843	38173	316857	255364
66	COMMUNICA., EXC. BRDCAST.	231574	408974	624314	222784	115259	307176	6953	116226	67976
67	RADIO, TV BROADCASTING	23935	63674	77097	3276	10997	42274	142364	15493	263603
68	ELEC., GAS, WATER, SAN. SER.	477373	739190	1233011	483609	267965	571994	375834	135409	180461
69	WHOLESALE, RETAIL TRADE	1836661	3586326	4833148	2319635	752856	3190089	74705	957806	64061
70	FINANCE, INSURANCE	447229	1372536	1029999	633694	173357	840941	206416	288748	0
71	REAL ESTATE, RENTAL	1498298	2075821	2877745	1452251	385929	1855551	51421	484580	34043
72	HOTELS, PERSONAL SERV.	224574	455466	574872	251176	98330	356472	35506	107335	248782
73	BUSINESS SERVICES	367246	821601	1188670	441491	78635	550082	43660	122753	25051
74	RESEARCH, DEVELOPMENT	212823	292457	502003	192120	86386	257005	12515	90511	16545
75	AUTO. REPAIR, SERVICES	124273	167345	212968	80397	21856	113171	49245	40775	10145
76	AMUSEMENTS	707581	2445793	248090	519333	90818	870353	20799	170095	
77	MED., EDUC. SERVICES	89338	178189	157742	95509	46752	147627	25618	46631	
78	FEDERAL GOVT. ENTERPRISE	91683	202896	353681	127521	33417	88769		160009	
79	STATE, LOCAL GOVT. ENT.									
80	IMPORTS	0	0	0	0	0	0	0	0	0
81	BUS., TRAVEL, ENT., GIFTS.	0	0	0	0	0	0	0	0	0
82	OFFICE SUPPLIES	0	0	0	0	0	0	0	0	0
83	SCRAP, USED GOODS	0	0	0	0	0	0	0	0	0
84	GOVERNMENT INDUSTRY	1171873	1459191	1850911	776146	513072	965960	218526	399222	145206
85	REST OF WORLD INDUSTRY	-30124	-47903	-91435	-46166	-9423	-37367	-4138	-12129	-18571
86	HOUSEHOLD INDUSTRY	75073	86259	118488	49273	73454	67734	8325	21766	6846
87	INVENTORY VALUATION ADJ.									
88	STATE TOTAL	16941568	30411849	54107701	19444688	6972759	25408389	3448988	8586024	2566904

163

TABLE C-3

STATE ESTIMATES OF 1963 OUTPUTS
(THOUSANDS OF CURRENT DOLLARS)

INDUSTRY TITLE	28 NEW HAMPSHIRE	29 NEW JERSEY	30 NEW MEXICO	31 NEW YORK	32 NORTH CAROLINA	33 NORTH DAKOTA	34 OHIO	35 OKLAHOMA	36 OREGON
1 LIVESTOCK, PRODS.	58039	191662	218518	804447	486531	299154	835670	534229	255643
2 OTHER AGRICULTURE PRODS.	20291	188219	139910	533789	1103939	594535	855092	420207	310036
3 FORESTRY, FISHERIES	2920	14497	1321	20367	35751	55	5010	1448	167046
4 AGRI.,FORES.,FISH. SERV.	2729	5707	6518	13428	43985	7899	22495	21158	10149
5 IRON, FERRO. ORES MINING		5481	2436	36069	2885		0	0	2203
6 NONFERROUS ORES MINING		5668	156652	18383	207	1174	260	2013	359
7 COAL MINING			9180			9209	169229	5248	0
8 CRUDE PETRO.,NATURAL GAS			462097	9156		74530	25714	780891	511
9 STONE, CLAY MINING	3076	62271	10381	92743	38138	3995	94887	19420	25263
10 CHEM.,FERT. MIN. MINING			100089	12421	3521		13531		29
11 NEW CONSTRUCTION	159572	1927017	437185	5045863	1000997	186738	2943049	970743	707139
12 MAINT., REPAIR CONSTR.	62198	571917	126501	1675894	385430	136416	1223710	259764	244943
13 ORDNANCE, ACCESSORIES		1901	67886	75332	33513		155856	255	342
14 FOOD, KINDRED PRODS.	108339	2874697	128206	516133	1046837	151116	3140787	578547	675398
15 TOBACCO MANUFACTURES				11422	3638584		36623		
16 FABRICS	163890	37619	170	278277	3601811		27170	1518	48976
17 TEXTILE PRODS.	12257	299031		207223	179121		123370	208	6461
18 APPAREL	54509	142889	2468	6393061	1224146		400477	47533	52375
19 MISC. TEXTILE PRODS.	6222	844802	2321	571218	131029	304	43518	3962	22821
20 LUMBER, WOOD PRODS.	71147	194256	30150	233608	304957	1604	150678	27088	1853178
21 WOODEN CONTAINERS	4519	73875	90	14691	9456		10834	0	5108
22 HOUSEHOLD FURNITURE	20672	12300	1468	272248	583863	241	140777	11642	32692
23 OTHER FURNITURE	7966	111721	2169	242229	52440	187	170485	4936	4123
24 PAPER, ALLIED PRODS.	159408	47082		951158	305896		665350	12284	209867
25 PAPERBOARD CONTAINERS	11614	500490	202	435382	86001	202	331383	16025	18628
26 PRINTING, PUBLISHING	44613	320050	20454	4044426	133454	15856	1007275	81783	81230
27 CHEMICALS,SELECT. PRODS.	13401	591919	10156	710811	138868	3031	674118	22925	53258
28 PLASTICS, SYNTHETICS	16961	1708659	117	242731	166607		284448	874	4762
29 DRUGS, COSMETICS	2130	290825	458	1261376	61853		525323	3608	6572
30 PAINT, ALLIED PRODS.	458	1484733		132639	21288		221308	5955	11231
31 PETROLEUM, RELATED INDS.	1584	1384942	60226	251919	7167	36282	935172	756516	18183
32 RUBBER, MISC. PLASTICS	49020	530245	4755	467588	72808		1971168	102074	8843
33 LEATHER TANNING, PRODS.	33086	61305	1373	89112	7789		31050	0	1536
34 FOOTWEAR, LEATHER PRODS.	192600	109756	165	577392	16267		87775	4184	4227
35 GLASS, GLASS PRODS.	1339	231092	31786	169373	48477		413800	65945	8325
36 STONE, CLAY PRODS.	41813	432021		642260	122560	9936	772396	81667	66658
37 PRIMARY IRON, STEEL MFR.	17181	284098		994924	29997	79	4101625	28233	61376
38 PRIMARY NONFERROUS MFR.	19632	1056145	41446	1136189	93077		956096	84693	121855

#	Industry	C1	C2	C3	C4	C5	C6	C7	C8	C9
39	METAL CONTAINERS	0	261080	0	121305	483	0	133204	2810	18918
40	FABRICATED METAL PRDTS.	11267	326633	6494	568951	98269	5645	875297	146655	76510
41	SCREW MACH. PRDTS., ETC.	7080	207290	1318	314590	17204	259	645406	6083	3635
42	OTHER FAB. METAL PRDTS.	10229	445809	946	518697	43260	218	826110	54058	24796
43	ENGINES, TURBINES	101	3934	0	196443	101	0	52534	101	598
44	FARM MACH., EQUIP.	113	3727	338	49801	20276	7053	161379	6923	7175
45	CONSTRUC. MACH., EQUIP.	22499	43076	1333	32697	1509	123	387401	126088	9292
46	MATERIAL HANDLING MACH.	0	120047	0	123184	1580	256	196302	2245	35849
47	METALWORKING MACHINERY	11601	120879	1297	286401	8161	1413	820185	2058	1952
48	SPECIAL MACH., EQUIP.	50270	220461	760	290477	119709	358	342026	8568	39478
49	GENERAL MACH., EQUIP.	23143	321322	127	463648	6403	124	657136	48217	5526
50	MACHINE SHOP PRDTS.	5061	74760	5917	190161	13278	1129	193151	13044	19467
51	OFFICE, COMPUT. MACHINES	4194	135982	729	1024937	8168	0	225651	1585	139
52	SERVICE IND. MACHINES	4827	117371	1093	348843	21387	0	281049	17219	5489
53	ELECT. TRANSMISS. EQUIP.	62287	269179	233	643175	98018	0	789751	18716	50765
54	HOUSEHOLD APPLIANCES	162	48074	0	146166	46737	0	998776	2178	4195
55	ELECTRIC LIGHTING EQUIP.	3075	257822	3040	334175	22859	0	332004	444	1715
56	RADIO, TV, ETC., EQUIP.	55620	1232334	1170	1721999	232411	0	370742	172572	1662
57	ELECTRONIC COMPONENTS	45619	308192	247	523182	42873	0	143122	4728	830
58	MISC. ELECTRICAL MACH.	760	85741	2719	131514	62777	0	225599	5981	7976
59	MOTOR VEHICLES, EQUIP.	260	745989	121	1866915	38240	0	5237746	61976	87086
60	AIRCRAFT, PARTS	0	345913	537	1131283	18574	0	1011540	482787	18160
61	OTHER TRANSPORT. EQUIP.	1885	174817	3454	235989	22764	354	183971	14812	57577
62	PROFESS., SCIEN. INSTRU.	3142	242524	0	435337	32192	74	154274	9179	7345
63	MEDICAL, PHOTO. EQUIP.	6117	119080	0	1290239	20721	0	9072	178	9787
64	MISC. MANUFACTURING	23950	447165	4058	1526883	38514	4967	310569	16412	21228
65	TRANSPORT., WAREHOUSING	58877	1562516	150221	4703198	591745	89826	1870690	466291	464342
66	COMMUNICA.,EXC. BRDCAST.	34202	476454	57458	1573442	256293	45595	709944	169959	137271
67	RADIO, TV BROADCASTING	3646	12197	8853	541721	34438	5396	104323	18982	18948
68	ELEC.,GAS,WATER,SAN.SER.	82031	893730	161515	2247914	414547	54146	1760925	317367	159845
69	WHOLESALE, RETAIL TRADE	319283	4386241	441966	16061845	2261095	376744	5801781	1202456	1314288
70	FINANCE, INSURANCE	88762	1059332	94984	6502456	524723	68956	1423204	332199	271052
71	REAL ESTATE, RENTAL	178161	2945292	314909	11951645	968272	146402	3874216	798233	692414
72	HOTELS, PERSONAL SERV.	64516	561287	73256	2050793	287442	36250	704730	148650	152259
73	BUSINESS SERVICES	37137	828080	76824	6121343	215801	22740	1091731	208369	177300
74	RESEARCH, DEVELOPMENT	0	0	0	0	0	0	0	0	0
75	AUTO. REPAIR, SERVICES	36070	354992	53991	949400	202853	36319	527564	144369	133413
76	AMUSEMENTS	29708	233071	22166	2014205	70172	10382	285915	45968	45446
77	MED.,EDUC. SERVICES	163007	991290	65755	6154695	539494	39835	1609580	209252	233743
78	FEDERAL GOVT. ENTERPRISE	16238	159315	29038	582769	108009	20253	229583	70925	57328
79	STATE, LOCAL GOVT. ENT.	38832	161703	21973	782680	171869	8746	476327	72770	102565
80	IMPORTS	0	0	0	0	0	0	0	0	0
81	BUS.TRAVEL, ENT., GIFTS.	0	0	0	0	0	0	0	0	0
82	OFFICE SUPPLIES	0	0	0	0	0	0	0	0	0
83	SCRAP, USED GOODS	0	0	0	0	0	0	0	0	0
84	GOVERNMENT INDUSTRY	216995	1580420	424222	4904783	1293308	216859	2023815	809486	481283
85	REST OF WORLD INDUSTRY	-9151	-53643	-16385	-354838	-21222	-8625	-73885	-17569	-18588
86	HOUSEHOLD INDUSTRY	11328	119459	14220	451466	129142	8109	143230	37888	27685
87	INVENTORY VALUATION ADJ.	0	0	0	0	0	0	0	0	0
88	STATE TOTAL	3086086	39826531	4107754	115545792	24303702	2732450	61695185	11218718	10069090

165

TABLE C-3

STATE ESTIMATES OF 1963 OUTPUTS
(THOUSANDS OF CURRENT DOLLARS)

INDUSTRY TITLE	37 PENNSYL-VANIA	38 RHODE ISLAND	39 SOUTH CAROLINA	40 SOUTH DAKOTA	41 TENNESSEE	42 TEXAS	43 UTAH	44 VERMONT	45 VIRGINIA
1 LIVESTOCK, PRODS.	806437	17360	157263	674203	408001	1458908	165371	145950	384917
2 OTHER AGRICULTURE PRODS.	474773	11244	382994	438535	481564	1748170	76595	51488	336142
3 FORESTRY, FISHERIES	9491	4976	24745	485	7081	46230	420	2402	42240
4 AGRI.,FORES.,FISH. SERV.	24983	2576	15487	9553	14011	171192	3854	545	17748
5 IRON,FERRO. ORES MINING	46159	0	0	27	114	7789	13213	0	940
6 NONFERROUS ORES MINING	3328	0	272	25887	1437	4897	229759	0	5792
7 COAL MINING	681809	0	0	98	27301	1288	33540	0	159572
8 CRUDE PETRO.,NATURAL GAS	49704	0	0	152	107	4068350	105409	0	618
9 STONE, CLAY MINING	94522	2659	27624	9970	49600	63212	7326	11016	56523
10 CHEM.,FERT. MIN. MINING	5096	0	453	29	34919	67291	8903	0	511
11 NEW CONSTRUCTION	2211964	237175	327279	203777	1008802	4040992	460565	66006	1614012
12 MAINT., REPAIR CONSTR.	899318	58058	152453	135017	202444	1234860	105234	38133	345474
13 ORDNANCE, ACCESSORIES	97737	73	0	0	57406	50093	117708	0	681
14 FOOD, KINDRED PRODTS.	3770379	169103	383365	468884	1442595	3189502	348881	166612	945241
15 TOBACCO MANUFACTURES	392309	49	99665	0	59441	5406	0	0	1431152
16 FABRICS	560886	351708	2968891	0	254044	115275	699	7784	471252
17 TEXTILE PRODS.	269393	52990	218236	0	63023	14391	484	2881	74397
18 APPAREL	1884319	59978	270786	0	746798	410622	24388	21962	300980
19 MISC. TEXTILE PRDTS.	116848	4876	33008	798	41782	53552	1448	404	23777
20 LUMBER, WOOD PRDTS.	193798	4886	178325	10501	179557	232619	14149	41116	245905
21 WOODEN CONTAINERS	10096	444	8772	102	18765	8482	180	1550	13407
22 HOUSEHOLD FURNITURE	202054	1552	37744	874	197001	103363	8385	23055	284238
23 OTHER FURNITURE	153175	12700	5399	182	25910	51728	3711	187	36327
24 PAPER, ALLIED PRDTS.	712864	18792	210919	181	293907	214017	4436	63320	318453
25 PAPERBOARD CONTAINERS	345027	18302	65077	871	62656	101800	2494	1077	51492
26 PRINTING, PUBLISHING	1085976	56953	45286	19564	212563	425331	44980	28097	147960
27 CHEMICALS,SELECT. PRDTS.	561416	42271	56800	3129	458179	2599076	16234	4630	263781
28 PLASTICS, SYNTHETICS	394710	42778	208006	0	530307	453889	0	3625	707808
29 DRUGS, COSMETICS	628262	8600	3601	967	10829	115324	2817	408	87005
30 PAINT, ALLIED PRDTS.	155656	7008	3471	0	21863	113773	1723	3894	11283
31 PETROLEUM, RELATED INDS.	1337564	30323	19059	371	42892	5719294	161761	371	73239
32 RUBBER, MISC. PLASTICS	511945	149534	58368	3313	178644	201529	11097	21123	76790
33 LEATHER TANNING, PRDTS.	64284	259	1059	0	37121	3115	410	3854	12278
34 FOOTWEAR, LEATHER PRODTS.	297133	12717	0	0	188718	31716	486	5440	46054
35 GLASS, GLASS PRDTS.	394642	32693	53843	0	108907	33959	248	0	21579
36 STONE, CLAY PRDTS.	681485	13101	60689	15395	158089	519928	66911	40219	178702
37 PRIMARY IRON, STEEL MFR.	5530478	72304	23563	79	106746	354629	166348	3184	86714
38 PRIMARY NONFERROUS MFR.	711516	201487	17938	0	318201	597094	147936	11637	82021

166

#	Industry									
39	METAL CONTAINERS	163189	0	683	0	13067	110646	6775	0	10216
40	FABRICATED METAL PRDTS.	878453	16078	46552	11739	189824	399017	53774	5026	140874
41	SCREW MACH. PRDTS., ETC.	438509	32726	10819	913	36558	25115	801	763	3531
42	OTHER FAB. METAL PRDTS.	678346	70014	13361		57297	242559	4604	2776	47197
43	ENGINES, TURBINES	283325	101	0	0	101	17314	0	0	0
44	FARM MACH., EQUIP.	101582	113	2761	4260	62848	26536	1649	451	7977
45	CONSTRUC. MACH., EQUIP.	151957	283	406	0	6653	421344	30864	1660	5498
46	MATERIAL HANDLING MACH.	153920	606	5106	4161	21834	21766	244	0	4981
47	METALWORKING MACHINERY	339193	55950	30509	3250	9446	23807	1439	68578	1834
48	SPECIAL MACH., EQUIP.	255395	46990	75758	239	19729	69771	3475	3710	11292
49	GENERAL MACH., EQUIP.	414554	15285	15987	3079	23378	80920	8295	729	15563
50	MACHINE SHOP PRDTS.	105424	8989	8526	3098	17606	60377	3867	1637	9786
51	OFFICE, COMPUT. MACHINES	181521	282	9791			9343	268	25559	48035
52	SERVICE IND. MACHINES	217708	2860	2415	0	34676	139344	9462	4293	23058
53	ELECT. TRANSMISS. EQUIP.	749300	5283	28263	0	63247	54006	5769	1812	112583
54	HOUSEHOLD APPLIANCES	100930	3267	7287	0	142023	24181	0	0	606
55	ELECTRIC LIGHTING EQUIP.	310980	51697	1194	0	21324	18362	796	7037	1348
56	RADIO, TV, ETC., EQUIP.	281157	13871	1414	109	145687	287728	14547	14572	113886
57	ELECTRONIC COMPONENTS	513983	22410	37155	2077	16403	46099	9368	6838	85974
58	MISC. ELECTRICAL MACH.	108254	10155	387	0	15806	32816	254		4211
59	MOTOR VEHICLES, EQUIP.	1005311	12374	6246	997	90799	666706	3518		239908
60	AIRCRAFT, PARTS	792699	8328	3004	0	66719	658187	238319	74184	23690
61	OTHER TRANSPORT. EQUIP.	567339	7742	13004	2852	63507	156744	8601	356	112216
62	PROFESS., SCIEN. INSTRU.	438275	32333	23038	162	46656	56105	1200	9208	9259
63	MEDICAL, PHOTO. EQUIP.	40027	11320	14003	0	272	8692	382	4824	24249
64	MISC. MANUFACTURING	467724	276618	52761	1994	90368	70194	13166	7078	67941
65	TRANSPORT., WAREHOUSING	2325645	110395	200751	62057	525887	2160606	19203	56865	750823
66	COMMUNICA.,EXC. BRDCAST.	701265	63906	118757	33985	291747	774675	80983	17842	259185
67	RADIO, TV BROADCASTING	126202	10305	15926	6586	33221	88734	8130	2936	31111
68	ELEC.,GAS,WATER,SAN.SER.	1690452	97706	208176	59949	174668	1368716	166411	43331	496624
69	WHOLESALE, RETAIL TRADE	6445870	510654	898070	351497	1907989	5840274	529106	189195	1924405
70	FINANCE, INSURANCE	1850699	167016	248062	73765	489511	1683084	121687	48827	490538
71	REAL ESTATE, RENTAL	3878744	313118	414403	175028	872878	3038462	364388	90356	1380724
72	HOTELS, PERSONAL SERV.	846450	65057	123623	39703	235386	750623	64195	37364	284079
73	BUSINESS SERVICES	1314676	73369	103527	25520	261079	989407	76127	18167	272544
74	RESEARCH, DEVELOPMENT	0	0	0	0	0	0	0	0	0
75	AUTO. REPAIR, SERVICES	620972	38721	96499	37174	179728	611792	57465	22705	194094
76	AMUSEMENTS	238807	37079	29124	18282	60493	196261	28826	14631	67051
77	MED.,EDUC. SERVICES	2482999	189905	154877	54852	481443	1000462	199121	141081	440271
78	FEDERAL GOVT. ENTERPRISE	267554	28997	63592	18668	250840	278693	23699	10896	161868
79	STATE, LOCAL GOVT. ENT.	488781	14346	44276	18355	239455	355233	40531	17500	195412
80	IMPORTS	0	0	0	0	0	0	0	0	0
81	BUS.TRAVEL, ENT., GIFTS.	0	0	0	0	0	0	0	0	0
82	OFFICE SUPPLIES	0	0	0	0	0	0	0	0	0
83	SCRAP, USED GOODS	0	0	0	0	0	0	0	0	0
84	GOVERNMENT INDUSTRY	235309	223339	645406	191708	696642	3105681	360050	78809	1644651
85	REST OF WORLD INDUSTRY	-82654	-6053	-9469	-6712	-24428	-104693	-8444	-6080	-25989
86	HOUSEHOLD INDUSTRY	188151	13830	72732	10416	86632	247775	8979	12126	101645
87	INVENTORY VALUATION ADJ.	0	0	0	0	0	0	0	0	0
88	STATE TOTAL	6180514	4356709	9988597	3232709	16240731	54746192	5093997	1818611	18751754

TABLE C-3

STATE ESTIMATES OF 1963 OUTPUTS
(THOUSANDS OF CURRENT DOLLARS)

INDUSTRY TITLE	46 WASHINGTON	47 WEST VIRGINIA	48 WISCONSIN	49 WYOMING	50 ALASKA	51 HAWAII	52 NO STATE ALLOCATION	53 NATIONAL TOTAL
1 LIVESTOCK, PRDTS.	290008	112882	1270359	183608	4330	44721	0	26474838
2 OTHER AGRICULTURE PRDTS.	524369	71745	555249	77140	220	266485	0	27005120
3 FORESTRY, FISHERIES	94630	4684	8381	468	59613	3177	0	1041929
4 AGRI.,FORES.,FISH. SERV.	12546	6852	14631	1533	31	26001	0	1221890
5 IRON, FERRO. ORES MINING	796	0	955	18347	382	0	0	874556
6 NONFERROUS ORES MINING	10734	0	1810	61998	6072	0	0	1281255
7 COAL MINING	4695	738667	0	10394	2820	0	0	2633681
8 CRUDE PETRO.,NATURAL GAS	7985	75872	0	382623	14641	0	0	10899284
9 STONE, CLAY MINING	20026	21029	47421	17312	1281	6545	0	1766409
10 CHEM.,FERT. MIN. MINING	51	103	0	17732	0	0	0	580180
11 NEW CONSTRUCTION	1381119	276827	1183412	209988	174119	379980	0	65518990
12 MAINT., REPAIR CONSTR.	368361	148439	426113	78597	23533	79152	0	19794446
13 ORDNANCE, ACCESSORIES	7495	89982	17009	0	0	0	0	4712322
14 FOOD, KINDRED PRDTS.	1114172	207177	2736578	76351	81029	517212	0	71774202
15 TOBACCO MANUFACTURES	0	25722	675	0	0	0	0	7332966
16 FABRICS	10828	5695	12504	0	0	206	0	12537783
17 TEXTILE PRDTS.	2648	120	41510	0	0	340	0	2948960
18 APPAREL	51481	43554	143832	0	0	24087	0	17907727
19 MISC. TEXTILE PRDTS.	14166	1512	13525	69	0	1606	0	2492699
20 LUMBER, WOOD PRDTS.	970588	65735	223028	17473	25152	8291	0	9554579
21 WOODEN CONTAINERS	9227	967	11142	75	0	0	0	378932
22 HOUSEHOLD FURNITURE	27878	7595	49927	67	0	6136	0	3965211
23 OTHER FURNITURE	12019	4721	39671	0	0	3382	0	1788205
24 PAPER, ALLIED PRDTS.	651878	24971	1021542	0	0	7227	0	11629051
25 PAPERBOARD CONTAINERS	60790	12920	168487	0	0	3858	0	4597296
26 PRINTING, PUBLISHING	124311	50987	359921	8572	3901	24237	0	16083476
27 CHEMICALS,SELECT. PRDTS.	220572	1202407	70938	1291	0	19080	0	14316680
28 PLASTICS, SYNTHETICS	17795	312745	22091	0	0	0	0	5501364
29 DRUGS, COSMETICS	5162	8092	159281	0	0	1599	0	8439910
30 PAINT, ALLIED PRDTS.	15808	1723	42483	0	0	0	0	2369505
31 PETROLEUM, RELATED INDS.	222594	68311	56105	368411	0	31058	0	20458961
32 RUBBER, MISC. PLASTICS	10539	6358	178969	110	0	884	0	9125828
33 LEATHER TANNING, PRDTS.	821	12971	122044	0	0	0	0	898144
34 FOOTWEAR, LEATHER PRDTS.	2931	4195	143239	0	0	1794	0	3352036
35 GLASS, GLASS PRDTS.	7463	245169	4135	0	0	495	0	2798138
36 STONE, CLAY PRDTS.	113870	79406	169375	20015	6062	26257	0	9164492
37 PRIMARY IRON, STEEL MFR.	51271	524857	383900	0	0	5438	0	23353859
38 PRIMARY NONFERROUS MFR.	458073	225092	149896	407	0	59	0	12742006

#	Industry							
39	METAL CONTAINERS	48798	15165	96704	0	0	0	20433	2369319
40	FABRICATED METAL PRDTS.	80836	67789	287849	729	0	0	5856	8218062
41	SCREW MACH. PRDTS., ETC.	6642	18501	225474	542	0	0	0	4420132
42	OTHER FAB. METAL PRDTS.	21003	57819	125074	618	0	0	1198	7406011
43	ENGINES, TURBINES	304	0	396876	0	0	0	0	2063858
44	FARM MACH. EQUIP.	7094	8946	288532	756	0	0	658	2812754
45	CONSTRUC. MACH., EQUIP.	25382	42186	346538	0	0	0	0	3672836
46	MATERIAL HANDLING MACH.	22276	4059	31998	0	0	0	127	1376976
47	METALWORKING MACHINERY	7395	15731	161410	0	0	0	195	4439358
48	SPECIAL MACH., EQUIP.	25096	2376	207314	0	0	0	4536	3241073
49	GENERAL MACH., EQUIP.	6366	914	240780	127	0	0	127	4615773
50	MACHINE SHOP PRDTS.	24835	9143	49708	1004	0	0	1403	2091509
51	OFFICE, COMPUT. MACHINES	5223	0	9482	0	0	0	0	3688446
52	SERVICE IND. MACHINES	8481	4113	119789	0	0	0	258	2779971
53	ELECT. TRANSMISS. EQUIP.	16893	22155	465130	499	0	0	132	5785838
54	HOUSEHOLD APPLIANCES	6983	1576	167782	0	0	0	0	4177433
55	ELECTRIC LIGHTING EQUIP.	11416	77662	24387	93	0	0	253	2798180
56	RADIO, TV, ETC., EQUIP.	15013	505	188834	0	0	0	240	11573385
57	ELECTRONIC COMPONENTS	2341	7805	33699	0	0	0	56	3845834
58	MISC. ELECTRICAL MACH.	1933		88435	0	0	0	0	1939165
59	MOTOR VEHICLES, EQUIP.	66178	26647	2349946	0	0	0	901	39319165
60	AIRCRAFT, PARTS	486939	121	5707	1828	0	0	0	13630173
61	OTHER TRANSPORT. EQUIP.	220508	42762	115301	89	0	0	1453	4667627
62	PROFESS., SCIEN. INSTRU.	2203	11241	114934	1257	0	0	0	3683490
63	MEDICAL, PHOTO. EQUIP.	1942	3707	4565	0	0	0	110	2286962
64	MISC. MANUFACTURING	27561	10857	135467	78	0	0	2557	6418348
65	TRANSPORT., WAREHOUSING	728530	316289	575765	103638	109953	0	185376	37162424
66	COMMUNICA.,EXC. BRDCAST.	228267	97412	21171	19939	5745	0	48447	13494968
67	RADIO, TV BROADCASTING	28029	13869	3852	3347	3338	0	7473	2307967
68	ELEC.,GAS,WATER,SAN.SER.	186739	394060	532895	97124	15677	0	58592	25027807
69	WHOLESALE, RETAIL TRADE	1869341	685138	2252259	172890	117039	0	334316	16384716
70	FINANCE, INSURANCE	427885	144700	555673	32852	24631	0	130435	33578817
71	REAL ESTATE, RENTAL	1375247	393234	1392517	108288	60317	0	391754	75594261
72	HOTELS, PERSONAL SERV.	219631	94002	279477	41362	19506	0	74310	15367860
73	BUSINESS SERVICES	273128	112694	344251	19730	24594	0	75174	25530613
74	RESEARCH, DEVELOPMENT								
75	AUTO. REPAIR, SERVICES	187313	62536	206318	21622	8815	0	36722	10717429
76	AMUSEMENTS	78544	47337	82200	8984	6640	0	22550	7680102
77	MED.,EDUC. SERVICES	365117	164225	289838	18735	18607	0	119496	33159869
78	FEDERAL GOVT. ENTERPRISE	150087	30507	80047	9122	53063	120588	60064	5864000
79	STATE, LOCAL GOVT. ENT.	323928	55536	67792	14506	13428	0	16278	7236000
80	IMPORTS	0	0	0	0	0	0	0	0
81	BUS.TRAVEL, ENT., GIFTS.	0	0	0	0	0	0	0	0
82	OFFICE SUPPLIES	0	0	0	0	0	0	0	0
83	SCRAP, USED GOODS	0	0	0	0	0	0	0	0
84	GOVERNMENT INDUSTRY	1157883	263669	829711	123142	287290	2456000	537477	55029532
85	REST OF WORLD INDUSTRY	-42252	-10387	-30760	-4626	-5212	5284000*	-7239	3259001*
86	HOUSEHOLD INDUSTRY	45668	19738	46432	4550	3287	0	13025	3823999
87	INVENTORY VALUATION ADJ.						-502000		-502000
88	STATE TOTAL	15652423	8026424	23883294	2354808	1169905	7358588	3634051	1063356523

*These figures exclude the value of secondary production. They therefore differ from those obtained by adding the corresponding values of final demand given in Appendix C of Volume I of this series. (See page 152)

TABLE C-4

STATE ESTIMATES OF 1947 EMPLOYMENT
(NUMBER OF EMPLOYEES)

INDUSTRY TITLE	1 ALABAMA	2 ARIZONA	3 ARKANSAS	4 CALIFORNIA	5 COLORADO	6 CONNECTICUT	7 DELAWARE	8 DISTRICT OF COLUMBIA	9 FLORIDA
1 LIVESTOCK, PRDTS.	20208	4330	30488	38189	8412	5385	3871	0	8718
2 OTHER AGRICULTURE PRDTS.	39792	11670	67512	122811	15588	4615	2129	0	21282
3 FORESTRY, FISHERIES	1540	11	909	9265	85	449	812	0	3587
4 AGRI.+FORES.+FISH. SERV.	2300	1004	3117	7392	978	1057	1183	0	979
5 IRON, FERRO. ORES MINING	1354	3	12	73	10	0	0	0	0
6 NONFERROUS ORES MINING	0	12819	512	7661	2160	0	0	0	388
7 COAL MINING	21908	0	1919	0	6045	0	0	0	0
8 CRUDE PETRO.,NATURAL GAS	13	0	2310	17488	1102	0	0	0	83
9 STONE, CLAY MINING	2252	252	234	3835	340	377	72	0	1212
10 CHEM.+FERT. MIN. MINING	0	14	777	405	83	0	0	0	1949
11 NEW CONSTRUCTION	19973	10580	14016	170122	12555	23964	4874	14938	47438
12 MAINT.+ REPAIR CONSTR.	7894	4211	4718	63455	7691	12746	3140	5937	17151
13 ORDNANCE, ACCESSORIES	10	1	1	132	111	9730	3	3	0
14 FOOD, KINDRED PRDTS.	13169	3690	11355	123197	15161	8314	5926	5146	20133
15 TOBACCO MANUFACTURES	693	0	345	894	9	520	145	0	8720
16 FABRICS	39589	2	982	1720	284	25317	797	2	12
17 TEXTILE PRDTS.	6435	0	292	1810	42	5850	273	1	68
18 APPAREL	11201	164	2619	40248	1314	22646	2000	732	2083
19 MISC. TEXTILE PRDTS.	1764	40	45	5154	330	1884	25	211	382
20 LUMBER, WOOD PRDTS.	36131	2321	25931	35256	2087	1092	631	115	12030
21 WOODEN CONTAINERS	1258	138	2127	3430	225	490	660	31	3699
22 HOUSEHOLD FURNITURE	1306	178	3012	13428	305	1283	21	31	1476
23 OTHER FURNITURE	306	87	126	4620	386	806	20	105	509
24 PAPER, ALLIED PRDTS.	5067	136	2577	6494	263	4780	549	299	4839
25 PAPERBOARD CONTAINERS	213	37	148	5470	386	3693	473	489	855
26 PRINTING, PUBLISHING	3805	1573	2254	41993	4696	11099	782	9864	6317
27 CHEMICALS,SELECT. PRDTS.	5958	216	2452	12536	1012	2731	1941	20	3957
28 PLASTICS, SYNTHETICS	0	0	2267	754	167	1293	3828	0	581
29 DRUGS, COSMETICS	118	39	39	6833	281	3167	44	104	163
30 PAINT, ALLIED PRDTS.	189	33	15	4565	281	586	16	30	155
31 PETROLEUM, RELATED INDS.	308	82	1189	21344	295	117	137	1	156
32 RUBBER, MISC. PLASTICS	4713	5	503	16709	877	16861	1571	30	780
33 LEATHER TANNING. PRDTS.	0	0	0	1304	9	295	2722	0	180
34 FOOTWEAR, LEATHER PRDTS.	347	46	1320	4479	1107	1320	0	0	203
35 GLASS, GLASS PRDTS.	42	9	1024	5279	393	1740	0	0	37
36 STONE, CLAY PRDTS.	6262	911	1703	21485	2147	4180	301	273	2991
37 PRIMARY IRON, STEEL MFR.	38570	262	279	23951	4698	11613	1343	1	224
38 PRIMARY NONFERROUS MFR.	4570	4028	2186	9497	1021	27619	14	0	98

170

Industry									
39 METAL CONTAINERS	186	0	203	6329	149	97	68	0	713
40 FABRICATED METAL PRDTS.	5380	663	391	25149	1552	6870	646	385	1341
41 SCREW MACH. PRDTS., ETC.	864	1	12	5721	25	13331	839	144	33
42 OTHER FAB. METAL PRDTS.	2729	93	538	15107	747	33394	507	0	622
43 ENGINES, TURBINES	6	1	0	4216	41	867	19	0	6
44 FARM MACH., EQUIP.	891	17	605	4115	365	467		0	294
45 CONSTRUC. MACH., EQUIP.	505	0	254	7906	1662	1028		0	193
46 MATERIAL HANDLING MACH.	135	23	118	895	265	357		2	23
47 METALWORKING MACHINERY	41	46	0	2996	42	17255		7	23
48 SPECIAL MACH., EQUIP.	920	0	185	8018	1143	7092	1078	81	579
49 GENERAL MACH., EQUIP.	804	96	96	7935	481	23747	2104	10	369
50 MACHINE SHOP PRDTS.	198	41	38	3549	210	1555	122	9	106
51 OFFICE, COMPUT. MACHINES	9	0	0	3601	68	17836	117	0	11
52 SERVICE IND. MACHINES	142	145	69	2860	60	1072	0	0	4
53 ELECT. TRANSMISS. EQUIP.	350	0	0	6543	149	5250	39	0	105
54 HOUSEHOLD APPLIANCES	820	144	62	7548	32	13915	22	2	39
55 ELECTRIC LIGHTING EQUIP.	402	13	14	4296	94	8604	47	139	66
56 RADIO, TV, ETC., EQUIP.	546	29	0	4135	326	6172	1	32	73
57 ELECTRONIC COMPONENTS	135	7	0	958	7	1485	0	33	18
58 MISC. ELECTRICAL MACH.	32	0	0	1427	61	1434	0	20	467
59 MOTOR VEHICLES, EQUIP.	635	364	126	15007	355	2911	284	1	717
60 AIRCRAFT, PARTS	0	25	0	82737	50	24110	90	0	90
61 OTHER TRANSPORT. EQUIP.	6280	175	188	21144	825	2811	892	150	5308
62 PROFESS., SCIEN. INSTRU.	89	70	339	5530	141	16830	97	12	125
63 MEDICAL, PHOTO. EQUIP.	1	1	2	1575	227	620	12	189	47
64 MISC. MANUFACTURING	613	101	833	10644	1553	23946	722		1250
65 TRANSPORT., WAREHOUSING	53167	14205	21457	240403	29192	27821	10345	19339	51393
66 COMMUNICA.,EXC. BRDCAST.	5721	2824	3877	61038	7553	10037	883	8371	10426
67 RADIO, TV BROADCASTING	758	390	355	3665	379	546	75	749	899
68 ELEC.,GAS,WATER,SAN.SER.	6422	3317	3743	36100	4407	6976	761	4357	5806
69 WHOLESALE, RETAIL TRADE	119443	40907	69523	755343	93665	125623	21725	89325	182304
70 FINANCE, INSURANCE	14157	3828	5467	121064	10273	34242	3850	9895	15762
71 REAL ESTATE, RENTAL	3779	2286	1996	28886	5410	3910	1168	12076	12428
72 HOTELS, PERSONAL SERV.	20727	8673	12519	105774	13325	16735	2636	20840	39276
73 BUSINESS SERVICES	3323	1225	1561	43108	3439	4904	656	5788	7492
74 RESEARCH, DEVELOPMENT	229	18	16	3320	78	163	93	127	175
75 AUTO. REPAIR, SERVICES	2321	647	1064	14587	1855	2241	320	1600	3690
76 AMUSEMENTS	4349	2109	3024	78818	4846	6284	893	3889	11063
77 MED.,EDUC. SERVICES	20562	8958	11638	236912	17201	26540	3048	34402	29086
78 FEDERAL GOVT. ENTERPRISE	10190	1787	4857	36777	4472	6360	898	7834	6679
79 STATE, LOCAL GOVT. ENT.	1384	634	349	28985	1276	751	190	1115	3363
80 IMPORTS	0	0	0	0	0	0	0	0	0
81 BUS.TRAVEL, ENT., GIFTS.	0	0	0	0	0	0	0	0	0
82 OFFICE SUPPLIES	0	0	0	0	0	0	0	0	0
83 SCRAP, USED GOODS	0	0	0	0	0	0	0	0	0
84 GOVERNMENT INDUSTRY	87835	34432	44300	613821	71063	60271	8803	207056	145927
85 REST OF WORLD INDUSTRY	0	0	0	0	0	0	0	0	0
86 HOUSEHOLD INDUSTRY	72822	9038	25335	127724	11743	24271	6781	24067	73647
87 INVENTORY VALUATION ADJ.	0	0	0	0	0	0	0	0	0
88 STATE TOTAL	749180	196129	406470	3649544	383462	808350	111121	490409	785474

TABLE C-4

STATE ESTIMATES OF 1947 EMPLOYMENT
(NUMBER OF EMPLOYEES)

INDUSTRY TITLE	10 GEORGIA	11 IDAHO	12 ILLINOIS	13 INDIANA	14 IOWA	15 KANSAS	16 KENTUCKY	17 LOUISIANA	18 MAINE
1 LIVESTOCK, PRDTS.	24933	6571	15762	22190	26406	10806	32964	21099	4926
2 OTHER AGRICULTURE PRDTS.	52067	14429	37238	23810	25594	21194	44036	40901	10074
3 FORESTRY, FISHERIES	498	85	281	178	131	75	777	4419	2927
4 AGRI.,FORES.,FISH. SERV.	3174	706	4984	3937	4957	2304	1000	1527	531
5 IRON, FERRO. ORES MINING	51	7	0	0	0	0	0	0	0
6 NONFERROUS ORES MINING	211	5116	90	0	0	1730	1	0	0
7 COAL MINING	89	0	31182	10184	1644	1103	60835	0	0
8 CRUDE PETRO.,NATURAL GAS	0	0	5960	749	0	8261	2728	809	0
9 STONE, CLAY MINING	5917	226	3052	2707	1398	879	1527	437	621
10 CHEM.,FERT. MIN. MINING	28	292	1007	340	426	426	198	2521	0
11 NEW CONSTRUCTION	32277	5173	95275	38340	22392	23571	19186	32636	8980
12 MAINT., REPAIR CONSTR.	12381	3345	51202	21974	13040	10467	8417	12370	5086
13 ORDNANCE, ACCESSORIES	10	2266	752	293	24	1	0	0	0
14 FOOD, KINDRED PRDTS.	28954	6018	143382	44817	47592	28182	24905	29688	8761
15 TOBACCO MANUFACTURES	686	0	491	1452	11	0	9048	784	16
16 FABRICS	81943	0	3362	1264	268	13	2961	528	23929
17 TEXTILE PRDTS.	10861	0	4811	768	5	7	257	306	1782
18 APPAREL	28327	0	56238	18652	4787	1460	12751	5459	2427
19 MISC. TEXTILE PRDTS.	5994	29	6911	1298	732	585	716	1316	1506
20 LUMBER, WOOD PRDTS.	30739	7533	9983	8186	4439	772	9425	26437	10509
21 WOODEN CONTAINERS	3223	102	3158	1004	257	188	2288	2632	1654
22 HOUSEHOLD FURNITURE	4916	37	19902	18473	1322	750	6736	1156	263
23 OTHER FURNITURE	668	40	9071	2383	833	288	342	185	307
24 PAPER, ALLIED PRDTS.	4086	1	16447	4537	651	469	483	12640	16190
25 PAPERBOARD CONTAINERS	1469	37	12827	4414	704	693	795	1759	191
26 PRINTING, PUBLISHING	6265	957	91693	15721	9622	5656	6168	4014	2003
27 CHEMICALS,SELECT. PRDTS.	5529	172	16742	3210	725	2750	1244	9463	596
28 PLASTICS, SYNTHETICS	2267	0	1900	273	172	0	1774	1995	39
29 DRUGS, COSMETICS	764	40	15906	14521	1675	1370	123	211	35
30 PAINT, ALLIED PRDTS.	362	1	7157	1238	376	36	1467	382	39
31 PETROLEUM, RELATED INDS.	438	56	15108	12684	95	4610	1004	12678	52
32 RUBBER, MISC. PLASTICS	1222	0	11689	12460	2992	1204	2627	21	242
33 LEATHER TANNING, PRDTS.	296	0	5118	401	0	0	312	34	672
34 FOOTWEAR, LEATHER PRDTS.	2182	28	23667	2224	768	137	3270	158	15047
35 GLASS, GLASS PRDTS.	24	0	10772	10926	109	5	219	631	87
36 STONE, CLAY PRDTS.	7252	442	19749	11420	4879	3543	3904	2424	560
37 PRIMARY IRON, STEEL MFR.	2671	49	80806	76933	2968	1021	6328	647	245
38 PRIMARY NONFERROUS MFR.	589	1111	26985	10698	467	483	3966	450	134

Industry									
39 METAL CONTAINERS	74	0	13462	937	195	0	50	763	195
40 FABRICATED METAL PRDTS.	2074	136	23495	14839	3404	2757	9410	2298	703
41 SCREW MACH. PRDTS., ETC.	605	3	30162	7976	287	123	525	223	33
42 OTHER FAB. METAL PRDTS.	520	0	51640	10092	2162	251	2727	160	729
43 ENGINES, TURBINES	0	235	10480	8223	189	55	0	0	0
44 FARM MACH., EQUIP.	1464	48	60577	9689	14348	1334	1577	341	40
45 CONSTRUC. MACH., EQUIP.	897	3	20820	3630	6760	1591	498	467	127
46 MATERIAL HANDLING MACH.	435	1	4840	674	611	193	460	19	22
47 METALWORKING MACHINERY	94	56	24856	5632	1378	203	453	40	47
48 SPECIAL MACH., EQUIP.	2195	16	18204	4328	2131	764	558	585	6286
49 GENERAL MACH., EQUIP.	269	0	18353	12975	1487	131	1091	138	10
50 MACHINE SHOP PRDTS.	35	0	5018	5106	756	381	393	148	39
51 OFFICE, COMPUT. MACHINES	17	0	7904	248	15	0	79	0	9
52 SERVICE IND. MACHINES	340	0	8803	14830	321	184	478	68	22
53 ELECT. TRANSMISS. EQUIP.	777	0	18791	16257	1427	216	242	49	0
54 HOUSEHOLD APPLIANCES	568	0	33535	14157	5712	1012	1007	0	68
55 ELECTRIC LIGHTING EQUIP.	56	0	15055	7021	164	308	722	0	54
56 RADIO, TV, ETC., EQUIP.	843	0	74125	15421	1617	72	34	34	0
57 ELECTRONIC COMPONENTS	135	0	8476	5277	312	34	9	146	0
58 MISC. ELECTRICAL MACH.	477	0	6139	14430	1462	17	1735	0	0
59 MOTOR VEHICLES, EQUIP.	2787	19	19097	57522	920	272	439	1	16
60 AIRCRAFT, PARTS	1	0	1995	8981	1044	2895	2389	8868	13
61 OTHER TRANSPORT. EQUIP.	942	89	27835	11062	1092	6241	1	47	1
62 PROFESS., SCIEN. INSTRU.	195	1	22931	2874	191	1018	1493	12	3485
63 MEDICAL, PHOTO. EQUIP.	2	34	7984	325	309	169	567	74	165
64 MISC. MANUFACTURING	1647	152	33066	9184	5570	3	2	915	74
65 TRANSPORT., WAREHOUSING	54016	11870	248217	80840	47000	738	1469	61333	1680
66 COMMUNICA.,EXC. BRDCAST.	11557	2119	52828	15483	10398	48550	49649	7860	13292
67 RADIO, TV BROADCASTING	1430	283	1796	771	1034	8278	5557	814	4149
68 ELEC.,GAS,WATER,SAN.SER.	9169	1794	30861	11297	7026	589	644	9156	366
69 WHOLESALE, RETAIL TRADE	168074	35320	680088	239073	162635	6947	6522	134845	2925
70 FINANCE, INSURANCE	20646	2557	100061	26043	18782	110755	114579	15060	47878
71 REAL ESTATE, RENTAL	4327	912	62589	7645	4914	9880	11358	3534	4834
72 HOTELS, PERSONAL SERV.	29503	4476	96749	29626	16082	2778	2589	19599	1811
73 BUSINESS SERVICES	5955	804	43137	6642	4606	12901	18144	6140	6442
74 RESEARCH, DEVELOPMENT	36	22	1289	63	56	3336	2842	91	1048
75 AUTO. REPAIR, SERVICES	3400	343	9143	3714	1989	37	29	2277	66
76 AMUSEMENTS	6205	2001	35514	10942	7779	1663	2051	6957	852
77 MED.,EDUC. SERVICES	22510	7612	126642	49259	30660	5264	5524	20090	2216
78 FEDERAL GOVT. ENTERPRISE	7832	1627	38199	11266	8747	16005	16809	5225	5795
79 STATE, LOCAL GOVT. ENT.	2112	142	5246	1958	1294	7110	7732	1997	3390
80 IMPORTS	0	0	0	0	0	470	857	0	309
81 BUS.TRAVEL, ENT., GIFTS.	0	0	0	0	0	0	0	0	0
82 OFFICE SUPPLIES	0	0	0	0	0	0	0	0	0
83 SCRAP, USED GOODS	0	0	0	0	0	0	0	0	0
84 GOVERNMENT INDUSTRY	139803	22501	280240	113895	80313	85111	90986	93161	37292
85 REST OF WORLD INDUSTRY	0	0	0	0	0	0	0	0	0
86 HOUSEHOLD INDUSTRY	98595	4440	75388	35800	23055	17143	31992	59104	10103
87 INVENTORY VALUATION ADJ.	0	0	0	0	0	0	0	0	0
88 STATE TOTAL	965982	154486	3316290	1310326	662269	492784	671045	703292	276949

TABLE C-4

STATE ESTIMATES OF 1947 EMPLOYMENT
(NUMBER OF EMPLOYEES)

INDUSTRY TITLE	19 MARYLAND	20 MASSA- CHUSETTS	21 MICHIGAN	22 MINNESOTA	23 MISSISSIPPI	24 MISSOURI	25 MONTANA	26 NEBRASKA	27 NEVADA
1 LIVESTOCK, PRDTS.	9314	8226	21074	43686	28280	35162	6157	10373	2100
2 OTHER AGRICULTURE PRDTS.	9686	6774	21926	10314	72720	19838	10843	18627	900
3 FORESTRY, FISHERIES	1395	5950	1541	447	1003	643	193	88	7
4 AGRI.+FORES.+FISH. SERV.	1921	967	1983	3768	3476	4537	537	2053	84
5 IRON, FERRO. ORES MINING	0	0	5640	13285	0	91	344	0	275
6 NONFERROUS ORES MINING	0	0	1075	0	0	6125	5416	0	1183
7 COAL MINING	1854	0	124	0	0	2071	1175	0	0
8 CRUDE PETRO.,NATURAL GAS	0	363	2568	0	1604	170	600	6	0
9 STONE, CLAY MINING	1003	0	3002	989	130	3701	228	409	448
10 CHEM.+FERT. MIN. MINING	0	1482	311	0	0	280	205	0	60
11 NEW CONSTRUCTION	36233	48472	57768	27691	17234	36972	5419	11293	3295
12 MAINT.+ REPAIR CONSTR.	15857	19024	24602	12951	5967	20837	3449	7622	1683
13 ORDNANCE, ACCESSORIES	61	3102	155	518	7	7	0	7	0
14 FOOD, KINDRED PRDTS.	32820	45209	48333	47839	10446	51335	4167	25844	621
15 TOBACCO MANUFACTURES	186	885	906	22	0	1645	0	0	0
16 FABRICS	3193	105152	1322	849	2922	639	0	21	0
17 TEXTILE PRDTS.	743	14082	2991	851	411	542	0	31	0
18 APPAREL	23584	49692	8967	10775	12356	34978	12	798	0
19 MISC. TEXTILE PRDTS.	1534	6011	2570	1246	80	3730	0	450	11
20 LUMBER, WOOD PRDTS.	3278	5332	14212	5701	25833	6149	4872	355	420
21 WOODEN CONTAINERS	990	2368	2208	819	2759	1365	0	127	0
22 HOUSEHOLD FURNITURE	1911	7811	12923	2115	1360	4192	22	482	0
23 OTHER FURNITURE	678	3043	6989	687	153	2795	33	516	0
24 PAPER, ALLIED PRDTS.	3407	24899	20258	6664	4774	3975	0	440	53
25 PAPERBOARD CONTAINERS	2081	9821	5426	2130	106	5033	0	226	0
26 PRINTING, PUBLISHING	9913	34912	22102	18547	1665	20450	1278	4070	413
27 CHEMICALS,SELECT. PRDTS.	7223	6388	18330	921	2455	5785	449	287	376
28 PLASTICS, SYNTHETICS	6676	3820	1171					6	0
29 DRUGS, COSMETICS	2220	5808	9213	2187	185	6920	2	1278	0
30 PAINT, ALLIED PRDTS.	773	1694	3796	734	15	2363	0	23	0
31 PETROLEUM, RELATED INDS.	1775	1808	2063	1625	108	2506	571	195	1
32 RUBBER, MISC. PLASTICS	5371	32745	17819	5263	2098	2510	0	743	1
33 LEATHER TANNING, PRDTS.	235	12920	2555	274	27	324	0	138	0
34 FOOTWEAR, LEATHER PRDTS.	2973	58163	1725	1299	1	42227	10	238	4
35 GLASS, GLASS PRDTS.	2214	1763	1439	835	365	2002	4	5	0
36 STONE, CLAY PRDTS.	4519	9688	12946	3190	1373	11865	593	1399	369
37 PRIMARY IRON, STEEL MFR.	25876	16775	80451	5428	281	10589	800	559	1
38 PRIMARY NONFERROUS MFR.	2938	7649	17831	847	0	4552	2845	366	439

#	Industry									
39	METAL CONTAINERS	4948	778	135	509	48	2161	0	188	0
40	FABRICATED METAL PRDTS.	5555	7713	19152	5501	254	9508	215	1035	79
41	SCREW MACH. PRDTS., ETC.	4529	9277	27276	2150	0	2407	0	11	0
42	OTHER FAB. METAL PRDTS.	1566	23659	44822	2285	276	6626	75	351	0
43	ENGINES, TURBINES	13	5890	14677	1343	0	1798	1	41	0
44	FARM MACH., EQUIP.	1087	401	9050	6538	88	1151	22	1447	8
45	CONSTRUC. MACH., EQUIP.	595	276	6032	3820	170	876	48	210	0
46	MATERIAL HANDLING MACH.	158	1016	3122	650	7	158	100	25	3
47	METALWORKING MACHINERY	1551	15373	35624	1658	0	1875	2	115	0
48	SPECIAL MACH., EQUIP.	2638	32185	8379	1991	418	3302	6	45	3
49	GENERAL MACH., EQUIP.	1229	10341	16196	950	234	1942	16	185	1
50	MACHINE SHOP PRDTS.	2135	2155	9274	712	22	2860	0	30	31
51	OFFICE, COMPUT. MACHINES	6	1308	7694	25	0	207	0	0	0
52	SERVICE IND. MACHINES	736	5653	11141	3603	0	2852	14	325	0
53	ELECT. TRANSMISS. EQUIP.	956	25295	10202	7965	33	11026	0	253	0
54	HOUSEHOLD APPLIANCES	1182	5455	18952	4721	0	5634	13	353	0
55	ELECTRIC LIGHTING EQUIP.	411	9578	1493	117	338	3130	0	122	0
56	RADIO, TV, ETC., EQUIP.	6139	11914	4522	3758	0	724	0	1247	0
57	ELECTRONIC COMPONENTS	785	6386	987	148	0	84	0	89	0
58	MISC. ELECTRICAL MACH.	553	2352	2821	920	0	820	0	65	0
59	MOTOR VEHICLES, EQUIP.	3611	4317	376376	2479	469	19965	39	477	20
60	AIRCRAFT, PARTS	16234	4674	1980	1364	0	1345	1	0	0
61	OTHER TRANSPORT. EQUIP.	12711	8749	7691	1769	3011	4920	17	277	0
62	PROFESS., SCIEN. INSTRU.	897	10195	5616	1437	15	1714	34	423	0
63	MEDICAL, PHOTO. EQUIP.	91	6661	1270	478	21	761	1	168	0
64	MISC. MANUFACTURING	3699	30996	11910	4816	321	7867	184	1175	75
65	TRANSPORT., WAREHOUSING	64033	115484	88824	69627	18959	96385	19161	33695	6911
66	COMMUNICA.+EXC. BRDCAST.	9743	26611	27419	11559	4308	18395	1785	6454	833
67	RADIO, TV BROADCASTING	518	1888	1710	929	328	983	255	510	32
68	ELEC.,GAS,WATER,SAN.SER.	8892	16993	21443	7732	3157	12762	2126	1233	580
69	WHOLESALE, RETAIL TRADE	144759	345044	394651	209218	69008	293781	36569	88331	10480
70	FINANCE, INSURANCE	20727	62776		26752	5804	37303	2869	14112	507
71	REAL ESTATE, RENTAL	8590	18259	31396	8795	1080	19210	1320	2770	311
72	HOTELS, PERSONAL SERV.	19577	45682	48479	21103	13205	39647	5020	10520	4118
73	BUSINESS SERVICES	5611	15626	22276	6375	2026	11655	697	2656	422
74	RESEARCH, DEVELOPMENT	343	590	130	194	35	144	7	19	18
75	AUTO. REPAIR, SERVICES	2321	5171	6557	2553	1011	4558	476	1271	222
76	AMUSEMENTS	7067	16752	22537	9773	1561	13369	1548	4295	3740
77	MED.,EDUC. SERVICES	17853	58830	73423	43370	8122	49026	8618	16129	1977
78	FEDERAL GOVT. ENTERPRISE	5687	19540	17631	7910	4210	16614	1758	5193	385
79	STATE, LOCAL GOVT. ENT.	2999	5213	13631	1037	127	3494	102	196	9
80	IMPORTS	0	0	0	0	0	0	0	0	0
81	BUS.TRAVEL, ENT., GIFTS.	0	0	0	0	0	0	0	0	0
82	OFFICE SUPPLIES	0	0	0	0	0	0	0	0	0
83	SCRAP, USED GOODS	0	0	0	0	0	0	0	0	0
84	GOVERNMENT INDUSTRY	113144	179840	179394	96335	71628	125016	26019	55031	12497
85	REST OF WORLD INDUSTRY	0	0	0	0	0	0	0	0	0
86	HOUSEHOLD INDUSTRY	41796	44027	53445	23703	45125	40897	3674	10453	253
87	INVENTORY VALUATION ADJ.	0	0	0	0	0	0	0	0	0
88	STATE TOTAL	772110	1783721	2156759	843169	455607	1236857	163018	350600	56256

TABLE C-4

STATE ESTIMATES OF 1947 EMPLOYMENT
(NUMBER OF EMPLOYEES)

INDUSTRY TITLE	28 NEW HAMPSHIRE	29 NEW JERSEY	30 NEW MEXICO	31 NEW YORK	32 NORTH CAROLINA	33 NORTH DAKOTA	34 OHIO	35 OKLAHOMA	36 OREGON
1 LIVESTOCK, PRDTS.	3261	6726	6029	30688	36575	3658	26520	30507	15597
2 OTHER AGRICULTURE PRDTS.	1739	7274	6971	23312	117425	15342	23480	42493	29403
3 FORESTRY, FISHERIES	335	1630	33	2856	974	10	738	325	1651
4 AGRI.,FORES.,FISH. SERV.	869	1306	625	2278	2711	904	3052	2241	951
5 IRON, FERRO. ORES MINING	0	0	43	1116	90	0	0	0	0
6 NONFERROUS ORES MINING	0	576	2236	1772	425	0	0	1621	52
7 COAL MINING	0	0	1418		0	421	21445	1720	0
8 CRUDE PETRO., NATURAL GAS	0	0	1740	4170	0	1	4927	18146	0
9 STONE, CLAY MINING	73	2278	124	2951	1572	81	5746	1633	2412
10 CHEM.,FERT. MIN. MINING	0	0	1535	669	0	0	0	0	0
11 NEW CONSTRUCTION	4956	55746	12557	145416	35111	2816	83435	27989	20474
12 MAINT., REPAIR CONSTR.	3077	22960	5828	82169	14980	2333	40034	8036	7853
13 ORDNANCE, ACCESSORIES	0	352	0	2962	31	0	130	0	1
14 FOOD, KINDRED PRDTS.	1995	49146	1883	137472	18057	3648	69492	15403	17888
15 TOBACCO MANUFACTURES	539	4870		2208	32074	0	2796	0	1
16 FABRICS	17458	41647	8	33784	149208	68	5798	501	1495
17 TEXTILE PRDTS.	1256	9652		24238	12253	19	3210	65	239
18 APPAREL	3078	71710	105	377704	56015	26	29836	1227	2661
19 MISC. TEXTILE PRDTS.	226	8414	73	39862	7542	6	3800	226	456
20 LUMBER, WOOD PRDTS.	4889	4608	1823	14718	27980	18	7893	2519	50241
21 WOODEN CONTAINERS	1584	1983	32	2882	3035	0	2885	83	1300
22 HOUSEHOLD FURNITURE	1152	4884	120	22773	25945	0	10439	667	2985
23 OTHER FURNITURE	161	2022	23	13772	1896	0	13068	206	497
24 PAPER, ALLIED PRDTS.	4853	12946	1	41125	7475	0	21078	263	4258
25 PAPERBOARD CONTAINERS	242	9018		23930	1543	0	11047	354	320
26 PRINTING, PUBLISHING	2409	20317	744	167090	5292	959	50057	5027	4506
27 CHEMICALS,SELECT. PRDTS.	154	37548	468	26362	2832	80	17253	612	681
28 PLASTICS, SYNTHETICS	74	9223	0	5501	2632	0	3746	0	0
29 DRUGS, COSMETICS	82	26591	0	28606	798	0	8173	79	89
30 PAINT, ALLIED PRDTS.	13	7203		6119	239	33	6638	151	271
31 PETROLEUM, RELATED INDS.	12	15290	289	4757	36	30	5748	7492	250
32 RUBBER, MISC. PLASTICS	889	22673	0	19055	1259	0	91019	2493	268
33 LEATHER TANNING, PRDTS.	1339	3343	0	5194	1291	5	2337	234	27
34 FOOTWEAR, LEATHER PRDTS.	18504	6907	80	64559	404	0	15932		344
35 GLASS, GLASS PRDTS.	0	10504	0	12540	319	0	19689	2898	54
36 STONE, CLAY PRDTS.	639	17675	370	25871	5155	171	40088	1920	1205
37 PRIMARY IRON, STEEL MFR.	651	21366	49	56741	1452	10	162212	1722	4800
38 PRIMARY NONFERROUS MFR.	129	24859	875	27727	1091	0	21826	3092	1084

#	Industry									
39	METAL CONTAINERS	0	4279	0	4635	0	0	6238	203	197
40	FABRICATED METAL PRDTS.	442	9997	268	26879	1999	102	39697	3207	2756
41	SCREW MACH. PRDTS., ETC.	462	5263	0	17368	49	4	38831	142	105
42	OTHER FAB. METAL PRDTS.	549	20941	1	31998	870	46	34111	797	545
43	ENGINES, TURBINES	6	3624	1	9756	3	1	9589	40	0
44	FARM MACH., EQUIP.	16	1151	16	9492	900	69	11899	415	205
45	CONSTRUC. MACH., EQUIP.	442	2714	0	1687	193	0	18886	3823	378
46	MATERIAL HANDLING MACH.	28	3413	0	3359	231	1	5925	79	1019
47	METALWORKING MACHINERY	1183	9125	29	15993	92	1	44870	99	215
48	SPECIAL MACH., EQUIP.	4196	11611	30	28671	2011	1	21998	132	1025
49	GENERAL MACH., EQUIP.	135	16222	1	19692	272	11	32634	825	274
50	MACHINE SHOP PRDTS.	97	2670	0	4420	379	1	4854	142	621
51	OFFICE, COMPUT. MACHINES	0	0	0	26886	9	0	17118	17	84
52	SERVICE IND. MACHINES	19	2756	0	7899	123	446	19265	77	388
53	ELECT. TRANSMISS. EQUIP.	831	16247	0	29974	153	0	46142	175	566
54	HOUSEHOLD APPLIANCES	18	12091	0	12502	127	0	40500	204	25
55	ELECTRIC LIGHTING EQUIP.	33	14735	1	16339	50	1	14879	34	60
56	RADIO, TV, ETC., EQUIP.	0	42661	0	33317	1635	0	9154	0	15
57	ELECTRONIC COMPONENTS	0	11718	0	10090	403	0	1953	0	130
58	MISC. ELECTRICAL MACH.	209	5102	0	9781	222	32	17947	64	420
59	MOTOR VEHICLES, EQUIP.	0	14229	0	41212	793	0	70461	601	0
60	AIRCRAFT, PARTS	11	9617	289	1767	1	0	15244	207	0
61	OTHER TRANSPORT. EQUIP.	14	19012	0	31615	452	5	9947	225	2390
62	PROFESS., SCIEN. INSTRU.	561	13654	1	36231	117	0	8183	468	140
63	MEDICAL, PHOTO. EQUIP.	65	3951	0	50056	10	1	1783	45	107
64	MISC. MANUFACTURING	2176	34082	307	89707	787	75	28560	719	1033
65	TRANSPORT., WAREHOUSING	6186	100493	12599	366638	39352	10528	193197	31855	31481
66	COMMUNICA., EXC. BRDCAST.	2975	27246	1571	94479	6661	1618	29574	8764	7012
67	RADIO, TV BROADCASTING	221	340	242	5335	1387	452	2905	524	557
68	ELEC.,GAS,WATER,SAN.SER.	1983	18110	1515	56318	6772	3099	27009	7203	5305
69	WHOLESALE, RETAIL TRADE	28373	271610	28801	1184711	176810	36206	534633	114138	101284
70	FINANCE, INSURANCE	3653	48411	2041	274855	15692	2548	58528	11659	7493
71	REAL ESTATE, RENTAL	681	15439	956	172350	3734	639	24181	5717	2847
72	HOTELS, PERSONAL SERV.	4163	46485	5932	182769	30621	3465	65833	16765	12394
73	BUSINESS SERVICES	629	12677	921	123100	4233	378	21128	4804	3922
74	RESEARCH, DEVELOPMENT	25	520	62	1389	25	155	337	136	27
75	AUTO. REPAIR, SERVICES	528	5070	538	18526	3090	280	8466	2404	1967
76	AMUSEMENTS	1281	14456	1520	70517	5700	1288	28310	4959	4825
77	MED.,EDUC. SERVICES	6714	43797	4439	213743	15838	4526	93950	21134	25760
78	FEDERAL GOVT. ENTERPRISE	1867	13423	1534	72412	7460	2456	23937	6613	4296
79	STATE, LOCAL GOVT. ENT.	272	2903	103	63030	1166	34	11743	1153	1531
80	IMPORTS	0	0	0	0	0	0	0	0	0
81	BUS.,TRAVEL, ENT., GIFTS.	0	0	0	0	0	0	0	0	0
82	OFFICE SUPPLIES	0	0	0	0	0	0	0	0	0
83	SCRAP, USED GOODS	0	0	0	0	0	0	0	0	0
84	GOVERNMENT INDUSTRY	15783	179483	38154	503654	137430	20076	245613	90507	53721
85	REST OF WORLD INDUSTRY	0	0	0	0	0	0	0	0	0
86	HOUSEHOLD INDUSTRY	5827	8579	881	191981	74347	3407	77506	24712	14752
87	INVENTORY VALUATION ADJ.									
88	STATE TOTAL	169293	1649192	148835	5667986	1117916	122590	2853085	547732	466186

TABLE C-4

STATE ESTIMATES OF 1947 EMPLOYMENT
(NUMBER OF EMPLOYEES)

INDUSTRY TITLE	37 PENNSYL-VANIA	38 RHODE ISLAND	39 SOUTH CAROLINA	40 SOUTH DAKOTA	41 TENNESSEE	42 TEXAS	43 UTAH	44 VERMONT	45 VIRGINIA
1 LIVESTOCK, PRDTS.	37863	625	17546	6183	34960	52972	4702	8286	32760
2 OTHER AGRICULTURE PRDTS.	27137	375	54454	11817	46040	114028	4298	3714	37240
3 FORESTRY, FISHERIES	1148	405	372	14	575	1183	6	187	3458
4 AGRI.,FORES.,FISH. SERV.	2997	112	1679	1260	1842	11157	414	273	1845
5 IRON,FERRO. ORES MINING	2158	0	0	0	417	88	95	0	7
6 NONFERROUS ORES MINING	9	0	0	2145	1241	4	12162	187	953
7 COAL MINING	189223	0	0	73	7750	6	4735	0	17695
8 CRUDE PETRO.,NATURAL GAS	10064	0	0	0	2	56293	8	0	3
9 STONE, CLAY MINING	5921	53	752	2262	2246	2118	519	1251	2724
10 CHEM.,FERT. MIN. MINING	0	0	0	0	789	4699	14	0	0
11 NEW CONSTRUCTION	110462	8350	18691	4357	32611	149879	6991	3699	38273
12 MAINT., REPAIR CONSTR.	45171	2985	6817	3230	12255	50560	3519	2048	16046
13 ORDNANCE, ACCESSORIES	413	4	0	0	0	50	0	4	10
14 FOOD, KINDRED PRDTS.	104095	4634	8649	7192	24633	62828	8058	2281	22267
15 TOBACCO MANUFACTURES	19449	15	1109	0	1941	838		0	16522
16 FABRICS	58504	54660	113092	0	13435	6255		3674	24433
17 TEXTILE PRDTS.	19492	5896	10496	0	1296	1495	4	142	2610
18 APPAREL	186555	2970	8707	0	36799	20112	248	2379	17778
19 MISC. TEXTILE PRDTS.	7731	586	2719	38	2083	2961	1529	68	3124
20 LUMBER, WOOD PRDTS.	13822	440	20244	949	16095	27857	80	4890	20644
21 WOODEN CONTAINERS	2701	184	1478	25	3102	2894	616	608	2488
22 HOUSEHOLD FURNITURE	13137	355	2364	0	7415	3604	47	1321	13415
23 OTHER FURNITURE	4022	351	90	0	258	2183	275	329	327
24 PAPER, ALLIED PRDTS.	22518	643	3924	0	3247	3027	100	2145	9123
25 PAPERBOARD CONTAINERS	12925	1425	1135	52	1785	1946	73	328	1264
26 PRINTING, PUBLISHING	54962	3151	2149	1139	9283	17644	1831	1099	5859
27 CHEMICALS,SELECT. PRDTS.	18372	419	2958	58	7997	13960	532	106	7813
28 PLASTICS, SYNTHETICS	11450	261	2	0	15323	2538	0	153	23026
29 DRUGS, COSMETICS	8456	340	69	40	2612	1300	71	186	1348
30 PAINT, ALLIED PRDTS.	4218	287	71	0	470	957	38	15	246
31 PETROLEUM, RELATED INDS.	18724	357	88	15	446	37412	698	134	148
32 RUBBER, MISC. PLASTICS	20761	6746	437	0	5069	1450	13	1074	1281
33 LEATHER TANNING, PRDTS.	8373	263	20	0	433	223	0	65	846
34 FOOTWEAR, LEATHER PRDTS.	22673	463	46	0	9950	1540	20	267	3999
35 GLASS, GLASS PRDTS.	29962	449	48	0	1086	1310	1	87	719
36 STONE, CLAY PRDTS.	42887	224	2335	377	7205	9342	1147	2124	3905
37 PRIMARY IRON, STEEL MFR.	254797	3572	896	6	7372	6939	5073	623	3610
38 PRIMARY NONFERROUS MFR.	22681	3958	23	0	4119	5139	2025	44	537

39 METAL CONTAINERS	157	0	299	2354	302	0	0	870	5019
40 FABRICATED METAL PRDTS.	3652	389	598	8694	10195	311	392	3045	44188
41 SCREW MACH. PRDTS., ETC.	12	14	4	457	981	0	0	5619	33406
42 OTHER FAB. METAL PRDTS.	1051	372	44	1951	1063	61	62	0	37894
43 ENGINES, TURBINES	66	451	1	117	12	0	1	41	12962
44 FARM MACH., EQUIP.	313	13	34	1649	1169	171	39	23	6606
45 CONSTRUC. MACH., EQUIP.	193	0	373	14116	481	14	0	8776	11037
46 MATERIAL HANDLING MACH.	213	3260	121	122	403	0	39	4935	3830
47 METALWORKING MACHINERY	15	787	31	275	82	20	10	242	16314
48 SPECIAL MACH., EQUIP.	465	22	64	2165	960	54	1167	951	21306
49 GENERAL MACH., EQUIP.	154	89	1	1430	834	11	239	9	20402
50 MACHINE SHOP PRDTS.	141	939	16	680	367	5	10	246	6434
51 OFFICE, COMPUT. MACHINES	6	7	35	15	635	0	0	145	285
52 SERVICE IND. MACHINES	26	101	41	995	368	28	1	159	11327
53 ELECT. TRANSMISS. EQUIP.	756	35	0	510	2984	39	0	1981	48503
54 HOUSEHOLD APPLIANCES	429	213	18	1347	387	34	1	213	18656
55 ELECTRIC LIGHTING EQUIP.	42	52	25	590	322	0	6	52	8351
56 RADIO, TV, ETC., EQUIP.	565	3	25	129	0	0	0	1788	15003
57 ELECTRONIC COMPONENTS	135	9	0	24	330	0	2	134	9924
58 MISC. ELECTRICAL MACH.	149	0	0	735	4109	18	0	0	5473
59 MOTOR VEHICLES, EQUIP.	730	31	39	2508	27	0	253	153	24307
60 AIRCRAFT, PARTS	1	104	0	13565	1590	9	0	894	3911
61 OTHER TRANSPORT. EQUIP.	15915	1	84	5305	1507	20	681	1089	37721
62 PROFESS., SCIEN. INSTRU.	119	638	23	464	13	156	15	898	20687
63 MEDICAL, PHOTO. EQUIP.	1072	6037	1	351	2937	94	27	22460	1848
64 MISC. MANUFACTURING	1537	1895	354	3032	48692	8725	898	9437	28139
65 TRANSPORT., WAREHOUSING	66686	91	17579	174326	8989	2041	17475	167	263150
66 COMMUNICA., EXC. BRDCAST.	9333	1287	2608	29461	1212	278	3342	3444	39916
67 RADIO, TV BROADCASTING	857	19206	467	2721	2439	1339	567	50867	1518
68 ELEC.,GAS,WATER,SAN.SER.	6375	2121	2262	25571	160637	37558	4077	8177	40897
69 WHOLESALE, RETAIL TRADE	165202	241	74439	470699	18681	3430	78992	2309	666500
70 FINANCE, INSURANCE	19893	2800	4235	51496	7727	849	7134	6357	92456
71 REAL ESTATE, RENTAL	7998	310	1725	17668	28454	3451	1002	1794	26149
72 HOTELS, PERSONAL SERV.	28905	18	5649	76390	4646	647	14322	22	79806
73 BUSINESS SERVICES	4172	307	1061	21450	122	19	1801	815	27470
74 RESEARCH, DEVELOPMENT	174	784	17	467	2894	345	54	2462	420
75 AUTO. REPAIR, SERVICES	2859	2421	654	8709	5682	1624	1716	8268	10303
76 AMUSEMENTS	6808	1658	2349	19096	28076	3967	2139	2392	30693
77 MED.,EDUC. SERVICES	28283	173	6624	77248	16811	2669	7851	1163	152749
78 FEDERAL GOVT. ENTERPRISE	8438		1867	18637	6434	129	3837		28321
79 STATE, LOCAL GOVT. ENT.	2579		401	12618			578		5894
80 IMPORTS	0	0	0	0	0	0	0	0	0
81 BUS.TRAVEL, ENT., GIFTS.	0	0	0	0	0	0	0	0	0
82 OFFICE SUPPLIES	0	0	0	0	0	0	0	0	0
83 SCRAP, USED GOODS	0	0	0	0	0	0	0	0	0
84 GOVERNMENT INDUSTRY	242600	11782	39410	338898	89560	26648	73667	45230	320079
85 REST OF WORLD INDUSTRY	0	0	0	0	0	0	0	0	0
86 HOUSEHOLD INDUSTRY	58929	5993	3925	142475	55463	532	53464	6310	102687
87 INVENTORY VALUATION ADJ.	0	0	0	0	0	0	0	0	0
88 STATE TOTAL	1026331	108445	227453	2230301	842768	136528	559322	312840	3758374

TABLE C-4

STATE ESTIMATES OF 1947 EMPLOYMENT
(NUMBER OF EMPLOYEES)

INDUSTRY TITLE	46 WASHINGTON	47 WEST VIRGINIA	48 WISCONSIN	49 WYOMING	50 ALASKA	51 HAWAII	52 NO STATE ALLOCATION	53 NATIONAL TOTAL
1 LIVESTOCK, PRDTS.	15021	20805	39303	5000	0	0	0	885217
2 OTHER AGRICULTURE PRDTS.	39979	9195	15697	3000	0	0	0	1360783
3 FORESTRY, FISHERIES	4014	741	902	12	0	0	0	58865
4 AGRI.,FORES.,FISH. SERV.	1260	414	2262	227	0	0	0	101135
5 IRON, FERRO. ORES MINING	1	0	1619	333	0	0	0	27688
6 NONFERROUS ORES MINING	541	0	211	44	0	0	0	71312
7 COAL MINING	1409	118083	0	4294	0	0	0	508768
8 CRUDE PETRO.,NATURAL GAS	0	5576	0	1710	0	0	0	155091
9 STONE, CLAY MINING	2705	1413	2836	295	0	0	0	78695
10 CHEM.,FERT. MIN. MINING	0	16	0	27	0	0	0	16305
11 NEW CONSTRUCTION	35084	18718	30287	5090	0	0	0	1691659
12 MAINT., REPAIR CONSTR.	10622	5859	14857	2273	0	0	0	740729
13 ORDNANCE, ACCESSORIES	1	0	38	0	0	0	0	2180
14 FOOD, KINDRED PRDTS.	26312	6429	55590	1580	0	0	0	1484536
15 TOBACCO MANUFACTURES	1	863	395	0	0	0	0	111083
16 FABRICS	146	1968	1886	0	0	0	0	825271
17 TEXTILE PRDTS.	90	0	1504	0	0	0	0	147221
18 APPAREL	2257	3685	16104	0	0	0	0	1195481
19 MISC. TEXTILE PRDTS.	633	26	1179	0	0	0	0	126400
20 LUMBER, WOOD PRDTS.	42428	7911	13405	919	0	0	0	574686
21 WOODEN CONTAINERS	623	340	2541	16	0	0	0	68031
22 HOUSEHOLD FURNITURE	2746	769	9397	7	0	0	0	229187
23 OTHER FURNITURE	459	129	1911	0	0	0	0	77798
24 PAPER, ALLIED PRDTS.	11259	947	23891	0	0	0	0	317701
25 PAPERBOARD CONTAINERS	1544	750	4399	0	0	0	0	133556
26 PRINTING, PUBLISHING	6729	3008	16726	492	0	0	0	718305
27 CHEMICALS,SELECT. PRDTS.	1395	15486	2055	181	0	0	0	270790
28 PLASTICS, SYNTHETICS	84	4794	311	0	0	0	0	107934
29 DRUGS, COSMETICS	196	300	2261	0	0	0	0	154729
30 PAINT, ALLIED PRDTS.	327	32	1190	17	0	0	0	54861
31 PETROLEUM, RELATED INDS.	241	812	640	2230	0	0	0	175855
32 RUBBER, MISC. PLASTICS	86	295	4674	4	0	0	0	320602
33 LEATHER TANNING, PRDTS.	11	1136	5521	0	0	0	0	58238
34 FOOTWEAR, LEATHER PRDTS.	419	394	15759	10	0	0	0	325447
35 GLASS, GLASS PRDTS.	460	18171	446	0	0	0	0	138680
36 STONE, CLAY PRDTS.	2971	12067	4411	282	0	0	0	322739
37 PRIMARY IRON, STEEL MFR.	3309	20668	22051	1	0	0	0	971289
38 PRIMARY NONFERROUS MFR.	6421	2675	4957	0	0	0	0	264645

180

#	Description								
39	METAL CONTAINERS	715	845	403	0	0	0	0	57814
40	FABRICATED METAL PRDTS.	2419	3288	17526	73	0	0	0	328447
41	SCREW MACH. PRDTS., ETC.	178	3384	9914	0	0	0	0	220049
42	OTHER FAB. METAL PRDTS.	775	1809	7548	0	0	0	0	349932
43	ENGINES, TURBINES	82	0	18599	0	0	0	0	103158
44	FARM MACH., EQUIP.	512	225	16185	34	0	0	0	167324
45	CONSTRUC. MACH., EQUIP.	1613	1686	15693	12	0	0	0	131754
46	MATERIAL HANDLING MACH.	283	86	1253	0	0	0	0	34716
47	METALWORKING MACHINERY	546	41	10724	1	0	0	0	222067
48	SPECIAL MACH., EQUIP.	1161	244	11896	1	0	0	0	218990
49	GENERAL MACH., EQUIP.	423	81	9461	1	0	0	0	202591
50	MACHINE SHOP PRDTS.	534	147	1894	9	0	0	0	59412
51	OFFICE, COMPUT. MACHINES	18	0	214	0	0	0	0	87400
52	SERVICE IND. MACHINES	104	23	2133	11	0	0	0	100007
53	ELECT. TRANSMISS. EQUIP.	214	218	18792	33	0	0	0	269347
54	HOUSEHOLD APPLIANCES	968	225	7966	14	0	0	0	213923
55	ELECTRIC LIGHTING EQUIP.	163	963	1265	0	0	0	0	111913
56	RADIO, TV, ETC., EQUIP.	357	0	832	0	0	0	0	236331
57	ELECTRONIC COMPONENTS	15	517	200	0	0	0	0	62171
58	MISC. ELECTRICAL MACH.	417	40	4045	0	0	0	0	80723
59	MOTOR VEHICLES, EQUIP.	1618	736	26301	0	0	0	0	702740
60	AIRCRAFT, PARTS	8028	26	600	0	0	0	0	219890
61	OTHER TRANSPORT. EQUIP.	6430	1214	5302	25	0	0	0	270748
62	PROFESS., SCIEN. INSTRU.	144	35	6883	1	0	0	0	161092
63	MEDICAL, PHOTO. EQUIP.	40	61	337	0	0	0	0	81695
64	MISC. MANUFACTURING	1253	1573	8621	30	0	0	0	384327
65	TRANSPORT., WAREHOUSING	54988	37808	55223	14290	0	0	0	3161973
66	COMMUNICA.,EXC. BRDCAST.	11611	4749	15468	1038	0	0	0	650660
67	RADIO, TV BROADCASTING	1014	618	732	99	0	0	0	45000
68	ELEC.,GAS,WATER,SAN.SER.	5727	11965	10667	863	0	0	0	476731
69	WHOLESALE, RETAIL TRADE	152765	86637	214467	16423	0	0	0	9453904
70	FINANCE, INSURANCE	17482	6978	24005	1452	0	0	0	1318133
71	REAL ESTATE, RENTAL	11340	3571	8295	908	0	0	0	571095
72	HOTELS, PERSONAL SERV.	18460	12452	23607	2828	0	0	0	1353286
73	BUSINESS SERVICES	5954	2305	7047	531	0	0	0	464330
74	RESEARCH, DEVELOPMENT	112	88	127	25	0	0	0	11729
75	AUTO. REPAIR, SERVICES	2419	1208	2392	189	0	0	0	153576
76	AMUSEMENTS	8662	4254	11452	930	0	0	0	508112
77	MED.,EDUC. SERVICES	47046	26821	38965	3072	0	0	0	1822389
78	FEDERAL GOVT. ENTERPRISE	8834	4312	10450	855	0	0	0	492989
79	STATE, LOCAL GOVT. ENT.	6790	696	1364	6	0	0	0	200000
80	IMPORTS	0	0	0	0	0	0	0	0
81	BUS.,TRAVEL, ENT., GIFTS	0	0	0	0	0	0	0	0
82	OFFICE SUPPLIES	0	0	0	0	0	0	0	0
83	SCRAP, USED GOODS	0	0	0	0	0	0	0	0
84	GOVERNMENT INDUSTRY	172305	51006	105766	19745	0	0	0	5896831
85	REST OF WORLD INDUSTRY	0	0	0	0	0	0	0	0
86	HOUSEHOLD INDUSTRY	19940	16439	26497	1933	0	0	0	1891000
87	INVENTORY VALUATION ADJ.	0	0	0	0	0	0	0	0
88	STATE TOTAL	796243	573909	1082327	93476	0	0	0	48442791

181

TABLE C-5

STATE ESTIMATES OF 1958 EMPLOYMENT
(NUMBER OF EMPLOYEES)

INDUSTRY TITLE	1 ALABAMA	2 ARIZONA	3 ARKANSAS	4 CALIFORNIA	5 COLORADO	6 CONNECTICUT	7 DELAWARE	8 DISTRICT OF COLUMBIA	9 FLORIDA
1 LIVESTOCK, PRDTS.	18032	10552	33033	65648	8257	6326	2963	0	14150
2 OTHER AGRICULTURE PRDTS.	13968	34874	57967	161352	8743	3917	2037	0	35850
3 FORESTRY, FISHERIES	1754	191	672	13193	115	254	367	0	9667
4 AGRI.,FORES.,FISH. SERV.	2556	1386	1929	9141	1004	2336	856	0	2663
5 IRON, FERRO. ORES MINING	2547	387	241	751	1626	31	0	0	0
6 NONFERROUS ORES MINING	170	13884	655	1033	4173	0	0	0	584
7 COAL MINING	7484	16	252	0	2016	0	0	0	0
8 CRUDE PETRO.,NATURAL GAS	222	10	2110	18461	3871	0	0	0	134
9 STONE, CLAY MINING	1479	536	988	6194	834	847	96	0	2732
10 CHEM.,FERT. MIN. MINING	0	16	342	2715	232	0	11	0	3256
11 NEW CONSTRUCTION	40153	26960	16059	246106	30954	39617	9371	17046	111117
12 MAINT., REPAIR CONSTR.	10490	4216	6337	73587	9664	10941	2323	5270	24110
13 ORDNANCE, ACCESSORIES	1086	5980	5	73653	4378	6561	41	41	3305
14 FOOD, KINDRED PRDTS.	19717	5392	13627	157243	16937	14140	6273	5733	36360
15 TOBACCO MANUFACTURES	425	0	0	14	0	1388	0	0	7635
16 FABRICS	32353	0	1030	1249	0	11200	1582	0	287
17 TEXTILE PRDTS.	1928	0	440	3099	20	2549	394	0	212
18 APPAREL	25817	1430	7458	48711	1100	17553	1184	26	6300
19 MISC. TEXTILE PRDTS.	1492	136	30	8389	306	1994	147	174	882
20 LUMBER, WOOD PRDTS.	23076	2730	19926	48398	2541	948	497	106	11368
21 WOODEN CONTAINERS	697	90	1334	3171	101	415	185	0	2162
22 HOUSEHOLD FURNITURE	2667	456	6155	20225	712	2122	24	75	5704
23 OTHER FURNITURE	259	215	707	7211	635	1409	6	64	1274
24 PAPER, ALLIED PRDTS.	9417	86	3165	12073	62	3048	413	399	11316
25 PAPERBOARD CONTAINERS	401	75	1160	12279	461	4319	166	188	2469
26 PRINTING, PUBLISHING	5077	2795	2907	64196	6797	14141	1238	12148	12709
27 CHEMICALS,SELECT. PRDTS.	5164	527	3036	13960	1227	2848	2352	80	7279
28 PLASTICS, SYNTHETICS	2639	0	0	2581	0	1916	2076	0	6720
29 DRUGS, COSMETICS	255	70	20	10422	155	3820	415	56	572
30 PAINT, ALLIED PRDTS.	271	77	95	5713	373	267	75	25	588
31 PETROLEUM, RELATED INDS.	424	100	1703	20616	792	414	637	0	662
32 RUBBER, MISC. PLASTICS	5782	343	925	23702	5121	15590	1860	58	709
33 LEATHER TANNING, PRDTS.	0	0	0	1158	4	237	1545	0	112
34 FOOTWEAR, LEATHER PRDTS.	787	78	3925	1649	1961	3203	160	0	464
35 GLASS, GLASS PRDTS.	408	10	1001	7073	10	696	10	10	787
36 STONE, CLAY PRDTS.	7040	2092	1632	34083	4020	5263	704	582	11508
37 PRIMARY IRON, STEEL MFR.	32699	264	10	29149	6885	6444	2578	0	473
38 PRIMARY NONFERROUS MFR.	5347	1953	2637	19008	658	19233	205	0	882

#	Industry	1	2	3	4	5	6	7	8	9
39	METAL CONTAINERS	292	0	119	9008	159	7	52	0	1643
40	FABRICATED METAL PRODTS.	7343	1464	875	36549	2511	4668	686	472	113
41	SCREW MACH. PRODTS., ETC.	1298	20	220	11417	130	12159	395	10	359
42	OTHER FAB. METAL PRODTS.	3442	185	1164	27998	1518	26431	794	57	2096
43	ENGINES, TURBINES	0	68	0	4264	0	870	0	0	37
44	FARM MACH., EQUIP.	587	43	46	2880	320	69	47	0	260
45	CONSTRUC. MACH., EQUIP.	318	5	5	7604	1696	81	10	0	113
46	MATERIAL HANDLING MACH.	1034	8	351	3323	320	245	0	0	55
47	METALWORKING MACHINERY	169	366	170	9285	112	14956	270	0	531
48	SPECIAL MACH., EQUIP.	1018	30	50	7328	310	4196	1486	0	469
49	GENERAL MACH., EQUIP.	420	90	237	12689	435	21345	65	9	667
50	MACHINE SHOP PRODTS.	643	515	311	15895	1081	4313	123	9	1266
51	OFFICE, COMPUT. MACHINES	10	750	0	9805	20	12183	10	147	147
52	SERVICE IND. MACHINES	315	1097	122	5521	105	1196	175	10	344
53	ELECT. TRANSMISS. EQUIP.	354	8	1531	22790	1541	6917	7	9	880
54	HOUSEHOLD APPLIANCES	21	0	493	6726	20	6773	52	34	120
55	ELECTRIC LIGHTING EQUIP.	1065	70	562	9665	52	8617	55	16	337
56	RADIO, TV, ETC., EQUIP.	0	1534	410	23304	18	4085	11	8	1272
57	ELECTRONIC COMPONENTS	2099	737	45	19956	121	4566	8	138	1121
58	MISC. ELECTRICAL MACH.	0	44	16	2999	133	817	8	8	1317
59	MOTOR VEHICLES, EQUIP.	1779	70	337	24338	635	2475	5535	0	494
60	AIRCRAFT, PARTS	14131	5000	0	224785	1656	58687	350	20	2275
61	OTHER TRANSPORT. EQUIP.	4744	65	770	15539	329	9589	299	9	6858
62	PROFESS., SCIEN. INSTRU.	100	402	1560	14823	410	16109	439	88	348
63	MEDICAL, PHOTO. EQUIP.	8	0	7	7	15	1171	8	8	308
64	MISC. MANUFACTURING	750	406	1731	17843	1446	16397	727	147	2391
65	TRANSPORT., WAREHOUSING	33905	13523	19412	219105	28429	23228	7545	25017	61192
66	COMMUNICA.,EXC. BRDCAST.	8162	5145	4106	84103	8899	10986	1584	889	21123
67	RADIO, TV BROADCASTING	1287	821	691	1075	956	1050	261	928	2550
68	ELEC.,GAS,WATER+SAN.SER.	6840	4736	3828	47296	5472	8994	792	1298	9273
69	WHOLESALE, RETAIL TRADE	138152	72439	75375	998529	113854	153268	30048	80662	317310
70	FINANCE, INSURANCE	23801	10435	10800	191920	19250	46715	4550	16489	49735
71	REAL ESTATE, RENTAL	4129	1916	1327	41244	3708	4376	835	10819	16210
72	HOTELS, PERSONAL SERV.	21636	13043	12545	139467	16959	19068	3191	19876	67267
73	BUSINESS SERVICES	6814	5424	3215	117719	9706	13182	2055	13771	25080
74	RESEARCH, DEVELOPMENT	623	86	34	11659	278	527	207	380	739
75	AUTO. REPAIR, SERVICES	3773	2302	1722	31119	3500	3736	605	2432	8866
76	AMUSEMENTS	3701	3857	2446	71639	5443	5205	1012	3363	13626
77	MED.,EDUC. SERVICES	34797	16876	17576	290965	34803	65812	8427	46092	67723
78	FEDERAL GOVT. ENTERPRISE	11779	3420	4913	54255	6419	8378	1206	12806	15008
79	STATE, LOCAL GOVT. ENT.	5001	1858	1552	32331	2784	3128	553	1566	8235
80	IMPORTS	0	0	0	0	0	0	0	0	0
81	BUS.TRAVEL, ENT., GIFTS.	0	0	0	0	0	0	0	0	0
82	OFFICE SUPPLIES	0	0	0	0	0	0	0	0	0
83	SCRAP, USED GOODS	0	0	0	0	0	0	0	0	0
84	GOVERNMENT INDUSTRY	155613	71357	71995	1015348	118632	89902	23267	130437	248645
85	REST OF WORLD INDUSTRY	0	0	0	0	0	0	0	0	0
86	HOUSEHOLD INDUSTRY	93350	16362	35711	293313	19435	28185	6957	24166	110314
87	INVENTORY VALUATION ADJ.	0	0	0	0	0	0	0	0	0
88	STATE TOTAL	879386	374504	471895	5425455	540365	930649	147423	434262	1405719

TABLE C-5

STATE ESTIMATES OF 1958 EMPLOYMENT
(NUMBER OF EMPLOYEES)

INDUSTRY TITLE	10 GEORGIA	11 IDAHO	12 ILLINOIS	13 INDIANA	14 IOWA	15 KANSAS	16 KENTUCKY	17 LOUISIANA	18 MAINE
1 LIVESTOCK, PRDTS.	27264	8768	22053	15793	25124	8824	24417	28935	10808
2 OTHER AGRICULTURE PRDTS.	24736	12232	29947	13207	14876	18176	22583	33065	10808
3 FORESTRY, FISHERIES	2588	347	818	285	148	18	950	2804	871
4 AGRI.,FORES.,FISH. SERV.	4430	315	5452	3510	3631	1731	1684	930	466
5 IRON, FERRO. ORES MINING	64	381	0	0	0	0	0	0	7
6 NONFERROUS ORES MINING	40	2986	181	0	0	78	0	0	0
7 COAL MINING	14		11139	4106	424	252	28512	21740	0
8 CRUDE PETRO.,NATURAL GAS	2	8	6279	1179	0	9698	3264	1381	0
9 STONE, CLAY MINING	4948	352	5270	3010	2486	1357	2543	3032	285
10 CHEM.,FERT. MIN. MINING	151	183	830			175	130	175	0
11 NEW CONSTRUCTION	48361	9422	147222	55814	23965	33995	32632	79929	10484
12 MAINT., REPAIR CONSTR.	12050	4125	59182	25218	15399	12510	9150	14777	3165
13 ORDNANCE, ACCESSORIES	152	50	4291	2181	2112	1	1	657	1145
14 FOOD, KINDRED PRDTS.	41300	7781	129029	48012	52567	22954	27999	30545	11483
15 TOBACCO MANUFACTURES	825	0	424	583		0	7992	525	0
16 FABRICS	71140	0	1689	38	169	204	1096	22	12888
17 TEXTILE PRDTS.	14893	0	4770	572	9	11	187	526	508
18 APPAREL	42742	8	38735	12186	2139	2230	1830	4050	2400
19 MISC. TEXTILE PRDTS.	5591	242	7076	1410	988	549	954	1041	400
20 LUMBER, WOOD PRDTS.	23179	10262	10150	8770	4449	644	7675	15850	12693
21 WOODEN CONTAINERS	3307	110	1603	616	210	120	1246	975	304
22 HOUSEHOLD FURNITURE	6059	58	16870	15946	1611	593	4442	1136	432
23 OTHER FURNITURE	852	63	7694	2928	1078	435	320	230	65
24 PAPER, ALLIED PRDTS.	12476	945	15263	5750	386	344	946	13958	16419
25 PAPERBOARD CONTAINERS	4344	80	16478	5401	1235	1674	1070	2601	342
26 PRINTING, PUBLISHING	9497	1309	94445	19940	11229	7727	7864	5151	2047
27 CHEMICALS,SELECT. PRDTS.	5873	2255	17700	5254	1028	3807	4812	13964	597
28 PLASTICS, SYNTHETICS	1551		1607	741	1455		3193	1702	0
29 DRUGS, COSMETICS	1526	10	18314	14346	1485	1863	345	148	20
30 PAINT, ALLIED PRDTS.	843	20	8548	1072	473	105	1530	345	5
31 PETROLEUM, RELATED INDS.	616	9	14140	9933	181	4376	1328	14287	125
32 RUBBER, MISC. PLASTICS	1233	4	22623	17359	4070	1745	992	177	1208
33 LEATHER TANNING, PRDTS.	405	46	3170	226	0	0	172	41	1428
34 FOOTWEAR, LEATHER PRDTS.	3071		16045	2289	312	127	2111	127	20002
35 GLASS, GLASS PRDTS.	665	6	13324	8619	20	128	817	874	0
36 STONE, CLAY PRDTS.	8672	901	24695	18384	5906	5578	4546	5814	889
37 PRIMARY IRON, STEEL MFR.	2368	55	66521	73110	2836	617	6452	1314	92
38 PRIMARY NONFERROUS MFR.	1003	1439	22824	14765	2118	507	1401	2078	237

Sector	1	2	3	4	5	6	7	8	9
39 METAL CONTAINERS	221	0	13174	923	10	172	102	1703	374
40 FABRICATED METAL PRDTS.	4751	120	29554	15096	4281	2792	3222	3705	542
41 SCREW MACH. PRDTS., ETC.	1244	10	33336	8974	1180	167	1432	140	140
42 OTHER FAB. METAL PRDTS.	694	13	51683	14801	3138	898	3386	316	113
43 ENGINES, TURBINES	0	0	8585	3937	1832	0	0	65	69
44 FARM MACH., EQUIP.	1304	237	26730	4850	18888	1953	3486	305	469
45 CONSTRUC. MACH., EQUIP.	759	31	38385	4380	5122	1382	116	929	0
46 MATERIAL HANDLING MACH.	818	8	6780	785	744	394	857	102	155
47 METALWORKING MACHINERY	404	20	26998	7228	1254	376	555	80	2110
48 SPECIAL MACH., EQUIP.	2750	10	14257	2856	1305	648	130	394	30
49 GENERAL MACH., EQUIP.	551	420	19140	12399	662	897	1248	237	332
50 MACHINE SHOP PRDTS.	629	73	8627	5072	510	1341	1643	977	0
51 OFFICE, COMPUT. MACHINES	114	10	6770	148	12	12	2333	0	142
52 SERVICE IND. MACHINES	678	0	8144	4390	618	1447	1784	142	25
53 ELECT. TRANSMISS. EQUIP.	2701	0	25242	16219	1095	11	1401	25	39
54 HOUSEHOLD APPLIANCES	9	0	23518	8666	5015	112	8947	39	54
55 ELECTRIC LIGHTING EQUIP.	435	0	17281	5886	61	53	2012	7	336
56 RADIO, TV, ETC., EQUIP.	11	0	74284	19268	5837	21	392	64	119
57 ELECTRONIC COMPONENTS	120	0	17321	10295	1794	700	1580	35	231
58 MISC. ELECTRICAL MACH.	564	57	4609	15638	764	586	66	49	54
59 MOTOR VEHICLES, EQUIP.	8526	0	22011	45057	1200	3379	3352	458	31
60 AIRCRAFT, PARTS	10000	172	11041	25804	1750	40882	125	0	1516
61 OTHER TRANSPORT. EQUIP.	1525	180	11447	9038	705	702	864	6541	3736
62 PROFESS., SCIEN. INSTRU.	1290	5	22158	2947	1807	192	400	107	108
63 MEDICAL, PHOTO. EQUIP.	24	0	8804	403	79	59	15	120	92
64 MISC. MANUFACTURING	3608	377	30580	7654	4149	704	871	1345	1218
65 TRANSPORT., WAREHOUSING	48127	10281	171419	67013	33328	39154	42380	65673	11970
66 COMMUNICA.,EXC. BRDCAST.	12701	2067	48736	16354	10878	8769	7722	10227	3469
67 RADIO, TV BROADCASTING	1749	423	4250	1694	1528	1020	1145	1407	739
68 ELEC.,GAS,WATER,SAN.SER.	10021	1930	36343	15424	9686	8818	8450	11635	2074
69 WHOLESALE, RETAIL TRADE	207937	39511	699066	269631	163745	120690	132482	169483	52149
70 FINANCE, INSURANCE	37449	4924	145301	47176	26093	19874	21016	27378	7740
71 REAL ESTATE, RENTAL	4963	607	48660	6708	3547	2552	3282	5339	1323
72 HOTELS, PERSONAL SERV.	31682	4753	99520	32847	17076	14980	19168	24946	9466
73 BUSINESS SERVICES	14062	1732	82607	12783	7628	6120	6800	13762	1901
74 RESEARCH, DEVELOPMENT	97	23	4477	172	117	85	265		161
75 AUTO. REPAIR, SERVICES	5590	714	13221	5724	3160	2691	3043	3969	1431
76 AMUSEMENTS	5605	1431	25291	9373	6033	4685	4820	5882	1661
77 MED.,EDUC. SERVICES	39746	8693	215667	73013	48138	33011	36658	39843	15622
78 FEDERAL GOVT. ENTERPRISE	11341	1950	41350	12106	8504	8476	7222	8798	3713
79 STATE, LOCAL GOVT. ENT.	6167	702	26028	6274	3989	3174	6072	2706	1497
80 IMPORTS	0	0	0	0	0	0	0	0	0
81 BUS.TRAVEL, ENT., GIFTS.	0	0	0	0	0	0	0	0	0
82 OFFICE SUPPLIES	0	0	0	0	0	0	0	0	0
83 SCRAP, USED GOODS	0	0	0	0	0	0	0	0	0
84 GOVERNMENT INDUSTRY	224673	33381	376225	165629	100671	130816	134529	143746	56641
85 REST OF WORLD INDUSTRY	121318	7668	83784	46920	30099	24922	37316	86017	12537
86 HOUSEHOLD INDUSTRY	0	0	0	0	0	0	0	0	0
87 INVENTORY VALUATION ADJ.	0	0	0	0	0	0	0	0	0
88 STATE TOTAL	1215789	187317	3548805	1454108	722151	632854	747565	942297	318406

TABLE C-5

STATE ESTIMATES OF 1958 EMPLOYMENT
(NUMBER OF EMPLOYEES)

INDUSTRY TITLE	19 MARYLAND	20 MASSA-CHUSETTS	21 MICHIGAN	22 MINNESOTA	23 MISSISSIPPI	24 MISSOURI	25 MONTANA	26 NEBRASKA	27 NEVADA
1 LIVESTOCK, PRDTS.	11911	11246	19765	21848	27996	27890	6661	9780	1655
2 OTHER AGRICULTURE PRDTS.	9089	6963	22235	17152	31004	19110	7339	14220	451
3 FORESTRY, FISHERIES	1598	4896	1298	607	591	622	123	17	31
4 AGRI.,FORES.,FISH. SERV.	2129	808	2263	3365	1052	4405	185	1900	228
5 IRON, FERRO. ORES MINING	14	0	6214	15043	0	483	996	0	425
6 NONFERROUS ORES MINING	2	0	2746	118	0	2906	4375	5	1995
7 COAL MINING	560	0	0	0		1204	179	0	0
8 CRUDE PETRO.,NATURAL GAS	23	0	1061		2128	150	1628	902	5
9 STONE, CLAY MINING	1610	998	4052	1970	850	3241	403	993	583
10 CHEM.,FERT. MIN. MINING			447			305	363		55
11 NEW CONSTRUCTION	53296	61083	74902	43937	21958	56299	8890	14300	5189
12 MAINT., REPAIR CONSTR.	14186	18768	29553	15251	7748	19423	4132	8137	1966
13 ORDNANCE, ACCESSORIES	4231	10448	11169	4579		9411	0	654	0
14 FOOD, KINDRED PRDTS.	35609	49006	57744	51377	12988	52539	3940	26495	812
15 TOBACCO MANUFACTURES	150	303	591	10		259	0	0	0
16 FABRICS	2359	36113	250	325	911	951	0	10	0
17 TEXTILE PRDTS.	125	11175	1560	534	879	878	35	10	0
18 APPAREL	19955	57961	4468	8041	25754	29769	8	667	2
19 MISC. TEXTILE PRDTS.	2234	7295	6510	1557	1000	2866	20	100	10
20 LUMBER, WOOD PRDTS.	4022	4886	10662	6778	17206	6243	6553	418	302
21 WOODEN CONTAINERS	794	1014	785	407	2429	689	45	65	0
22 HOUSEHOLD FURNITURE	2224	9079	8914	1585	4681	3398	33	580	30
23 OTHER FURNITURE	2617	1704	9118	885	265	2358	7	508	56
24 PAPER, ALLIED PRDTS.	3697	25107	17881	9322	6850	6035	71	517	10
25 PAPERBOARD CONTAINERS	5477	10437	8911	2209	446	5801		312	10
26 PRINTING, PUBLISHING	11848	37166	27823	20513	2214	26386	1885	4844	703
27 CHEMICALS,SELECT. PRDTS.	6165	5189	17941	2069	2602	9818	963	865	717
28 PLASTICS, SYNTHETICS	3366	4019	4075	146	52	50	8	8	0
29 DRUGS, COSMETICS	2836	4615	9623	1957	851	6195		644	0
30 PAINT, ALLIED PRDTS.	1180	1706	3808	784	50	2466	21	100	0
31 PETROLEUM, RELATED INDS.	1227	957	2807	1365	307	2853	1065	537	10
32 RUBBER, MISC. PLASTICS	7251	35847	14113	2107	1279	2838		1049	9
33 LEATHER TANNING, PRDTS.	172	7889	1430	374	10	238	5	0	0
34 FOOTWEAR, LEATHER PRDTS.	2231	53147	1418	1254	1666	33637	21	109	10
35 GLASS, GLASS PRDTS.	2585	305	2538	60	883	1991		20	10
36 STONE, CLAY PRDTS.	6226	10723	14486	6725	2992	12144	518	1745	918
37 PRIMARY IRON, STEEL MFR.	30371	12958	51463	4163	250	9595	231	317	0
38 PRIMARY NONFERROUS MFR.	5539	9621	16851	930	440	3953	4393	813	814

186

No.	Industry	1	2	3	4	5	6	7	8	9
39	METAL CONTAINERS	4321	494	79	1014	8	2253	0	432	0
40	FABRICATED METAL PRDTS.	5258	8806	19129	5164	1946	11493	285	2537	88
41	SCREW MACH. PRDTS., ETC.	2058	10018	21650	2257	85	2766	17	130	130
42	OTHER FAB. METAL PRDTS.	2415	21434	38171	3889	333	7393	43	382	69
43	ENGINES, TURBINES	0	8496	11309	889	0	444		0	0
44	FARM MACH., EQUIP.	137	69	4786	4404	432	1922	5	1661	0
45	CONSTRUC. MACH., EQUIP.	175	415	4972	3339	416	790	3	178	0
46	MATERIAL HANDLING MACH.	246	1325	6719	1122	396	568		106	0
47	METALWORKING MACHINERY	2628	14997	42599	2189	40	2197		85	0
48	SPECIAL MACH., EQUIP.	2645	20879	6311	1452	505	1820	73	80	0
49	GENERAL MACH., EQUIP.	1722	9055	16157	1868	105	1618		913	0
50	MACHINE SHOP PRDTS.	1439	3903	13032	2150	371	4571		203	73
51	OFFICE, COMPUT. MACHINES	376	2323	9098	5838	0	81		12	0
52	SERVICE IND. MACHINES	1151	4775	9461	4392	85	6758		150	5
53	ELECT. TRANSMISS. EQUIP.	1684	15725	8582	3474	287	12267		17	10
54	HOUSEHOLD APPLIANCES	826	1375	8368	3616	2057	2447		0	0
55	ELECTRIC LIGHTING EQUIP.	194	752	1088	193	1127	3618		0	0
56	RADIO, TV, ETC., EQUIP.	12635	17107	3181	1359	186	681		2004	185
57	ELECTRONIC COMPONENTS	377	29333	2281	1796	410	1108	10	1242	10
58	MISC. ELECTRICAL MACH.	517	2571	3587	477	8	1686		65	0
59	MOTOR VEHICLES, EQUIP.	3932	2928	231259	3291	1350	17857	11	818	10
60	AIRCRAFT, PARTS	27200	8724	12403	4187	750	31627		0	10
61	OTHER TRANSPORT. EQUIP.	12299	11224	8570	1386	9554	2728	39	1289	0
62	PROFESS., SCIEN. INSTRU.	1655	13513	7059	10853	48	1518	20	322	0
63	MEDICAL, PHOTO. EQUIP.	312	7423	1436	1699	42	722		37	0
64	MISC. MANUFACTURING	3714	26613	10577	3986	713	6855	168	486	139
65	TRANSPORT., WAREHOUSING	62944	68356	76260	61464	15025	66718	15565	29672	6367
66	COMMUNICA.,EXC. BRDCAST.	10187	28009	29070	12072	4656	19306	3178	6761	1794
67	RADIO, TV BROADCASTING	918	1827	2660	1738	744	2119	454	820	194
68	ELEC.,GAS,WATER,SAN.SER.	11069	14483	18674	7929	5130	13541	2301	1679	840
69	WHOLESALE, RETAIL TRADE	183395	362244	442047	217962	77142	301207	41504	88914	17163
70	FINANCE, INSURANCE	30880	86535	66888	41260	10780	55583	5058	18628	2091
71	REAL ESTATE, RENTAL	9469	14500	12630	7163	1417	13560	1033	2123	609
72	HOTELS, PERSONAL SERV.	23543	48058	56868	25129	13354	40178	5223	11225	12816
73	BUSINESS SERVICES	13861	36896	41016	15713	3924	21693	1956	4112	1471
74	RESEARCH, DEVELOPMENT	1094	1710	490	779	67	447	17	53	69
75	AUTO. REPAIR, SERVICES	3958	7180	11186	4099	1479	7231	748	862	273
76	AMUSEMENTS	12967	11134	19042	7878	2256	9799	1407	3987	12196
77	MED.,EDUC. SERVICES	54148	158133	128965	72969	13941	88551	1373	26851	2650
78	FEDERAL GOVT. ENTERPRISE	8482	21113	19957	12766	4627	19746	2157	5313	1040
79	STATE, LOCAL GOVT. ENT.	4342	12922	12780	5254	1831	4713	898	6086	337
80	IMPORTS	0	0	0	0	0	0		0	0
81	BUS.TRAVEL, ENT., GIFTS.	0	0	0	0	0	0		0	0
82	OFFICE SUPPLIES	0	0	0	0	0	0		0	0
83	SCRAP, USED GOODS	0	0	0	0	0	0		0	0
84	GOVERNMENT INDUSTRY	171362	242873	266636	126414	49949	195979	39128	77136	23405
85	REST OF WORLD INDUSTRY	0	0	0	0	0	0		0	0
86	HOUSEHOLD INDUSTRY	42854	40069	81363	36801	66605	44663	7507	16706	3119
87	INVENTORY VALUATION ADJ.	0	0	0	0	0	0		0	0
88	STATE TOTAL	994298	1921053	2253871	983021	474513	1402221	195275	405718	104029

TABLE C-5

STATE ESTIMATES OF 1958 EMPLOYMENT
(NUMBER OF EMPLOYEES)

INDUSTRY TITLE	28 NEW HAMPSHIRE	29 NEW JERSEY	30 NEW MEXICO	31 NEW YORK	32 NORTH CAROLINA	33 NORTH DAKOTA	34 OHIO	35 OKLAHOMA	36 OREGON
1 LIVESTOCK, PRDTS.	3503	11260	11531	41548	32594	5960	20932	17562	12311
2 OTHER AGRICULTURE PRDTS.	1051	9740	10043	23452	71406	16040	19068	21438	16689
3 FORESTRY, FISHERIES	345	2129	108	3852	1927	8	1495	240	2326
4 AGRI.,FORES.,FISH. SERV.	331	1993	635	4293	2048	261	5239	1736	166
5 IRON,FERRO. ORES MINING	0	850	230	1266	215		0	0	60
6 NONFERROUS ORES MINING	0	185	3976	860	231	14	28	261	181
7 COAL MINING	0		156	0	0	310	10036	820	0
8 CRUDE PETRO.,NATURAL GAS		0	5376	987	0	587	3024	25216	
9 STONE, CLAY MINING	228	2527	530	4460	3120	185	6466	1221	925
10 CHEM.,FERT. MIN. MINING	6	0	3551	512	180		0	4	2
11 NEW CONSTRUCTION	7455	80001	22151	207277	46510	9359	135632	39962	19678
12 MAINT., REPAIR CONSTR.	2297	23052	4032	60987	18552	3406	40953	8551	6782
13 ORDNANCE, ACCESSORIES	21	644	3910	30313	8815	3	3783	2	19
14 FOOD, KINDRED PRDTS.	3126	61117	3537	147525	30046	3779	85875	15442	19826
15 TOBACCO MANUFACTURES	175	1866		588	26937		1449	0	0
16 FABRICS	9868	19360	30	16033	143436	0	1912	1107	928
17 TEXTILE PRDTS.	381	6865		11950	3291	0	4299	12	100
18 APPAREL	4124	71863	219	340380	87500	0	20777	2307	1747
19 MISC. TEXTILE PRDTS.	162	11272	339	35793	4166	0	3488	242	940
20 LUMBER, WOOD PRDTS.	4519	3688	1556	15237	29821	20	7359	1981	66976
21 WOODEN CONTAINERS	770	1251	0	1323	1432	50	1552	20	1043
22 HOUSEHOLD FURNITURE	1270	5989	62	21258	35914	0	8154	908	1602
23 OTHER FURNITURE	57	2594	69	14975	3701	7	10695	279	355
24 PAPER, ALLIED PRDTS.	5775	14947	0	39504	7887	4	22916	209	5291
25 PAPERBOARD CONTAINERS	315	13544		25910	2988	10	12904	421	849
26 PRINTING, PUBLISHING	2821	30795	1438	175119	8832	10	57902	5918	5287
27 CHEMICALS,SELECT. PRDTS.	117	35485	406	22862	3470	1230	26320	871	814
28 PLASTICS, SYNTHETICS	9	7308	0	5497	5663	7	4889	0	44
29 DRUGS, COSMETICS	127	29382	0	31798	1093	0	8186	255	132
30 PAINT, ALLIED PRDTS.	13	7197	10	4161	484	10	6067	305	264
31 PETROLEUM, RELATED INDS.	162	11377	616	3021	214	10	7672	6547	279
32 RUBBER, MISC. PLASTICS	1395	24719	0	20853	1920	317	76613	0117	366
33 LEATHER TANNING, PRDTS.	1914	3010	0	4217	396	8	1563	0	46
34 FOOTWEAR, LEATHER PRDTS.	19840	9093	82	54548	104	0	9325	361	167
35 GLASS, GLASS PRDTS.	10	12434	30	11564	842	5	19369	3387	199
36 STONE, CLAY PRDTS.	1446	20118	1076	29291	7012	343	45137	3399	2377
37 PRIMARY IRON, STEEL MFR.	770	13925		42226	1381	20	125457	1407	2664
38 PRIMARY NONFERROUS MFR.	939	23388	174	26077	1621	0	27726	1677	1563

39	METAL CONTAINERS	0	6811	0	4202	9	0	3851	41	736
40	FABRICATED METAL PRDTS.	583	15091	328	34676	2995	256	41271	5937	3186
41	SCREW MACH. PRDTS., ETC.	430	9955	0	17021	330	0	30942	115	125
42	OTHER FAB. METAL PRDTS.	628	21431	10	9992	2064	21	37434	1488	1130
43	ENGINES, TURBINES	0	1935	0	2629	37	308	3999	11	0
44	FARM MACH., EQUIP.	11	263	7	738	849	0	5273	263	288
45	CONSTRUC. MACH., EQUIP.	879	2202	140	3280	120	9	16649	5170	277
46	MATERIAL HANDLING MACH.	0	5270	0	16564	172	9	7651	64	998
47	METALWORKING MACHINERY	537	8182	50	17870	149	53	42748	157	132
48	SPECIAL MACH., EQUIP.	3906	10336	0	22934	5013	0	14250	603	1180
49	GENERAL MACH., EQUIP.	1370	14278	30	9458	680	0	30627	1628	260
50	MACHINE SHOP PRDTS.	221	5429	309	42457	1050	57	9339	1112	886
51	OFFICE, COMPUT. MACHINES	207	3830	60	13087	414	0	18957	10	30
52	SERVICE IND. MACHINES	55	5720	10	32297	447	7	7968	207	165
53	ELECT. TRANSMISS. EQUIP.	2579	19568	8	7189	1696	0	38435	409	1867
54	HOUSEHOLD APPLIANCES	8	5959	0	18382	1061	0	29859	53	185
55	ELECTRIC LIGHTING EQUIP.	18	12391	61	46335	640	8	12399	15	67
56	RADIO, TV, ETC., EQUIP.	1857	42275	297	23243	5131	0	6948	834	69
57	ELECTRONIC COMPONENTS	3064	24093	11	11238	2714	0	7695	697	235
58	MISC. ELECTRICAL MACH.	0	3410	45	35163	1589	0	12786	209	132
59	MOTOR VEHICLES, EQUIP.	0	14701	0	57116	1418	65	84259	716	777
60	AIRCRAFT, PARTS	6	22494	130	12373	226	0	60674	8500	800
61	OTHER TRANSPORT. EQUIP.	51	13843	0	35128	770	0	6681	1000	2051
62	PROFESS., SCIEN. INSTRU.	113	22772	0	49504	1404	10	9089	602	224
63	MEDICAL, PHOTO. EQUIP.	214	4085			0	0	571	7	347
64	MISC. MANUFACTURING	1858	24073	354	88873	1600	215	20489	921	997
65	TRANSPORT., WAREHOUSING	5138	104328	11311	364356	41632	9055	150401	28541	30861
66	COMMUNICA., EXC. BRDCAST.	2607	22173	3355	107096	10322	1928	34731	9166	7824
67	RADIO, TV BROADCASTING	293	529	485	17290	2088	531	3725	1206	948
68	ELEC., GAS, WATER, SAN. SER.	2202	22426	4892	56780	9026	1922	26086	9551	5056
69	WHOLESALE, RETAIL TRADE	33094	352603	46891	1228942	214186	36061	581629	126671	107916
70	FINANCE, INSURANCE	6036	73626	6716	369487	32130	4415	94319	19364	17213
71	REAL ESTATE, RENTAL	803	16370	1101	136025	4633	495	21176	4034	3474
72	HOTELS, PERSONAL SERV.	6036	53731	7575	198145	36558	3804	72126	18418	13561
73	BUSINESS SERVICES	1660	35755	5407	213530	9576	1117	49063	9252	8994
74	RESEARCH, DEVELOPMENT	69	1725	253	4643	65	322	1143	278	74
75	AUTO, REPAIR, SERVICES	793	8962	1312	25351	5564	529	13783	3537	2554
76	AMUSEMENTS	1512	12230	1691	68170	5833	1084	24066	4519	3827
77	MED., EDUC. SERVICES	14724	97937	9140	424361	49587	11161	184790	31590	32433
78	FEDERAL GOVT. ENTERPRISE	2029	16875	2938	81358	9890	2447	29825	7447	5790
79	STATE, LOCAL GOVT. ENT.	942	6616	1010	64295	4674	3745	14057	3556	2963
80	IMPORTS	0	0	0	0	0	0	0	0	0
81	BUS. TRAVEL, ENT., GIFTS.	0	0	0	0	0	0	0	0	0
82	OFFICE SUPPLIES	0	0	0	0	0	0	0	0	0
83	SCRAP, USED GOODS	0	0	0	0	0	0	0	0	0
84	GOVERNMENT INDUSTRY	25236	254497	76130	704028	158920	31803	34701	148134	84074
85	REST OF WORLD INDUSTRY	0	0	0	0	0	0	0	0	0
86	HOUSEHOLD INDUSTRY	6723	55745	11077	190552	97983	7003	96309	28017	21107
87	INVENTORY VALUATION ADJ.									
88	STATE TOTAL	203834	2031493	269017	6380038	1320994	160403	3151036	650235	538812

TABLE C-5

STATE ESTIMATES OF 1958 EMPLOYMENT
(NUMBER OF EMPLOYEES)

INDUSTRY TITLE	37 PENNSYL-VANIA	38 RHODE ISLAND	39 SOUTH CAROLINA	40 SOUTH DAKOTA	41 TENNESSEE	42 TEXAS	43 UTAH	44 VERMONT	45 VIRGINIA
1 LIVESTOCK, PRODS.	27117	851	22757	7320	26695	51848	7681	8535	30729
2 OTHER AGRICULTURE PRODS.	13883	284	43243	5680	22305	121152	2845	1708	26271
3 FORESTRY, FISHERIES	1121	702	1427	42	711	2949	25	417	2968
4 AGRI.,FORES.,FISH. SERV.	4976	118	796	759	1584	7403	316	266	1709
5 IRON,FERRO. ORES MINING	1665	0	0	2	1573	247	469	0	106
6 NONFERROUS ORES MINING	209	0	38	1971	902	96	7020	7	538
7 COAL MINING	60169	0	0	10	2688	163	848	0	13858
8 CRUDE PETRO.,NATURAL GAS	4221	0	0	1	9	75248	1100	0	22
9 STONE, CLAY MINING	6309	148	1531	588	2653	4604	209	691	3352
10 CHEM.,FERT. MIN. MINING	205	0	13	0	825	2118		0	152
11 NEW CONSTRUCTION	136976	8438	28531	6632	34825	180532	14758	4312	52350
12 MAINT., REPAIR CONSTR.	48997	2995	7201	3330	12905	52884	3070	1248	16151
13 ORDNANCE, ACCESSORIES	6556	230		15	1922	1058	1279	7	129
14 FOOD, KINDRED PRODS.	113562	7257	10243	8761	29639	76272	9706	0903	31855
15 TOBACCO MANUFACTURES	12875	10	1343	0	1231	385	0	0	13156
16 FABRICS	31108	22157	121215	0	9841	5610	24	728	24682
17 TEXTILE PRODS.	10950	4914	4275	0	2290	4907	7	85	2257
18 APPAREL	185192	4424	24596	10	52293	30696	1385	2023	26852
19 MISC. TEXTILE PRODS.	7709	473	1421	50	2120	3334	115	20	1904
20 LUMBER, WOOD PRODS.	11383	176	15711	927	15869	15419	682	3800	20123
21 WOODEN CONTAINERS	868	10	852	10	1645	1740	10	26	2162
22 HOUSEHOLD FURNITURE	15408	145	3116	50	11314	6658	452	1464	14292
23 OTHER FURNITURE	7631	434	180	10	694	3651	69	0	1933
24 PAPER, ALLIED PRODS.	22299	180	3718	45	6884	7097	75	2133	9321
25 PAPERBOARD CONTAINERS	15866	1303	2702		2461	2706	136	315	1829
26 PRINTING, PUBLISHING	64279	3716	3115	1417	12232	26379	1854	2128	9737
27 CHEMICALS,SELECT. PRODS.	15223	572	10190	85	18175	30144	1004	86	9656
28 PLASTICS, SYNTHETICS	11209	330	3136		16959	4790		52	18790
29 DRUGS, COSMETICS	12425	169	420	72	2549	2012	155	74	2165
30 PAINT, ALLIED PRODS.	5108	297	105	0	452	1940	85	35	357
31 PETROLEUM, RELATED INDS.	16741	267	300	0	596	42824	1082	45	428
32 RUBBER, MISC. PLASTICS	20087	7642	835	83	4967	5103	402	952	2505
33 LEATHER TANNING, PRODS.	4528	9	65	7	735	174	4	184	708
34 FOOTWEAR, LEATHER PRODS.	27812	756	9	0	11159	2646	39	475	539
35 GLASS, GLASS PRODS.	22439	1291	1886		2561	1486	10	375	585
36 STONE, CLAY PRODS.	40288	590	3268	465	7327	19456	2610	3900	7262
37 PRIMARY IRON, STEEL MFR.	202776	2033	349	10	4825	15001	7083	100	3212
38 PRIMARY NONFERROUS MFR.	23927	6383	170	0	6033	9055	2449	338	1762

190

	(1)	(2)	(3)	(4)	(5)	(6)	(7)	(8)	(9)
39 METAL CONTAINERS	5607	0	0	0	173	2688	147	0	0
40 FABRICATED METAL PRDTS.	54336	989	1612	370	10581	18152	2433	214	6037
41 SCREW MACH. PRDTS., ETC.	22802	1974	85	85	710	941	85	10	20
42 OTHER FAB. METAL PRDTS.	19779	5070	110	64	1948	7050	13	31	644
43 ENGINES, TURBINES	20493	12	0	0	65	65	112	0	0
44 FARM MACH., EQUIP.	3885	8	8	49	2371	1473	112	69	282
45 CONSTRUC. MACH., EQUIP.	8553	11	7	0	610	20006	965	198	113
46 MATERIAL HANDLING MACH.	6947	18	83	52	858	642	15	0	200
47 METALWORKING MACHINERY	17874	4038	30	118	333	450	0	4206	135
48 SPECIAL MACH., EQUIP.	16076	2222	2817	16	1064	3149	105	430	840
49 GENERAL MACH., EQUIP.	20727	903	220	16	555	3028	40	110	215
50 MACHINE SHOP PRDTS.	6980	489	490	155	1425	3579	197	106	576
51 OFFICE, COMPUT. MACHINES	3311	12	10	0	0	19	20	886	771
52 SERVICE IND. MACHINES	7427	645	124	16	700	4318	205	85	885
53 ELECT. TRANSMISS. EQUIP.	37099	264	7	35	16	895	63	404	210
54 HOUSEHOLD APPLIANCES	5196	0	656	0	5966	426	0	0	52
55 ELECTRIC LIGHTING EQUIP.	12396	1621	0	16	820	373	9	336	8
56 RADIO, TV, ETC., EQUIP.	10078	18	399	0	1947	3604	0	0	798
57 ELECTRONIC COMPONENTS	27081	374	775	11	300	2210	459	529	1215
58 MISC. ELECTRICAL MACH.	4390	916	0	0	424	1101	67	166	99
59 MOTOR VEHICLES, EQUIP.	19001	432	201	10	2804	6004	166	166	1842
60 AIRCRAFT, PARTS	16572	149	0	0	125	50544	1319	75	259
61 OTHER TRANSPORT. EQUIP.	19056	270	527	190	2819	8279	153	43	14884
62 PROFESS., SCIEN. INSTRU.	21716	699	331	8	2690	3589	35	443	206
63 MEDICAL, PHOTO. EQUIP.	1576	937	43	0	48	359	4	35	1351
64 MISC. MANUFACTURING	25453	22604	873	83	4266	3697	429	418	1785
65 TRANSPORT., WAREHOUSING	167937	8265	16734	5664	42924	157643	15584	4270	65285
66 COMMUNICA.,EXC. BROCAST.	32497	3285	5092	2073	11403	34019	3656	1425	11915
67 RADIO, TV BROADCASTING	4416	261	1033	366	2118	4774	654	219	1820
68 ELEC.,GAS,WATER,SAN.SER.	47242	2701	4531	1652	3084	40037	2428	1091	8836
69 WHOLESALE, RETAIL TRADE	672785	51753	94554	36939	184201	589739	52251	19938	205361
70 FINANCE, INSURANCE	127772	11459	14805	4709	27755	101121	7885	3544	33188
71 REAL ESTATE, RENTAL	23088	1854	1567	684	4445	16052	1871	275	7601
72 HOTELS, PERSONAL SERV.	83069	6614	15687	3968	28985	93882	6442	3444	34188
73 BUSINESS SERVICES	56431	3358	4225	1073	13105	43652	3568	637	15827
74 RESEARCH, DEVELOPMENT	1262	48	147	34	414	1059	67	23	621
75 AUTO. REPAIR, SERVICES	16523	1143	2690	669	4559	16220	1185	461	4609
76 AMUSEMENTS	22920	2589	2635	1492	5489	17523	1884	759	6582
77 MED.,EDUC. SERVICES	269785	20199	17741	10482	50340	124296	14620	10416	51957
78 FEDERAL GOVT. ENTERPRISE	37104	2738	5237	2478	19366	28140	2737	1671	11894
79 STATE, LOCAL GOVT. ENT.	17208	1351	2073	1125	8919	16976	1230	546	5466
80 IMPORTS	0	0	0	0	0	0	0	0	0
81 BUS.TRAVEL, ENT., GIFTS.	0	0	0	0	0	0	0	0	0
82 OFFICE SUPPLIES	0	0	0	0	0	0	0	0	0
83 SCRAP, USED GOODS	0	0	0	0	0	0	0	0	0
84 GOVERNMENT INDUSTRY	375704	59852	143072	38686	139470	526386	57637	14746	302189
85 REST OF WORLD INDUSTRY	108140	6019	68582	8926	69897	178668	6380	6731	71268
86 HOUSEHOLD INDUSTRY	0	0	0	0	0	0	0	0	0
87 INVENTORY VALUATION ADJ.	0	0	0	0	0	0	0	0	0
88 STATE TOTAL	3692411	307460	728570	160660	994475	2956615	259002	118397	1228441

TABLE C-5

STATE ESTIMATES OF 1958 EMPLOYMENT
(NUMBER OF EMPLOYEES)

INDUSTRY TITLE	46 WASHINGTON	47 WEST VIRGINIA	48 WISCONSIN	49 WYOMING	50 ALASKA	51 HAWAII	52 NO STATE ALLOCATION	53 NATIONAL TOTAL
1 LIVESTOCK, PRDTS.	12730	10500	25674	5693	0	0	0	865030
2 OTHER AGRICULTURE PRDTS.	26270	3500	6326	1675	0	0	0	1089970
3 FORESTRY, FISHERIES	3052	326	905	27	0	0	0	71927
4 AGRI.,FORES.,FISH. SERV.	377	402	2186	124	0	0	0	98073
5 IRON, FERRO. ORES MINING	4	1	850	299	0	0	0	37009
6 NONFERROUS ORES MINING	572	0	180	1069	0	0	0	54307
7 COAL MINING	276	62110	0	549	0	0	0	210129
8 CRUDE PETRO.,NATURAL GAS	2	4132	0	3960	0	0	0	196509
9 STONE, CLAY MINING	1058	1342	2514	485	0	0	0	96075
10 CHEM.,FERT. MIN. MINING	2	0	0	534	0	0	0	20556
11 NEW CONSTRUCTION	40202	18040	41995	8820	0	0	0	2463496
12 MAINT., REPAIR CONSTR.	11724	5611	15681	2806	0	0	0	774893
13 ORDNANCE, ACCESSORIES	21	37	90	0	0	0	0	204944
14 FOOD, KINDRED PRDTS.	26700	8740	64115	1430	0	0	0	1699058
15 TOBACCO MANUFACTURES	0	821	72	0	0	0	0	82032
16 FABRICS	337	349	1080	0	0	0	0	585691
17 TEXTILE PRDTS.	118	0	1075	0	0	0	0	103070
18 APPAREL	2868	4316	10756	0	0	0	0	1253328
19 MISC. TEXTILE PRDTS.	876	45	887	10	0	0	0	128779
20 LUMBER, WOOD PRDTS.	40919	6639	14935	667	0	0	0	538769
21 WOODEN CONTAINERS	649	143	1300	0	0	0	0	39680
22 HOUSEHOLD FURNITURE	2363	945	3805	20	0	0	0	251007
23 OTHER FURNITURE	572	171	4496	7	0	0	0	95540
24 PAPER, ALLIED PRDTS.	14172	789	29891	10	0	0	0	369064
25 PAPERBOARD CONTAINERS	1635	625	6267	0	0	0	0	181177
26 PRINTING, PUBLISHING	8066	3561	20718	623	0	0	0	861766
27 CHEMICALS,SELECT. PRDTS.	10138	18164	2398	24	0	0	0	344303
28 PLASTICS, SYNTHETICS	129	4415	419	0	0	0	0	121536
29 DRUGS, COSMETICS	130	265	2176	4	0	0	0	174172
30 PAINT, ALLIED PRDTS.	351	55	1128	0	0	0	0	58954
31 PETROLEUM, RELATED INDS.	1373	710	702	2411	0	0	0	179166
32 RUBBER, MISC. PLASTICS	378	254	7534	9	0	0	0	346741
33 LEATHER TANNING, PRDTS.	21	350	4551	0	0	0	0	41105
34 FOOTWEAR, LEATHER PRDTS.	310	328	11638	0	0	0	0	299070
35 GLASS, GLASS PRDTS.	426	14424	183	0	0	0	0	136372
36 STONE, CLAY PRDTS.	4664	7206	6139	0	0	0	0	412631
37 PRIMARY IRON, STEEL MFR.	2744	17010	20487	471	0	0	0	804695
38 PRIMARY NONFERROUS MFR.	7937	4246	4708	0	0	0	0	289822

39 METAL CONTAINERS	748	221	2084	0	0	0	0	63878
40 FABRICATED METAL PRDTS.	4379	1970	14128	148	0	0	0	393122
41 SCREW MACH. PRDTS., ETC.	189	1515	10507	0	0	0	0	209296
42 OTHER FAB. METAL PRDTS.	1075	2712	6167	10	0	0	0	354073
43 ENGINES, TURBINES	11	0	18218	0	0	0	0	95569
44 FARM MACH., EQUIP.	322	293	14305	0	0	0	0	108588
45 CONSTRUC. MACH., EQUIP.	755	1123	13799	13	0	0	0	144034
46 MATERIAL HANDLING MACH.	528	145	1486	0	0	0	0	54724
47 METALWORKING MACHINERY	343	1615	7809	6	0	0	0	233196
48 SPECIAL MACH., EQUIP.	1107	95	8195	0	0	0	0	162322
49 GENERAL MACH., EQUIP.	603	265	9808	0	0	0	0	211267
50 MACHINE SHOP PRDTS.	1334	667	2289	73	0	0	0	115534
51 OFFICE, COMPUT. MACHINES	70	0	513	0	0	0	0	121619
52 SERVICE IND. MACHINES	205	230	5075	19	0	0	0	100474
53 ELECT. TRANSMISS. EQUIP.	415	48	24007	10	0	0	0	283134
54 HOUSEHOLD APPLIANCES	235	52	6800	0	0	0	0	142951
55 ELECTRIC LIGHTING EQUIP.	349	2165	1348	9	0	0	0	123336
56 RADIO, TV, ETC., EQUIP.	67	11	565	0	0	0	0	288984
57 ELECTRONIC COMPONENTS	80	385	2403	0	0	0	0	195275
58 MISC. ELECTRICAL MACH.	100	16	5142	0	0	0	0	78371
59 MOTOR VEHICLES, EQUIP.	1394	659	26325	0	0	0	0	577188
60 AIRCRAFT, PARTS	62306	126	1199	75	0	0	0	765482
61 OTHER TRANSPORT. EQUIP.	5971	851	5242	14	0	0	0	215089
62 PROFESS., SCIEN. INSTRU.	551	332	9494	0	0	0	0	208027
63 MEDICAL, PHOTO. EQUIP.	183	42	394	0	0	0	0	83277
64 MISC. MANUFACTURING	1573	876	8553	61	0	0	0	355646
65 TRANSPORT., WAREHOUSING	45824	30956	47425	10174	0	0	0	2687380
66 COMMUNICA.,EXC. BRDCAST.	11867	5935	13687	1445	0	0	0	718454
67 RADIO, TV BROADCASTING	1719	1039	1786	264	0	0	0	92612
68 ELEC.,GAS,WATER,SAN.SER.	2970	11322	7210	1112	0	0	0	540713
69 WHOLESALE, RETAIL TRADE	170063	85824	232599	18515	0	0	0	10708422
70 FINANCE, INSURANCE	27241	11479	36788	2191	0	0	0	2061592
71 REAL ESTATE, RENTAL	6428	2920	6880	365	0	0	0	486190
72 HOTELS, PERSONAL SERV.	22069	11296	27027	3774	0	0	0	1554303
73 BUSINESS SERVICES	13413	4401	15559	1085	0	0	0	995691
74 RESEARCH, DEVELOPMENT	324	230	421	46	0	0	0	37993
75 AUTO. REPAIR, SERVICES	3932	1690	3315	383	0	0	0	254378
76 AMUSEMENTS	6826	3323	9917	785	0	0	0	461395
77 MED.,EDUC. SERVICES	53085	25983	70668	3278	0	0	0	3229616
78 FEDERAL GOVT. ENTERPRISE	10970	4625	10661	1159	0	0	0	614224
79 STATE, LOCAL GOVT. ENT.	11813	1682	3627	346	0	0	0	337000
80 IMPORTS	0	0	0	0	0	0	0	0
81 BUS.TRAVEL, ENT., GIFTS.	0	0	0	0	0	0	0	0
82 OFFICE SUPPLIES	0	0	0	0	0	0	0	0
83 SCRAP, USED GOODS	0	0	0	0	0	0	0	0
84 GOVERNMENT INDUSTRY	190699	58789	140588	21716	0	0	0	8379446
85 REST OF WORLD INDUSTRY	0	0	0	0	0	0	0	0
86 HOUSEHOLD INDUSTRY	35256	18163	34480	4113	0	0	0	2550000
87 INVENTORY VALUATION ADJ.	0	0	0	0	0	0	0	0
88 STATE TOTAL	923558	496643	1186354	102916	0	0	0	56974311

TABLE C-6

STATE ESTIMATES OF 1963 EMPLOYMENT
(NUMBER OF EMPLOYEES)

INDUSTRY TITLE	1 ALABAMA	2 ARIZONA	3 ARKANSAS	4 CALIFORNIA	5 COLORADO	6 CONNECTICUT	7 DELAWARE	8 DISTRICT OF COLUMBIA	9 FLORIDA
1 LIVESTOCK, PRDTS.	16490	10638	28577	75973	10491	4427	3212	0	17186
2 OTHER AGRICULTURE PRDTS.	16510	19362	55423	129027	6509	3573	1788	0	59814
3 FORESTRY, FISHERIES	1250	166	655	10825	53	663	270	0	7073
4 AGRI.,FORES.,FISH. SERV.	2605	1534	2905	13045	448	2033	942	0	6091
5 IRON, FERRO. ORES MINING	917	10	15	949	2124	0	0	0	0
6 NONFERROUS ORES MINING	45	13705	561	666	2955	57	0	0	455
7 COAL MINING	5741	6	109	6	1374	0	0	0	0
8 CRUDE PETRO.,NATURAL GAS	132	15	1346	14478	2825	0	0	0	175
9 STONE, CLAY MINING	1799	928	1487	7939	1067	770	55	0	2604
10 CHEM.,FERT. MIN. MINING	0	0	347	2765	80	0	7	0	3219
11 NEW CONSTRUCTION	35516	24969	20818	284840	28405	39058	9530	20289	96100
12 MAINT., REPAIR CONSTR.	10001	6123	8707	58064	9188	9992	2116	4249	22533
13 ORDNANCE, ACCESSORIES	5051	4165	9	136342	3065	8099	0	0	11330
14 FOOD, KINDRED PRDTS.	22469	6601	17820	155731	18637	11302	6066	4634	39797
15 TOBACCO MANUFACTURES	1250	0	0	42	0	226	0	0	5435
16 FABRICS	27695	6	987	896	15	9009	1490	0	403
17 TEXTILE PRDTS.	2709	8	938	4139	40	2852	468	0	80
18 APPAREL	35437	10	10950	53936	1324	15721	3574	39	10053
19 MISC. TEXTILE PRDTS.	1274	2379	21	11384	542	2007	247	159	1321
20 LUMBER, WOOD PRDTS.	19200	240	19858	49011	2236	1478	826	166	10050
21 WOODEN CONTAINERS	719	2950	1340	2895	178	240	41	0	1918
22 HOUSEHOLD FURNITURE	3038	55	7229	22666	727	2152	16	66	5483
23 OTHER FURNITURE	563	617	1098	9459	390	1894	107	48	1208
24 PAPER, ALLIED PRDTS.	10635	330	5814	13848	526	3694	324	498	12158
25 PAPERBOARD CONTAINERS	945	451	1445	15042	676	3826	571	209	2957
26 PRINTING, PUBLISHING	5302	190	3902	72637	7620	17226	1455	13180	16332
27 CHEMICALS,SELECT. PRDTS.	5195	4147	3204	14592	1143	3062	2216	98	8871
28 PLASTICS, SYNTHETICS	2919	741	14	2540	11	1981	4929	0	6517
29 DRUGS, COSMETICS	147	0	14	11856	228	5849	384	25	900
30 PAINT, ALLIED PRDTS.	296	80	63	6672	286	209	9	63	835
31 PETROLEUM, RELATED INDS.	750	66	1453	19017	925	350	839	0	774
32 RUBBER, MISC. PLASTICS	5784	72	1753	29229	5764	16863	3144	5	1487
33 LEATHER TANNING, PRDTS.	0	312	0	1076	7	104	1086	0	69
34 FOOTWEAR, LEATHER PRDTS.	827	0	6434	4607	2716	2197	530	0	1807
35 GLASS, GLASS PRDTS.	109	56	608	9094	56	663	32	5	956
36 STONE, CLAY PRDTS.	7158	3189	2838	36598	4815	5794	812	840	11589
37 PRIMARY IRON, STEEL MFR.	33281	745	354	29636	7887	8256	2954	0	1123
38 PRIMARY NONFERROUS MFR.	6896	11469	3500	20415	463	17630	355	0	1197

	Industry									
39	METAL CONTAINERS	197	0	124	8920	261	71	0	0	1676
40	FABRICATED METAL PRDTS.	7875	2035	1706	34444	2285	4572	753	358	9688
41	SCREW MACH. PRDTS., ETC.	1320	47	101	12810	152	12545	329		530
42	OTHER FAB. METAL PRDTS.	4381	483	1833	33376	1497	23177	428	116	2631
43	ENGINES, TURBINES		0	0	2844	131	1886	0	0	56
44	FARM MACH., EQUIP.	898	203	284	3122	425	44	55	0	426
45	CONSTRUC. MACH., EQUIP.	432	7	18	7528	1944	84	11	0	134
46	MATERIAL HANDLING MACH.	288	6	458	3199	137	255		0	174
47	METALWORKING MACHINERY	338	240	332	10567	129	15804	247	0	904
48	SPECIAL MACH., EQUIP.	1127	52	185	8182	303	4207	743	18	1227
49	GENERAL MACH., EQUIP.	567	119	335	18908	541	20834	28		534
50	MACHINE SHOP PRDTS.	736	1023	366	18769	1195	4812	195	128	1613
51	OFFICE, COMPUT. MACHINES	11	2986	411	14358	71	9746	0	76	1927
52	SERVICE IND. MACHINES	734	1300	786	5578	115	1180	147	8	487
53	ELECT. TRANSMISS. EQUIP.	510	139	2954	21280	2687	6276	9	53	432
54	HOUSEHOLD APPLIANCES	22	10	2126	6763	15	7949	136	8	109
55	ELECTRIC LIGHTING EQUIP.	1274	19	849	7943	163	7495	163	18	377
56	RADIO, TV, ETC., EQUIP.	624	3171	2186	102604	178	7638	9	66	10138
57	ELECTRONIC COMPONENTS	921	5776	11	45845	257	11403	42	42	2218
58	MISC. ELECTRICAL MACH.	500	13	13	3530	213	1674	154	7	1952
59	MOTOR VEHICLES, EQUIP.	1922	133	682	27000	1043	3208	5816	142	843
60	AIRCRAFT, PARTS	8626	5315	53	158683	15358	65193	550	0	10378
61	OTHER TRANSPORT. EQUIP.	5185	277	1619	18200	288	16344	171	4	7192
62	PROFESS., SCIEN. INSTRU.	185	1462	1907	17028	720	14096	316	83	1395
63	MEDICAL, PHOTO. EQUIP.		49	12	5489	142	2532	0	47	810
64	MISC. MANUFACTURING	1613	458	3151	24644	1551	16146	259	243	3140
65	TRANSPORT., WAREHOUSING	31556	12394	17483	213616	25969	22242	6368	13940	64020
66	COMMUNICA.,+EXC. BRDCAST.	8265	5735	4496	95295	9499	11215	1374	1578	22577
67	RADIO, TV BROADCASTING	1551	977	803	11822	1172	1086	349	1669	3171
68	ELEC.,GAS,WATER,SAN.SER.	7822	4996	6626	45983	6552	8832	362	1314	13007
69	WHOLESALE, RETAIL TRADE	148464	92084	83060	1177143	128303	168682	32798	79602	359119
70	FINANCE, INSURANCE	27957	15652	12980	245467	24647	50309	5619	17039	66144
71	REAL ESTATE, RENTAL	3966	3931	1856	52295	4954	4951	1070	13757	21709
72	HOTELS, PERSONAL SERV.	22141	16277	13184	163931	18778	19742	3125	20788	74432
73	BUSINESS SERVICES	13022	10515	5094	185122	13429	20834	3393	19060	31459
74	RESEARCH, DEVELOPMENT	744	119	30	20061	595	704	57	927	2364
75	AUTO. REPAIR, SERVICES	4148	2623	1958	36907	3567	4425	711	2907	984
76	AMUSEMENTS	3466	4197	2357	77511	4557	4480	819	2937	14969
77	MED.,EDUC. SERVICES	38930	25495	23434	359007	44594	80480	10468	60170	88735
78	FEDERAL GOVT. ENTERPRISE	13007	4342	4946	66919	7382	8873	1495	16646	18897
79	STATE, LOCAL GOVT. ENT.	14246	7972	1518	43862	3104	3245	847	2114	11503
80	IMPORTS	0	0	0	0	0	0	0	0	0
81	BUS.TRAVEL, ENT., GIFTS.	0	0	0	0	0	0	0	0	0
82	OFFICE SUPPLIES	0	0	0	0	0	0	0	0	0
83	SCRAP, USED GOODS	0	0	0	0	0	0	0	0	0
84	GOVERNMENT INDUSTRY	169374	88942	77570	1231635	148658	105415	28032	188627	318299
85	REST OF WORLD INDUSTRY	64843	11365	24806	203734	13500	897451	4833	16786	76623
86	HOUSEHOLD INDUSTRY	0	0	0	0	0	0	0	0	0
87	INVENTORY VALUATION ADJ.									
88	STATE TOTAL	904443	449369	517299	6183860	616857	1875394	162676	505851	1618903

TABLE C-6

STATE ESTIMATES OF 1963 EMPLOYMENT
(NUMBER OF EMPLOYEES)

INDUSTRY TITLE	10 GEORGIA	11 IDAHO	12 ILLINOIS	13 INDIANA	14 IOWA	15 KANSAS	16 KENTUCKY	17 LOUISIANA	18 MAINE
1 LIVESTOCK, PRDTS.	21385	7344	19022	11162	22480	12514	20813	17623	6373
2 OTHER AGRICULTURE PRDTS.	24615	12656	28978	14838	17520	10486	32287	41377	5627
3 FORESTRY, FISHERIES	2311	395	366	263	96	0	287	2516	1015
4 AGRI.,FORES.,FISH. SERV.	4554	496	5523	3422	4299	2783	481	1069	371
5 IRON, FERRO. ORES MINING	120	4	0	0	0	0	0	0	0
6 NONFERROUS ORES MINING	19	2768	340	0	0	1	0	0	5
7 COAL MINING	6	0	8993	2970	290	264	20785	0	0
8 CRUDE PETRO.,NATURAL GAS	0	0	4359	1042	0	7697	2710	18533	0
9 STONE, CLAY MINING	5432	246	4926	2861	2388	1413	2746	1336	210
10 CHEM.,FERT. MIN. MINING	133	229	536	0	0	189	240	1987	0
11 NEW CONSTRUCTION	52769	6031	122740	47165	21974	26957	38345	71653	8381
12 MAINT., REPAIR CONSTR.	13709	3471	48732	21131	14323	13874	12551	11557	4034
13 ORDNANCE, ACCESSORIES	128	163	5200	5676	2736	0	0	3294	640
14 FOOD, KINDRED PRDTS.	41913	8955	116462	45401	50225	21192	23821	29667	11689
15 TOBACCO MANUFACTURES	672	0	410	444	0	0	9885	104	104
16 FABRICS	67634	0	1546	0	193	11	671	0	11403
17 TEXTILE PRDTS.	17996	0	3596	503	8	8	216	326	680
18 APPAREL	58061	23	34013	11815	2644	3015	22425	5026	3035
19 MISC. TEXTILE PRDTS.	6951	22	7995	1714	648	817	1304	873	433
20 LUMBER, WOOD PRDTS.	20316	10236	10080	9841	3108	829	7558	13876	11636
21 WOODEN CONTAINERS	2425	55	1008	384	162	47	796	806	218
22 HOUSEHOLD FURNITURE	7314	66	13314	18657	1386	807	4725	1011	488
23 OTHER FURNITURE	948	58	10186	3711	977	614	575	289	208
24 PAPER, ALLIED PRDTS.	13205	569	16213	6563	1387	802	2021	12940	16209
25 PAPERBOARD CONTAINERS	5946	54	19364	6086	1702	2130	1814	2234	367
26 PRINTING, PUBLISHING	10162	1354	95476	22558	11988	8734	8791	5355	2390
27 CHEMICALS,SELECT. PRDTS.	6439	3203	19035	4899	1313	3699	5559	13018	554
28 PLASTICS, SYNTHETICS	1660	0	1214	836	1553	479	3953	2153	9
29 DRUGS, COSMETICS	2014	0	18115	14937	1529	1919	75	216	20
30 PAINT, ALLIED PRDTS.	905	11	9104	1470	518	137	1572	240	14
31 PETROLEUM, RELATED INDS.	717	7	11346	7333	121	3954	857	11126	63
32 RUBBER, MISC. PLASTICS	2463	10	28789	22255	5292	2467	2216	189	1949
33 LEATHER TANNING, PRDTS.	70	0	2148	154	1167		291	29	2059
34 FOOTWEAR, LEATHER PRDTS.	3634	36	13900	2796	8	249	2495	6	22666
35 GLASS, GLASS PRDTS.	1746	0	11258	8907	5916	49	46	804	75
36 STONE, CLAY PRDTS.	10600	760	24972	16331	3092	6319	4935	5469	1279
37 PRIMARY IRON, STEEL MFR.	3524	113	72887	75848	3396	1652	7924	1176	35
38 PRIMARY NONFERROUS MFR.	1531	1343	24816	17708		474	1738	1873	141

#	Industry	C1	C2	C3	C4	C5	C6	C7	C8	C9
39	METAL CONTAINERS	377	1794	77	181	59	986	12133	37	674
40	FABRICATED METAL PRDTS.	572	4027	5582	3945	4404	16203	25369	391	6629
41	SCREW MACH. PRDTS., ETC.	316	316	1815	247	1067	9925	35118	30	1903
42	OTHER FAB. METAL PRDTS.	60	1613	4938	1152	3778	16105	51341	0	1554
43	ENGINES, TURBINES	555	56	0	0	1472	5994	8551	303	10
44	FARM MACH., EQUIP.	44	515	4090	1967	21605	5222	23567	29	1653
45	CONSTRUC. MACH., EQUIP.	452	975	72	1166	5159	3878	46059	64	749
46	MATERIAL HANDLING MACH.	0	121	1267	444	605	591	6531	9	582
47	METALWORKING MACHINERY	171	51	757	314	1658	8023	30443	46	449
48	SPECIAL MACH., EQUIP.	566	594	967	877	1573	2942	14477	102	3129
49	GENERAL MACH., EQUIP.	154	168	1705	1121	1744	16503	20311	0	634
50	MACHINE SHOP PRDTS.	290	1124	1767	1732	701	5872	10872	50	713
51	OFFICE, COMPUT. MACHINES	0	65	1916	16	8	151	7837	0	132
52	SERVICE IND. MACHINES	194	252	2082	858	1051	5394	9925	0	883
53	ELECT. TRANSMISS. EQUIP.	149	75	2999	121	915	15824	25181	0	3551
54	HOUSEHOLD APPLIANCES	16	51	75	13	3573	9287	24026	0	93
55	ELECTRIC LIGHTING EQUIP.	304	30	10587	78	42	6574	16160	0	860
56	RADIO, TV, ETC., EQUIP.	134	71	2370	316	9321	29811	72889	63	112
57	ELECTRONIC COMPONENTS	982	42	508	1736	3205	10917	23525	0	139
58	MISC. ELECTRICAL MACH.	170	79	4836	708	797	18692	6419	93	578
59	MOTOR VEHICLES, EQUIP.	70	539	387	3833	1292	60206	22409	175	10314
60	AIRCRAFT, PARTS	1530	3298	4528	28638	375	20519	6282	528	15559
61	OTHER TRANSPORT. EQUIP.	3169	8189	55	1830	1046	10458	11892	18	2771
62	PROFESS., SCIEN. INSTRU.	51	373	1099	274	2307	3205	27638	0	1073
63	MEDICAL, PHOTO. EQUIP.	9	57	1499	61	115	1403	8955	232	66
64	MISC. MANUFACTURING	998	0096	68	751	5317	8330	31869	0	4637
65	TRANSPORT., WAREHOUSING	8876	60264	1837	33386	27997	54514	172055	8569	49823
66	COMMUNICA.,EXC. BRDCAST.	3190	9729	34268	7248	8869	14805	43525	2391	14112
67	RADIO, TV BROADCASTING	634	1777	7321	1214	1646	2056	4675	480	2250
68	ELEC.,GAS,WATER,SAN.SER.	3035	11989	1305	8899	8533	11255	33181	1610	9627
69	WHOLESALE, RETAIL TRADE	52420	168327	6865	124925	168292	288311	740369	41661	229015
70	FINANCE, INSURANCE	8618	31137	140168	21295	29880	52898	156772	5780	45545
71	REAL ESTATE, RENTAL	1263	5117	23136	2685	3470	6825	44756	704	6435
72	HOTELS, PERSONAL SERV.	6578	22839	2936	16118	19178	33087	98447	4783	33218
73	BUSINESS SERVICES	2716	19375	20095	9295	11909	18715	105052	2364	20962
74	RESEARCH, DEVELOPMENT	100	368	110	97	397	847	3663	1498	420
75	AUTO. REPAIR, SERVICES	1232	7786	3235	2650	2892	6132	13709	764	6354
76	AMUSEMENTS	1287	5457	5633	4141	4922	7393	24173	1236	5887
77	MED.,EDUC. SERVICES	20164	48582	48453	39449	57724	83161	257746	9969	48713
78	FEDERAL GOVT. ENTERPRISE	3865	7967	10580	8284	8938	13794	44752	2242	14469
79	STATE, LOCAL GOVT. ENT.	1420	6582	3488	3657	3751	6892	28709	809	6255
80	IMPORTS	0	0	0	0	0	0	0	0	0
81	BUS.TRAVEL, ENT., GIFTS.	0	0	0	0	0	0	0	0	0
82	OFFICE SUPPLIES	0	0	0	0	0	0	0	0	0
83	SCRAP, USED GOODS	0	0	0	0	0	0	0	0	0
84	GOVERNMENT INDUSTRY	65508	165702	154431	147724	118685	199875	434472	39641	257799
85	REST OF WORLD INDUSTRY	0	0	0	0	0	0	0	0	0
86	HOUSEHOLD INDUSTRY	8709	59749	25920	17311	20908	32591	58198	5326	84270
87	INVENTORY VALUATION ADJ.	0	0	0	0	0	0	0	0	0
88	STATE TOTAL	314908	938069	799638	637367	755619	1537867	3660995	192675	1308628

TABLE C-6

STATE ESTIMATES OF 1963 EMPLOYMENT
(NUMBER OF EMPLOYEES)

INDUSTRY TITLE	19 MARYLAND	20 MASSA-CHUSETTS	21 MICHIGAN	22 MINNESOTA	23 MISSISSIPPI	24 MISSOURI	25 MONTANA	26 NEBRASKA	27 NEVADA
1 LIVESTOCK, PRDTS.	10066	6572	17368	18623	21710	18050	5089	11785	1257
2 OTHER AGRICULTURE PRDTS.	6934	5428	23632	17377	43290	17950	6911	10215	743
3 FORESTRY, FISHERIES	1636	6807	1539	418	672	589	249	9	8
4 AGRI.,FORES.,FISH. SERV.	2291	493	2756	2673	1924	4518	305	982	448
5 IRON, FERRO. ORES MINING	0	0	3883	11161	0	811	70	0	179
6 NONFERROUS ORES MINING	1	0	2507	111	0	1754	4257	2	1887
7 COAL MINING	413	0	0	0	0	1137	82	0	0
8 CRUDE PETRO.,NATURAL GAS	35	0	1146	0	1972	195	1125	454	3
9 STONE, CLAY MINING	1881	1459	3666	1739	890	3478	431	1189	545
10 CHEM.,FERT. MIN. MINING	0	0	191	0	0	371	478	0	47
11 NEW CONSTRUCTION	64186	63767	75066	38931	22610	52674	8466	16252	14443
12 MAINT., REPAIR CONSTR.	13051	16479	24703	16926	10372	22250	5738	10610	1929
13 ORDNANCE, ACCESSORIES	1278	6403	2182	5930	0	11024	0	119	0
14 FOOD, KINDRED PRDTS.	35755	40795	52524	48648	14646	48213	4057	26820	1025
15 TOBACCO MANUFACTURES	85	59	377	0	0	360	0	0	0
16 FABRICS	1692	25815	306	178	698	839	0	57	0
17 TEXTILE PRDTS.	75	9757	2022	524	1933	1519	0	0	0
18 APPAREL	21798	52786	5077	7528	33887	31004	0	1460	4
19 MISC. TEXTILE PRDTS.	1938	9060	11523	1941	1000	3112	9	59	18
20 LUMBER, WOOD PRDTS.	3889	5045	11840	252	18862	6194	8267	878	371
21 WOODEN CONTAINERS	776	649	412	1588	2052	710	0	47	0
22 HOUSEHOLD FURNITURE	2669	9432	8191	767	6569	2688	35	595	41
23 OTHER FURNITURE	2243	2212	10234	0	564	2567	56	1127	50
24 PAPER, ALLIED PRDTS.	3627	24049	17281	10477	3964	5425	211	384	9
25 PAPERBOARD CONTAINERS	5594	10501	10058	2930	607	6082	0	565	0
26 PRINTING, PUBLISHING	14603	40578	27804	21933	2301	27197	1530	5486	1157
27 CHEMICALS,SELECT. PRDTS.	6094	4719	16668	2562	3096	10296	309	800	795
28 PLASTICS, SYNTHETICS	3284	5760	4595	382	124	77	0	0	0
29 DRUGS, COSMETICS	4129	3650	8536	2093	780	6664	15	1144	56
30 PAINT, ALLIED PRDTS.	1276	1712	3843	606	63	2508	0	47	11
31 PETROLEUM, RELATED INDS.	1181	1454	2781	1474	652	2166	877	250	43
32 RUBBER, MISC. PLASTICS	10605	33596	19005	3283	3005	5514	10	1732	0
33 LEATHER TANNING, PRDTS.	303	6126	1007	361	0	221	0	62	0
34 FOOTWEAR, LEATHER PRDTS.	2207	42300	2739	1094	2160	27013	5	246	0
35 GLASS, GLASS PRDTS.	2827	310	5462	2410	601	255	0	8	0
36 STONE, CLAY PRDTS.	6740	10890	13527	10418	3987	11132	817	2255	1756
37 PRIMARY IRON, STEEL MFR.	26932	11035	64519	4549	363	9146	87	277	41
38 PRIMARY NONFERROUS MFR.	6554	11154	17255	1374	205	3623	4913	1766	4227

	Industry	C1	C2	C3	C4	C5	C6	C7	C8	C9
39	METAL CONTAINERS	3749	438	219	1347	88	2750	0	269	0
40	FABRICATED METAL PRDTS.	5253	8764	17534	4612	2370	10392	272	2751	209
41	SCREW MACH. PRDTS., ETC.	1685	9887	25638	3160	976	2747	21	111	6
42	OTHER FAB. METAL PRDTS.	2591	20524	43288	4396	1741	8638	0	623	16
43	ENGINES, TURBINES	0	7955	12747	693	0	287	0	0	0
44	FARM MACH. EQUIP.	55	44	5230	5476	1496	2080	39	1582	0
45	CONSTRUC. MACH., EQUIP.	195	329	4822	4232	555	1365	4	213	4
46	MATERIAL HANDLING MACH.	420	1463	7187	1072	595	696	5	43	0
47	METALWORKING MACHINERY	3070	14991	49673	1835	14	3098	0	115	0
48	SPECIAL MACH., EQUIP.	2991	20233	6978	1892	387	1968	0	16	6
49	GENERAL MACH., EQUIP.	1059	9261	16185	2512	152	2268	0	1076	8
50	MACHINE SHOP PRDTS.	2308	5349	13896	3075	508	6176	57	201	57
51	OFFICE, COMPUT. MACHINES	249	4204	9365	12060		691	0		0
52	SERVICE IND. MACHINES	1343	3652	8402	4913	493	7449	0	73	50
53	ELECT. TRANSMISS. EQUIP.	1585	11874	10097	4551	665	9879	0	86	27
54	HOUSEHOLD APPLIANCES	475	1377	7568	2335	2111	2761	0	45	0
55	ELECTRIC LIGHTING EQUIP.	167	8845	1756	617	1384	4263	0	0	0
56	RADIO, TV, ETC., EQUIP.	22460	42534	2997	9314	367	4933	0	4242	202
57	ELECTRONIC COMPONENTS	1187	28953	3047	2412	498	819	0	1579	11
58	MISC. ELECTRICAL MACH.	628	2933	6665	748	132	1437	0	126	7
59	MOTOR VEHICLES, EQUIP.	7021	3331	263074	3539	2160	23467	50	1662	14
60	AIRCRAFT, PARTS	14315	9610	10099	3517	686	31539	0	10	10
61	OTHER TRANSPORT. EQUIP.	10347	6256	8164	1082	5506	4097	83	1440	5
62	PROFESS., SCIEN. INSTRU.	1408	18177	12779	7024	349	3027	91	1217	0
63	MEDICAL, PHOTO. EQUIP.	494	10255	538	1103	6	951		29	
64	MISC. MANUFACTURING	3138	26340	11724	6014	2262	6858	168	1516	232
65	TRANSPORT., WAREHOUSING	52775	60839	70635	52283	13937	70496	11350	25789	6099
66	COMMUNICA., EXC. BRDCAST.	10548	25878	25760	10871	4845	17913	2633	6790	2826
67	RADIO, TV BROADCASTING	1151	1946	3050	1974	875	2237	497	1162	298
68	ELEC., GAS, WATER, SAN. SER.	4341	17182	26457	9478	5770	14276	2490	1802	1620
69	WHOLESALE, RETAIL TRADE	201393	375014	453876	228884	82122	303616	39860	95647	25932
70	FINANCE, INSURANCE	36969	103025	74281	46202	13752	62130	5714	20835	4251
71	REAL ESTATE, RENTAL	11239	16181	11973	8534	2066	12813	940	2806	2074
72	HOTELS, PERSONAL SERV.	25195	46384	54702	26119	13533	39942	5030	12242	17096
73	BUSINESS SERVICES	22808	46256	33762	23409	5890	33407	2679	7418	3780
74	RESEARCH, DEVELOPMENT	3810	3279	667	241	189	288	138	143	56
75	AUTO. REPAIR, SERVICES	5078	8536	12790	4344	1946	7088	648	1898	1012
76	AMUSEMENTS	6857	10808	15381	6604	1972	9247	1083	3423	23626
77	MED., EDUC. SERVICES	71939	198569	157345	85973	17090	106060	12317	29836	4048
78	FEDERAL GOVT. ENTERPRISE	10042	24307	21254	13550	5012	23486	2241	5949	1596
79	STATE, LOCAL GOVT. ENT.	5123	14475	12305	4099	2355	5706	876	6137	430
80	IMPORTS	0	0	0	0	0	0	0	0	0
81	BUS. TRAVEL, ENT., GIFTS.	0	0	0	0	0	0	0	0	0
82	OFFICE SUPPLIES	0	0	0	0	0	0	0	0	0
83	SCRAP, USED GOODS	0	0	0	0	0	0	0	0	0
84	GOVERNMENT INDUSTRY	209024	272233	341884	159917	113592	211971	47061	88541	30625
85	REST OF WORLD INDUSTRY	0	0	0	0	0	0	0	0	0
86	HOUSEHOLD INDUSTRY	29767	28389	56516	25563	46265	31024	5214	11604	2166
87	INVENTORY VALUATION ADJ.									
88	STATE TOTAL	1064900	2001732	2408535	1049586	562271	1445658	195960	438737	159492

TABLE C-6

STATE ESTIMATES OF 1963 EMPLOYMENT
(NUMBER OF EMPLOYEES)

INDUSTRY TITLE	28 NEW HAMPSHIRE	29 NEW JERSEY	30 NEW MEXICO	31 NEW YORK	32 NORTH CAROLINA	33 NORTH DAKOTA	34 OHIO	35 OKLAHOMA	36 OREGON
1 LIVESTOCK, PRDTS.	2126	8354	7987	26400	31622	4795	15433	13507	11954
2 OTHER AGRICULTURE PRDTS.	874	9646	6013	20600	84378	11205	18567	12493	17046
3 FORESTRY, FISHERIES	407	2995	73	5267	1790	3	980	132	2317
4 AGRI.+FORES.+FISH. SERV.	427	1321	403	3889	2466	488	4925	2159	158
5 IRON, FERRO. ORES MINING	0	0	62	1421	67	0	14	0	66
6 NONFERROUS ORES MINING	0	362	4142	726	25	23		269	50
7 COAL MINING	0	555	317	0	0	342	8483	354	0
8 CRUDE PETRO.+NATURAL GAS	0	0	4982	829	0	511	1573	20357	11
9 STONE, CLAY MINING	215	0	595	4573	2418	240	5673	1249	1799
10 CHEM.+FERT. MIN. MINING		2960	3557	253	79	0	408	0	2
11 NEW CONSTRUCTION	7146	86578	17989	205738	57475	6388	104858	40625	22198
12 MAINT.+ REPAIR CONSTR.	2890	26468	5164	70943	22700	4705	44868	9669	7954
13 ORDNANCE, ACCESSORIES	69	69	2711	4877	1493	0	6212	9	20
14 FOOD, KINDRED PRDTS.	2962	61098	3586	128882	32858	3060	76096	14254	20015
15 TOBACCO MANUFACTURES	0	1020		493	28215	0	1028	0	0
16 FABRICS	7703	13648	9	12674	146417	0	1504	51	647
17 TEXTILE PRDTS.	637	5238	0	8543	6396	0	3911	11	146
18 APPAREL	4160	72226	28	314971	108357	0	19297	4611	3198
19 MISC. TEXTILE PRDTS.	283	13096	200	35647	6960	22	3003	290	1012
20 LUMBER, WOOD PRDTS.	4042	4002	2120	14087	26297	88	8020	2014	69543
21 WOODEN CONTAINERS	484	960	9	1187	1106	0	939	0	432
22 HOUSEHOLD FURNITURE	1635	6185	194	17933	44371	10	7984	881	2170
23 OTHER FURNITURE	592	2687	63	14901	4100	8	9440	282	330
24 PAPER, ALLIED PRDTS.	4919	16603	0	36911	9719	0	23425	351	5970
25 PAPERBOARD CONTAINERS	585	15484	0	23476	3746	6	14374	477	705
26 PRINTING, PUBLISHING	3717	34790	1470	171596	10141	1366	58801	5900	5264
27 CHEMICALS,SELECT. PRDTS.	184	38443	255	19783	3972	155	22758	969	859
28 PLASTICS, SYNTHETICS	322	6626	8	6453	8657	0	6131	14	66
29 DRUGS, COSMETICS	67	32344	11	31256	1333	0	8177	144	260
30 PAINT, ALLIED PRDTS.	14	7022	560	3731	684	0	6246	182	349
31 PETROLEUM, RELATED INDS.	59	9045	226	2434	190	378	6810	5579	368
32 RUBBER, MISC. PLASTICS	3301	27925	0	28078	3476	0	80213	2303	409
33 LEATHER TANNING, PRDTS.	1983	2247	109	3332	361	0	1321	0	43
34 FOOTWEAR, LEATHER PRDTS.	18363	9099	9	48627	1337	0	8259	378	256
35 GLASS, GLASS PRDTS.	76	14229	1289	10286	2370	0	19643	4015	390
36 STONE, CLAY PRDTS.	1673	20353	0	27764	8142	474	41986	3240	2545
37 PRIMARY IRON, STEEL MFR.	938	12689	163	41187	1744	11	129258	1651	2560
38 PRIMARY NONFERROUS MFR.	786	23319		27357	1852	0	26847	2206	1876

#	Industry									
39	METAL CONTAINERS	0	7483	0	3703	9	0	3686	50	425
40	FABRICATED METAL PRDTS.	714	16069	309	30373	4496	249	39104	6145	2910
41	SCREW MACH. PRDTS., ETC.	295	11015	0	18223	1423	11	32066	282	160
42	OTHER FAB. METAL PRDTS.	980	24805	36	34309	3297	19	42011	1416	1460
43	ENGINES, TURBINES	9	220	0	7551	10	0	2282	10	45
44	FARM MACH., EQUIP.	7	198	7	1940	1299	350	6400	369	284
45	CONSTRUC. MACH., EQUIP.	823	1816	58	1279	112	10	14842	5666	352
46	MATERIAL HANDLING MACH.	0	4632	0	5999	112	16	8859	156	1473
47	METALWORKING MACHINERY	716	8129	86	17566	553	60	45583	133	151
48	SPECIAL MACH., EQUIP.	3411	11337	46	15142	7000	39	16256	466	1587
49	GENERAL MACH., EQUIP.	2025	14909	8	24566	376	8	31214	2237	240
50	MACHINE SHOP PRDTS.	468	5635	383	9290	1144	98	10019	1118	1207
51	OFFICE, COMPUT. MACHINES	132	4615	47	36466	461	0	19913	143	8
52	SERVICE IND. MACHINES	194	5381	58	11602	1056	0	10021	852	202
53	ELECT. TRANSMISS. EQUIP.	3207	16014	11	29601	4220	0	36656	1175	5052
54	HOUSEHOLD APPLIANCES	16	3781	0	7238	2072	0	32127	162	146
55	ELECTRIC LIGHTING EQUIP.	154	14248	0	19015	1229	0	13636	23	65
56	RADIO, TV, ETC., EQUIP.	3277	64960	254	87806	9963	0	16160	7906	98
57	ELECTRONIC COMPONENTS	4795	24595	74	35201	3650	0	9435	203	37
58	MISC. ELECTRICAL MACH.	68	4140	13	7117	2047	0	9168	128	359
59	MOTOR VEHICLES, EQUIP.	10	12874	115	39648	1987	0	112368	1542	1413
60	AIRCRAFT, PARTS	0	16613	5	52694	1489	0	47782	5001	858
61	OTHER TRANSPORT. EQUIP.	93	9908	23	9902	1266	7	6335	643	2602
62	PROFESS., SCIEN. INSTRU.	257	12678	151	25611	2319	12	10596	557	461
63	MEDICAL, PHOTO. EQUIP.	416	4581	0	50155	774	0	601	22	499
64	MISC. MANUFACTURING	1831	28581	360	89657	2745	245	19574	1115	1522
65	TRANSPORT., WAREHOUSING	3171	84158	9929	327699	42834	6828	125390	25808	27536
66	COMMUNICA.,EXC. BRDCAST.	2623	25974	3469	95677	12050	1751	32819	8169	7593
67	RADIO, TV BROADCASTING	342	513	651	16400	2778	568	4584	1394	1159
68	ELEC.,GAS,WATER,SAN.SER.	1801	22729	4596	54895	9671	1914	32790	9465	5956
69	WHOLESALE, RETAIL TRADE	35749	411142	51028	1270894	236844	36721	598829	131029	123948
70	FINANCE, INSURANCE	6927	77630	8865	384166	41384	5608	102458	22881	19677
71	REAL ESTATE, RENTAL	890	17656	1506	131873	5638	453	20703	3979	3899
72	HOTELS, PERSONAL SERV.	5548	53431	8600	198456	36018	4306	71804	17924	15036
73	BUSINESS SERVICES	2348	56559	5370	261678	15782	1452	61899	15408	11710
74	RESEARCH, DEVELOPMENT	120	2779	467	8533	149	51	1841	211	127
75	AUTO. REPAIR, SERVICES	840	9893	1259	29295	6453	459	15221	3357	348
76	AMUSEMENTS	1202	12903	1986	72647	5830	1067	19949	4311	3712
77	MED.,EDUC. SERVICES	17983	124892	12072	524880	65520	12297	223048	40911	39915
78	FEDERAL GOVT. ENTERPRISE	2170	21141	3018	84086	12109	2700	32612	8357	6232
79	STATE, LOCAL GOVT. ENT.	839	8162	1135	67476	4958	443	22702	3108	3297
80	IMPORTS	0	0	0	0	0	0	0	0	0
81	BUS.TRAVEL, ENT., GIFTS.	0	0	0	0	0	0	0	0	0
82	OFFICE SUPPLIES	0	0	0	0	0	0	0	0	0
83	SCRAP, USED GOODS	28905	301414	90859	796702	184994	38162	397152	166315	104706
84	GOVERNMENT INDUSTRY	0	0	0	0	0	0	0	0	0
85	REST OF WORLD INDUSTRY	4670	38722	7694	132358	68061	4865	66898	19461	14661
86	HOUSEHOLD INDUSTRY									
87	INVENTORY VALUATION ADJ.									
88	STATE TOTAL	213596	2188601	278861	6506453	1473496	155047	3224858	670234	596116

201

TABLE C-6

STATE ESTIMATES OF 1963 EMPLOYMENT
(NUMBER OF EMPLOYEES)

INDUSTRY TITLE	37 PENNSYL-VANIA	38 RHODE ISLAND	39 SOUTH CAROLINA	40 SOUTH DAKOTA	41 TENNESSEE	42 TEXAS	43 UTAH	44 VERMONT	45 VIRGINIA
1 LIVESTOCK, PRDTS.	16545	568	13975	6233	23872	61435	5827	4241	25163
2 OTHER AGRICULTURE PRDTS.	11455	432	40025	4767	33128	86565	3173	1759	25837
3 FORESTRY, FISHERIES	1794	464	1594	27	996	2276	66	509	3067
4 AGRI.,FORES.,FISH. SERV.	5287	269	1118	590	2207	9436	679	129	1444
5 IRON,FERRO.ORES MINING	1814	0	0	2	9	343	285	0	26
6 NONFERROUS ORES MINING	182	0	14	1914	1027	110	6386	0	378
7 COAL MINING	36196	0	0	0	1846	135	1726	0	11525
8 CRUDE PETRO.,NATURAL GAS	3853	0	0	2	8	60981	567	0	7
9 STONE, CLAY MINING	5725	203	1604	633	2718	4584	895	894	3672
10 CHEM.,FERT. MIN. MINING	176	0	24	0	1373	1810	317	0	30
11 NEW CONSTRUCTION	115729	10437	25276	7826	44250	175936	15795	3732	75766
12 MAINT., REPAIR CONSTR.	49042	2651	12045	5386	11931	48558	3688	2277	16654
13 ORDNANCE, ACCESSORIES	3713	0	0	0	2024	6590	3038	0	44
14 FOOD, KINDRED PRDTS.	107695	6027	11018	7895	31937	75309	8676	2710	32031
15 TOBACCO MANUFACTURES	9540	6	1848	0	990	106	0	0	14030
16 FABRICS	26013	17640	121200	0	9862	5353	56	604	24690
17 TEXTILE PRDTS.	9214	3765	5933	0	2182	920	27	185	2475
18 APPAREL	196134	4929	35754	0	68102	37537	2299	1748	32982
19 MISC. TEXTILE PRDTS.	9215	401	2285	65	2298	3166	93	23	1555
20 LUMBER, WOOD PRDTS.	11648	469	13781	671	15164	16398	944	3146	19120
21 WOODEN CONTAINERS	689	42	980	7	1410	863	9	214	1794
22 HOUSEHOLD FURNITURE	13916	108	3080	83	16342	6870	544	1691	17929
23 OTHER FURNITURE	9200	1173	173	15	1560	3637	304	10	2085
24 PAPER, ALLIED PRDTS.	23136	548	5462	6	7202	8457	154	1943	9844
25 PAPERBOARD CONTAINERS	17133	1565	3267	45	2840	3723	118	354	2236
26 PRINTING, PUBLISHING	63416	4043	3415	1590	14461	29565	2667	2295	10793
27 CHEMICALS,SELECT. PRDTS.	14556	911	9749	117	19556	32981	642	80	10610
28 PLASTICS, SYNTHETICS	12609	1556	5625	0	16582	5409	0	52	21888
29 DRUGS, COSMETICS	13825	202	747	64	3094	2533	77	36	2267
30 PAINT, ALLIED PRDTS.	4652	274	169	0	578	2615	66	86	418
31 PETROLEUM, RELATED INDS.	14156	120	281	9	503	35963	975	9	506
32 RUBBER, MISC. PLASTICS	23035	8074	2043	206	7698	6757	416	1702	4671
33 LEATHER TANNING, PRDTS.	2928	25	86	0	1103	115	7	231	592
34 FOOTWEAR, LEATHER PRDTS.	28447	1422	0	0	14130	2532	30	529	3713
35 GLASS, GLASS PRDTS.	20882	2220	2205	0	4825	1642	9	0	930
36 STONE, CLAY PRDTS.	36426	454	4192	830	8489	23170	2458	3225	8770
37 PRIMARY IRON, STEEL MFR.	187248	2302	951	4	6573	15892	4719	279	3892
38 PRIMARY NONFERROUS MFR.	22915	6736	180	0	6728	11556	1968	412	2219

202

39 METAL CONTAINERS	155	0	135	2687	292	0	18	0	5046
40 FABRICATED METAL PRDTS.	6419	215	2264	20558	10126	465	2175	942	44904
41 SCREW MACH. PRDTS., ETC.	123	81	40	1281	1786	0	555	2125	21679
42 OTHER FAB. METAL PRDTS.	3161	348	180	9188	5114	82	1157	4580	33848
43 ENGINES, TURBINES	0	0	0	465	10	0	0	8	16078
44 FARM MACH., EQUIP.	527	44	139	1428	2738	192	100	7	2952
45 CONSTRUC. MACH., EQUIP.	198	57	1283	20118	302	0	22	27	6515
46 MATERIAL HANDLING MACH.	163	0	15	1211	1098	125	199	50	7329
47 METALWORKING MACHINERY	106	4427	93	1512	803	159	1415	4271	18499
48 SPECIAL MACH., EQUIP.	746	360	166	3517	1082	11	4889	2936	15790
49 GENERAL MACH., EQUIP.	636	55	491	3490	1227	142	703	750	21913
50 MACHINE SHOP PRDTS.	825	129	362	4381	1436	209	929	830	8083
51 OFFICE, COMPUT. MACHINES	1992	1222	16	527			476	13	4726
52 SERVICE IND. MACHINES	983	0	470	5510			59	200	10722
53 ELECT. TRANSMISS. EQUIP.	4546	261	158	2298	1347	0	2200	539	36797
54 HOUSEHOLD APPLIANCES	47	279	0	809	2409	0	458	148	4361
55 ELECTRIC LIGHTING EQUIP.	56	0	39	834	6322	0	112	3095	13114
56 RADIO, TV, ETC., EQUIP.	5820	296	830	10517	882	0	66	746	15938
57 ELECTRONIC COMPONENTS	5870	0	622	9338	5898	10	3586	1830	32235
58 MISC. ELECTRICAL MACH.	129	1361	13	1209	1142	131	39	424	4565
59 MOTOR VEHICLES, EQUIP.	2332	365	192	7917	454	0	234	613	18879
60 AIRCRAFT, PARTS	1488	192	12072	34341	4107	23	0	539	26901
61 OTHER TRANSPORT. EQUIP.	21618	2113	429	7830	3432	141	699	547	20553
62 PROFESS., SCIEN. INSTRU.	713	49	74	3601	3655	13	1166	2235	21529
63 MEDICAL, PHOTO. EQUIP.	1024	746	7	597	1392	0	711	1019	2496
64 MISC. MANUFACTURING	3630	331	633	5355	18	190	2859	21212	26618
65 TRANSPORT., WAREHOUSING	55432	525	13502	140074	5942	5178	14810	8210	158206
66 COMMUNICA.,EXC. BRDCAST.	13053	3672	3804	34442	38341	1856	5374	3019	38263
67 RADIO, TV BROADCASTING	1977	1512	639	5191	10207	492	1544	396	4640
68 ELEC.,GAS,WATER,SAN.SER.	9118	244	2462	40047	2457	1725	4786	3015	42350
69 WHOLESALE, RETAIL TRADE	222943	913	60301	625689	3200	38237	100818	53465	671905
70 FINANCE, INSURANCE	38520	20629	10056	118604	194996	5566	17958	12191	132224
71 REAL ESTATE, RENTAL	10107	3928	2110	18597	35466	731	1990	2127	23490
72 HOTELS, PERSONAL SERV.	36134	403	6813	97829	5408	4294	16569	6472	84413
73 BUSINESS SERVICES	18033	3689	5437	63427	30571	1716	7743	5243	76076
74 RESEARCH, DEVELOPMENT	1587	1015	374	2688	22461	126	195	79	2886
75 AUTO. REPAIR, SERVICES	5216	45	1355	16365	511	664	3616	1412	17918
76 AMUSEMENTS	6479	355	2211	17712	5104	1180	2599	2247	18307
77 MED.,EDUC. SERVICES	67267	1027	20862	166926	4955	11976	24122	23778	299131
78 FEDERAL GOVT. ENTERPRISE	15073	13377	3127	31813	63132	2622	6182	3471	39690
79 STATE, LOCAL GOVT. ENT.	6470	1672	1329	20833	19925	647	2574	1245	17913
80 IMPORTS	0	411	0	0	11905	0	0	0	0
81 BUS.TRAVEL, ENT., GIFTS.	0	0	0	0	0	0	0	0	0
82 OFFICE SUPPLIES	0	0	0	0	0	0	0	0	0
83 SCRAP, USED GOODS		0			0				
84 GOVERNMENT INDUSTRY	344242	16349	71066	612091	160130	45677	159673	63101	438637
85 REST OF WORLD INDUSTRY	0	0	0	0	0	0	0	0	0
86 HOUSEHOLD INDUSTRY	49504	4675	4432	124104	48552	6200	47638	4181	75113
87 INVENTORY VALUATION ADJ.	0	0	0	0	0	0	0	0	0
88 STATE TOTAL	1360115	122285	300303	3088779	1109943	169771	773117	323383	3713371

TABLE C-6

STATE ESTIMATES OF 1963 EMPLOYMENT
(NUMBER OF EMPLOYEES)

INDUSTRY TITLE	46 WASHINGTON	47 WEST VIRGINIA	48 WISCONSIN	49 WYOMING	50 ALASKA	51 HAWAII	52 NO STATE ALLOCATION	53 NATIONAL TOTAL
1 LIVESTOCK, PRDTS.	12476	5723	18494	4016	291	1785	0	739052
2 OTHER AGRICULTURE PRDTS.	26524	4277	9506	1984	18	12507	0	1055549
3 FORESTRY, FISHERIES	3215	271	1214	39	55	46	0	69756
4 AGRI.,FORES.,FISH. SERV.	478	443	2373	143	0	421	0	110244
5 IRON, FERRO. ORES MINING	2	0	853	627	2	0	0	26185
6 NONFERROUS ORES MINING	576	0	118	1169	296	0	0	50069
7 COAL MINING	194	41553	0	364	194	0	0	145407
8 CRUDE PETRO.,NATURAL GAS	120	3517	0	3158	257	0	0	158975
9 STONE, CLAY MINING	1026	1299	2772	577	61	328	0	100198
10 CHEM.,FERT. MIN. MINING	3	6	0	674	0	0	0	19533
11 NEW CONSTRUCTION	36985	13331	41347	8368	4175	12881	0	2452764
12 MAINT., REPAIR CONSTR.	10101	7381	15496	3271	601	2758	0	783614
13 ORDNANCE, ACCESSORIES	445	1278	568	0	0	0	0	245934
14 FOOD, KINDRED PRDTS.	26626	7275	58432	1408	2877	15214	0	1642806
15 TOBACCO MANUFACTURES	0	631	75	0	0	0	0	77331
16 FABRICS	358	371	741	0	0	8	0	541095
17 TEXTILE PRDTS.	108	8	1455	0	0	43	0	101596
18 APPAREL	3555	4542	10876	0	8	2113	0	1354441
19 MISC. TEXTILE PRDTS.	781	187	795	4	8	149	0	148142
20 LUMBER, WOOD PRDTS.	41938	5951	15137	941	943	464	0	532278
21 WOODEN CONTAINERS	493	96	1039	9	9	0	0	30947
22 HOUSEHOLD FURNITURE	1755	814	3717	5	8	477	0	270272
23 OTHER FURNITURE	353	293	2508	6	95	91	0	106389
24 PAPER, ALLIED PRDTS.	16477	904	29997	0	1425	283	0	387020
25 PAPERBOARD CONTAINERS	1842	684	6342	0	0	116	0	201022
26 PRINTING, PUBLISHING	8450	3430	21999	712	432	1730	0	913241
27 CHEMICALS,SELECT. PRDTS.	9961	15545	1952	6	11	354	0	346599
28 PLASTICS, SYNTHETICS	271	6862	600	0	0	0	0	144713
29 DRUGS, COSMETICS	262	174	2251	0	0	78	0	184574
30 PAINT, ALLIED PRDTS.	433	63	1137	0	0	0	0	61266
31 PETROLEUM, RELATED INDS.	1332	629	575	2060	61	314	0	153498
32 RUBBER, MISC. PLASTICS	484	196	6946	10	10	59	0	414959
33 LEATHER TANNING, PRDTS.	7	508	4225	0	0	0	0	34287
34 FOOTWEAR, LEATHER PRDTS.	357	367	11207	0	0	108	0	293202
35 GLASS, GLASS PRDTS.	389	14580	1875	0	0	39	0	146959
36 STONE, CLAY PRDTS.	4643	5799	7424	680	172	896	0	426830
37 PRIMARY IRON, STEEL MFR.	1932	15576	23186	0	0	182	0	820210
38 PRIMARY NONFERROUS MFR.	5741	5136	5613	0	0	0	0	319626

#	Industry								
39	METAL CONTAINERS	834	217	2180	0	0	406	0	63753
40	FABRICATED METAL PRDTS.	3908	3220	14547	76	74	243	0	393500
41	SCREW MACH. PRDTS., ETC.	275	1152	11652	40	0	0	0	226759
42	OTHER FAB. METAL PRDTS.	1000	2934	7598	26	0	94	0	408469
43	ENGINES, TURBINES	10		17224	0	0	0	0	86604
44	FARM MACH., EQUIP.	341	341	12480	12	0	46	0	112614
45	CONSTRUC. MACH., EQUIP.	1277	1262	14186	0	0	0	0	150633
46	MATERIAL HANDLING MACH.	1018	243	1420	0	0	5	0	60326
47	METALWORKING MACHINERY	418	598	10482	0	0	9	0	259001
48	SPECIAL MACH., EQUIP.	1574	72	9247	0	0	166	0	171526
49	GENERAL MACH., EQUIP.	389	98	11024	0	0	0	0	233245
50	MACHINE SHOP PRDTS.	1508	660	3291	8	60	9	0	135820
51	OFFICE, CUMPUT. MACHINES	187	206	458	57	0	61	0	137138
52	SERVICE IND. MACHINES	361	439	5394	0	0	0	0	112841
53	ELECT. TRANSMISS. EQUIP.	658	46	24985	25	0	11	0	293193
54	HOUSEHOLD APPLIANCES	325	2541	6379	0	0	5	0	145893
55	ELECTRIC LIGHTING EQUIP.	529	57	1459	6	0	0	0	133092
56	RADIO, TV, ETC., EQUIP.	966	905	9609	0	8	8	0	567725
57	ELECTRONIC COMPONENTS	151	0	2802	0	0	11	0	288434
58	MISC. ELECTRICAL MACH.	92	664	4629	0	7	5	0	83528
59	MOTOR VEHICLES, EQUIP.	1891	10	37721	175	0	0	0	693026
60	AIRCRAFT, PARTS	63088	1508	354	9	5	85	0	679333
61	OTHER TRANSPORT. EQUIP.	7299	453	5399	71	89	0	0	227926
62	PROFESS., SCIEN. INSTRU.	44	278	5909	10	10	80	0	208300
63	MEDICAL, PHOTO. EQUIP.	59	842	374	56	29	0	0	97154
64	MISC. MANUFACTURING	1735		8520			314	0	388614
65	TRANSPORT., WAREHOUSING	41383	22642	43825	7095	5519	10607	0	2443392
66	COMMUNICA.,EXC. BRDCAST.	11267	5376	13366	1368	334	1086	0	713740
67	RADIO, TV BROADCASTING	1908	850	240	318	229	497	0	101838
68	ELEC.,GAS,WATER,SAN.SER.	4764	10456	13146	1240	456	2041	0	557440
69	WHOLESALE, RETAIL TRADE	184394	79698	246151	19954	9825	44626	0	11498905
70	FINANCE, INSURANCE	33307	11030	42068	2497	1448	7328	0	2349797
71	REAL ESTATE, RENTAL	7963	2620	6654	446	430	3804	0	524783
72	HOTELS, PERSONAL SERV.	19794	10985	28436	3668	1442	8652	0	1617868
73	BUSINESS SERVICES	17649	7139	21232	1522	1503	4979	0	1365608
74	RESEARCH, DEVELOPMENT	267	119	291	65	65	226	0	65714
75	AUTO. REPAIR, SERVICES	2160	1571	3308	397	219	1418	0	274527
76	AMUSEMENTS	6105	3267	7660	747	370	2468	0	455364
77	MED.,EDUC. SERVICES	63914	27524	89148	3482	2340	13198	0	3980146
78	FEDERAL GOVT. ENTERPRISE	12681	4712	11123	1206	3166	4324	0	698023
79	STATE, LOCAL GOVT. ENT.	11846	2159	4599	394	326	1749	0	398000
80	IMPORTS	0	0	0	0	0	0	0	0
81	BUS.TRAVEL, ENT., GIFTS.	0	0	0	0	0	0	0	0
82	OFFICE SUPPLIES	0	0	0	0	0	0	0	0
83	SCRAP, USED GOODS	0	0	0	0	0	0	0	0
84	GOVERNMENT INDUSTRY	215345	66342	172206	25240	60371	100092	0	10075004
85	REST OF WORLD INDUSTRY	0	0	0	0	0	0	0	0
86	HOUSEHOLD INDUSTRY	24490	12617	23951	2857	1976	4889	0	2656000
87	INVENTORY VALUATION ADJ.	0	0	0	0	0	0	0	0
88	STATE TOTAL	969867	457553	1269572	103279	102302	266986	0	61745179

TABLE C-7

STATE ESTIMATES OF 1947 PAYROLLS
(THOUSANDS OF CURRENT DOLLARS)

INDUSTRY TITLE	1 ALABAMA	2 ARIZONA	3 ARKANSAS	4 CALIFORNIA	5 COLORADO	6 CONNECTICUT	7 DELAWARE	8 DISTRICT OF COLUMBIA	9 FLORIDA
1 LIVESTOCK, PRDTS.	10104	10824	19288	95117	15772	14540	3871	0	21214
2 OTHER AGRICULTURE PRDTS.	19896	29176	42712	305883	29228	12460	2129	0	51786
3 FORESTRY, FISHERIES	2531	17	1494	15231	139	738	1335	0	5896
4 AGRI.,FORES.,FISH. SERV.	3782	1651	5124	12151	1608	1738	1944	0	1609
5 IRON, FERRO. ORES MINING	6192	6	17	269	35	0	0	0	0
6 NONFERROUS ORES MINING	0	28497	1838	15416	6776	0	0	0	1756
7 COAL MINING	59704	0	5500	0	21388	0	0	0	0
8 CRUDE PETRO.,NATURAL GAS	45	0	6712	65824	4103	0	0	0	296
9 STONE, CLAY MINING	3729	492	463	12407	941	1194	438	0	2964
10 CHEM.,FERT. MIN. MINING	0	137	1956	1490	250	0	0	0	4965
11 NEW CONSTRUCTION	36932	25231	25745	539568	31717	63113	11018	36679	108594
12 MAINT., REPAIR CONSTR.	14591	10042	8476	198375	19153	33569	7101	14619	39250
13 ORDNANCE, ACCESSORIES	24	0	0	367	322	29153	0	7	4
14 FOOD, KINDRED PRDTS.	26941	9546	20505	364799	37977	22547	12269	14496	43529
15 TOBACCO MANUFACTURES	1027	0	511	2057	13	984	290	0	13172
16 FABRICS	85190	3	1783	3852	637	65543	1957	7	22
17 TEXTILE PRDTS.	13249	0	528	4996	85	15669	615	4	145
18 APPAREL	18574	399	3889	104038	2391	54770	3330	1164	3648
19 MISC. TEXTILE PRDTS.	2906	80	65	12153	664	4496	55	450	804
20 LUMBER, WOOD PRDTS.	47672	6206	43163	114316	4509	2297	1031	385	20372
21 WOODEN CONTAINERS	1846	374	3530	9689	617	1165	976	56	5591
22 HOUSEHOLD FURNITURE	2230	412	6107	40530	689	3219	44	68	3306
23 OTHER FURNITURE	638	230	279	14611	853	2281	45	240	1215
24 PAPER, ALLIED PRDTS.	13349	463	7416	19875	838	14584	1751	755	13520
25 PAPERBOARD CONTAINERS	489	88	335	15996	922	11436	1205	1245	1938
26 PRINTING, PUBLISHING	10425	4556	5244	145837	11783	33797	2297	32565	18200
27 CHEMICALS,SELECT. PRDTS.	14630	733	6985	40768	3600	9019	5848	59	10261
28 PLASTICS, SYNTHETICS	0	0	5986	2727	0	4199	10540	0	2162
29 DRUGS, COSMETICS	268	120	90	22408	390	8154	111	236	352
30 PAINT, ALLIED PRDTS.	573	114	46	16037	847	1850	48	92	474
31 PETROLEUM, RELATED INDS.	822	283	3501	74528	1007	409	436	63	451
32 RUBBER, MISC. PLASTICS	15268	10	1187	52500	2264	48536	3712	0	2091
33 LEATHER TANNING, PRDTS.	0	0	0	3911	22	782	7627	0	505
34 FOOTWEAR, LEATHER PRDTS.	620	123	1814	11677	2723	2744	0	0	401
35 GLASS, GLASS PRDTS.	77	27	2937	16912	1353	4365	0	0	117
36 STONE, CLAY PRDTS.	13426	2095	3451	60202	5123	12735	672	521	6490
37 PRIMARY IRON, STEEL MFR.	102088	857	705	76392	14212	36487	3896	2	547
38 PRIMARY NONFERROUS MFR.	12060	11708	4566	28814	3042	81214	55	0	374

39 METAL CONTAINERS	519	0	522	19560	469	236	171	0	1627
40 FABRICATED METAL PRDTS.	13770	1900	1054	84168	4436	20261	1975	1104	3607
41 SCREW MACH. PRDTS., ETC.	1959	1	25	17579	62	38954	2042	0	73
42 OTHER FAB. METAL PRDTS.	6860	253	1122	46549	1858	92569	1265	334	1546
43 ENGINES, TURBINES	17			13054	121	2701			17
44 FARM MACH., EQUIP.	2412	50	1480	12863	1076	1369	48	0	717
45 CONSTRUC. MACH., EQUIP.	1438	0	706	26552	4584	3212		0	502
46 MATERIAL HANDLING MACH.	460		182	3209	737	1117			51
47 METALWORKING MACHINERY	102	64	3	9542	118	58014	2991	5	56
48 SPECIAL MACH., EQUIP.	2105	129	370	24371	3481	23969	6997	19	1500
49 GENERAL MACH., EQUIP.	2076		248	25860	1316	73231	375	153	1090
50 MACHINE SHOP PRDTS.	479	110	110	10948	563	4418	276	24	252
51 OFFICE, COMPUT. MACHINES	27	0		10586	188	50492		27	30
52 SERVICE IND. MACHINES	339	368	183	9069	174	3399	92		9
53 ELECT. TRANSMISS. EQUIP.	934	0	0	19976	407	15106	45	0	286
54 HOUSEHOLD APPLIANCES	1927	364	154	24132	90	42221	117	0	85
55 ELECTRIC LIGHTING EQUIP.	1011	34	27	12752	277	21807	1	4	154
56 RADIO, TV, ETC., EQUIP.	1260	72	0	12174	881	15642			200
57 ELECTRONIC COMPONENTS	311	18	0	2611	18	3371	0	380	49
58 MISC. ELECTRICAL MACH.	81	0	0	4680	214	3799		88	1405
59 MOTOR VEHICLES, EQUIP.	1634	839	260	47724	1045	8106	814	82	2028
60 AIRCRAFT, PARTS	0	63	0	267820	127	76075	262	37	262
61 OTHER TRANSPORT. EQUIP.	19175	445	302	68487	2390	7747	2798		13934
62 PROFESS., SCIEN. INSTRU.	217	172	1185	16396	300	46122	238	353	310
63 MEDICAL, PHOTO. EQUIP.	1		2	4679	670	1779	0	33	100
64 MISC. MANUFACTURING	1149	298	1549	30452	3621	67062	1876	498	2663
65 TRANSPORT., WAREHOUSING	127000	42000	59000	769000	82000	82000	30000	58000	149000
66 COMMUNICA.,EXC. BRDCAST.	13358	6444	8071	108514	18834	29059	2413	26137	24583
67 RADIO, TV BROADCASTING	2283	1249	887	12416	1425	2281	284	3925	3120
68 ELEC.,GAS,WATER,SAN.SER.	17015	9308	8967	129679	12616	24209	2791	15508	17250
69 WHOLESALE, RETAIL TRADE	215076	94733	122141	2087061	208448	300600	51724	269749	375224
70 FINANCE, INSURANCE	35920	9328	12757	286700	20815	96639	10839	26563	42319
71 REAL ESTATE, RENTAL	5516	4272	2898	113455	8608	7447	1984	19475	23807
72 HOTELS, PERSONAL SERV.	26252	15154	15904	228850	22632	32320	4581	38918	63508
73 BUSINESS SERVICES	6784	2952	2980	117066	6895	11601	1742	15755	17107
74 RESEARCH, DEVELOPMENT	992	63	51	19814	170	902	509	574	856
75 AUTO. REPAIR, SERVICES	4255	1565	1774	40714	4142	5093	637	3947	8447
76 AMUSEMENTS	6375	3448	4513	35508	8228	11142	1819	9454	30284
77 MED.,EDUC. SERVICES	28369	16802	15434	575699	24462	41907	4374	95511	51148
78 FEDERAL GOVT. ENTERPRISE	27565	4623	12567	95213	11564	16429	2319	20344	17303
79 STATE, LOCAL GOVT. ENT.	2486	1655	549	86512	2430	1821	385	2745	6809
80 IMPORTS	0	0	0	0	0	0	0	0	0
81 BUS.,TRAVEL, ENT., GIFTS.	0	0	0	0	0	0	0	0	0
82 OFFICE SUPPLIES	0	0	0	0	0	0	0	0	0
83 SCRAP, USED GOODS	0	0	0	0	0	0	0	0	0
84 GOVERNMENT INDUSTRY	192850	82978	87318	1651509	164426	139832	21092	532744	341894
85 REST OF WORLD INDUSTRY	57455	11501	19527	197836	14325	43508	10065	38124	84713
86 HOUSEHOLD INDUSTRY	0	0	0	0	0	0	0	0	0
87 INVENTORY VALUATION ADJ.	0	0	0	0	0	0	0	0	0
88 STATE TOTAL	1371712	457818	628770	10283062	869236	2129365	256587	1284430	1677946

TABLE C-7

STATE ESTIMATES OF 1947 PAYROLLS
(THOUSANDS OF CURRENT DOLLARS)

INDUSTRY TITLE	10 GEORGIA	11 IDAHO	12 ILLINOIS	13 INDIANA	14 IOWA	15 KANSAS	16 KENTUCKY	17 LOUISIANA	18 MAINE
1 LIVESTOCK, PROTS.	14895	12516	28848	22673	45194	17560	17980	14973	9195
2 OTHER AGRICULTURE PROTS.	31105	27484	68152	24327	43806	34440	24020	29027	18805
3 FORESTRY, FISHERIES.	818	140	462	293	215	124	1277	7264	4811
4 AGRI.,FORES.,FISH. SERV.	5218	1160	8192	6471	8149	3787	1643	2510	874
5 IRON, FERRO. ORES MINING	123	25	120	0	0	0	4	0	0
6 NONFERROUS ORES MINING	359	15575	0	0	0	0		0	0
7 COAL MINING	128	0	110604	34224	3936	2201	162572	0	0
8 CRUDE PETRO.,NATURAL GAS	0	0	0	1905	0	22238	5693	31363	0
9 STONE, CLAY MIN. MINING	13324	576	15763	7001	3532	2436	3466	2853	1401
10 CHEM.,FERT. MIN. MINING	51	795	9097			827	411	5074	
11 NEW CONSTRUCTION	59000	12838	277178	95036	48996	37786	38591	76047	19928
12 MAINT., REPAIR CONSTR.	22638	8301	149187	54396	28534	20635	16955	24899	11287
13 ORDNANCE, ACCESSORIES	24	6461	1941	728	51	3		0	
14 FOOD, KINDRED PROTS.	57672	15338	421555	119739	128252	75821	61257	58296	17225
15 TOBACCO MANUFACTURES	1038	0	851	2544	19		1620	1162	31
16 FABRICS	166610	0	8228	2697	515	0	5915	952	56158
17 TEXTILE PROTS.	21320	0	14101	1464	12	28	474	574	7760
18 APPAREL	46894	0	139189	35817	8104	17	21115	8725	4179
19 MISC. TEXTILE PROTS.	9724	69	16039	2822	1487	2284	1083	2294	3418
20 LUMBER, WOOD PROTS.	40106	21320	28121	19600	11435	1234	16342	42608	19326
21 WOODEN CONTAINERS	4572	251	7170	2181	705	1768	4856	4668	3440
22 HOUSEHOLD FURNITURE	8603	86	54722	43767	3449	411	16610	2227	504
23 OTHER FURNITURE	1372	118	27306	6278	2077	1695	770	418	910
24 PAPER, ALLIED PROTS.	11238	8	47745	12322	1915	708	1112	34165	48611
25 PAPERBOARD CONTAINERS	3630	88	35162	12193	1633	1141	2372	4379	367
26 PRINTING, PUBLISHING	17140		322532	46241	24987	1968	16969	11094	4670
27 CHEMICALS,SELECT. PROTS.	10856	2586	51208	9495	1955	13300	3869	27586	1596
28 PLASTICS, SYNTHETICS	5110	429	5718	939	438	8126	5565	6917	104
29 DRUGS, COSMETICS	2145	99	47399	47254	4668	4724	288	489	96
30 PAINT, ALLIED PROTS.	1102	2	25969	4135	1173	134	5035	979	129
31 PETROLEUM, RELATED INUS.	1363	201	51277	47245	268	15172	3298	49210	166
32 RUBBER, MISC. PLASTICS	3259	0	33027	34604	10623	4513	7866	63	467
33 LEATHER TANNING, PROTS.	823	0	16414	1080	0	0	875	93	1578
34 FOOTWEAR, LEATHER PROTS.	3779	71	50594	4206	1360	270	5970	331	30893
35 GLASS, GLASS PROTS.	76	0	30333	27833	204	9	487	1981	219
36 STONE, CLAY PROTS.	15015	1168	55607	29703	13093	8764	8406	5149	1516
37 PRIMARY IRON, STEEL MFR.	7153	138	264501	252744	8216	2839	18635	1878	615
38 PRIMARY NONFERROUS MFR.	2174	3429	82459	31180	1137	1451	10223	1103	421

		1	2	3	4	5	6	7	8	9
39	METAL CONTAINERS	190	0	39153	2447	621	0	128	2046	473
40	FABRICATED METAL PRDTS.	5148	420	75369	44165	10730	8094	24699	5872	1847
41	SCREW MACH. PRDTS., ETC.	1266	0	94030	22110	755	325	1292	489	84
42	OTHER FAB. METAL PRDTS.	1259	8	160311	27996	5867	571	6919	359	1882
43	ENGINES, TURBINES	0	0	33108	25783	556	163	0	0	0
44	FARM MACH., EQUIP.	3036	686	181939	26742	39962	3551	4190	740	117
45	CONSTRUC. MACH., EQUIP.	2240	161	63405	11543	19255	4186	1329	1298	400
46	MATERIAL HANDLING MACH.	996	10	15619	1892	1636	501	1327	51	70
47	METALWORKING MACHINERY	226	2	87224	19789	4429	564	1075	100	118
48	SPECIAL MACH., EQUIP.	5903	2	63854	13973	5736	2014	1473	1563	17043
49	GENERAL MACH., EQUIP.	764	175	59649	40394	4170	384	3240	339	30
50	MACHINE SHOP PRDTS.	78	42	14895	12774	1899	909	926	331	87
51	OFFICE, COMPUT. MACHINES	55	0	23190	831	49	0	250	0	28
52	SERVICE IND. MACHINES	812	0	26635	44230	784	533	1312	180	66
53	ELECT. TRANSMISS. EQUIP.	1069	0	50918	45290	3928	651	576	0	154
54	HOUSEHOLD APPLIANCES	1290	0	102142	40593	17225	3078	2832	117	0
55	ELECTRIC LIGHTING EQUIP.	121	0	43845	18587	368	698	1662	0	0
56	RADIO, TV, ETC., EQUIP.	2069	0	227652	38293	3620	176	101	22	0
57	ELECTRONIC COMPONENTS	311	0	21998	12403	661	40	3853	0	0
58	MISC. ELECTRICAL MACH.	1170	0	16630	40899	2993	649	1335	87	34
59	MOTOR VEHICLES, EQUIP.	7843	53	59923	18639	2407	8084	7019	384	36
60	AIRCRAFT, PARTS	2	0	6467	29922	3549	21287	0	0	1
61	OTHER TRANSPORT. EQUIP.	2912	260	92441	33400	2964	3126	4338	24391	9568
62	PROFESS., SCIEN. INSTRU.	363	3	44700	7836	484	426	1481	101	461
63	MEDICAL, PHOTO. EQUIP.	3	101	23957	911	773	6	31	31	186
64	MISC. MANUFACTURING	3232	402	91119	23233	12211	1606	3197	1991	3910
65	TRANSPORT., WAREHOUSING	145000	34000	768000	244000	124000	138000	136000	143000	32000
66	COMMUNICA.,EXC. BROCAST.	30440	4670	141361	34725	20207	15412	12650	18528	8722
67	RADIO, TV BROADCASTING	4573	878	8340	2781	3383	1883	2088	2759	1204
68	ELEC.,GAS,WATER,SAN.SER.	22488	5111	92539	35002	18330	18090	15926	26159	7803
69	WHOLESALE, RETAIL TRADE	338861	74812	1755844	510775	325546	215754	225004	268366	94491
70	FINANCE, INSURANCE	52858	5564	260666	63919	41079	21277	25973	35278	12056
71	REAL ESTATE, RENTAL	6306	1260	102401	11710	7174	4185	3510	5969	2650
72	HOTELS, PERSONAL SERV.	38732	8045	196762	50548	25502	18711	27131	26405	11208
73	BUSINESS SERVICES	14112	1499	134878	18234	8701	6945	6104	13927	1711
74	RESEARCH, DEVELOPMENT	167	120	8073	254	136	118	92	338	362
75	AUTO. REPAIR, SERVICES	6342	717	25273	8027	4317	3548	3805	4456	1730
76	AMUSEMENTS	11089	3214	78007	19191	10402	6747	10694	13796	2780
77	MED.,EDUC. SERVICES	33166	11918	245943	77213	42247	21987	23991	30250	7068
78	FEDERAL GOVT. ENTERPRISE	20302	4203	98684	29100	22588	18383	20070	13513	8754
79	STATE, LOCAL GOVT. ENT.	3415	170	13170	4419	2335	827	1428	3528	582
80	IMPORTS	0	0	0	0	0	0	0	0	0
81	BUS.TRAVEL,ENT., GIFTS.	0	0	0	0	0	0	0	0	0
82	OFFICE SUPPLIES	0	0	0	0	0	0	0	0	0
83	SCRAP, USED GOODS	0	0	0	0	0	0	0	0	0
84	GOVERNMENT INDUSTRY	256485	47726	726713	257144	15630	159221	173174	191614	69810
85	REST OF WORLD INDUSTRY	0	0	0	0	0	0	0	0	0
86	HOUSEHOLD INDUSTRY	76212	4194	100426	37690	24135	18796	28180	51941	12688
87	INVENTORY VALUATION ADJ.	0	0	0	0	0	0	0	0	0
88	STATE TOTAL	1693363	341691	8985773	3222550	1390662	1023452	1298590	1351670	582914

TABLE C-7

STATE ESTIMATES OF 1947 PAYROLLS
(THOUSANDS OF CURRENT DOLLARS)

INDUSTRY TITLE	19 MARYLAND	20 MASSA-CHUSETTS	21 MICHIGAN	22 MINNESOTA	23 MISSISSIPPI	24 MISSOURI	25 MONTANA	26 NEBRASKA	27 NEVADA
1 LIVESTOCK, PRDTS.	17157	17000	26465	5744	13440	45390	14850	17527	7700
2 OTHER AGRICULTURE PRDTS.	17843	14000	27535	65256	34560	25610	26150	31473	3300
3 FORESTRY, FISHERIES	2292	9780	2534	734	1649	1057	318	144	12
4 AGRI.,FORES.,FISH. SERV.	3158	1590	3259	6195	5713	7457	882	3375	138
5 IRON, FERRO. ORES MINING	0	0	20392	51325	0	313	1057	0	979
6 NONFERROUS ORES MINING	0	0	2864	0	0	17872	17176	0	4397
7 COAL MINING	4968	0	356	0	0	5604	4208	0	0
8 CRUDE PETRO.,NATURAL GAS	0	1352	7435	0	5601	642	2077	18	
9 STONE, CLAY MINING	2309	0	8703	2406	246	8363	709	984	1553
10 CHEM.,FERT. MIN. MINING	0	3614	2623	0	0	419	662	0	147
11 NEW CONSTRUCTION	83410	128830	161582	70700	30889	90162	13095	24050	10668
12 MAINT., REPAIR CONSTR.	36504	50563	68816	33064	9157	50813	7873	16226	5447
13 ORDNANCE, ACCESSORIES	199	8955	428	1296	0	16	0	17	0
14 FOOD, KINDRED PRDTS.	74805	119740	135658	131885	18316	137961	11228	68778	1833
15 TOBACCO MANUFACTURES	283	1902	1689	38	0	3495	0	0	0
16 FABRICS	7298	258583	3098	2194	5455	1409	0	41	0
17 TEXTILE PRDTS.	1677	37553	7736	1773	798	2545	0	57	0
18 APPAREL	49178	108300	18467	23242	16720	69364	30	1272	0
19 MISC. TEXTILE PRDTS.	3558	12595	6449	2311	113	7763		941	26
20 LUMBER, WOOD PRDTS.	6001	13985	33619	13404	38124	12174	13592	754	1365
21 WOODEN CONTAINERS	2522	5316	5386	1739	4373	2998	0	291	0
22 HOUSEHOLD FURNITURE	4193	20267	35224	5351	2428	9494	59	1181	0
23 OTHER FURNITURE	1641	8178	21153	1969	327	6920	104	1210	0
24 PAPER, ALLIED PRDTS.	8916	71316	65825	19819	12861	10004	0	998	0
25 PAPERBOARD CONTAINERS	4986	24281	15661	6058	243	11747	0	574	159
26 PRINTING, PUBLISHING	29619	103025	75812	65201	3837	58990	3361	9944	1289
27 CHEMICALS,SELECT. PRDTS.	20250	18965	61220	2611	5726	17405	1465	773	1226
28 PLASTICS, SYNTHETICS	17228	11882	4519	0	0	0	0	10	
29 DRUGS, COSMETICS	6330	17649	27599	5299	408	18936	6	3893	0
30 PAINT, ALLIED PRDTS.	2357	5519	13034	2083	25	7669	0	52	0
31 PETROLEUM, RELATED INDS.	5738	6497	7690	5162	340	4438	2048	630	3
32 RUBBER, MISC. PLASTICS	14767	89237	61308	15156	6617	7918	0	2021	2
33 LEATHER TANNING, PRDTS.	656	38855	7818	748	74	706	0	377	0
34 FOOTWEAR, LEATHER PRDTS.	5659	132232	3633	2611	1	82559	26	483	5
35 GLASS, GLASS PRDTS.	5273	5197	4398	2570	864	5992	12	9	0
36 STONE, CLAY PRDTS.	10774	28812	37184	7592	2520	32021	1485	3412	1089
37 PRIMARY IRON, STEEL MFR.	74747	51594	267107	16262	687	31064	2399	1471	4
38 PRIMARY NONFERROUS MFR.	9033	22352	55997	2271	0	12722	9039	1135	1430

Industry									
39 METAL CONTAINERS	12121	1889	542	1269	135	5707	0	546	0
40 FABRICATED METAL PRDTS.	17386	23860	63748	16586	648	27674	641	3100	242
41 SCREW MACH. PRDTS., ETC.	11105	26608	90368	6351	0	5695	169	25	0
42 OTHER FAB. METAL PRDTS.	3949	65055	136367	6018	649	18031	1	931	0
43 ENGINES, TURBINES	37	18464	51183	4024	0	4825	64	121	23
44 FARM MACH., EQUIP.	2895	997	29293	18913	216	3040	161	3407	0
45 CONSTRUC. MACH., EQUIP.	1582	872	18911	10827	499	2611	275	657	7
46 MATERIAL HANDLING MACH.	440	3452	10385	1641	21	472	16	73	0
47 METALWORKING MACHINERY	3176	46915	138844	5179	3	7836	2	404	0
48 SPECIAL MACH., EQUIP.	8250	95424	29798	6056	1088	9846	42	135	2
49 GENERAL MACH., EQUIP.	3610	30821	55029	2784	600	5940	0	457	85
50 MACHINE SHOP PRDTS.	5979	5616	26765	1847	51	7351	0	73	0
51 OFFICE, COMPUT. MACHINES	16	3720	25874	85	0	701	0	0	0
52 SERVICE IND. MACHINES	1899	17709	33583	9729	0	7744	0	880	0
53 ELECT. TRANSMISS. EQUIP.	2138	73606	30125	22357	88	30939	37	720	0
54 HOUSEHOLD APPLIANCES	2873	17286	58882	12547	99	15153	0	976	0
55 ELECTRIC LIGHTING EQUIP.	975	23487	4700	272	2	8149	99	280	0
56 RADIO, TV, ETC., EQUIP.	18615	29069	11947	10108	774	1839	2	3688	0
57 ELECTRONIC COMPONENTS	2556	14667	2576	455	0	203	0	217	0
58 MISC. ELECTRICAL MACH.	1581	5804	7931	2362	0	1725	0	164	0
59 MOTOR VEHICLES, EQUIP.	10335		1205339	6929	1329	57825	110	1280	56
60 AIRCRAFT, PARTS	47200	12550	6539	4604	0	4542	4	0	0
61 OTHER TRANSPORT. EQUIP.	41956	27464	22638	5022	8720	12863	50	743	0
62 PROFESS., SCIEN. INSTRU.	2551	35552	17126	4268	34	4377	84	1382	0
63 MEDICAL, PHOTO. EQUIP.	261	17071	3970	1160	48	1914	1	411	0
64 MISC. MANUFACTURING	7973	78916	31656	12162	756	18704	462	2605	212
65 TRANSPORT., WAREHOUSING	169000	223000	253000	197000	45000	278000	5400	92000	20000
66 COMMUNICA., EXC. BRDCAST.	25351	67414	68083	25468	9076	42762	4117	13901	2072
67 RADIO, TV BROADCASTING	1521	7920	8001	2790	859	4162	788	1735	114
68 ELEC.,GAS,WATER,SAN.SER.	27689	52341	83856	23090	7417	37206	6599	3808	1812
69 WHOLESALE, RETAIL TRADE	317490	808007	961064	463243	112981	669030	80234	180296	27185
70 FINANCE, INSURANCE	51080	163828	99804	62555	13236	89686	6182	30648	1168
71 REAL ESTATE, RENTAL	14580	31838	36388	13280	1476	27532	1645	3973	694
72 HOTELS, PERSONAL SERV.	33211	82419	94092	38409	15635	64508	8259	15659	10017
73 BUSINESS SERVICES	13788	39787	65202	14342	4170	29286	1488	4769	897
74 RESEARCH, DEVELOPMENT	1858	3054	678	862	143	600	18	99	97
75 AUTO. REPAIR, SERVICES	4901	11567	15811	5809	1790	10005	1181	2595	683
76 AMUSEMENTS	13906	30448	42748	16880	2185	26151	1934	5848	15972
77 MED.,EDUC. SERVICES	27447	87635	122286	78137	11407	75797	13838	22726	3322
78 FEDERAL GOVT. ENTERPRISE	14718	50466	45548	20462	10884	42924	4542	13414	996
79 STATE, LOCAL GOVT. ENT.	7179	21357	40773	2529	179	6954	190	419	22
80 IMPORTS	0	0	0	0	0	0	0	0	0
81 BUS.TRAVEL, ENT., GIFTS.	0	0	0	0	0	0	0	0	0
82 OFFICE SUPPLIES	0	0	0	0	0	0	0	0	0
83 SCRAP, USED GOODS	0	0	0	0	0	0	0	0	0
84 GOVERNMENT INDUSTRY	370409	431443	480220	227159	122703	260914	56548	112524	22590
85 REST OF WORLD INDUSTRY	0	0	0	0	0	0	0	0	0
86 HOUSEHOLD INDUSTRY	56251	76411	66751	23589	30913	41912	4029	11178	1985
87 INVENTORY VALUATION ADJ.	0	0	0	0	0	0	0	0	0
88 STATE TOTAL	1897167	4331328	5908700	1963228	627825	2783147	381727	732988	153025

TABLE C-7

STATE ESTIMATES OF 1947 PAYROLLS
(THOUSANDS OF CURRENT DOLLARS)

INDUSTRY TITLE	28 NEW HAMPSHIRE	29 NEW JERSEY	30 NEW MEXICO	31 NEW YORK	32 NORTH CAROLINA	33 NORTH DAKOTA	34 OHIO	35 OKLAHOMA	36 OREGON
1 LIVESTOCK, PRDTS.	5870	21618	9276	76720	14725	10202	33946	16716	21143
2 OTHER AGRICULTURE PRDTS.	3130	23382	10724	58280	47275	42798	30054	23284	39857
3 FORESTRY, FISHERIES	550	2660	55	4695	1602	16	1213	535	2714
4 AGRI.,FORES.,FISH. SERV.	1429	2145	1026	3745	4455	1486	5017	3683	1563
5 IRON, FERRO. ORES MINING	0	2078	151	4838	320	0	0	0	0
6 NONFERROUS ORES MINING	0	4405	7635	2286	452	0	0	5771	253
7 COAL MINING	0	0	4360	0	0	1044	66536	4812	0
8 CRUDE PETRO.,NATURAL GAS	0	0	5501	0	0	0	14938	56137	0
9 STONE, CLAY MINING	148	6569	347	13311	3101	1	15913	3690	6722
10 CHEM.,FERT. MIN. MINING	0	0	5506	9995		223	0	0	0
11 NEW CONSTRUCTION	10559	155597	30055	433712	64270	6602	231033	64124	54632
12 MAINT., REPAIR CONSTR.	6555	64085	12805	244968	27425	5469	111142	16602	20959
13 ORDNANCE, ACCESSORIES	976	976		6882	68		309	309	3
14 FOOD, KINDRED PRDTS.	5182	149457	4456	404976	37816	9345	186980	35688	46299
15 TOBACCO MANUFACTURES	1043	9759	0	4245	65309	0	5286	0	2
16 FABRICS	42624	126390	13	90446	300514	177	14172	908	3763
17 TEXTILE PRDTS.	3102	28017	0	67589	24304	0	8097	118	523
18 APPAREL	5734	165674	151	1119655	102938	39	72240	1792	5884
19 MISC. TEXTILE PRDTS.	427	20150	124	93663	14541	64	8481	417	1016
20 LUMBER, WOOD PRDTS.	10292	13502	4081	36318	41785	0	19819	5158	160488
21 WOODEN CONTAINERS	3444	4771	87	21549	5340	14	6717	153	3528
22 HOUSEHOLD FURNITURE	2687	13883	228	65469	49642	44	26682	1337	8436
23 OTHER FURNITURE	434	5504	65	43206	4185	0	39243	450	1540
24 PAPER, ALLIED PRDTS.	12970	43589	1	117843	22794	0	65132	603	13897
25 PAPERBOARD CONTAINERS	518	25674	0	66034	3244		30151	804	839
26 PRINTING, PUBLISHING	6348	68597	1808	571911	13574	2233	155397	12867	13614
27 CHEMICALS,SELECT. PRDTS.	400	127984	1517	88674	5515	212	51011	1714	2153
28 PLASTICS, SYNTHETICS	238	29500	0	18626	6594	0	11671	0	0
29 DRUGS, COSMETICS	210	83116	0	80617	2240	107	24900	171	277
30 PAINT, ALLIED PRDTS.	44	23718	0	21901	727	91	23189	463	774
31 PETROLEUM, RELATED INDS.	28	57102	1038	16195	99	0	20896	23484	839
32 RUBBER, MISC. PLASTICS	2060	66292	0	53869	3353	0	271525	7678	794
33 LEATHER TANNING, PRDTS.	3679	11135	0	15928	2728	0	6550	0	68
34 FOOTWEAR, LEATHER PRDTS.	40205	15783	211	158882	698		33161	420	792
35 GLASS, GLASS PRDTS.	0	25739	0	32733	772	9	54145	8110	162
36 STONE, CLAY PRDTS.	1645	49303	782	75925	9750	371	102547	4054	3475
37 PRIMARY IRON, STEEL MFR.	1710	67697	136	179915	3607	27	510949	4745	14627
38 PRIMARY NONFERROUS MFR.	369	77664	2871	87357	3148		71077	7919	3226

39	METAL CONTAINERS	0	12566	0	12244	0	0	16933	522	604
40	FABRICATED METAL PRDTS.	1038	32846	785	87272	4920	333	122369	8930	8968
41	SCREW MACH. PRDTS., ETC.	1265	15741	0	52828	118	10	114902	281	276
42	OTHER FAB. METAL PRDTS.	1307	60060	2	89773	1892	139	97383	0103	1700
43	ENGINES, TURBINES	16	10112	1	31681	5	1	30786	120	0
44	FARM MACH., EQUIP.	46	3624	47	28131	1908	186	3608	1099	659
45	CONSTRUC. MACH., EQUIP.	1392	8547	0	5412	502	0	59522	11803	1182
46	MATERIAL HANDLING MACH.	89	12275	83	11076	605	0	19059	222	3223
47	METALWORKING MACHINERY	3729	29648	96	5610	214	3	154407	201	622
48	SPECIAL MACH., EQUIP.	12087	40312	2	95016	5156	1	72971	306	3387
49	GENERAL MACH., EQUIP.	335	51386	0	60561	835	28	94136	2351	871
50	MACHINE SHOP PRDTS.	212	7505	0	12758	973	3	14047	339	2096
51	OFFICE, COMPUT. MACHINES	0	8496	0	82901	17	0	59045	55	265
52	SERVICE IND. MACHINES	59	7840	0	23987	314	1808	61150	234	1031
53	ELECT. TRANSMISS. EQUIP.	2066	48088	0	88115	203	0	138641	442	1642
54	HOUSEHOLD APPLIANCES	57	36376	1	36224	313	0	120022	453	74
55	ELECTRIC LIGHTING EQUIP.	83	38066	0	46458	99	2	3673	78	144
56	RADIO, TV, ETC., EQUIP.	0	136609	0	95383	3544	0	21938	0	36
57	ELECTRONIC COMPONENTS	512	31161	0	27173	873	0	4627	162	411
58	MISC. ELECTRICAL MACH.	29	15391	0	26584	526	81	5372	1694	1324
59	MOTOR VEHICLES, EQUIP.	31	45715	800	122523	2059	0	226511	590	7713
60	AIRCRAFT, PARTS		31233	0	58885	0	0	49701	537	371
61	OTHER TRANSPORT. EQUIP.	193	62505	3	101256	1053	11	30038	1286	314
62	PROFESS., SCIEN. INSTRU.		43580		110707	250		24754	128	
63	MEDICAL, PHOTO. EQUIP.		11748		148547	25	1	5056		
64	MISC. MANUFACTURING	4381	93530	750	236046	1557	205	75226	1416	2885
65	TRANSPORT., WAREHOUSING	16000	302000	3094	1131000	105000	29000	552000	85000	103000
66	COMMUNICA., EXC. BRDCAST.	6176	70849	722	287829	14747	3090	75696	17850	18519
67	RADIO, TV BROADCASTING	667	1433	4092	26717	4129	1415	12364	1745	1970
68	ELEC.,GAS,WATER,SAN.SER.	6154	57763	55790	183634	18467	6842	85664	19507	16717
69	WHOLESALE, RETAIL TRADE	55436	668406	4248	3444648	324357	73731	1257745	227543	253489
70	FINANCE, INSURANCE	8935	131681	1453	799337	41755	5241	153658	26053	24943
71	REAL ESTATE, RENTAL	921	24882	8554	305212	5378	667	44543	9211	8217
72	HOTELS, PERSONAL SERV.	8621	95203	1922	385580	42035	4673	120021	24633	24796
73	BUSINESS SERVICES	1103	28942	337	400282	8967	814	57461	11047	10107
74	RESEARCH, DEVELOPMENT	137	2795	1186	8092	85	844	1571	635	101
75	AUTO. REPAIR, SERVICES	1077	12197	1965	49309	5550	540	19323	5137	5394
76	AMUSEMENTS	1659	29489	6679	219716	9728	1655	53224	8033	10043
77	MED.,EDUC. SERVICES	7580	67894	3969	434285	23419	7053	148129	31549	51339
78	FEDERAL GOVT. ENTERPRISE	4823	34721	188	187014	19357	6341	61824	17113	11098
79	STATE, LOCAL GOVT. ENT.	431	6087	0	167800	1869	57	30247	1998	3529
80	IMPORTS	0	0	0	0	0	0	0	0	0
81	BUS.,TRAVEL, ENT., GIFTS.	0	0	0	0	0	0	0	0	0
82	OFFICE SUPPLIES	0	0	0	0	0	0	0	0	0
83	SCRAP, USED GOODS									0
84	GOVERNMENT INDUSTRY	45172	432573	77011	1517539	281386	44126	602353	176799	133473
85	REST OF WORLD INDUSTRY							0		0
86	HOUSEHOLD INDUSTRY	6624	95593	6034	357779	67217	3578	93418	22719	17700
87	INVENTORY VALUATION ADJ.									
88	STATE TOTAL	376086	4551022	317924	16044938	1890319	273053	7442245	1036331	1169095

TABLE C-7

STATE ESTIMATES OF 1947 PAYROLLS
(THOUSANDS OF CURRENT DOLLARS)

INDUSTRY TITLE	37 PENNSYL- VANIA	38 RHODE ISLAND	39 SOUTH CAROLINA	40 SOUTH DAKOTA	41 TENNESSEE	42 TEXAS	43 UTAH	44 VERMONT	45 VIRGINIA
1 LIVESTOCK, PRDTS.	53590	1875	8042	11679	15106	88816	9403	12429	24804
2 OTHER AGRICULTURE PRDTS.	38410	1125	24958	22321	19894	191184	8597	5571	28196
3 FORESTRY, FISHERIES	1887	665	611	22	945	1944	10	307	5685
4 AGRI.,FORES.,FISH. SERV.	4926	184	2760	2072	3028	18341	680	449	3032
5 IRON, FERRO. ORES MINING	7787	0	0	0	1158	134	392	0	17
6 NONFERROUS ORES MINING	14	0	0	7319	2789	14	40962	350	1906
7 COAL MINING	577812	0	0	168	20320	4	17620	0	52192
8 CRUDE PETRO.,NATURAL GAS	22915	0	0		3	189629	26	0	11
9 STONE, CLAY MINING	16078	0	1439	5898	4465	4826	1628	3563	5221
10 CHEM.,FERT. MIN. MINING	0	89	0	0	2735	16015	119	0	0
11 NEW CONSTRUCTION	279588	21534	31021	8691	62285	343093	16822	7130	74552
12 MAINT., REPAIR CONSTR.	113687	7699	11314	6430	23410	97390	8449	3947	31255
13 ORDNANCE, ACCESSORIES	1057	10	0	0	0	130	0	10	24
14 FOOD, KINDRED PRDTS.	267088	12694	17307	18842	54031	142208	18593	5676	44684
15 TOBACCO MANUFACTURES	31217	29	1659	0	3127	1317	6	0	32176
16 FABRICS	138995	137930	237781	0	28774	12926	639	9132	56451
17 TEXTILE PRDTS.	49836	15419	21334	0	2898	2896		352	6258
18 APPAREL	375119	5802	14291	79	58443	32672	2687	4293	30061
19 MISC. TEXTILE PRDTS.	14698	1229	5995	2432	3747	5281	150	131	5770
20 LUMBER, WOOD PRDTS.	27929	1085	27946	73	25645	47217	1370	9481	30392
21 WOODEN CONTAINERS	5609	442	1975	0	5733	4220	127	1439	4093
22 HOUSEHOLD FURNITURE	31580	987	4486	0	14426	7507	691	2898	27771
23 OTHER FURNITURE	10102	1036	201	0	499	4749	308	864	920
24 PAPER, ALLIED PRDTS.	65643	1923	11123	0	8564	8828	0	5718	22667
25 PAPERBOARD CONTAINERS	31350	3203	2702	133	3765	4417	174	769	2765
26 PRINTING, PUBLISHING	170909	8881	5418	2697	23468	47927	4684	2655	15836
27 CHEMICALS,SELECT. PRDTS.	55508	1239	5632	138	22728	42949	1382	280	19753
28 PLASTICS, SYNTHETICS	34847	747	5	0	39963	8642		369	64780
29 DRUGS, COSMETICS	23699	1038	208	149	5868	3424	194	483	3746
30 PAINT, ALLIED PRDTS.	13724	1064	186	0	1329	2920	130	48	802
31 PETROLEUM, RELATED INDS.	67739	1329	278	44	1207	138449	2456	425	455
32 RUBBER, MISC. PLASTICS	64402	16502	1143	0	15279	4612	19	2402	3507
33 LEATHER TANNING, PRDTS.	22721	671	55	0	985	622	0	173	2014
34 FOOTWEAR, LEATHER PRDTS.	43182	958	93	0	18837	2821	53	479	6928
35 GLASS, GLASS PRDTS.	77372	1044	153	0	2899	3277	27	219	1815
36 STONE, CLAY PRDTS.	113151	608	4285	894	15125	20183	2979	5721	8132
37 PRIMARY IRON, STEEL MFR.	784044	10340	2351	16	19872	19243	15592	1564	9121
38 PRIMARY NONFERROUS MFR.	65149	10841	77	0	11177	13887	6331	123	1929

#	Industry									
39	METAL CONTAINERS	11863	0	0	0	765	6080	942	0	344
40	FABRICATED METAL PRDTS.	130403	2534	957	918	25035	23514	1630	1055	9844
41	SCREW MACH. PRDTS., ETC.	95323	8372	0	0	1736	1087	9	38	35
42	OTHER FAB. METAL PRDTS.	101246	15184	130	175	2863	5322	125	854	2611
43	ENGINES, TURBINES	43403	0	2	0	34	341	0	1340	181
44	FARM MACH. EQUIP.	20856	121	96	468	3095	4324	100	38	548
45	CONSTRUC. MACH., EQUIP.	33953	0	67	40	1253	44992	1199	0	502
46	MATERIAL HANDLING MACH.	12145	71	20	53	1069	279	342	0	379
47	METALWORKING MACHINERY	52463	23648	3112	144	201	768	88	10207	36
48	SPECIAL MACH., EQUIP.	67509	14331	605	27	2324	6023	163	1970	1317
49	GENERAL MACH., EQUIP.	60555	589	24	12	2155	4026	2	59	396
50	MACHINE SHOP PRDTS.	18544	2184	0	0	765	1941	42	195	331
51	OFFICE, COMPUT. MACHINES	636	28	1	69	27	33	96	2425	16
52	SERVICE IND. MACHINES	31091	821	0	143	1219	2307	122	19	58
53	ELECT. TRANSMISS. EQUIP.	160996	360	0	86	999	1345	50	257	2065
54	HOUSEHOLD APPLIANCES	52714	505	11	0	6207	3331	73	89	915
55	ELECTRIC LIGHTING EQUIP.	21057	4632	0	0	880	1396	79	541	84
56	RADIO, TV, ETC., EQUIP.	37923	541	0	0	888	374	0	133	1304
57	ELECTRONIC COMPONENTS	22078	133	0	0	0	66	0	0	311
58	MISC. ELECTRICAL MACH.	14634	3875	7	0	873	1836	0	9	355
59	MOTOR VEHICLES, EQUIP.	76580	311	701	54	11683	7014	110	24	2062
60	AIRCRAFT, PARTS	12394	0	1	0	68	39748	0	0	1
61	OTHER TRANSPORT. EQUIP.	112612	396	2202	17	4428	15679	177	85	50065
62	PROFESS., SCIEN. INSTRU.	65374	2122	34	47	3739	1203	51	268	278
63	MEDICAL, PHOTO. EQUIP.	3986	2813	51	390	33	748	1	2	2069
64	MISC. MANUFACTURING	71782	52701	1714	261	4967	6795	937	1388	2981
65	TRANSPORT., WAREHOUSING	764000	26000	44000	21000	141000	442000	52000	17000	192000
66	COMMUNICA.,EXC. BROCAST.	100923	10177	7307	4035	21048	62550	6258	3668	23168
67	RADIO, TV BROADCASTING	6004	596	1577	732	2899	9026	1438	261	2805
68	ELEC.,GAS,WATER,SAN.SER.	125221	10883	9790	3102	5635	69586	6057	3590	17228
69	WHOLESALE, RETAIL TRADE	1477937	138021	138021	70910	309071	962467	99878	37722	255402
70	FINANCE, INSURANCE	241000	20508	18214	6778	45990	119772	9734	6542	51531
71	REAL ESTATE, RENTAL	44685	4135	1402	1091	11005	28033	2993	370	12292
72	HOTELS, PERSONAL SERV.	135850	12410	18080	5220	38986	110496	9844	4663	42643
73	BUSINESS SERVICES	69456	4054	3478	1062	10334	53581	2666	412	8122
74	RESEARCH, DEVELOPMENT	1882	88	359	45	662	2170	31	99	950
75	AUTO. REPAIR, SERVICES	21061	1709	2913	634	5497	18223	1470	571	5472
76	AMUSEMENTS	54606	4621	3447	1889	9745	32993	4036	1050	11535
77	MED.,EDUC. SERVICES	211026	10815	10744	5943	41986	121190	9588	3122	39358
78	FEDERAL GOVT. ENTERPRISE	73186	6191	9935	6902	46229	48268	4826	4283	21912
79	STATE, LOCAL GOVT. ENT.	13052	1880	922	220	14494	23751	665	288	4772
80	IMPORTS	0	0	0	0	0	0	0	0	0
81	BUS.TRAVEL, ENT., GIFTS.	0	0	0	0	0	0	0	0	0
82	OFFICE SUPPLIES	0	0	0	0	0	0	0	0	0
83	SCRAP, USED GOODS	0	0	0	0	0	0	0	0	0
84	GOVERNMENT INDUSTRY	819147	99948	171674	50917	178517	668292	95808	24857	646516
85	REST OF WORLD INDUSTRY	0	0	0	0	0	0	0	0	0
86	HOUSEHOLD INDUSTRY	155760	11757	42820	4339	50966	132216	4011	6670	55894
87	INVENTORY VALUATION ADJ.	0	0	0	0	0	0	0	0	0
88	STATE TOTAL	9350280	741907	941248	277820	1555917	4619800	480942	225614	2100409

TABLE C-7

STATE ESTIMATES OF 1947 PAYROLLS
(THOUSANDS OF CURRENT DOLLARS)

INDUSTRY TITLE	46 WASHINGTON	47 WEST VIRGINIA	48 WISCONSIN	49 WYOMING	50 ALASKA	51 HAWAII	52 NO STATE ALLOCATION	53 NATIONAL TOTAL
1 LIVESTOCK, PRDTS.	19936	8322	55739	15000	0	0	0	1074794
2 OTHER AGRICULTURE PRDTS.	53064	3678	22261	9000	0	0	0	1747206
3 FORESTRY, FISHERIES	6598	1217	1483	19	0	0	0	96758
4 AGRI.,FORES.,FISH. SERV.	2071	681	3718	373	0	0	0	166242
5 IRON, FERRO. ORES MINING	4	0	7111	1130	0	0	0	105853
6 NONFERROUS ORES MINING	1603	0	513	24	0	0	0	191147
7 COAL MINING	4880	380460	0	14720	0	0	0	1563004
8 CRUDE PETRO.,NATURAL GAS	0	11338	0	6097	0	0	0	489622
9 STONE,CLAY MIN. MINING	7674	3556	6677	757	0	0	0	203780
10 CHEM.,FERT. MIN. MINING	0	44	0	88	0	0	0	49220
11 NEW CONSTRUCTION	93593	41690	77042	13218	0	0	0	4278326
12 MAINT., REPAIR CONSTR.	28242	12957	37792	5527	0	0	0	1858580
13 ORDNANCE, ACCESSORIES	3	0	97	0	0	0	0	59566
14 FOOD, KINDRED PRDTS.	69052	15537	145818	4301	0	0	0	3903998
15 TOBACCO MANUFACTURES	2	1421	751	0	0	0	0	204661
16 FABRICS	370	4400	4252	0	0	0	0	1888655
17 TEXTILE PRDTS.	209	0	3803	0	0	0	0	368084
18 APPAREL	4887	5825	33405	0	0	0	0	2786636
19 MISC. TEXTILE PRDTS.	1503	66	2560	0	0	0	0	273666
20 LUMBER, WOOD PRDTS.	134457	14044	30604	2053	0	0	0	1219757
21 WOODEN CONTAINERS	1647	802	5500	43	0	0	0	152015
22 HOUSEHOLD FURNITURE	7144	1565	25831	13	0	0	0	559742
23 OTHER FURNITURE	1214	291	5187	0	0	0	0	221893
24 PAPER, ALLIED PRDTS.	38248	2343	69999	0	0	0	0	932584
25 PAPERBOARD CONTAINERS	4126	1499	12161	0	0	0	0	353324
26 PRINTING, PUBLISHING	21776	7392	50007	1313	0	0	0	2284633
27 CHEMICALS,SELECT. PRDTS.	4237	51172	6603	619	0	0	0	828084
28 PLASTICS, SYNTHETICS	333	15834	639	0	0	0	0	316832
29 DRUGS, COSMETICS	579	713	7104	0	0	0	0	458147
30 PAINT, ALLIED PRDTS.	1146	98	3783	59	0	0	0	185690
31 PETROLEUM, RELATED INDUS.	829	2627	2036	8255	0	0	0	628086
32 RUBBER, MISC. PLASTICS	206	920	15029	6	0	0	0	946677
33 LEATHER TANNING, PRDTS.	30	2574	17103	0	0	0	0	169980
34 FOOTWEAR, LEATHER PRDTS.	1015	709	34668	26	0	0	0	704706
35 GLASS, GLASS PRDTS.	1556	48115	1176	0	0	0	0	370568
36 STONE, CLAY PRDTS.	8364	30211	12286	725	0	0	0	838547
37 PRIMARY IRON, STEEL MFR.	10306	64725	73388	4	0	0	0	3031219
38 PRIMARY NONFERROUS MFR.	18673	7235	15208	0	0	0	0	793650

#	Sector	1	2	3	4	5	6	7	8	9
39	METAL CONTAINERS	2235	2122	1060	0	0	0	0	0	158671
40	FABRICATED METAL PRDTS.	7906	9221	56130	223	0	0	0	0	999335
41	SCREW MACH. PRDTS., ETC.	514	7753	27243	0	0	0	0	0	648729
42	OTHER FAB. METAL PRDTS.	2240	4256	20605	0	0	0	0	0	998667
43	ENGINES, TURBINES	245	0	56056	100	0	0	0	0	328501
44	FARM MACH., EQUIP.	1527	604	47706	37	0	0	0	0	491417
45	CONSTRUC. MACH., EQUIP.	5505	4840	49564	2	0	0	0	0	407176
46	MATERIAL HANDLING MACH.	858	227	3919	1	0	0	0	0	110529
47	METALWORKING MACHINERY	1774	108	34995	1	0	0	0	0	751663
48	SPECIAL MACH., EQUIP.	3886	616	37279	24	0	0	0	0	693122
49	GENERAL MACH., EQUIP.	1426	212	30710	0	0	0	0	0	624007
50	MACHINE SHOP PRDTS.	1531	348	5011	32	0	0	0	0	165815
51	OFFICE, COMPUT. MACHINES	41	0	726	88	0	0	0	0	270691
52	SERVICE IND. MACHINES	308	42	6288	39	0	0	0	0	297800
53	ELECT. TRANSMISS. EQUIP.	642	432	53397	0	0	0	0	0	798212
54	HOUSEHOLD APPLIANCES	2843	473	24083	0	0	0	0	0	630928
55	ELECTRIC LIGHTING EQUIP.	486	2041	3371	0	0	0	0	0	298641
56	RADIO, TV, ETC., EQUIP.	953	0	1747	63	0	0	0	0	679776
57	ELECTRONIC COMPONENTS	36	1175	418	1	0	0	0	0	154626
58	MISC. ELECTRICAL MACH.	1318	82	10570	0	0	0	0	0	224223
59	MOTOR VEHICLES, EQUIP.	4795	2077	79052	54	0	0	0	0	2215654
60	AIRCRAFT, PARTS	25815	64	2072		0	0	0	0	704571
61	OTHER TRANSPORT. EQUIP.	20656	3857	14929		0	0	0	0	836682
62	PROFESS., SCIEN. INSTRU.	378	83	18910		0	0	0	0	461968
63	MEDICAL, PHOTO. EQUIP.	114	136	972		0	0	0	0	235399
64	MISC. MANUFACTURING	3592	3023	20586		0	0	0	0	990292
65	TRANSPORT., WAREHOUSING	173000	112000	145000	40000	0	0	0	0	9018000
66	COMMUNICA.,EXC. BRDCAST.	30677	11558	32555	2318	0	0	0	0	1656564
67	RADIO, TV BROADCASTING	2033	1874	2702	242	0	0	0	0	167000
68	ELEC.,GAS,WATER,SAN.SER.	18148	32295	32474	2542	0	0	0	0	1458000
69	WHOLESALE, RETAIL TRADE	397710	176333	453270	35109	0	0	0	0	22038962
70	FINANCE, INSURANCE	46438	18175	59639	2615	0	0	0	0	3421524
71	REAL ESTATE, RENTAL	22882	5249	12161	1232	0	0	0	0	1012047
72	HOTELS, PERSONAL SERV.	39381	18932	42452	5454	0	0	0	0	2411899
73	BUSINESS SERVICES	15934	4754	15370	1263	0	0	0	0	1273853
74	RESEARCH, DEVELOPMENT	480	478	519	138	0	0	0	0	63498
75	AUTO. REPAIR, SERVICES	6762	2289	5482	441	0	0	0	0	355368
76	AMUSEMENTS	18502	6556	16507	1238	0	0	0	0	1245000
77	MED.,EDUC. SERVICES	94476	34746	55176	4176	0	0	0	0	3210797
78	FEDERAL GOVT. ENTERPRISE	23351	11139	26993	2211	0	0	0	0	1279164
79	STATE, LOCAL GOVT. ENT.	18079	1606	3184	13	0	0	0	0	510000
80	IMPORTS	0	0	0	0	0	0	0	0	0
81	BUS.TRAVEL, ENT., GIFTS.	0	0	0	0	0	0	0	0	0
82	OFFICE SUPPLIES	0	0	0	0	0	0	0	0	0
83	SCRAP, USED GOODS					0	0	0	0	
84	GOVERNMENT INDUSTRY	396133	110342	234450	33295	0	0	0	1556000	15730000
85	REST OF WORLD INDUSTRY	22121	17736	2662	2151	0	0	0	0	0
86	HOUSEHOLD INDUSTRY	0	0	0		0	0	0	0	2348000
87	INVENTORY VALUATION ADJ.					0	0	0	0	0
88	STATE TOTAL	1967308	1353915	2563329	218473	0	0	0	1556000	118682703

TABLE C-8

STATE ESTIMATES OF 1958 PAYROLLS
(THOUSANDS OF CURRENT DOLLARS)

INDUSTRY TITLE	1 ALABAMA	2 ARIZONA	3 ARKANSAS	4 CALIFORNIA	5 COLORADO	6 CONNECTICUT	7 DELAWARE	8 DISTRICT OF COLUMBIA	9 FLORIDA
1 LIVESTOCK, PRDTS.	18596	10454	26499	109896	20885	14205	4741	0	30847
2 OTHER AGRICULTURE PRDTS.	14404	34546	46501	270104	22115	8795	3259	0	78153
3 FORESTRY, FISHERIES	3620	693	1608	52457	294	926	1594	0	25474
4 AGRI.,FORES.,FISH. SERV.	5277	5028	4619	36347	2556	8524	3720	0	7018
5 IRON, FERRO. ORES MINING	12168	1688	560	4001	8612	0	0	0	0
6 NONFERROUS ORES MINING	814	76509	3504	5062	18203	180	0	0	3945
7 COAL MINING	35606	25	1219	0	9628	0	0	0	0
8 CRUDE PETRO.,NATURAL GAS	1355	40	10878	124133	25517	0	0	0	853
9 STONE, CLAY MINING	4988	1815	3368	34515	3986	4586	757	0	11429
10 CHEM.,FERT. MIN. MINING	0	96	1485	17242	1757	0	160	0	15896
11 NEW CONSTRUCTION	125546	138896	48406	1330586	146873	201914	44354	76797	442684
12 MAINT., REPAIR CONSTR.	32896	21682	18920	397754	45717	55749	10991	23819	96060
13 ORDNANCE, ACCESSORIES	7553	40626	19	554517	29590	34580	260	260	25141
14 FOOD, KINDRED PRDTS.	69748	26328	42726	756183	82248	65170	20676	27584	131084
15 TOBACCO MANUFACTURES	1185	0	0	52	0	3381	0	0	20710
16 FABRICS	90682	0	3419	4633	70	41607	6230	0	942
17 TEXTILE PRDTS.	5434	0	1422	13961	0	9435	1581	0	703
18 APPAREL	59149	3896	16288	160898	3702	55880	3422	78	17218
19 MISC. TEXTILE PRDTS.	3899	335	96	28454	1003	6530	365	581	2732
20 LUMBER, WOOD PRDTS.	48410	11588	48160	232055	8686	4357	942	547	30262
21 WOODEN CONTAINERS	1656	277	3670	14316	350	1277	569	0	5409
22 HOUSEHOLD FURNITURE	8056	1751	18230	92610	3201	8930	90	341	18460
23 OTHER FURNITURE	965	950	2362	36574	3062	6467	22	286	5209
24 PAPER, ALLIED PRDTS.	50101	469	17681	62579	342	17600	2122	2060	58690
25 PAPERBOARD CONTAINERS	1037	414	4796	64307	2109	20801	829	969	10234
26 PRINTING, PUBLISHING	21977	12501	11528	351578	31580	72727	6888	66166	58411
27 CHEMICALS,SELECT. PRDTS.	24163	2800	17411	80283	5843	17247	15056	431	32391
28 PLASTICS, SYNTHETICS	14643	0	0	14321		10331	11519	0	37287
29 DRUGS, COSMETICS	1383	376	106	59644	738	20103	2212	324	1280
30 PAINT, ALLIED PRDTS.	1359	413	523	32004	1880	1512	413	142	2612
31 PETROLEUM, RELATED INDS.	1881	610	10050	122465	4754	2272	5192	0	3483
32 RUBBER, MISC. PLASTICS	32436	1508	4736	121932	26856	73314	8817	255	2578
33 LEATHER TANNING, PRDTS.	0	0	0	5418	16	970	6583	0	476
34 FOOTWEAR, LEATHER PRDTS.	2124	278	9211	5557	7426	10869	610	0	1307
35 GLASS, GLASS PRDTS.	1912	46	5900	32426	46	3134	46	46	2911
36 STONE, CLAY PRDTS.	28338	11006	6491	173287	18460	27098	2727	2923	44582
37 PRIMARY IRON, STEEL MFR.	186661	1434	61	174594	40316	33664	14189	0	2056
38 PRIMARY NONFERROUS MFR.	30046	10961	14613	106808	3272	104302	1070	0	3589

218

#	Industry	C1	C2	C3	C4	C5	C6	C7	C8	C9
39	METAL CONTAINERS	1606	0	667	50849	890	38	286	0	10087
40	FABRICATED METAL PRDTS.	35772	7710	3698	211347	13564	24636	3576	2494	9571
41	SCREW MACH. PRDTS., ETC.	6461	104	1131	64710	672	61570	2031	52	1308
42	OTHER FAB. METAL PRDTS.	15085	641	5134	138771	7175	122338	3852	245	9190
43	ENGINES, TURBINES	0	393	0	24616	0	5023	0	0	214
44	FARM MACH., EQUIP.	2123	218	233	14613	1559	350	238	0	963
45	CONSTRUC. HANDLING MACH.	1660	26	38	42455	9018	427	52	0	605
46	MATERIAL HANDLING MACH.	5908	46	1974	20311	1748	1117	0	0	313
47	METALWORKING MACHINERY	828	2383	1004	56079	492	85604	1419	53	2581
48	SPECIAL MACH., EQUIP.	4617	158	158	40946	1631	23875	9458	0	2067
49	GENERAL MACH., EQUIP.	2272	487	263	79184	2347	106146	352	53	2572
50	MACHINE SHOP PRDTS.	2928	2554	487	88175	5118	21675	608	731	5200
51	OFFICE, COMPUT. MACHINES	1602	4116	910	58098	534	52287	0	55	602
52	SERVICE IND. MACHINES	1908	4275	1185	29916	6712	5899	890	53	1424
53	ELECT. TRANSMISS. EQUIP.	107	43	0	127595	102	33803	38	164	3430
54	HOUSEHOLD APPLIANCES	4872	320	551	37214	238	32807	266	0	429
55	ELECTRIC LIGHTING EQUIP.	0	8569	6099	48187	91	39378	253	73	1542
56	RADIO, TV, ETC., EQUIP.	7297	3736	2523	135323	345	19713	73	35	7125
57	ELECTRONIC COMPONENTS	0	215	2571	108175	560	20975	657	657	4689
58	MISC. ELECTRICAL MACH.	7789	376	2295	14653	2905	3992	39	39	5960
59	MOTOR VEHICLES, EQUIP.	87612	30263	194	132717	10096	12387	31074	129	1868
60	AIRCRAFT, PARTS	25094	263	78	1383667	1366	363859	2170	53	9890
61	OTHER TRANSPORT. EQUIP.	433	2394	993	82392	2181	57971	1333	372	29847
62	PROFESS., SCIEN. INSTRU.	31	0	0	83399	65	74236	2345	36	1234
63	MEDICAL, PHOTO. EQUIP.	2612	1756	3426	4273	5637	5796	36	638	1263
64	MISC. MANUFACTURING			6928	75161		72424	2841		8971
65	TRANSPORT., WAREHOUSING	146000	71000	79000	1204000	149000	113000	34000	89000	315000
66	COMMUNICA.,EXC. BRDCAST.	35798	16639	17438	439956	42717	55369	7656	5435	100958
67	RADIO, TV BROADCASTING	6002	4077	2677	73658	5576	6792	1531	7538	13695
68	ELEC.,GAS,WATER,SAN.SER.	41350	27835	17743	319283	35177	57668	4571	6669	52418
69	WHOLESALE, RETAIL TRADE	376501	219192	189776	3694709	360592	511111	109147	278322	914508
70	FINANCE, INSURANCE	96453	43488	41015	912190	84612	225354	22032	76211	211969
71	REAL ESTATE, RENTAL	10813	6969	2445	141744	11911	12981	3623	25174	49168
72	HOTELS, PERSONAL SERV.	40422	33035	22888	419089	43289	54048	8724	53222	164526
73	BUSINESS SERVICES	28819	22132	8920	530592	40444	55959	7584	64704	96952
74	RESEARCH, DEVELOPMENT	2696	296	108	69584	603	2922	1128	1721	3608
75	AUTO. REPAIR, SERVICES	10004	7905	4672	111772	11633	13238	2096	8092	28289
76	AMUSEMENTS	6700	6296	4566	419093	17069	11807	3218	11981	36075
77	MED.,EDUC. SERVICES	79556	49055	36911	999832	94774	210547	24988	184392	180191
78	FEDERAL GOVT. ENTERPRISE	55032	15496	22181	243826	28800	38211	5430	59912	65174
79	STATE, LOCAL GOVT. ENT.	16096	8654	4495	172557	9545	12914	2043	7305	29195
80	IMPORTS	0	0	0	0	0	0	0	0	0
81	BUS.TRAVEL, ENT., GIFTS.	0	0	0	0	0	0	0	0	0
82	OFFICE SUPPLIES	0	0	0	0	0	0	0	0	0
83	SCRAP, USED GOODS	0	0	0	0	0	0	0	0	0
84	GOVERNMENT INDUSTRY	636078	336200	224938	4413711	504463	400312	104858	798800	1004928
85	REST OF WORLD INDUSTRY	0	0	0	0	0	0	0	0	0
86	HOUSEHOLD INDUSTRY	95071	21052	36181	307555	24096	62988	13481	47779	166266
87	INVENTORY VALUATION ADJ.	0	0	0	0	0	0	0	0	0
88	STATE TOTAL	2852131	1380755	1172054	23309592	2121150	4041984	601011	1935745	4787981

219

TABLE C-8

STATE ESTIMATES OF 1958 PAYROLLS
(THOUSANDS OF CURRENT DOLLARS)

	INDUSTRY TITLE	10 GEORGIA	11 IDAHO	12 ILLINOIS	13 INDIANA	14 IOWA	15 KANSAS	16 KENTUCKY	17 LOUISIANA	18 MAINE
1	LIVESTOCK, PRDTS.	29361	17118	35624	22873	42083	12092	18702	19601	20000
2	OTHER AGRICULTURE PRDTS.	26639	23882	48376	19127	24917	24908	17298	22399	20000
3	FORESTRY, FISHERIES	5925	736	2775	833	395	38	2317	6951	2690
4	AGRI.,FORES.,FISH. SERV.	10144	669	18509	10255	9707	3651	4109	2306	1439
5	IRON, FERRO. ORES MINING	229	2018	0	0	0	0	0	0	0
6	NONFERROUS ORES MINING	132	16123	356	0	0	158	0	0	21
7	COAL MINING	35	3	66595	22858	1453	1507	122365	0	0
8	CRUDE PETRO.,NATURAL GAS	10	16	29625	5347	0	46516	12357	138080	0
9	STONE, CLAY MINING	18814	1400	27060	13686	11089	6351	9956	5678	1033
10	CHEM.,FERT. MIN. MINING	468	860	2628	0	0	584	464	10516	0
11	NEW CONSTRUCTION	153208	43255	780150	252957	96682	127305	117544	330729	42349
12	MAINT., REPAIR CONSTR.	38235	18945	314087	114441	62018	46069	33291	55378	12780
13	ORDNANCE, ACCESSORIES	668	208	20662	11335	11009	5	0	3702	6027
14	FOOD, KINDRED PRDTS.	137399	28875	644265	224914	260189	103999	122242	113755	37264
15	TOBACCO MANUFACTURES	2043	0	1582	2204	0	0	33749	1295	0
16	FABRICS	201275	0	6190	119	493	577	3259	80	41349
17	TEXTILE PRDTS.	43186	0	21717	2147	25	30	730	1910	1542
18	APPAREL	109906	19	127269	32393	5668	5489	47101	10434	6393
19	MISC. TEXTILE PRDTS.	14047	527	25957	4979	3406	1941	2725	2677	1282
20	LUMBER, WOOD PRDTS.	49024	47295	43562	34834	18444	2750	19208	41138	37971
21	WOODEN CONTAINERS	8007	338	5884	1952	664	369	5004	3000	717
22	HOUSEHOLD FURNITURE	19754	227	74693	63076	6430	2332	16543	3477	1576
23	OTHER FURNITURE	3159	284	37896	12087	5674	1902	1293	926	291
24	PAPER, ALLIED PRDTS.	62962	5186	77038	27339	2033	1932	3051	73490	96502
25	PAPERBOARD CONTAINERS	18854	387	80915	25608	5979	8297	4391	11336	1203
26	PRINTING, PUBLISHING	44298	5820	535550	95825	51120	32384	39145	22966	8343
27	CHEMICALS,SELECT. PRDTS.	24016	13363	97597	28329	4877	20803	28201	84278	2307
28	PLASTICS, SYNTHETICS	8606	0	10207	4112	8073	0	21626	10627	0
29	DRUGS, COSMETICS	7759	62	97285	94853	7947	9764	1870	467	114
30	PAINT, ALLIED PRDTS.	4166	62	48706	5952	2497	736	8579	1643	28
31	PETROLEUM, RELATED INDS.	3136	120	86351	64289	812	26563	8101	94243	622
32	RUBBER, MISC. PLASTICS	4931	40	111001	87264	22206	9707	3980	783	4481
33	LEATHER TANNING, PRDTS.	1637	16	15908	895	0	0	681	186	5423
34	FOOTWEAR, LEATHER PRDTS.	7854	132	47559	7395	758	433	6033	371	62551
35	GLASS, GLASS PRDTS.	3116	27	69177	40367	91	600	3828	5305	0
36	STONE, CLAY PRDTS.	29587	3889	125767	86366	27109	26391	18982	24448	3623
37	PRIMARY IRON, STEEL MFR.	12333	305	400981	444645	14244	2555	41501	8198	372
38	PRIMARY NONFERROUS MFR.	4458	8126	126286	79951	11106	2662	7670	11629	1276

#	Industry	1	2	3	4	5	6	7	8	9
39	METAL CONTAINERS	1233	0	76587	5165	55	946	567	9488	2095
40	FABRICATED METAL PRDTS.	19976	615	161748	80447	22407	14519	15813	17734	3282
41	SCREW MACH. PRDTS., ETC.	4405	52	178113	47311	5630	769	6889	720	0
42	OTHER FAB. METAL PRDTS.	3061	56	253317	69762	14297	4076	16380	1497	551
43	ENGINES, TURBINES	0	0	49561	22728	10576	0	0	375	0
44	FARM MACH., EQUIP.	5109	942	144615	23980	103659	7703	17688	1229	350
45	CONSTRUC. MACH., EQUIP.	3959	162	193775	22066	27118	7245	623	4776	2465
46	MATERIAL HANDLING MACH.	3633	41	38203	4168	3986	2198	4239	559	0
47	METALWORKING MACHINERY	2108	118	159080	43323	6957	1756	2723	473	813
48	SPECIAL MACH., EQUIP.	11720	53	81754	15812	6059	3365	—	2014	11000
49	GENERAL MACH., EQUIP.	2441	2272	106574	66759	3260	4507	6478	1179	162
50	MACHINE SHOP PRDTS.	3130	363	42925	25237	2076	6672	6187	4531	1328
51	OFFICE, COMPUT. MACHINES	626	51	35675	597	66	66	12805	625	0
52	SERVICE IND. MACHINES	2731	0	43025	22684	2697	7037	6116	107	276
53	ELECT. TRANSMISS. EQUIP.	14257	0	125450	79099	4417	59	45790	200	1537
54	HOUSEHOLD APPLIANCES	46	0	118689	42580	26593	386	8247	32	525
55	ELECTRIC LIGHTING EQUIP.	1990	0	82729	30251	279	242	1817	358	779
56	RADIO, TV, ETC., EQUIP.	62	0	373706	95980	31785	106	6816	129	264
57	ELECTRONIC COMPONENTS	518	0	67802	42559	6532	3020	322	239	166
58	MISC. ELECTRICAL MACH.	2587	0	20260	76407	3733	2773	17867	2243	7553
59	MOTOR VEHICLES, EQUIP.	43312	224	123574	253451	5382	18111	775	31973	21078
60	AIRCRAFT, PARTS	62125	410	65962	157962	10850	253468	4267	546	602
61	OTHER TRANSPORT. EQUIP.	6563	926	64205	43725	2913	3253	1612	509	436
62	PROFESS., SCIEN. INSTRU.	5301	26	106430	13618	10307	1061	68	5374	4222
63	MEDICAL, PHOTO. EQUIP.	98	0	46555	1617	381	231	509	68	50000
64	MISC. MANUFACTURING	14428	1337	132042	34523	15686	2955	3653	5374	14723
65	TRANSPORT., WAREHOUSING	45000	45000	1053000	331000	160000	185000	178000	265000	3756
66	COMMUNICA., EXC. BRDCAST.	60390	9209	245662	72406	41936	33946	33318	45920	9549
67	RADIO, TV BROADCASTING	8661	2030	30544	9467	7737	5035	5751	7377	146214
68	ELEC.,GAS,WATER,SAN.SER.	50763	11055	248652	97680	55444	47147	46052	69158	30687
69	WHOLESALE, RETAIL TRADE	606754	114213	2476628	837551	473361	346200	369266	493703	3184
70	FINANCE, INSURANCE	161673	19847	683942	200036	106638	77758	83405	113230	19838
71	REAL ESTATE, RENTAL	12883	1480	150890	17397	8337	6407	7595	14569	7184
72	HOTELS, PERSONAL SERV.	64513	12082	291464	83147	38587	32865	43145	53831	877
73	BUSINESS SERVICES	50915	6137	422454	53251	27251	21993	27953	54272	4293
74	RESEARCH, DEVELOPMENT	454	126	28038	694	287	221	271	984	3186
75	AUTO. REPAIR, SERVICES	16346	2464	51581	17813	10278	8811	8781	11740	39253
76	AMUSEMENTS	11771	2055	79601	19003	9908	7252	11299	13298	16715
77	MED.,EDUC. SERVICES	102711	19837	689592	201040	113545	80064	—	93081	4816
78	FEDERAL GOVT. ENTERPRISE	51244	8920	190038	55680	39151	38159	40047	32604	0
79	STATE, LOCAL GOVT. ENT.	18299	2080	132009	25654	13136	11217	8320	19055	0
80	IMPORTS	0	0	0	0	0	0	0	0	0
81	BUS.TRAVEL, ENT., GIFTS.	0	0	0	0	0	0	0	0	0
82	OFFICE SUPPLIES	0	0	0	0	0	0	0	0	0
83	SCRAP, USED GOODS	0	0	0	0	0	0	0	0	0
84	GOVERNMENT INDUSTRY	977741	11731	1642819	636044	361690	534678	569085	558479	182603
85	REST OF WORLD INDUSTRY	0	0	0	0	0	0	0	0	0
86	HOUSEHOLD INDUSTRY	132510	8318	144407	59194	35605	31316	43620	99282	17989
87	INVENTORY VALUATION ADJ.	0	0	0	0	0	0	0	0	0
88	STATE TOTAL	3886428	626565	15719487	5984475	2549790	2345993	2562880	3156495	1035900

TABLE C-8

STATE ESTIMATES OF 1958 PAYROLLS
(THOUSANDS OF CURRENT DOLLARS)

INDUSTRY TITLE	19 MARYLAND	20 MASSA-CHUSETTS	21 MICHIGAN	22 MINNESOTA	23 MISSISSIPPI	24 MISSOURI	25 MONTANA	26 NEBRASKA	27 NEVADA
1 LIVESTOCK, PRDTS.	17016	19146	24942	27450	24674	36197	17129	16300	5500
2 OTHER AGRICULTURE PRDTS.	12984	11854	28058	21550	27326	24803	18871	23700	1500
3 FORESTRY, FISHERIES	3632	23835	3907	1792	1138	1522	309	40	143
4 AGRI.,FORES.,FISH. SERV.	4839	3935	6808	9935	2025	10771	464	4462	1049
5 IRON, FERRO. ORES MINING	61	0	33282	86602	0	2466	4566	0	2364
6 NONFERROUS ORES MINING	14	0	15722	733	0	12549	20843	0	11014
7 COAL MINING	1982	0	0	0	0	6757	804	20	
8 CRUDE PETRO.,NATURAL GAS	118	0	5383	0	13255	313	10055	0	15
9 STONE, CLAY MINING	6642	4876	20287	9340	2859	13142	2098	5333	3372
10 CHEM.,FERT. MIN. MINING			6498	0	788	788	2011	4116	235
11 NEW CONSTRUCTION	214099	297981	386206	209815	68378	236720	40261	56634	29023
12 MAINT., REPAIR CONSTR.	56926	91496	152284	72826	22845	81616	18441	32203	11229
13 ORDNANCE, ACCESSORIES	28648	59605	86199	23868		54501		2677	0
14 FOOD, KINDRED PRDTS.	139804	212132	280812	247097	42235	250728	16901	124714	3990
15 TOBACCO MANUFACTURES	528	855	2143	35		967	0	0	0
16 FABRICS	7726	131133	1056	1165	2551	3595	0	31	0
17 TEXTILE PRDTS.	494	46708	7604	2031	2841	3300	111	31	0
18 APPAREL	60688	175525	12150	25134	58972	85658	19	1741	8
19 MISC. TEXTILE PRDTS.	7635	21787	34007	4890	2338	9479	59	253	
20 LUMBER, WOOD PRDTS.	12382	20253	37755	26629	38343	18946	28761	1836	1328
21 WOODEN CONTAINERS	2482	3317	2442	1544	6380	1900	138	200	0
22 HOUSEHOLD FURNITURE	7847	35642	36347	7578	14665	12760	154	2875	134
23 OTHER FURNITURE	9523	7315	48448	3850	1011	9607	25	2194	245
24 PAPER, ALLIED PRDTS.	19612	122199	96834	46656	1645	27281	382	2447	56
25 PAPERBOARD CONTAINERS	25210	43837	44394	11091	8240	25419		1355	56
26 PRINTING, PUBLISHING	57304	183163	154746	101964	10703	128008	8763	21798	3439
27 CHEMICALS,SELECT. PRDTS.	29026	27816	106286	11035	289	56458	5216	4430	4346
28 PLASTICS, SYNTHETICS	18677	22300	22611	810		278		44	0
29 DRUGS, COSMETICS	14046	24941	59932	9095	3664	29946	0	3472	0
30 PAINT, ALLIED PRDTS.	5789	8608	22993	4182	275	13605	113	550	0
31 PETROLEUM, RELATED INDS.	7240	5652	19755	8253	1068	15983	7031	2751	70
32 RUBBER, MISC. PLASTICS	32926	166830	74572	9565	7376	12979	0	5084	40
33 LEATHER TANNING, PRDTS.	687	37459	7324	1488	40	983	20	306	0
34 FOOTWEAR, LEATHER PRDTS.	6803	177589	4085	4631	5253	94622	18	91	0
35 GLASS, GLASS PRDTS.	13279	1388	13272	378	4138	12279	90		46
36 STONE, CLAY PRDTS.	28575	57687	71879	31148	10224	57830	2333	7288	5145
37 PRIMARY IRON, STEEL MFR.	182961	71842	318082	23814	1282	53447	1345	1470	
38 PRIMARY NONFERROUS MFR.	30510	45496	96168	4608	2421	20409	24769	4510	4548

39 METAL CONTAINERS	24017	2755	442	5539	44	13154	0	2420	0
40 FABRICATED METAL PRDTS.	26208	45024	107805	28206	7168	60698	1466	12923	494
41 SCREW MACH. PRDTS., ETC.	10618	47613	122663	11110	440	13135	0	671	0
42 OTHER FAB. METAL PRDTS.	10423	99790	196422	17943	990	35974	79	1784	331
43 ENGINES, TURBINES	0	49047	67248	5132	0	2563	0	0	0
44 FARM MACH., EQUIP.	695	350	25978	20717	2192	8567	218	6784	0
45 CONSTRUC. MACH., EQUIP.	912	2320	27511	18083	2236	3996	26	785	0
46 MATERIAL HANDLING MACH.	1399	6568	40297	5689	2172	3283	0	611	0
47 METALWORKING MACHINERY	11709	78542	297180	12497	236	12074	13	502	0
48 SPECIAL MACH., EQUIP.	14033	103260	39718	7409	2657	8273	0	421	0
49 GENERAL MACH., EQUIP.	9109	46393	97447	9662	568	8669	0	4256	0
50 MACHINE SHOP PRDTS.	7422	19420	64843	10760	1823	22591	363	923	363
51 OFFICE, COMPUT. MACHINES	2064	13745	49934	32042	445	445	0	66	0
52 SERVICE IND. MACHINES	5186	25995	53168	21332	432	33372	0	763	21
53 ELECT. TRANSMISS. EQUIP.	7308	88308	47914	18810	1547	61529	0	75	56
54 HOUSEHOLD APPLIANCES	4227	7037	45214	18507	10528	8616	0	0	0
55 ELECTRIC LIGHTING EQUIP.	887	31501	5760	991	5107	16552	0	0	0
56 RADIO, TV, ETC., EQUIP.	75808	84212	15015	6717	1041	3217	49	11218	1026
57 ELECTRONIC COMPONENTS	1742	117695	10483	8347	1769	3204	0	5328	56
58 MISC. ELECTRICAL MACH.	2526	12562	19065	1874	39	8238	0	316	0
59 MOTOR VEHICLES, EQUIP.	20727	16229	1376156	17510	5563	91341	46	3753	66
60 AIRCRAFT, PARTS	165640	54089	75350	23208	4650	196037	0	66	66
61 OTHER TRANSPORT. EQUIP.	67002	66117	38685	5847	51902	13675	153	5586	0
62 PROFESS., SCIEN. INSTRU.	8480	66803	40140	61643	157	6774	103	1938	56
63 MEDICAL, PHOTO. EQUIP.	1283	33722	8030	9043	220	2857	0	200	0
64 MISC. MANUFACTURING	14916	107303	46784	15590	2475	25298	734	2040	673
65 TRANSPORT., WAREHOUSING	244000	299000	402000	308000	64000	449000	77000	142000	38000
66 COMMUNICA., EXC. BRDCAST.	55984	132660	146324	50512	20021	89617	14293	28887	8643
67 RADIO, TV BROADCASTING	4172	11857	19255	2563	3021	13870	2169	4315	1058
68 ELEC.,GAS,WATER,SAN.SER.	64854	87222	129901	51541	25967	85689	13529	8161	4992
69 WHOLESALE, RETAIL TRADE	540299	1171985	1493045	708046	186806	980746	124146	258682	58633
70 FINANCE, INSURANCE	128616	386552	302160	178000	41000	229137	20726	77359	9041
71 REAL ESTATE, RENTAL	28600	43971	41973	21648	3220	37156	2440	5558	1721
72 HOTELS, PERSONAL SERV.	58795	127925	154085	65987	23568	99545	12666	23551	44074
73 BUSINESS SERVICES	56836	178671	221270	71273	13605	99648	7261	20151	6772
74 RESEARCH, DEVELOPMENT	5927	8848	2561	3466	272	1864	42	273	376
75 AUTO. REPAIR, SERVICES	13209	23696	35536	13767	3928	24704	2586	2951	1157
76 AMUSEMENTS	20738	31208	44479	13447	3451	24030	2362	7349	55775
77 MED.,EDUC. SERVICES	150264	500147	210393		30884	235726	28037	62272	8696
78 FEDERAL GOVT. ENTERPRISE	38022	96374	91761	58560	20080	90260	9863	24226	4689
79 STATE, LOCAL GOVT. ENT.	17446	57771	63590	20949	4692	16802	2996	25085	1362
80 IMPORTS	0	0	0	0	0	0	0	0	0
81 BUS.TRAVEL, ENT., GIFTS.	0	0	0	0	0	0	0	0	0
82 OFFICE SUPPLIES	0	0	0	0	0	0	0	0	0
83 SCRAP, USED GOODS	0	0	0	0	0	0	0	0	0
84 GOVERNMENT INDUSTRY	89110	1062859	1235590	512161	328301	711783	142306	285878	105825
85 REST OF WORLD INDUSTRY	0	0	0	0	0	0	0	0	0
86 HOUSEHOLD INDUSTRY	71787	83583	110989	48651	63845	64359	9015	19955	4452
87 INVENTORY VALUATION ADJ.	0	0	0	0	0	0	0	0	0
88 STATE TOTAL	395715	7694931	10159192	3787760	1366980	5346680	706787	1394972	447347

TABLE C-8

STATE ESTIMATES OF 1958 PAYROLLS
(THOUSANDS OF CURRENT DOLLARS)

INDUSTRY TITLE	28 NEW HAMPSHIRE	29 NEW JERSEY	30 NEW MEXICO	31 NEW YORK	32 NORTH CAROLINA	33 NORTH DAKOTA	34 OHIO	35 OKLAHOMA	36 OREGON
1 LIVESTOCK, PRDTS.	6923	23593	10156	75426	25072	8940	34538	17711	22923
2 OTHER AGRICULTURE PRDTS.	2077	20407	8844	42574	54928	24060	31462	20889	31077
3 FORESTRY, FISHERIES	1364	6640	322	12597	4359	17	4372	557	5848
4 AGRI.,FORES.,FISH. SERV.	1313	6213	1882	14041	4631	562	15320	4025	419
5 IRON, FERRO. ORES MINING	0	4569	1215	7925	1139	0	0	0	318
6 NONFERROUS ORES MINING	0	0	24996	7347	1288	29	144	1354	948
7 COAL MINING	0	0	588	0	0	1616	53872	4305	1
8 CRUDE PETRO.,NATURAL GAS	0	0	30393	0	0	3642	16251	139190	0
9 STONE, CLAY MINING	1003	12945	2402	5617	10295	867	31052	4975	4646
10 CHEM.,FERT. MIN. MINING	87	0	21123	25990	1117	0	0	58	29
11 NEW CONSTRUCTION	29220	403712	101227	1152690	131435	38338	667688	150821	96650
12 MAINT.,REPAIR CONSTR.	8986	116330	18076	339024	52417	13560	201665	30649	33338
13 ORDNANCE, ACCESSORIES	90	3955	26526	207181	47651	17	19004	11	90
14 FOOD, KINDRED PRDTS.	11653	306980	13505	708086	102249	15651	409923	60623	84608
15 TOBACCO MANUFACTURES	476	6006	0	1803	103979	0	4516	0	0
16 FABRICS	34914	87328	87	70989	428441	0	7016	2316	3323
17 TEXTILE PRDTS.	1457	30599		46440	10032	0	20735	39	395
18 APPAREL	11893	216503	578	1243703	223814	0	69267	5596	4403
19 MISC. TEXTILE PRDTS.	507	40567	791	118612	11685	0	12182	634	3159
20 LUMBER, WOOD PRDTS.	15125	15078	5454	60584	62153	53	29389	5715	324845
21 WOODEN CONTAINERS	2455	4257	0	4309	3501	152	5851	62	4002
22 HOUSEHOLD FURNITURE	4209	25019	248	90102	110480	0	36016	2721	6467
23 OTHER FURNITURE	255	12086	278	72369	12478	26	54234	1164	1734
24 PAPER, ALLIED PRDTS.	28143	80423	0	193035	42909	13	126315	1168	29532
25 PAPERBOARD CONTAINERS	1049	63916		118875	10570	50	61920	2047	4241
26 PRINTING, PUBLISHING	13184	157890	6240	994025	37709	43	307053	25536	26383
27 CHEMICALS,SELECT. PRDTS.	755	224336	2433	132031	13987	5280	145975	4860	4418
28 PLASTICS, SYNTHETICS	50	40550		30501	31422	31	27802	0	244
29 DRUGS, COSMETICS	551	163799	53	167496	4800	0	49800	1386	556
30 PAINT, ALLIED PRDTS.	56	41285	55	23120	2662	49	32879	1678	1117
31 PETROLEUM, RELATED INDS.	796	72535	3933	18802	1042	49	48268	36498	1521
32 RUBBER, MISC. PLASTICS	6033	116988	0	96584	8114	2328	412189	11603	1624
33 LEATHER TANNING, PRDTS.	8115	13365		18095	1317	47	6443	0	182
34 FOOTWEAR, LEATHER PRDTS.	56918	30684	172	176898	326	19	32722	1095	541
35 GLASS, GLASS PRDTS.	46	56580	137	52097	2826	0	101528	16002	932
36 STONE, CLAY PRDTS.	5887	99985	4556	150907	22715	1360	205297	14335	11416
37 PRIMARY IRON, STEEL MFR.	3912	75179	0	245172	5205	99	731501	6499	15639
38 PRIMARY NONFERROUS MFR.	5095	131064	979	138184	9000	0	152442	9220	9221

Sector	1	2	3	4	5	6	7	8	9
39 METAL CONTAINERS	4127	225	21336	0	49	21509	0	39021	0
40 FABRICATED METAL PRDTS.	16790	30558	225194	1210	13570	188128	1381	81010	2560
41 SCREW MACH. PRDTS., ETC.	643	537	163414	96	1697	81036	0	50994	2225
42 OTHER FAB. METAL PRDTS.	5035	6792	186106	0	7374	143665	49	103329	2494
43 ENGINES, TURBINES	0	64	23086	1563	214	57684	0	11171	0
44 FARM MACH., EQUIP.	1461	951	25157	49	2894	13340	36	1334	56
45 CONSTRUC. MACH., EQUIP.	1594	363	87825	52	643	3643	763	11528	4835
46 MATERIAL HANDLING MACH.	5794	28013	43251	224	833	18323	0	30925	2543
47 METALWORKING MACHINERY	611	736	253546	0	716	91135	295	44757	18357
48 SPECIAL MACH., EQUIP.	6761	2468	78884	0	19885	98719	0	59753	7410
49 GENERAL MACH., EQUIP.	1541	7549	162434	284	2504	122753	162	78525	869
50 MACHINE SHOP PRDTS.	4412	4801	48366	0	3992	45630	1513	25966	1136
51 OFFICE, COMPUT. MACHINES	165	55	103403	30	2272	226602	329	18472	280
52 SERVICE IND. MACHINES	839	936	40228	0	2123	69261	51	31839	13900
53 ELECT. TRANSMISS. EQUIP.	1063	1835	205882	0	7627	174371	43	100591	40
54 HOUSEHOLD APPLIANCES	947	271	175927	37	3604	30389	0	29506	82
55 ELECTRIC LIGHTING EQUIP.	326	69	59974	0	2928	76805	0	57263	8261
56 RADIO, TV, ETC., EQUIP.	376	3912	30716	0	28663	261537	341	246605	10744
57 ELECTRONIC COMPONENTS	1014	2985	29958	331	7310	108620	1736	106817	0
58 MISC. ELECTRICAL MACH.	638	1021	68179	0	7764	49219	54	15871	0
59 MOTOR VEHICLES, EQUIP.	4034	2954	510787	46	4924	199119	238	85229	19
60 AIRCRAFT, PARTS	4960	52700	386669	0	945	361830	0	134929	0
61 OTHER TRANSPORT. EQUIP.	11168	3889	34598	863	4271	64932	399	75897	399
62 PROFESS., SCIEN. INSTRU.	1153	2973	43364	0	4946	199760	743	133216	446
63 MEDICAL, PHOTO. EQUIP.	1712	37	2633	0	0	302546	0	21980	1120
64 MISC. MANUFACTURING	3902	3872	85245	0	4708	338781	1107	98972	6289
65 TRANSPORT., WAREHOUSING	163000	130000	744000	43000	190000	1797000	56000	500000	21000
66 COMMUNICA., EXC. BRDCAST.	39824	38584	173308	7866	43944	554732	14958	106687	11255
67 RADIO, TV BROADCASTING	5196	6206	24543	2573	9628	134019	2239	3453	1362
68 ELEC.,GAS,WATER,SAN.SER.	32832	49520	167163	11350	51446	379031	26840	148348	12326
69 WHOLESALE, RETAIL TRADE	378591	355967	1927013	110706	585814	4622637	134842	1230469	94227
70 FINANCE, INSURANCE	75069	76537	411077	17133	132582	1844146	27001	347824	24935
71 REAL ESTATE, RENTAL	9184	11979	63955	1167	11567	425318	3376	46002	1858
72 HOTELS, PERSONAL SERV.	37398	40604	198130	7995	71395	592432	17124	151490	16151
73 BUSINESS SERVICES	37067	38312	219491	3636	35183	1101409	24361	155437	5558
74 RESEARCH, DEVELOPMENT	279	1296	5333	1755	224	27057	1379	9278	376
75 AUTO. REPAIR, SERVICES	9510	10934	47337	1558	16185	93330	4236	31189	2600
76 AMUSEMENTS	8568	8713	67253	1478	10572	292273	3475	35213	3510
77 MED.,EDUC. SERVICES	91973	78847	524585	25796	126191	1405241	23958	280251	41696
78 FEDERAL GOVT. ENTERPRISE	26823	33444	137057	11264	44393	373995	12776	76356	9017
79 STATE, LOCAL GOVT. ENT.	14832	9632	77530	1325	13718	313764	3268	26632	2501
80 IMPORTS	0	0	0	0	0	0	0	0	0
81 BUS.TRAVEL, ENT., GIFTS.	0	0	0	0	0	0	0	0	0
82 OFFICE SUPPLIES	0	0	0	0	0	0	0	0	0
83 SCRAP, USED GOODS	0	0	0	0	0	0	0	0	0
84 GOVERNMENT INDUSTRY	314235	598370	1439661	106150	880516	3169285	338723	1104779	171004
85 REST OF WORLD INDUSTRY	0	0	0	0	110247	426124	0	0	10194
86 HOUSEHOLD INDUSTRY	25373	34219	140449	7943	0	0	12671	102495	0
87 INVENTORY VALUATION ADJ.	0	0	0	0	0	0	0	0	0
88 STATE TOTAL	2096610	2276023	13630418	484378	4067809	27768588	1003317	8763146	778232

TABLE C-8

STATE ESTIMATES OF 1958 PAYROLLS
(THOUSANDS OF CURRENT DOLLARS)

INDUSTRY TITLE	37 PENNSYL-VANIA	38 RHODE ISLAND	39 SOUTH CAROLINA	40 SOUTH DAKOTA	41 TENNESSEE	42 TEXAS	43 UTAH	44 VERMONT	45 VIRGINIA
1 LIVESTOCK, PRDTS.	52251	2250	13792	12388	20158	44356	10946	13333	30190
2 OTHER AGRICULTURE PRDTS.	26749	750	26208	9612	16842	103644	4054	2667	25810
3 FORESTRY, FISHERIES	3081	2542	2646	102	1439	7058	56	1285	9887
4 AGRI.,FORES.,FISH. SERV.	13681	428	1476	1829	3209	17715	703	819	5690
5 IRON, FERRO. ORES MINING	8944	0	0	11	6489	556	2889	0	561
6 NONFERROUS ORES MINING	503	0	257	10052	4221	504	40111	46	1928
7 COAL MINING	279517	0	0	194	9733	3170	15539	0	53797
8 CRUDE PETRO.,NATURAL GAS	17141	0	0	1	24	450985	5465	112	112
9 STONE, CLAY MINING	29216	578	5166	2670	9154	17923	6381	3207	11106
10 CHEM.,FERT. MIN. MINING	2980	0	189	0	4920	12437	3035	0	1224
11 NEW CONSTRUCTION	629707	40008	81970	24146	113269	726279	72120	17066	196729
12 MAINT., REPAIR CONSTR.	225217	14208	20681	12099	42095	193413	14790	4934	59899
13 ORDNANCE, ACCESSORIES	41149	800		61	9271	6299	5183	38	442
14 FOOD, KINDRED PRDTS.	494807	31031	33432	39649	116267	294612	41766	11903	106353
15 TOBACCO MANUFACTURES	36564	29	3788	0	4261	1326	0	0	50576
16 FABRICS	111862	79605	379860	0	31022	16411	64	2440	82747
17 TEXTILE PRDTS.	44946	19095	13254	0	7755	14211	18	336	7294
18 APPAREL	512774	12104	56645	27	125228	79090	3755	5554	45208
19 MISC. TEXTILE PRDTS.	22654	1570	3231	135	5563	9908	438	64	6368
20 LUMBER, WOOD PKDTS.	36867	786	32201	3117	37420	43367	2303	11108	44638
21 WOODEN CONTAINERS	2935	31	2115	31	4968	4018	31	60	4822
22 HOUSEHOLD FURNITURE	58611	543	8701	168	34656	22211	1723	5616	46916
23 OTHER FURNITURE	34824	1747	801	46	2395	14248	306	0	8968
24 PAPER, ALLIED PRDTS.	116665	892	20540	0	34999	36824	321	9393	48324
25 PAPERBOARD CONTAINERS	68740	4276	11961	200	9098	12267	552	1049	7304
26 PRINTING, PUBLISHING	326325	18603	13188	5492	55207	116664	8287	8579	41764
27 CHEMICALS,SELECT. PRDTS.	78763	2802	61844	392	108905	190800	5207	554	45667
28 PLASTICS, SYNTHETICS	62196	1831	17401	0	95770	31040	0	289	99024
29 DRUGS, COSMETICS	68611	944	2274	297	11043	10085	835	325	12175
30 PAINT, ALLIED PRDTS.	28036	1213	578	0	2084	10221	468	150	1647
31 PETROLEUM, RELATED INDS.	102236	1597	1262	0	2382	275217	6627	238	2824
32 RUBBER, MISC. PLASTICS	98725	32734	3734	371	25968	25999	1989	4296	8701
33 LEATHER TANNING, PRDTS.	18957	41	290	40	2912	624	16	729	2811
34 FOOTWEAR, LEATHER PRDTS.	80106	2642	34	21	30654	6841	115	1469	1851
35 GLASS, GLASS PRDTS.	106958	6056	8837	0	14825	6696	46	1710	1842
36 STONE, CLAY PRDTS.	192486	2763	11251	2131	28269	77505	12326	16289	29081
37 PRIMARY IRON, STEEL MFR.	1191923	11339	2121	51	23894	79243	43532	495	14270
38 PRIMARY NONFERROUS MFR.	124247	30442	931	0	33471	48638	13786	1867	9642

#	Industry	C1	C2	C3	C4	C5	C6	C7	C8	C9
39	METAL CONTAINERS	28847	0	0	0	968	15976	824	0	0
40	FABRICATED METAL PRDTS.	291055	4863	6476	1841	48890	80742	12449	1140	30058
41	SCREW MACH. PRDTS., ETC.	120552	8444	437	437	3653	4012	437	51	103
42	OTHER FAB. METAL PRDTS.	148963	21652	252	275	7575	31306	56	149	3092
43	ENGINES, TURBINES	121753	69	0	0	375	375	0	0	0
44	FARM MACH., EQUIP.	20583	0	41	249	12030	5063	257	350	967
45	CONSTRUC. MACH., EQUIP.	44698	57	38	0	3113	109546	5289	1035	605
46	MATERIAL HANDLING MACH.	37382	104	457	299	4618	3267	81	0	966
47	METALWORKING MACHINERY	99185	20481	177	491	1703	2152	0	21348	798
48	SPECIAL MACH., EQUIP.	79650	9834	10781	65	4950	15170	552	2262	3283
49	GENERAL MACH., EQUIP.	108883	4505	1190	65	2930	15127	216	595	778
50	MACHINE SHOP PRDTS.	33142	2433	2031	743	5606	16696	986	361	2317
51	OFFICE, COMPUT. MACHINES	17746	66	326	0	2469	104	110	4863	4232
52	SERVICE IND. MACHINES	34659	3280	55	65	86	18643	1042	432	4501
53	ELECT. TRANSMISS. EQUIP.	207848	1423	3357	55	1745	4319	332	2177	903
54	HOUSEHOLD APPLIANCES	24286	7415	38	155	27342	1767	0	266	266
55	ELECTRIC LIGHTING EQUIP.	54463	537	101	0	3374	1706	41	1537	37
56	RADIO, TV, ETC., EQUIP.	99036	2234	1011	62	9074	20109	0	366	4467
57	ELECTRONIC COMPONENTS	47703	2549	4476	0	1416	9534	2014	2304	5242
58	MISC. ELECTRICAL MACH.	121688	787	1753	0	1745	4789	327	811	484
59	MOTOR VEHICLES, EQUIP.	23677	1753	787	52	12154	31708	722	50	9081
60	AIRCRAFT, PARTS	112865	537	2234	0	775	307690	8178	375	1774
61	OTHER TRANSPORT. EQUIP.	106707	2287	2964	790	13458	38165	635	366	78320
62	PROFESS., SCIEN. INSTRU.	109633	3292	763	47	13348	17993	117	2022	887
63	MEDICAL, PHOTO. EQUIP.	6935	3352	188	293	1567	1567	10	117	5440
64	MISC. MANUFACTURING	101750	3201	76533	169	15234	12979	1751	1715	6587
65	TRANSPORT., WAREHOUSING	943000	37000	70000	23000	192000	699000	83000	20000	291000
66	COMMUNICA.,EXC. BRDCAST.	209996	16045	21828	8531	50128	152561	16223	5778	58084
67	RADIO, TV BROADCASTING	27041	1436	4454	1496	9940	24503	3108	984	9238
68	ELEC.,GAS,WATER,SAN.SER.	304127	15880	24006	8166	15333	218437	13985	5692	50570
69	WHOLESALE, RETAIL TRADE	2138910	155399	235108	101157	519733	1767506	162127	55062	568814
70	FINANCE, INSURANCE	553000	45841	58062	17875	113481	415984	34416	14462	134395
71	REAL ESTATE, RENTAL	74421	5942	3287	1550	11175	44806	4879	538	21091
72	HOTELS, PERSONAL SERV.	218609	16296	28401	7980	58756	206000	15561	8101	75497
73	BUSINESS SERVICES	257922	12489	15065	6985	54447	175356	14804	1997	69069
74	RESEARCH, DEVELOPMENT	5649	189	978	83	2256	4919	120	126	3384
75	AUTO. REPAIR, SERVICES	53337	3453	7344	1980	12856	50183	3950	1342	13942
76	AMUSEMENTS	51774	5422	4469	2358	11176	35554	3962	1602	11835
77	MED.,EDUC. SERVICES	732158	54930	40822	23534	126565	324272	41235	28864	136463
78	FEDERAL GOVT. ENTERPRISE	170527	11967	22459	11328	92413	125525	12553	7689	51726
79	STATE, LOCAL GOVT. ENT.	69397	4556	6067	3293	35856	59392	3876	1672	18299
80	IMPORTS	0	0	0	0	0	0	0	0	0
81	BUS.,TRAVEL, ENT., GIFTS.	0	0	0	0	0	0	0	0	0
82	OFFICE SUPPLIES	0	0	0	0	0	0	0	0	0
83	SCRAP, USED GOODS	0	0	0	0	0	0	0	0	0
84	GOVERNMENT INDUSTRY	1684315	179110	560595	141752	513667	2279372	239455	59127	1308055
85	REST OF WORLD INDUSTRY	0	0	0	0	0	0	0	0	0
86	HOUSEHOLD INDUSTRY	196240	12451	68255	9959	81617	225883	7088	9496	88359
87	INVENTORY VALUATION ADJ.	0	0	0	0	0	0	0	0	0
88	STATE TOTAL	15246066	1082668	2052182	502289	3187938	10592163	1022551	394383	4203201

TABLE C-8

STATE ESTIMATES OF 1958 PAYROLLS
(THOUSANDS OF CURRENT DOLLARS)

INDUSTRY TITLE	46 WASHINGTON	47 WEST VIRGINIA	48 WISCONSIN	49 WYOMING	50 ALASKA	51 HAWAII	52 NO STATE ALLOCATION	53 NATIONAL TOTAL
1 LIVESTOCK, PRDTS.	23501	8250	43324	15454	0	0	0	1156806
2 OTHER AGRICULTURE PRDTS.	48499	2750	10076	4546	0	0	0	1395194
3 FORESTRY, FISHERIES	9171	743	2884	46	0	0	0	222660
4 AGRI.,FORES.,FISH. SERV.	1131	915	6965	207	0	0	0	281340
5 IRON, FERRO. ORES MINING	21	5	6332	1507	0	0	0	201098
6 NONFERROUS ORES MINING	2369	0	653	3659	0	0	0	286688
7 COAL MINING	1360	309495	0	2157	0	0	0	1006180
8 CRUDE PETRO.,NATURAL GAS	4	15143	0	25336	0	0	0	1138504
9 STONE, CLAY MINING	5279	5797	11480	1971	0	0	0	430926
10 CHEM.,FERT. MIN. MINING	29	0	0	3032	0	0	0	115976
11 NEW CONSTRUCTION	211334	78507	204589	40162	0	0	0	11246570
12 MAINT., REPAIR CONSTR.	61498	24774	74835	12181	0	0	0	3513367
13 ORDNANCE, ACCESSORIES	81	127	446	0	0	0	0	1369822
14 FOOD, KINDRED PRDTS.	126141	33817	291469	5612	0	0	0	7553199
15 TOBACCO MANUFACTURES	0	2875	225	0	0	0	0	287153
16 FABRICS	1406	962	4215	0	0	0	0	1893190
17 TEXTILE PRDTS.	420	0	4828	0	0	0	0	388797
18 APPAREL	8918	10721	35977	0	0	0	0	3756856
19 MISC. TEXTILE PRDTS.	3069	145	2873	31	0	0	0	426257
20 LUMBER, WOOD PRDTS.	188967	14881	52818	2551	0	0	0	1854985
21 WOODEN CONTAINERS	2606	360	4178	0	0	0	0	122454
22 HOUSEHOLD FURNITURE	10149	2648	15613	82	0	0	0	940704
23 OTHER FURNITURE	2675	751	20761	25	0	0	0	443785
24 PAPER, ALLIED PRDTS.	76763	2906	160494	51	0	0	0	1921520
25 PAPERBOARD CONTAINERS	7666	2318	31388	0	0	0	0	835016
26 PRINTING, PUBLISHING	41708	14713	106124	2753	0	0	0	4468939
27 CHEMICALS,SELECT. PRDTS.	69946	116042	12622	142	0	0	0	1977224
28 PLASTICS, SYNTHETICS	716	25678	2501	0	0	0	0	683376
29 DRUGS, COSMETICS	634	1426	12648	19	0	0	0	961189
30 PAINT, ALLIED PRDTS.	1839	303	6031	0	0	0	0	324813
31 PETROLEUM, RELATED INDS.	8665	4142	3819	15175	0	0	0	1112654
32 RUBBER, MISC. PLASTICS	1661	1254	37422	40	0	0	0	1722287
33 LEATHER TANNING, PRDTS.	91	1387	22609	0	0	0	0	184234
34 FOOTWEAR, LEATHER PRDTS.	1031	1037	39883	0	0	0	0	928834
35 GLASS, GLASS PRDTS.	1996	71850	641	0	0	0	0	665544
36 STONE, CLAY PRDTS.	24770	26214	30129	2303	0	0	0	1905158
37 PRIMARY IRON, STEEL MFR.	15997	109021	111211	0	0	0	0	4718655
38 PRIMARY NONFERROUS MFR.	49629	25573	24607	0	0	0	0	1579302

39	METAL CONTAINERS	4193	1233	11548	0	0	0	0	358786
40	FABRICATED METAL PRDTS.	25093	9915	79188	478	0	0	0	2091490
41	SCREW MACH. PRDTS., ETC.	955	6709	49416	0	0	0	0	1083930
42	OTHER FAB. METAL PRDTS.	5211	12624	31386	49	0	0	0	1746694
43	ENGINES, TURBINES	64		96295	0	0	0	0	548251
44	FARM MACH., EQUIP.	1468	1487	72738	0	0	0	0	553098
45	CONSTRUC. MACH., EQUIP.	4679	6465	77739	81	0	0	0	764577
46	MATERIAL HANDLING MACH.	3152	833	8304	0	0	0	0	307467
47	METALWORKING MACHINERY	2059	9541	46815	27	0	0	0	1380034
48	SPECIAL MACH., EQUIP.	6298	500	46029	0	0	0	0	855543
49	GENERAL MACH., EQUIP.	3439	1433	57464	0	0	0	0	1143509
50	MACHINE SHOP PRDTS.	6579	3322	11389	0	0	0	0	570932
51	OFFICE, COMPUT. MACHINES	384	0	2816	363	0	0	0	646264
52	SERVICE IND. MACHINES	1042	1170	26356	0	0	0	0	513086
53	ELECT. TRANSMISS. EQUIP.	2212	259	135048	93	0	0	0	1503947
54	HOUSEHOLD APPLIANCES	1203	266	35419	51	0	0	0	736727
55	ELECTRIC LIGHTING EQUIP.	1838	10610	6650	0	0	0	0	568735
56	RADIO, TV, ETC., EQUIP.	376	62	2585	41	0	0	0	1543001
57	ELECTRONIC COMPONENTS	345	1661	8763	0	0	0	0	848607
58	MISC. ELECTRICAL MACH.	489	78	25124	0	0	0	0	381448
59	MOTOR VEHICLES, EQUIP.	7658	3458	144353	0	0	0	0	3318106
60	AIRCRAFT, PARTS	386297	661	6841	452	0	0	0	4720050
61	OTHER TRANSPORT. EQUIP.	33652	4797	23874	57	0	0	0	1130325
62	PROFESS., SCIEN. INSTRU.	3096	1507	53329	0	0	0	0	1092818
63	MEDICAL, PHOTO. EQUIP.	1001	220	1795	0	0	0	0	467482
64	MISC. MANUFACTURING	6441	2713	34345	262	0	0	0	1414544
65	TRANSPORT., WAREHOUSING	237000	134000	224000	46000	0	0	0	13375000
66	COMMUNICA.,EXC. BRDCAST.	59692	27626	59502	6245	0	0	0	3509634
67	RADIO, TV BROADCASTING	5334	4875	10204	984	0	0	0	557000
68	ELEC.,GAS,WATER,SAN.SER.	18991	64184	42011	6692	0	0	0	3337000
69	WHOLESALE, RETAIL TRADE	605470	244639	694122	54997	0	0	0	34783443
70	FINANCE, INSURANCE	126532	46565	157335	8448	0	0	0	9245831
71	REAL ESTATE, RENTAL	24527	6799	18319	1096	0	0	0	1466693
72	HOTELS, PERSONAL SERV.	63202	26406	69064	10839	0	0	0	4026342
73	BUSINESS SERVICES	55965	20150	69245	3596	0	0	0	4580547
74	RESEARCH, DEVELOPMENT	1392	1253	1725	251	0	0	0	207549
75	AUTO. REPAIR, SERVICES	14906	4943	11498	1195	0	0	0	848950
76	AMUSEMENTS	15158	6675	18305	1400	0	0	0	1479762
77	MED.,EDUC. SERVICES	163682	61899	184103	7654	0	0	0	9453075
78	FEDERAL GOVT. ENTERPRISE	49830	21283	49107	5342	0	0	0	2798115
79	STATE, LOCAL GOVT. ENT.	55369	6103	15898	3937	0	0	0	1455000
80	IMPORTS	0	0	0	0	0	0	0	0
81	BUS.,TRAVEL, ENT., GIFTS.	0	0	0	0	0	0	0	0
82	OFFICE SUPPLIES	0	0	0	0	0	0	0	0
83	SCRAP, USED GOODS	0	0	0	0	0	0	0	0
84	GOVERNMENT INDUSTRY	870247	175493	512590	73528	0	0	3029999	39029000
85	REST OF WORLD INDUSTRY	0	0	0	0	0	0	0	0
86	HOUSEHOLD INDUSTRY	42743	21020	42026	4802	0	0	0	3503000
87	INVENTORY VALUATION ADJ.	0	0	0	0	0	0	0	0
88	STATE TOTAL	3931004	1872967	4671933	378002	0	0	3029999	227966648

TABLE C-9

STATE ESTIMATES OF 1963 PAYROLLS
(THOUSANDS OF CURRENT DOLLARS)

INDUSTRY TITLE	1 ALABAMA	2 ARIZONA	3 ARKANSAS	4 CALIFORNIA	5 COLORADO	6 CONNECTICUT	7 DELAWARE	0 DISTRICT OF COLUMBIA	9 FLORIDA
1 LIVESTOCK, PRDTS.	17989	13829	28917	176035	29004	12175	5138	0	25445
2 OTHER AGRICULTURE PRDTS.	18011	25171	56083	298965	17996	9825	2862	0	88555
3 FORESTRY, FISHERIES	3196	138	1847	47988	44	2571	766	0	23316
4 AGRI.,FORES.,FISH. SERV.	6661	1281	8189	57829	374	7885	2676	0	20079
5 IRON, FERRO. ORES MINING	5077	221	298	7067	13950	0	0	0	0
6 NONFERROUS ORES MINING	208	99267	3361	3861	16227	290	0	0	3215
7 COAL MINING	30716	42	523	42	8118	0	0	0	0
8 CRUDE PETRO.,NATURAL GAS	857	69	7564	114937	23710	0	0	0	1264
9 STONE, CLAY MINING	7448	4234	6913	52307	5343	5207	271	0	12359
10 CHEM.,FERT. MIN. MINING	0	0	1704	20948	1085	0	139	0	16670
11 NEW CONSTRUCTION	143562	164296	86404	2098974	175323	246451	56666	124552	458090
12 MAINT., REPAIR CONSTR.	40433	40637	36302	429499	56975	63042	12592	26257	107626
13 ORDNANCE, ACCESSORIES	33793	31650	57	1209043	23296	49084	0	0	93181
14 FOOD, KINDRED PRDTS.	89183	34486	63596	926986	103746	63441	22897	29235	170176
15 TOBACCO MANUFACTURES	3722	0	0	137	0	815	0	0	17077
16 FABRICS	98863	50	3606	4218	75	42285	7380	0	1489
17 TEXTILE PRDTS.	10381	61	4170	22598	244	13816	1953	0	330
18 APPAREL	100891	7528	29938	204093	4107	56389	12922	106	30893
19 MISC. TEXTILE PRDTS.	3900	684	56	44875	1942	7031	767	518	4233
20 LUMBER, WOOD PRDTS.	52763	13986	62150	280078	9012	6975	2610	1013	34454
21 WOODEN CONTAINERS	2190	212	4439	15467	690	877	115	0	5678
22 HOUSEHOLD FURNITURE	10662	2507	24946	124487	3507	10283	71	284	20576
23 OTHER FURNITURE	2542	1850	4334	58815	2386	10091	410	280	5914
24 PAPER, ALLIED PRDTS.	72120	3173	34453	86022	2816	23210	2185	2769	76507
25 PAPERBOARD CONTAINERS	3870	942	7133	93507	3618	21183	3034	999	14693
26 PRINTING, PUBLISHING	26777	21585	17545	468279	43039	102195	8082	88743	83199
27 CHEMICALS,SELECT. PRDTS.	29412	4693	21310	100198	6666	22718	16796	476	51526
28 PLASTICS, SYNTHETICS	17426	0	51	18479	74	13105	34899	0	38241
29 DRUGS, COSMETICS	731	411	63	75674	1196	36335	2340	144	4205
30 PAINT, ALLIED PRDTS.	1685	417	354	45591	1709	1433	59	354	4154
31 PETROLEUM, RELATED INDS.	4350	416	9425	135366	6748	2275	6251	0	3885
32 RUBBER, MISC. PLASTICS	36362	1523	8639	168836	37521	90141	17521	20	6158
33 LEATHER TANNING, PRDTS.	0	0	0	6654	31	483	5263	0	466
34 FOOTWEAR, LEATHER PRDTS.	3051	317	19171	18787	13436	7486	1641	0	5854
35 GLASS, GLASS PRDTS.	603	279	3823	57326	279	3414	128	20	4596
36 STONE, CLAY PRDTS.	32712	18007	11927	231974	27931	35703	3974	4991	51763
37 PRIMARY IRON, STEEL MFR.	216992	4593	1510	210747	58671	53988	20005	0	6137
38 PRIMARY NONFERROUS MFR.	48230	78307	20964	132905	2445	115675	2256	0	6037

39 METAL CONTAINERS	953	0	912	63779	1886	429	0	0	13556
40 FABRICATED METAL PRDTS.	41611	11210	7484	227194	14438	27319	4315	2397	44592
41 SCREW MACH. PRDTS., ETC.	7206	206	463	81825	760	71638	1674		2603
42 OTHER FAB. METAL PRDTS.	21617	2310	7401	203645	9153	127125	2218	563	11663
43 ENGINES, TURBINES		0	0	22129	1020	13634	0	0	358
44 FARM MACH., EQUIP.	3881	1201	1224	18670	2401	244	254		1955
45 CONSTRUC. MACH., EQUIP.	2509	52	99	51424	12772	480	71		803
46 MATERIAL HANDLING MACH.	1343	58	2523	21976	939	1637	0		979
47 METALWORKING MACHINERY	2020	1471	1791	76559	790	110287	1330		5267
48 SPECIAL MACH., EQUIP.	5839	332	827	51772	1937	29537	7267	177	6874
49 GENERAL MACH., EQUIP.	3299	711	1543	140995	3674	131192	139		2763
50 MACHINE SHOP PRDTS.	3751	5812	1715	123422	5915	30117	1019	764	7505
51 OFFICE, COMPUT. MACHINES	74	22154	2761	106507	524	55473	0	511	12936
52 SERVICE IND. MACHINES	3479	7415	3325	34345	602	6841	741	40	2521
53 ELECT. TRANSMISS. EQUIP.	2980	522	11826	144210	14357	36857	36	311	2161
54 HOUSEHOLD APPLIANCES	128	36	8694	43087	54	44674	523	30	420
55 ELECTRIC LIGHTING EQUIP.	6626	96	3990	44652	947	41534	838	92	1558
56 RADIO, TV, ETC., EQUIP.	3181	20771	9945	776560	1092	51602	47	374	77626
57 ELECTRONIC COMPONENTS	4252	32456	55	284430	1032	60880	156	156	11389
58 MISC. ELECTRICAL MACH.	3000	77	77	21059	1263	9553	924	43	11855
59 MOTOR VEHICLES, EQUIP.	14362	615	2692	200197	5821	18134	45515	1370	3699
60 AIRCRAFT, PARTS	51577	44468	406	1319178	121827	462726	4126		76471
61 OTHER TRANSPORT. EQUIP.	30144	1240	7254	109515	1434	129468	1246	17	36218
62 PROFESS., SCIEN. INSTRU.	799	11345	6744	105211	4364	77602	1289	329	6785
63 MEDICAL, PHOTO. EQUIP.		298	45	40723	869	18103	0	318	3761
64 MISC. MANUFACTURING	6074	2176	12053	129101	7543	87169	691	1432	12407
65 TRANSPORT., WAREHOUSING	164000	85000	101000	1498000	172000	129000	36000	104000	386000
66 COMMUNICA.,EXC. BROCAST.	45031	31976	22830	592150	56155	74318	8807	10785	124048
67 RADIO, TV BROADCASTING	8002	5826	3612	95702	7146	7576	2308	15575	18051
68 ELEC.,GAS,WATER,SAN.SER.	59168	37551	39810	372021	46585	68694	2468	9268	90660
69 WHOLESALE, RETAIL TRADE	502827	345495	268119	5330599	510889	697492	140346	349148	1276474
70 FINANCE, INSURANCE	130424	81678	58821	1411632	130622	281307	29633	94308	80448
71 REAL ESTATE, RENTAL	12354	17646	5050	228925	17675	18200	4109	38883	80446
72 HOTELS, PERSONAL SERV.	48315	44775	26325	580000	57963	65906	9754	71180	199943
73 BUSINESS SERVICES	36554	48992	20934	1083721	67846	96397	14834	113544	136195
74 RESEARCH, DEVELOPMENT	4495	2659	109	154914	3146	5691	333	8255	14390
75 AUTO. REPAIR, SERVICES	13972	10724	7046	106770	14756	18131	2494	10792	3947
76 AMUSEMENTS	8060	9969	6154	491572	15882	13116	4101	12067	50194
77 MED.,EDUC. SERVICES	108154	90335	59232	1508390	152865	306932	34929	299337	283922
78 FEDERAL GOVT. ENTERPRISE	71951	23803	27398	364032	40561	49513	8167	93184	100551
79 STATE, LOCAL GOVT. ENT.	23712	15415	5171	280890	14439	16033	3328	10590	47699
80 IMPORTS	0	0	0	0	0	0	0	0	0
81 BUS.TRAVEL, ENT., GIFTS.	0	0	0	0	0	0	0	0	0
82 OFFICE SUPPLIES	0	0	0	0	0	0	0	0	0
83 SCRAP, USED GOODS	0	0	0	0	0	0	0	0	0
84 GOVERNMENT INDUSTRY	841379	489433	333848	6857315	754905	554375	133629	1185957	1461283
85 REST OF WORLD INDUSTRY	0	0	0	0	0	0	0	0	0
86 HOUSEHOLD INDUSTRY	99704	27229	40748	376514	27732	67637	14727	51286	189220
87 INVENTORY VALUATION ADJ.	0	0	0	0	0	0	0	0	0
88 STATE TOTAL	3576176	2112500	1715321	33884906	3011915	5252450	779101	2767844	6652472

TABLE C-9

STATE ESTIMATES OF 1963 PAYROLLS
(THOUSANDS OF CURRENT DOLLARS)

INDUSTRY TITLE	10 GEORGIA	11 IDAHO	12 ILLINOIS	13 INDIANA	14 IOWA	15 KANSAS	16 KENTUCKY	17 LOUISIANA	18 MAINE
1 LIVESTOCK, PRDTS.	26964	15790	33686	18889	42150	19044	18457	13740	12746
2 OTHER AGRICULTURE PRDTS.	31036	27210	51314	25111	32850	15956	28543	32260	11254
3 FORESTRY, FISHERIES	5956	1119	1409	854	279	73	240	7550	3521
4 AGRI.,FORES.,FISH. SERV.	11740	1407	21273	11129	12449	7383	401	3208	1286
5 IRON, FERRO. ORES MINING	418	88	0	0	0	0	0	0	0
6 NONFERROUS ORES MINING	86	16256	1964	0	0	36	0	0	38
7 COAL MINING	42	0	65382	19787	1308	1857	101490	0	0
8 CRUDE PETRO.,NATURAL GAS	0	0	23539	5698	0	42086	12224	141908	0
9 STONE, CLAY MINING	25971	1303	28298	14710	12281	6980	12356	5132	788
10 CHEM.,FERT. MIN. MINING	1636	5038	2705	0	0	766	920	13062	0
11 NEW CONSTRUCTION	205484	34346	817142	271849	116222	132510	175935	374343	39910
12 MAINT., REPAIR CONSTR.	53471	19847	326875	122694	75833	69636	58106	53657	19929
13 ORDNANCE, ACCESSORIES	1049	1239	34664	37840	18246	0	0	20976	3479
14 FOOD, KINDRED PRDTS.	168940	40811	696190	248487	303607	122570	127071	131848	45229
15 TOBACCO MANUFACTURES	1343	0	2040	1619	0	0	50102	318	0
16 FABRICS	242629	0	7187	0	724	47	2701	0	43635
17 TEXTILE PRDTS.	68377	0	19132	2410	35	35	813	0	2918
18 APPAREL	174044	64	127375	37999	7631	8808	65052	1548	9142
19 MISC. TEXTILE PRDTS.	20934	81	31832	6948	2408	2695	4335	14087	1798
20 LUMBER, WOOD PRDTS.	54438	53497	50001	44412	14062	3485	22410	43665	41923
21 WOODEN CONTAINERS	7798	212	4117	1188	578	167	3919	2564	686
22 HOUSEHOLD FURNITURE	25908	271	64301	85842	7126	3610	19122	3441	1943
23 OTHER FURNITURE	3813	226	57341	18278	5430	3468	2120	1168	1072
24 PAPER, ALLIED PRDTS.	80137	4384	95238	36884	7099	3802	7995	79853	106267
25 PAPERBOARD CONTAINERS	30366	297	110651	35207	9135	11579	9660	12769	1716
26 PRINTING, PUBLISHING	55866	6673	646998	126540	62702	44491	49958	26673	11670
27 CHEMICALS,SELECT. PRDTS.	32568	23596	130593	30700	7087	21548	37471	98357	2589
28 PLASTICS, SYNTHETICS	9737	0	8544	6727	10862	3350	32240	16199	49
29 DRUGS, COSMETICS	11831	0	112128	115875	9511	12493	365	836	94
30 PAINT, ALLIED PRDTS.	5330	70	59840	10120	3151	896	11285	1347	69
31 PETROLEUM, RELATED INDS.	4138	37	83577	58356	729	27652	5800	87606	399
32 RUBBER, MISC. PLASTICS	10603	41	159498	126138	35220	17399	11963	730	7673
33 LEATHER TANNING, PRDTS.	466	0	12387	745	0	0	1184	149	9244
34 FOOTWEAR, LEATHER PRDTS.	11571	126	49526	10450	3886	849	8378	21	82332
35 GLASS, GLASS PRDTS.	9038	0	65602	47511	39	240	170	5542	286
36 STONE, CLAY PRDTS.	44109	4091	146544	90202	33565	37322	24460	26959	6456
37 PRIMARY IRON, STEEL MFR.	22303	653	528752	561582	17649	8347	55970	6615	167
38 PRIMARY NONFERROUS MFR.	7056	8054	159859	119674	24248	2646	12338	12426	765

232

No.	Industry	(1)	(2)	(3)	(4)	(5)	(6)	(7)	(8)	(9)
39	METAL CONTAINERS	4287	231	85765	6458	328	1020	413	12847	2551
40	FABRICATED METAL PRDTS.	31799	2215	152105	96786	25016	21575	29928	22448	3222
41	SCREW MACH. PRDTS., ETC.	7938	0	221057	59082	5333	1505	10212	1385	280
42	OTHER FAB. METAL PRDTS.	7135	154	303349	91370	21016	5627	28031	8078	2396
43	ENGINES, TURBINES	63	0	59739	40554	9024	0	0	358	0
44	FARM MACH., EQUIP.	7322	1579	156967	28717	146413	9333	23719	2407	243
45	CONSTRUC. MACH., EQUIP.	4850	184	313374	23359	32405	7063	381	5653	2451
46	MATERIAL HANDLING MACH.	3140	430	45060	3268	3540	3245	7768	787	0
47	METALWORKING MACHINERY	2804	57	217357	57206	10800	1876	4440	275	776
48	SPECIAL MACH., EQUIP.	15479	294	100691	18428	8961	5298	5145	2995	2615
49	GENERAL MACH., EQUIP.	3131	0	134712	108196	9628	6828	11337	894	853
50	MACHINE SHOP PRDTS.	3376	531	65552	35694	3248	9489	8120	6211	1355
51	OFFICE, COMPUT. MACHINES	883	0	46170	1055	53	106	12861	436	0
52	SERVICE IND. MACHINES	4914	258	61370	30807	6514	4346	13344	1298	1193
53	ELECT. TRANSMISS. EQUIP.	20668	0	139595	91409	4405	603	14305	314	600
54	HOUSEHOLD APPLIANCES	358	0	144991	56897	21031	63	62548	209	93
55	ELECTRIC LIGHTING EQUIP.	4419	0	87370	44967	184	342	10587	141	1407
56	RADIO, TV, ETC., EQUIP.	551	256	421615	170404	56983	2004	2145	442	761
57	ELECTRONIC COMPONENTS	603	0	105651	54353	13787	6997	22281	156	4805
58	MISC. ELECTRICAL MACH.	3253	432	32826	132224	4791	4255	1768	474	823
59	MOTOR VEHICLES, EQUIP.	78687	1388	158056	412835	6599	21193	2193	1274	396
60	AIRCRAFT, PARTS	116707	2278	43924	154610	2757	210543	27295	25353	9516
61	OTHER TRANSPORT. EQUIP.	12392	113	80873	63632	4877	5342	9475	50053	22929
62	PROFESS., SCIEN. INSTRU.	4282	0	163870	17422	13112	1577	7818	1596	346
63	MEDICAL, PHOTO. EQUIP.	247	0	57081	7290	546	315	283	356	44
64	MISC. MANUFACTURING	18318	710	165145	47071	24348	3432	8859	4287	3529
65	TRANSPORT., WAREHOUSING	304000	50000	1198000	369000	162000	209000	206000	297000	51000
66	COMMUNICA.,EXC. BRDCAST.	86007	13034	266566	81541	46448	36349	39648	51657	17565
67	RADIO, TV BROADCASTING	11389	2464	36339	12430	8880	6486	7113	10807	3411
68	ELEC.,GAS,WATER,SAN.SER.	66539	10952	296110	84187	61442	57415	44425	78488	17991
69	WHOLESALE, RETAIL TRADE	851476	148777	3149354	1075192	593709	444759	477951	613866	184216
70	FINANCE, INSURANCE	232350	27209	872044	266686	146625	100765	108161	149324	40458
71	REAL ESTATE, RENTAL	21695	2011	165872	22234	9770	8946	8540	17016	3403
72	HOTELS, PERSONAL SERV.	77241	13249	317694	93213	46371	38155	48850	54968	21744
73	BUSINESS SERVICES	92105	9990	644903	88353	47372	40574	43061	89819	11058
74	RESEARCH, DEVELOPMENT	2316	10742	21034	4742	2233	433	456	2032	533
75	AUTO. REPAIR, SERVICES	22558	3021	62241	22892	11483	10634	11492	14870	4498
76	AMUSEMENTS	15509	2690	87142	20579	11540	9521	14656	15181	3756
77	MED.,EDUC. SERVICES	150727	28414	988565	279843	50856	116755	145676	145610	59021
78	FEDERAL GOVT. ENTERPRISE	77832	12491	252511	77660	50510	45432	58268	43753	21214
79	STATE, LOCAL GOVT. ENT.	21287	2948	172102	32198	16330	16104	13372	23615	5076
80	IMPORTS	0	0	0	0	0	0	0	0	0
81	BUS.TRAVEL, ENT., GIFTS.	0	0	0	0	0	0	0	0	0
82	OFFICE SUPPLIES	0	0	0	0	0	0	0	0	0
83	SCRAP, USED GOODS	0	0	0	0	0	0	0	0	0
84	GOVERNMENT INDUSTRY	1365582	171852	2479016	961739	536242	696498	768869	791726	257847
85	REST OF WORLD INDUSTRY	0	0	0	0	0	0	0	0	0
86	HOUSEHOLD INDUSTRY	149186	8663	145791	62554	39229	33022	46393	101618	18016
87	INVENTORY VALUATION ADJ.	0	0	0	0	0	0	0	0	0
88	STATE TOTAL	5372601	796444	19957053	7761592	3264841	2848886	3331241	3895609	1254564

TABLE C-9

STATE ESTIMATES OF 1963 PAYROLLS
(THOUSANDS OF CURRENT DOLLARS)

INDUSTRY TITLE	19 MARYLAND	20 MASSA-CHUSETTS	21 MICHIGAN	22 MINNESOTA	23 MISSISSIPPI	24 MISSOURI	25 MONTANA	26 NEBRASKA	27 NEVADA
1 LIVESTOCK, PRDTS.	15987	14788	24145	26382	20040	28078	13571	21964	5029
2 OTHER AGRICULTURE PRDTS.	11013	12212	32855	24618	39960	27922	18429	19036	2971
3 FORESTRY, FISHERIES	5015	32643	5852	1340	1544	1654	621	7	32
4 AGRI.,FORES.,FISH. SERV.	7027	2367	10480	8571	4423	12676	760	820	1700
5 IRON, FERRO. ORES MINING	3	0	28408	80334	0	4962	375	0	1207
6 NONFERROUS ORES MINING	0	0	19446	683	0	7322	26821	16	13875
7 COAL MINING	1455	0	0	0	0	7996	328	0	0
8 CRUDE PETRO.,NATURAL GAS	238	0	0	0	15000	332	7890	3276	26
9 STONE, CLAY MINING	10341	8182	6974	8482	3161	17191	2313	5699	3283
10 CHEM.,FERT. MIN. MINING	0	0	21008	0	0	4305	3027	0	221
11 NEW CONSTRUCTION	311361	399637	475505	241987	82092	311064	50758	83335	114145
12 MAINT.+ REPAIR CONSTR.	63517	103470	156881	105442	36205	131711	34837	54576	15278
13 ORDNANCE, ACCESSORIES	10513	34828	14909	39542	0	73501	0	513	0
14 FOOD, KINDRED PRDTS.	160443	207489	292202	274635	53940	273952	21220	151523	6286
15 TOBACCO MANUFACTURES	291	235	1632	0	0	1446	0	0	0
16 FABRICS	5911	110848	1385	658	2634	3524	0	279	0
17 TEXTILE PRDTS.	314	48399	12869	2481	8123	6713	0	0	0
18 APPAREL	77123	189321	16167	28170	90391	103266	0	4163	11
19 MISC. TEXTILE PRDTS.	8523	30497	72253	6556	3009	11730	32	159	65
20 LUMBER, WOOD PRDTS.	15027	23806	48351	28301	66334	21039	41992	4318	2378
21 WOODEN CONTAINERS	2489	2315	1406	1043	6390	2492	0	167	0
22 HOUSEHOLD FURNITURE	10718	40922	37458	7718	23473	11136	146	3300	167
23 OTHER FURNITURE	10351	11712	62164	4084	2187	14083	277	6238	151
24 PAPER, ALLIED PRDTS.	22908	140175	115032	62890	25640	28473	1540	1949	44
25 PAPERBOARD CONTAINERS	30322	55391	60176	17155	2510	31592	0	2679	0
26 PRINTING, PUBLISHING	84625	228535	176314	126521	9596	154546	7949	28094	6068
27 CHEMICALS,SELECT. PRDTS.	36124	30899	123035	17322	16161	72345	2313	4874	5654
28 PLASTICS, SYNTHETICS	19272	39230	36998	2672	735	538			0
29 DRUGS, COSMETICS	24917	23168	58757	12380	3139	40243	79	7389	290
30 PAINT, ALLIED PRDTS.	7663	10056	29030	4062	354	15638		307	70
31 PETROLEUM, RELATED INDS.	7408	9378	20905	10780	4933	14204	6453	1564	225
32 RUBBER, MISC. PLASTICS	52644	177083	112535	17700	17471	28805		9263	0
33 LEATHER TANNING, PRDTS.	1264	32752	5799	2058	0	1280	41	353	0
34 FOOTWEAR, LEATHER PRDTS.	6983	164285	10947	5004	6427	87421	18	828	0
35 GLASS, GLASS PRDTS.	16511	1585	35393	13168	3058	1299	0	39	
36 STONE, CLAY PRDTS.	37862	70887	83074	64424	16867	63540	4515	11331	12145
37 PRIMARY IRON, STEEL MFR.	185692	69789	493235	29074	1699	62334	535	1672	268
38 PRIMARY NONFERROUS MFR.	45456	61320	111165	8318	1319	22990	30875	12257	28360

234

#	Industry									
39	METAL CONTAINERS	27220	2918	1408	9512	467	19928	0	1960	0
40	FABRICATED METAL PRDTS.	29368	52330	105843	26943	11588	61966	1469	15098	1282
41	SCREW MACH. PRDTS., ETC.	9972	53998	165938	18227	4193	15774	104	668	38
42	OTHER FAB. METAL PRDTS.	13749	112790	276842	24067	7787	48915		3158	82
43	ENGINES, TURBINES	0	57515	90964	4248		1760	201	0	0
44	FARM MACH., EQUIP.	254	243	34918	29446	8675	10797	24	7182	0
45	CONSTRUC. MACH., EQUIP.	1262	2053	29876	25821	3123	8782	31	1098	24
46	MATERIAL HANDLING MACH.	2630	8920	53249	6253	2875	4615		336	
47	METALWORKING MACHINERY	16551	95575	407808	10963	74	19520		545	0
48	SPECIAL MACH., EQUIP.	19926	127362	49595	11866	2058	12499		70	38
49	GENERAL MACH., EQUIP.	7006	56751	117336	15909	729	14379	0	5932	48
50	MACHINE SHOP PRDTS.	14151	30878	84450	18319	2828	37697	323	1014	323
51	OFFICE, COMPUT. MACHINES	1670	22779	66107	83531	0	4790		53	
52	SERVICE IND. MACHINES	8134	25767	55455	30892	2337	42972		390	258
53	ELECT. TRANSMISS. EQUIP.	8001	78574	63793	27247	2556	54931		444	144
54	HOUSEHOLD APPLIANCES	1826	7966	46761	11436	12475	13521		220	0
55	ELECTRIC LIGHTING EQUIP.	858	40841	9630	3499	6166	24765		0	
56	RADIO, TV, ETC., EQUIP.	163168	282286	18402	58140	1803	31623	0	27317	1313
57	ELECTRONIC COMPONENTS	5943	146408	13734	11956	2294	2997	0	6195	43
58	MISC. ELECTRICAL MACH.	3768	15799	40976	3267	496	7171	0	757	43
59	MOTOR VEHICLES, EQUIP.	54421	23075	2099724	30967	17546	177190	233	11268	66
60	AIRCRAFT, PARTS	111418	75113	77260	23841	4104	231870		74	79
61	OTHER TRANSPORT. EQUIP.	65218	42621	46627	4818	31643	24791	288	7223	22
62	PROFESS., SCIEN. INSTRU.	7917	108914	87996	45511	1425	18256	460	5399	
63	MEDICAL, PHOTO. EQUIP.	1869	60192	3143	5381	18	4229		130	0
64	MISC. MANUFACTURING	14078	125014	64233	26475	8633	27406	988	5886	1445
65	TRANSPORT., WAREHOUSING	280000	345000	469000	321000	72000	492000	76000	151000	44000
66	COMMUNICA..EXC. BRDCAST.	71733	158649	164435	60484	25996	105119	14399	36535	16874
67	RADIO, TV BROADCASTING	8207	14808	20584	12319	4374	16419	2751	6420	1845
68	ELEC.,GAS,WATER,SAN.SER.	31138	131750	208524	71384	34643	108852	16533	10844	12751
69	WHOLESALE, RETAIL TRADE	751906	1509967	1821231	909151	261828	1222200	151716	343854	113917
70	FINANCE, INSURANCE	185429	502293	395371	236658	61951	306608	27770	103850	23327
71	REAL ESTATE, RENTAL	39820	45600	39189	29906	5448	41692	2542	9273	9554
72	HOTELS, PERSONAL SERV.	73286	149893	171614	76291	27428	114304	14000	29399	75613
73	BUSINESS SERVICES	121747	251893	158297	120082	22649	164963	10907	33790	21562
74	RESEARCH, DEVELOPMENT	27040	25226	3559	1505	994	1461	842	1080	236
75	AUTO. REPAIR, SERVICES	19336	33666	48819	18414	6259	28930	2980	7227	5052
76	AMUSEMENTS	29110	37844	50264	19474	4363	29593	2908	8469	91292
77	MED.,EDUC. SERVICES	254055	793800	548424	297593	45804	353451	36653	84681	16860
78	FEDERAL GOVT. ENTERPRISE	55283	136074	119251	76276	27322	131500	12355	33124	8713
79	STATE, LOCAL GOVT. ENT.	21370	76519	66332	20895	7095	23295	3578	31011	2296
80	IMPORTS	0	0	0	0	0	0	0	0	0
81	BUS.TRAVEL, ENT., GIFTS.	0	0	0	0	0	0	0	0	0
82	OFFICE SUPPLIES	0	0	0	0	0	0	0	0	0
83	SCRAP, USED GOODS	0	0	0	0	0	0	0	0	0
84	GOVERNMENT INDUSTRY	1171873	1459191	1850911	776146	513072	965960	218526	399222	145206
85	REST OF WORLD INDUSTRY	0	0	0	0	0	0	0	0	0
86	HOUSEHOLD INDUSTRY	75073	86259	118488	49273	73454	67734	8325	21766	6846
87	INVENTORY VALUATION ADJ.	0	0	0	0	0	0	0	0	0
88	STATE TOTAL	5114095	9806318	13184892	4949941	1899388	6800568	884621	1855950	821141

TABLE C-9

STATE ESTIMATES OF 1963 PAYROLLS
(THOUSANDS OF CURRENT DOLLARS)

INDUSTRY TITLE	28 NEW HAMPSHIRE	29 NEW JERSEY	30 NEW MEXICO	31 NEW YORK	32 NORTH CAROLINA	33 NORTH DAKOTA	34 OHIO	35 OKLAHOMA	36 OREGON
1 LIVESTOCK, PRDTS.	5670	18564	13122	52800	26715	7493	28142	17144	24320
2 OTHER AGRICULTURE PRDTS.	2330	21436	9878	41200	71285	17507	33858	15856	34680
3 FORESTRY, FISHERIES	1629	11666	61	20945	4959	3	3256	353	7442
4 AGRI.,FORES.,FISH. SERV.	1705	5153	336	15469	6835	407	16372	5782	506
5 IRON-,FERRO. ORES MINING	0	2884	529	9717	435	0	0	0	432
6 NONFERROUS ORES MINING	0	3449	28081	4839	132	163	99	976	336
7 COAL MINING	0	0	2164	0	0	2672	51342	1907	0
8 CRUDE PETRO.,NATURAL GAS	0	0	33073	5857	0	4479	7686	138813	79
9 STONE, CLAY MINING	1203	19190	3239	30285	9924	1260	31058	5590	10383
10 CHEM.,FERT. MIN. MINING	0	0	25258	5013	2566	0	8085	0	20
11 NEW CONSTRUCTION	35177	542567	93334	1454800	197060	37151	625939	188594	146740
12 MAINT., REPAIR CONSTR.	14233	166109	26898	502726	77929	27743	268687	44117	52844
13 ORDNANCE, ACCESSORIES	0	457	20601	30751	12277	0	44104	57	81
14 FOOD, KINDRED PRDTS.	14155	365836	16079	754857	128503	14270	424250	66338	99714
15 TOBACCO MANUFACTURES	0	4054	0	1914	131247	0	3852	0	0
16 FABRICS	31600	78211	48	65210	550674	0	6812	253	2468
17 TEXTILE PRDTS.	2724	29759	0	44477	24157	0	25783	52	618
18 APPAREL	12837	253796	77	1316617	324925	0	76556	13356	12940
19 MISC. TEXTILE PRDTS.	945	54742	532	139844	22708	58	11766	959	3910
20 LUMBER, WOOD PRDTS.	15187	18918	8383	65770	73584	379	35372	6961	387950
21 WOODEN CONTAINERS	1690	3920	35	4524	3332	0	3619	0	1631
22 HOUSEHOLD FURNITURE	6525	28803	658	85713	164149	51	39173	3158	11256
23 OTHER FURNITURE	3349	15525	305	84097	15241	51	56609	1393	1858
24 PAPER, ALLIED PRDTS.	28478	104780	0	214776	60359	0	155221	2108	39956
25 PAPERBOARD CONTAINERS	2704	89043	50	127588	17244	31	82736	2692	4294
26 PRINTING, PUBLISHING	19388	204846	7517	1156192	48751	6677	363037	29377	29061
27 CHEMICALS,SELECT. PRDTS.	1246	286754	1736	132868	18114	731	151988	6068	6041
28 PLASTICS, SYNTHETICS	1843	48551	0	45882	50262	0	41024	51	446
29 DRUGS, COSMETICS	330	217243	42	193870	6882	0	57046	642	1314
30 PAINT, ALLIED PRDTS.	69	47074	70	25217	4381	0	40573	1043	2159
31 PETROLEUM, RELATED INDS.	380	69501	3861	17995	881	2951	50384	36853	2345
32 RUBBER, MISC. PLASTICS	15638	152958	1297	137736	14857	0	533768	13834	2330
33 LEATHER TANNING, PRDTS.	9710	12718	0	16853	1650	0	6616	0	194
34 FOOTWEAR, LEATHER PRDTS.	64542	34856	326	175852	4283	0	32004	1209	989
35 GLASS, GLASS PRDTS.	289	75101	45	57701	10334	0	121271	23104	2454
36 STONE, CLAY PRDTS.	8388	125851	6680	176330	33109	2398	230338	15992	15525
37 PRIMARY IRON, STEEL MFR.	5169	79551	0	285963	9729	66	925605	8617	17127
38 PRIMARY NONFERROUS MFR.	4144	151354	972	173507	10682	0	176349	14104	12225

236

#	Industry									
39	METAL CONTAINERS	0	51948	0	24165	58	0	24240	362	2649
40	FABRICATED METAL PRDTS.	3280	97346	1517	188935	22175	1242	241563	34494	19228
41	SCREW MACH. PRDTS., ETC.	1528	67772	186	101427	6905	69	198881	1313	943
42	OTHER FAB. METAL PRDTS.	4675	151089		179361	14473	100	256609	7808	7629
43	ENGINES, TURBINES	64	992		57499	63	0	15436	63	349
44	FARM MACH., EQUIP.	40	1078	34	12170	5287	1587	36238	1899	1692
45	CONSTRUC. MACH., EQUIP.	4771	11061	384	7241	685	62	96160	33085	2178
46	MATERIAL HANDLING MACH.	0	33731		41911	610	85	58708	813	10199
47	METALWORKING MACHINERY	4217	55209	514	118979	2898	358	329966	727	808
48	SPECIAL MACH., EQUIP.	20805	78036	294	103414	33643	164	109140	2581	10867
49	GENERAL MACH., EQUIP.	11273	102131	48	159313	1851	44	204886	12795	1641
50	MACHINE SHOP PRDTS.	2397	32806	2371	53993	5222	559	55529	5517	7378
51	OFFICE, COMPUT. MACHINES	720	29211	341	267234	2159	0	140546	957	52
52	SERVICE IND. MACHINES	1193	33263	301	74909	5553	0	61306	3799	1391
53	ELECT. TRANSMISS. EQUIP.	16626	95756	61	206156	20750	0	243081	6261	29332
54	HOUSEHOLD APPLIANCES	93	26051		35702	7968	0	220018	663	738
55	ELECTRIC LIGHTING EQUIP.	709	77597		97718	6316	0	77138	108	319
56	RADIO, TV, ETC., EQUIP.	21560	485904	1312	647231	58738	0	92455	51434	543
57	ELECTRONIC COMPONENTS	20132	139414	299	204564	13614	0	47362	1134	198
58	MISC. ELECTRICAL MACH.	329	23343	77	33864	10425	0	54653	768	2207
59	MOTOR VEHICLES, EQUIP.	57	108814	669	303065	9248	0	834396	9409	8732
60	AIRCRAFT, PARTS	0	116931	19	427567	8518	0	370099	39225	6135
61	OTHER TRANSPORT. EQUIP.	518	67516	73	58052	4617	24	39956	2443	14620
62	PROFESS., SCIEN. INSTRU.	1222	87033	832	157971	9703	78	58457	2960	2617
63	MEDICAL, PHOTO. EQUIP.	2896	29583		392751	4081		3214	83	3354
64	MISC. MANUFACTURING	6804	129010	1535	391334	9389	1178	98021	4365	7067
65	TRANSPORT., WAREHOUSING	23000	636000	62000	2075000	239000	43000	836000	161000	190000
66	COMMUNICA.,EXC. BRDCAST.	15199	160111	19337	655556	61255	9562	198140	43545	45002
67	RADIO, TV BROADCASTING	1800	3872	3112	158170	14304	3095	32408	6830	6871
68	ELEC.,GAS,WATER,SAN.SER.	11924	179514	29806	449684	61441	13177	244977	57989	48674
69	WHOLESALE, RETAIL TRADE	126159	1722547	182186	5770710	828074	135063	2400430	466546	524067
70	FINANCE, INSURANCE	35187	435128	43800	2368188	202149	26207	543891	111534	10612
71	REAL ESTATE, RENTAL	2403	62547	5556	499431	17862	1349	72498	12574	12821
72	HOTELS, PERSONAL SERV.	19072	178813	21414	688438	88083	9685	217478	43839	45290
73	BUSINESS SERVICES	9626	273243	26649	1579000	65947	6446	318041	70631	56247
74	RESEARCH, DEVELOPMENT	855	19505	2616	67627	645	174	10490	1002	656
75	AUTO. REPAIR, SERVICES	3129	42337	4833	125554	22934	1529	57422	13450	1547
76	AMUSEMENTS	5552	48740	4722	392231	14367	2061	68852	9875	10361
77	MED.,EDUC. SERVICES	60337	445913	37214	2212108	205484	33772	761674	121828	134109
78	FEDERAL GOVT. ENTERPRISE	12014	117039	16012	473449	65027	14827	183801	46110	35063
79	STATE, LOCAL GOVT. ENT.	3257	37177	4626	366878	16309	1806	106853	11363	18818
80	IMPORTS	0	0	0	0	0	0	0	0	0
81	BUS.TRAVEL, ENT., GIFTS.	0	0	0	0	0	0	0	0	0
82	OFFICE SUPPLIES	0	0	0	0	0	0	0	0	0
83	SCRAP, USED GOODS	0	0	0	0	0	0	0	0	0
84	GOVERNMENT INDUSTRY	216995	1580421	424222	4904784	1299309	216859	2023816	809486	481283
85	REST OF WORLD INDUSTRY	0	0	0	0	0	0	0	0	0
86	HOUSEHOLD INDUSTRY	11328	119459	14220	451466	129142	8109	143230	37888	27685
87	INVENTORY VALUATION ADJ.	0	0	0	0	0	0	0	0	0
88	STATE TOTAL	997023	11540231	1218479	35262555	5730436	658812	16959539	2919909	2823640

TABLE C-9

STATE ESTIMATES OF 1963 PAYROLLS
(THOUSANDS OF CURRENT DOLLARS)

INDUSTRY TITLE	37 PENNSYL-VANIA	38 RHODE ISLAND	39 SOUTH CAROLINA	40 SOUTH DAKOTA	41 TENNESSEE	42 TEXAS	43 UTAH	44 VERMONT	45 VIRGINIA
1 LIVESTOCK, PRDTS.	36636	2271	9576	11332	18846	94643	9064	7775	27630
2 OTHER AGRICULTURE PRDTS.	25364	1729	27424	8668	26154	133357	4936	3225	28370
3 FORESTRY, FISHERIES	6329	2110	3921	22	3133	6618	163	1871	8501
4 AGRI.,FORES.,FISH. SERV.	18657	1224	2748	493	6945	27443	1672	476	4000
5 IRON, FERRO. ORES MINING	10631	0	0	12	50	1589	1483	0	170
6 NONFERROUS ORES MINING	1058	0	99	11797	5855	655	47092	0	1828
7 COAL MINING	201787	0	0	14	8112	950	9941	0	49009
8 CRUDE PETRO.,NATURAL GAS	19551	0	0	89	38	446581	4193	0	88
9 STONE, CLAY MINING	30232	1149	6627	2864	11389	20304	4814	4364	15802
10 CHEM.,FERT. MIN. MINING	3488	0	276	20	1664	7760	1200	0	395
11 NEW CONSTRUCTION	636339	58619	90857	35077	181874	856097	88329	18012	328825
12 MAINT., REPAIR CONSTR.	270257	14920	43403	24133	49251	224181	20733	10988	72336
13 ORDNANCE, ACCESSORIES	20546	50	0	0	13543	41959	22916	0	358
14 FOOD, KINDRED PRDTS.	559202	31183	41337	44775	143994	339065	42383	13248	127023
15 TOBACCO MANUFACTURES	32010	16	6221	0	4072	326	0	0	63251
16 FABRICS	105444	74472	472522	0	38930	17979	269	2088	94529
17 TEXTILE PRDTS.	44814	15441	22558	0	8685	3011	148	789	10418
18 APPAREL	642492	16591	101634	0	192702	117065	7129	5526	94901
19 MISC. TEXTILE PRDTS.	30853	1316	6800	174	7252	11033	341	95	5912
20 LUMBER, WOOD PRDTS.	44513	1858	37666	2748	44127	56716	3920	11158	55327
21 WOODEN CONTAINERS	2798	158	2735	24	5082	2658	35	723	5142
22 HOUSEHOLD FURNITURE	59784	439	11264	410	56004	26349	2490	7667	72484
23 OTHER FURNITURE	49063	5561	877	91	6189	16155	1685	63	11518
24 PAPER, ALLIED PRDTS.	146006	2669	35480	14	45084	49708	777	10245	59707
25 PAPERBOARD CONTAINERS	89561	5945	17076	220	13187	18708	644	1920	10756
26 PRINTING, PUBLISHING	374681	23815	16860	7179	75175	150883	14031	10838	54992
27 CHEMICALS,SELECT. PRDTS.	91098	5669	67472	541	137746	256770	4139	535	60068
28 PLASTICS, SYNTHETICS	83183	8895	31710	0	113924	41546		295	142744
29 DRUGS, COSMETICS	95661	1308	3944	321	15888	14544	395	152	17832
30 PAINT, ALLIED PRDTS.	30758	1493	847	0	3412	15811	417	411	2378
31 PETROLEUM, RELATED INDS.	103519	906	1715	57	2940	280097	7075	57	3617
32 RUBBER, MISC. PLASTICS	133332	39417	11133	988	44926	37572	2494	8346	19470
33 LEATHER TANNING, PRDTS.	14599	128	535	0	4290	499	31	1037	2411
34 FOOTWEAR, LEATHER PRDTS.	94352	5557	0	0	47466	7855	108	1811	11109
35 GLASS, GLASS PRDTS.	118635	12081	11625	0	31360	9219	45	0	4194
36 STONE, CLAY PRDTS.	205641	2485	17246	4215	37985	106973	13509	15818	40466
37 PRIMARY IRON, STEEL MFR.	1315586	13608	5576	22	32826	98838	34090	1340	20301
38 PRIMARY NONFERROUS MFR.	146642	34329	955	0	47165	74698	11714	2222	16024

Industry	1	2	3	4	5	6	7	8	9
39 METAL CONTAINERS	33323	0	101	0	1529	19400	842	0	1009
40 FABRICATED METAL PRDTS.	268647	4793	9841	2318	55690	104100	13480	1284	34067
41 SCREW MACH. PRDTS., ETC.	136827	10634	2826	0	7654	6309	228	424	590
42 OTHER FAB. METAL PRDTS.	189560	21564	5703	382	22259	51824	858	1595	16676
43 ENGINES, TURBINES	122409	57	424	0	63	2961	0	0	0
44 FARM MACH., EQUIP.	18517	40	132	866	18988	6254	621	243	2209
45 CONSTRUC. MACH., EQUIP.	42163	144	1129	975	1676	124766	7959	305	1167
46 MATERIAL HANDLING MACH.	48453	363	7629	949	5567	7013	98	29753	918
47 METALWORKING MACHINERY	120448	26416	22369	47	4223	8872	556	1486	732
48 SPECIAL MACH., EQUIP.	100128	17122	4572	783	5756	20787	1062	305	4176
49 GENERAL MACH., EQUIP.	143349	7552	3197	1192	6441	20133	2935	514	3230
50 MACHINE SHOP PRDTS.	44712	4221	298	0	6580	22951	1941	6682	3791
51 OFFICE, COMPUT. MACHINES	30976	74	11873	0	0	3537	118	1603	13366
52 SERVICE IND. MACHINES	63068	1102	1761	0	6055	27636	2452	655	4955
53 ELECT. TRANSMISS. EQUIP.	252829	2895	576	0	10615	14145	911	0	26135
54 HOUSEHOLD APPLIANCES	24280	855	374	0	25608	3309	0	1366	180
55 ELECTRIC LIGHTING EQUIP.	64192	14289	0	0	4587	3919	191	0	288
56 RADIO, TV, ETC., EQUIP.	100679	4919	0	67	29246	64487	5442	6660	34364
57 ELECTRONIC COMPONENTS	176032	7313	13527	514	5260	52156	3085	1763	30977
58 MISC. ELECTRICAL MACH.	27267	2045	234	0	2725	6385	77	0	548
59 MOTOR VEHICLES, EQUIP.	121767	2770	1123	211	17945	54786	1067	13144	17074
60 AIRCRAFT, PARTS	197052	3432	3868	0	20521	264869	95745	225	9606
61 OTHER TRANSPORT. EQUIP.	131695	2517	4616	483	19008	42126	2113	4384	143827
62 PROFESS., SCIEN. INSTRU.	132309	10865	3531	95	6127	17814	355	1652	3259
63 MEDICAL, PHOTO. EQUIP.	13617	4039	0	0	91	2607	45	1813	4178
64 MISC. MANUFACTURING	124138	84248	11250	793	22002	21073	2946	0	16135
65 TRANSPORT., WAREHOUSING	980000	44000	81000	27000	229000	777000	98000	20000	321000
66 COMMUNICA.,EXC. BRDCAST.	236698	17730	28096	9873	55372	186926	20246	7963	77144
67 RADIO, TV BROADCASTING	31510	2747	7310	2398	12434	28210	3177	1148	11204
68 ELEC.,GAS,WATER,SAN.SER.	325063	22519	29859	10635	19394	253936	17805	5354	61402
69 WHOLESALE, RETAIL TRADE	2550161	204347	323216	130177	690929	2301882	230791	71403	781744
70 FINANCE, INSURANCE	687698	58172	84121	25107	173769	581373	48784	18913	192061
71 REAL ESTATE, RENTAL	83385	8289	5627	2366	16142	61913	6836	1087	34786
72 HOTELS, PERSONAL SERV.	251273	20817	34632	10199	70181	241335	18808	10796	94315
73 BUSINESS SERVICES	393288	21475	33189	6716	87308	299746	22811	4360	84084
74 RESEARCH, DEVELOPMENT	19122	442	993	605	2523	14241	2043	244	10502
75 AUTO. REPAIR, SERVICES	66503	5277	9137	2516	18008	60360	5570	1255	18508
76 AMUSEMENTS	58355	6783	6334	3227	12647	46480	6062	4037	16225
77 MED.,EDUC. SERVICES	999076	81269	66147	33916	189802	502790	71707	46917	200151
78 FEDERAL GOVT. ENTERPRISE	223218	18197	32139	14543	110986	172859	17510	9449	78719
79 STATE, LOCAL GOVT. ENT.	77798	5134	8736	2508	131182	81990	5767	1691	25152
80 IMPORTS	0	0	0	0	0	0	0	0	0
81 BUS.TRAVEL, ENT., GIFTS	0	0	0	0	0	0	0	0	0
82 OFFICE SUPPLIES	0	0	0	0	0	0	0	0	0
83 SCRAP, USED GOODS	0	0	0	0	0	0	0	0	0
84 GOVERNMENT INDUSTRY	235310	223339	645406	191708	69642	3105682	360050	78809	1644651
85 REST OF WORLD INDUSTRY	0	0	0	0	0	0	0	0	0
86 HOUSEHOLD INDUSTRY	188151	13830	72732	10416	86632	247775	8979	12126	101645
87 INVENTORY VALUATION ADJ.	0	0	0	0	0	0	0	0	0
88 STATE TOTAL	18130148	1372652	2697899	649885	4396432	13554934	1454478	514503	5670637

TABLE C-9

STATE ESTIMATES OF 1963 PAYROLLS
(THOUSANDS OF CURRENT DOLLARS)

INDUSTRY TITLE	46 WASHINGTON	47 WEST VIRGINIA	48 WISCONSIN	49 WYOMING	50 ALASKA	51 HAWAII	52 NO STATE ALLOCATION	53 NATIONAL TOTAL
1 LIVESTOCK, PRDTS.	23673	5151	34346	12049	943	7619	0	1175506
2 OTHER AGRICULTURE PRDTS.	50327	3849	17654	5951	57	53381	0	1600494
3 FORESTRY, FISHERIES	10814	679	4983	99	292	141	0	249585
4 AGRI.,FORES.,FISH. SERV.	1606	1112	9741	365	0	1294	0	354415
5 IRON, FERRO. ORES MINING	16	0	7221	4343	16	0	0	181936
6 NONFERROUS ORES MINING	3457	0	768	7701	1914	0	0	333271
7 COAL MINING	1078	248939	0	1871	2226	0	0	821098
8 CRUDE PETRO.,NATURAL GAS	1111	15503	0	25100	3151	0	0	1112984
9 STONE, CLAY MINING	6237	7066	15159	2565	326	1754	0	524345
10 CHEM.,FERT. MIN. MINING	39	69	0	5244	0	0	0	137108
11 NEW CONSTRUCTION	246025	68090	252752	49226	41968	79187	0	14144585
12 MAINT., REPAIR CONSTR.	67467	38364	94818	18933	6205	17044	0	4468947
13 ORDNANCE, ACCESSORIES	3560	10513	3778	0	0	0	0	1956954
14 FOOD, KINDRED PRDTS.	151228	33872	312799	6874	16138	59195	0	8636507
15 TOBACCO MANUFACTURES	0	2482	272	0	0	0	0	330494
16 FABRICS	1728	1372	3151	0	0	50	0	2127938
17 TEXTILE PRDTS.	443	39	7617	0	0	163	0	469416
18 APPAREL	12670	14263	39738	0	29	7128	0	4662153
19 MISC. TEXTILE PRDTS.	3349	582	3350	16	0	472	0	577845
20 LUMBER, WOOD PRDTS.	223832	17306	60178	3869	6514	2603	0	2227319
21 WOODEN CONTAINERS	2151	267	4042	0	39	0	0	111804
22 HOUSEHOLD FURNITURE	8715	2567	15988	21	40	2329	0	1149962
23 OTHER FURNITURE	2145	1466	12930	26	514	387	0	577883
24 PAPER, ALLIED PRDTS.	109947	5292	193696	0	12026	1695	0	2401589
25 PAPERBOARD CONTAINERS	11186	3142	37380	0	0	525	0	1106816
26 PRINTING, PUBLISHING	50509	15805	127332	3393	2530	9405	0	5515137
27 CHEMICALS,SELECT. PRDTS.	83861	118732	11748	50	44	2100	0	2393150
28 PLASTICS, SYNTHETICS	1986	47870	4260	0	0	0	0	973900
29 DRUGS, COSMETICS	1373	1092	14690	0	0	390	0	1199553
30 PAINT, ALLIED PRDTS.	2509	354	7224	0	0	0	0	401244
31 PETROLEUM, RELATED INDS.	10104	4134	3667	15188	484	2197	0	1133768
32 RUBBER, MISC. PLASTICS	2779	1076	38243	41	41	243	0	2364093
33 LEATHER TANNING, PRDTS.	31	2068	25256	0	0	0	0	179204
34 FOOTWEAR, LEATHER PRDTS.	1512	1557	44029	0	0	408	0	1048620
35 GLASS, GLASS PRDTS.	2448	81354	14336	0	0	192	0	845737
36 STONE, CLAY PRDTS.	29923	26908	42385	3919	1441	5402	0	2366262
37 PRIMARY IRON, STEEL MFR.	13032	120743	151059	0	0	1352	0	5759179
38 PRIMARY NONFERROUS MFR.	41501	37027	34942	0	0	0	0	2066501

	C1	C2	C3	C4	C5	C6	C7	Total
39 METAL CONTAINERS	5941	1313	15394	0	0	2543	0	443645
40 FABRICATED METAL PRDTS.	26950	17253	91167	291	500	1644	0	2313346
41 SCREW MACH. PRDTS., ETC.	1753	5311	63460	228	0	460	0	1357057
42 OTHER FAB. METAL PRDTS.	6118	15108	42804	136	0	0	0	2339322
43 ENGINES, TURBINES	63		107934	0	0	0	0	609319
44 FARM MACH., EQUIP.	1886	1592	78940	0	0	271	0	689122
45 CONSTRUC. MACH., EQUIP.	9120	6924	97496	75	0	0	0	977547
46 MATERIAL HANDLING MACH.	7013	1468	9064	0	0	31	0	403751
47 METALWORKING MACHINERY	3130	3223	76228	0	0	57	0	1842034
48 SPECIAL MACH., EQUIP.	10594	709	62444	0	0	0	0	1094823
49 GENERAL MACH., EQUIP.	2611	486	78431	48	0	1117	0	1542490
50 MACHINE SHOP PRDTS.	9279	3511	19998	323	346	63	0	793629
51 OFFICE, COMPUT. MACHINES	1390	0	3227	0	0	347	0	945221
52 SERVICE IND. MACHINES	2288	1038	33061	0	0	0	0	674899
53 ELECT. TRANSMISS. EQUIP.	4212	2494	162752	121	0	70	0	1828538
54 HOUSEHOLD APPLIANCES	1679	178	37023	0	0	29	0	864147
55 ELECTRIC LIGHTING EQUIP.	2598	14593	8000	32	0	0	0	710084
56 RADIO, TV, ETC. EQUIP.	6888	339	66251	0	45	39	0	3852463
57 ELECTRONIC COMPONENTS	1251	3800	14403	0	0	30	0	1534988
58 MISC. ELECTRICAL MACH.	552		26668	0	43	28	0	494515
59 MOTOR VEHICLES, EQUIP.	12457	6417	264218	0	0	0	0	5188402
60 AIRCRAFT, PARTS	507362	75	2235	1388	20	515	0	5253607
61 OTHER TRANSPORT. EQUIP.	47028	10392	28022	26	573	0	0	1411002
62 PROFESS., SCIEN. INSTRU.	260	1906	34240	516	51	547	0	1238152
63 MEDICAL, PHOTO. EQUIP.	281	1257	1748	0	0	51	0	674316
64 MISC. MANUFACTURING	8875	3482	38824	283	155	67	0	1794164
65 TRANSPORT., WAREHOUSING	285000	135000	251000	43000	30000	941	0	15417000
66 COMMUNICA., EXC. BROCAST.	69759	30975	71689	7458	4280	60000	0	4298000
67 RADIO, TV BROADCASTING	12697	4050	11274	1308	1566	6945	0	715000
68 ELEC.,GAS,WATER,SAN.SER.	36145	68630	96712	9646	5481	2661	0	4145000
69 WHOLESALE, RETAIL TRADE	798172	279085	893010	69389	50210	15040	0	45732917
70 FINANCE, INSURANCE	183665	52917	212607	12252	10212	156157	0	12592669
71 REAL ESTATE, RENTAL	32068	7496	20946	1463	1788	38334	0	1892567
72 HOTELS, PERSONAL SERV.	67972	27126	82531	11650	6659	15435	0	4837074
73 BUSINESS SERVICES	92342	40055	102525	6191	10568	27194	0	7228196
74 RESEARCH, DEVELOPMENT	1970	627	1395	334	334	25564	0	460667
75 AUTO. REPAIR, SERVICES	11051	5052	13578	1559	1088	1266	0	1080425
76 AMUSEMENTS	18894	8782	20040	1690	1589	5224	0	1838826
77 MED.,EDUC. SERVICES	219710	81435	281724	9729	11140	5914	0	14210540
78 FEDERAL GOVT. ENTERPRISE	88619	26630	82632	6695	16856	51704	0	3862923
79 STATE, LOCAL GOVT. ENT.	69984	7480	23754	1664	2960	21600	0	1997000
80 IMPORTS	0	0	0	0	0	9413	0	0
81 BUS.,TRAVEL, ENT., GIFTS.	0	0	0	0	0	0	0	0
82 OFFICE SUPPLIES	0	0	0	0	0	0	0	0
83 SCRAP, USED GOODS	0	0	0	0	0	0	0	0
84 GOVERNMENT INDUSTRY	1157884	263369	829711	123142	287290	537477	2455987	55029532
85 REST OF WORLD INDUSTRY	0	0	0	0	0	0	0	0
86 HOUSEHOLD INDUSTRY	45668	19738	46432	4550	3287	13025	0	3824000
87 INVENTORY VALUATION ADJ.	0	0	0	0	0	0	0	0
88 STATE TOTAL	5035551	2102321	6137324	482031	543979	1258408	2455987	297720226

241

Bibliography*

1. American Gas Association. *The American Gas Rate Book*. New York, 1963.
2. ——. *Gas Facts, 1958*. New York, 1959.
3. ——. *Gas Facts, 1964*. New York, 1965
4. ——. *Historical Statistics of the Gas Industry, 1961*. New York, 1961.
5. ——. *Survey of Residential Gas Service by County, 1962*. New York, 1961.
6. American Hospital Association. *Hospitals, Guide Issue: Journal of the American Hospital Association* 41 (August 1, 1967), pt. 2.
7. American Petroleum Institute. "Joint Association Survey: Report on Expenditures for Drilling and Equipping Wells in 1953." *Survey and News Release*. New York, December 1953.
8. ——. "1963 Drilling by Counties." *Oil and Gas Journal* 62 (January 27, 1964).
9. ——. *Oil and Gas Journal* 45 (February 1947).
10. American Public Works Administration. *Refuse Collection Practice*. Danville, Illinois: Interstate Printers and Publishers, 1966.
11. American Veterinary Medical Association. *American Veterinary Medical Association Directory*. Chicago, Illinois, 1963.
12. American Water Works Association. *Journal* 40 (February 1948).
13. ——. *A Survey of Operating Data for Water Works in 1960*. New York, 1964.
14. Association of American Railroads. *Number of Employees of Class I Line-Haul Railroads and Switching and Terminal Companies by States and Metropolitan Areas, 1963*. Washington, D.C., May 1963.
15. ——. "Number of Employees in Class I Line-Haul Railways and Class I Companies by State as of Payroll Period Nearest July 15, 1947." Washington, D.C. Unpublished tabulation. n.d.
16. ——. *Railroad Mileage, Employment, Payroll, and Taxes by States, 1963*. Washington, D.C., September 1964.
17. ——. *Railroad Mileage, Employment, Payroll, and Taxes by States, 1964*. Washington, D.C., September 1965.
18. Automobile Repair and Services – IO-75. Unpublished statistics used for input-output industry IO-69.
19. Board of Governors of the Federal Reserve System. *Fiftieth Annual Report of the Board of Governors of the Federal Reserve System, 1963*. Washington, D.C., 1964.
20. ——. *Forty-Fourth Annual Report of the Board of Governors of the Federal Reserve System, 1958*. Washington, D.C. 1959.
21. ——. *Thirty-Third Annual Report of the Board of Governors of the Federal Reserve System, 1947*. Washington, D.C., 1948.

---

*Material published by the U.S. Government Printing Office, Washington, D.C. 20402, is cited as: GPO, [date].

22. Broadcasting Publications, Inc. *Broadcasting Yearbook, 1958*. Washington, D.C., 1958.
23. California Division of Mines and Geology. *Mineral Information Service*. January 1965.
24. Chilton Publishing Company. *The Spectator, 1963 Health Insurance Index*. 1963.
25. ——. *The Spectator, 1963 Property, Liability Insurance Index*. 1963.
26. Civil Service Commission. "1963 Employment — Regional Offices of Federal Deposit Insurance Corporation." Unpublished.
27. ——. "1963 Employment — Regional Office of the Federal Home Loan Bank Board." Unpublished.
28. ——. "1963 Post Office Employment in SMSA's." Unpublished.
29. ——. "Paid Civilian Employment in the Executive Branch of the Federal Government by Agency and State of Official Duty Station, December 1947." Unpublished.
30. ——. "Paid Civilian Employment of the Federal Government in the Continental United States by Agency and State of Official Duty Station, December 1958." Unpublished.
31. ——. "Paid Civilian Employment of the Federal Government in the United States by Agency and State of Official Duty Station, December 31, 1963." Unpublished.
32. CUNA International. *International Credit Union Yearbook, 1958*. Washington, D.C., 1958.
33. F. W. Dodge Corporation. "Construction Statistics, 1958." Special tabulation.
34. Enfield, George H. "Soil Testing Doubles in Ten Years." *Plant Food Review* 13 (1967): 17–18.
35. ——. "Soil Testing Gains Ground." *Plant Food Review* 10 (Winter 1964): 2, 3, 9.
36. ——. "Soil Testing in the United States." *Plant Food Review* 7 (1961): 7–8.
37. Ensminger, M. E. *The Stockman's Handbook*. Danville, Illinois: Printers and Publishers, Inc., 1962.
38. Executive Office of the President. *The Budget of the United States Government, Fiscal Year 1947*. GPO, 1946.
39. ——. *The Budget of the United States Government, Fiscal Year 1958*. GPO, 1957.
40. ——. *The Budget of the United States Government, Fiscal Year 1963*. GPO, 1962.
41. ——. Office of Emergency Planning. Unpublished documents.
42. Farm Credit Administration. *The Fifteenth Annual Report of the Farm Credit Administration, 1947–1948*. GPO, December 31, 1948.
43. ——. *The Fourteenth Annual Report of the Farm Credit Administration, 1946–1947*. GPO, November 17, 1947.
44. ——. *The Thirtieth Annual Report of the Farm Credit Administration, 1962–1963*. GPO, November 27, 1963.
45. [Jack] Faucett Associates, Inc. "Input-Output Transactions by Transportation. Mode, 1947 and 1958." Prepared for the Office of Transportation, U.S. Department of Transportation, April 1968.

46. [Jack] Faucett Associates, Inc. "1963 Manufacturing Industry Shipments Estimates for Counties, SMSA's, and States." Prepared for the Office of Civil Defense, U.S. Department of Defense, August 1968.

47. ——. "1963 Output Measures for Input-Output Sectors by Standard Metropolitan Statistical Areas and Non-Metropolitan State Areas." Prepared for the Institute for Defense Analyses, January 1967.

48. ——. "Unpublished Estimates of 1963 Mineral Production Prepared by Jack Faucett Associates, Inc." Prepared for the Bureau of Mines, U.S. Department of the Interior, October 1967.

49. Federal Communications Commission. *AM-FM Broadcast Financial Data, 1963*. Washington, D.C., October 9, 1964.

50. ——. *Broadcast Financial Data for Networks and AM, FM, and TV Stations, 1948*. Washington, D.C., 1950.

51. ——. *Final AM-FM Broadcast Financial Data, 1958*. Washington, D.C., September 23, 1957.

52. ——. *Final AM-FM Broadcast Financial Data, 1961*. Washington, D.C., December 6, 1962.

53. ——. *Final TV Broadcast Financial Data, 1958*. Washington, D.C., 1959.

54. ——. *Final TV Broadcast Financial Data, 1961*. Washington, D.C., August 14, 1962.

55. ——. *Financial and Operating Data Relative to Standard Broadcast Stations and Networks, 1947*. Washington, D.C., 1949.

56. ——. *Statistics of Communications Common Carriers for the Year Ended December 31, 1963*. GPO, 1965.

57. ——. *Statistics of Communications Common Carriers, Year Ended December 31, 1958*. GPO, 1960.

58. ——. *Statistics of the Communications Industry in the United States, Year Ended December 31, 1947*. GPO, 1949.

59. ——. *TV Broadcast Financial Data, 1963*. Washington, D.C., July 23, 1964.

60. Federal Deposit Insurance Corporation. *Annual Report of the Federal Deposit Insurance Corporation, 1947*. Washington, D.C., 1948.

61. ——. *Annual Report of the Federal Deposit Insurance Corporation, 1958*. Washington, D.C., 1959.

62. ——. *Annual Report of the Federal Deposit Insurance Corporation, 1963*. Washington, D.C., 1964.

63. Federal Home Loan Bank Board. *Combined Financial Statements, 1947*. Washington, D.C., October 1948.

64. ——. *Combined Financial Statements, 1958*. Washington, D.C., October 1959.

65. ——. *Combined Financial Statements, 1963*. Washington, D.C., February 1965.

66. ——. *Federal Home Loan Bank Board Annual Report, 1947*. Washington, D.C., March 1948.

67. ——. *Federal Home Loan Bank Board Annual Report, 1948*. Washington, D.C., March 1949.

68. ——. *Federal Home Loan Bank Board Annual Report, 1958*. Washington, D.C., June 1, 1959.

69. Federal National Mortgage Association. "1963 Employment-Regional

Offices of the Federal National Mortgage Association." Unpublished.
70. Federal Power Commission. *Electric Power Statistics.* Issued monthly.
71. ——. "Form #4." Unpublished returns of questionnaires, 1947 and 1958.
72. ——. *Statistics of Electric Utilities in the U.S., 1947.* GPO, 1949.
73. ——. *Statistics of Electric Utilities in the U.S., 1958.* GPO, 1960.
74. ——. *Statistics of Electric Utilities in the U.S., 1963.* GPO, 1965.
75. General Services Administration. "Contracts Awarded in 1958." Special tabulation.
76. ——. "General Services Administration Construction Contracts Awarded." Unpublished.
77. Harvard Economic Research Project. "A Multiregional Input-Output Model for the United States." Report No. 21. Prepared for the Economic Development Administration, U.S. Department of Commerce, December 1970.
78. ——. "1947 to 1958 SIC Code Concordance." Unpublished computer tabulation.
79. ——. "Preliminary Report on Price Index Research 1947–1958." Unpublished.
80. Health Insurance Institute. *Source Book of Health Insurance Data, 1959.* New York, 1959.
81. ——. *Source Book of Health Insurance Data, 1965.* New York, 1965.
82. Housing and Home Finance Agency [now HUD]. *First Annual Report of the Housing and Home Finance Agency, 1947.* GPO, 1948.
83. ——. *Twelfth Annual Report, Housing and Home Finance Agency, 1958.* GPO, 1959.
84. Hultgren, Thomas. *Cost, Prices, and Profits: Their Cyclical Relations.* New York: National Bureau of Economic Research, 1965, pp. 44–46.
85. Illinois State Geological Survey. *Illinois 1963 Mineral Production by Counties.* State of Illinois, Department of Registration and Education, February 1965.
86. International Oil Scout Association. *International Oil and Gas Development.* Austin, Texas, 1963.
—— Jack Faucett Associates, Inc.: See entries 45 through 48.
87. McGraw-Hill, Inc. *McGraw-Hill Directory of Electric Utilities, 1964.* New York: McGraw-Hill, Inc., 1964.
88. National Aeronautics and Space Administration. "Disbursements for Construction of Facilities by Site Location." Unpublished.
89. Ojibway Press, Inc. *Brown's Directory of North American Gas Companies.* Duluth, Minnesota, 1963.
90. Panama Canal Company. Canal Zone Government. *Annual Report for the Fiscal Year 1948.* Balboa Heights, Canal Zone, 1949.
91. ——. ——. *Annual Report, Fiscal Year Ended June 30, 1959.* Balboa Heights, Canal Zone, 1960.
92. Polenske, Karen R. et al. *State Estimates of the Gross National Product, 1947, 1958, 1963.* Lexington, Mass.: Lexington Books, D.C. Heath and Company, 1972.

93. Railroad Commission of Texas. *Annual Report of the Oil and Gas Division.*
1963.

94. State of Louisiana. Department of Conservation. *Annual Oil and Gas Report.*
1963.

95. Stoddard, Charles H. *The Small Private Forest in the United States.*
Washington, D.C.: Resources for the Future, Inc., 1961.

96. Tennessee Valley Authority. "Estimated Construction Expenditures."
Unpublished.

97. Transportation Association of America. *Transportation Facts and Trends.*
Washington, D.C., 1965.

98. U.S. Atomic Energy Commission. *1963 Financial Report of the Atomic
Energy Commission.* GPO, 1963.

99. U.S. Bureau of the Census. *Census of Agriculture, 1954.* GPO, 1956.

100. ——. *Census of Agriculture, 1959.* GPO, 1962.

101. ——. *Census of Agriculture, 1964.* GPO, 1967.

102. ——. *Census of Business, 1948.* Vols. I, II, and III, *Retail Trade.* GPO, 1952.

103. ——. *Census of Business, 1958.* Vols. I, II, and III, *Retail Trade.* GPO, 1961.

104. ——. *Census of Business, 1963.* Vols. II and III, *Retail Trade.* GPO, 1965.

105. ——. *Census of Business, 1963.* Vol. I, *Retail Trade – Merchandise Line
Sales.* GPO, 1965.

106. ——. *Census of Business, 1958.* Vols. V and VI, *Selected Services.* GPO,
1961.

107. ——. *Census of Business, 1963.* Vols. VI and VII, *Selected Services.* GPO,
1965.

108. ——. *Census of Business, 1948.* Vols. V and VII, *Service Trade.* GPO,
1952.

109. ——. *Census of Business, 1948.* Vols. IV and V, *Wholesale Trade.* GPO,
1952.

110. ——. *Census of Business, 1958.* Vol. IV, *Wholesale Trade – Area Statistics.*
GPO, 1961.

111. ——. *Census of Business, 1963.* Vols. IV and V, *Wholesale Trade.* GPO,
1965.

112. ——. *Census of Business, 1958.* Vol. III, *Wholesale Trade – Public Warehousing.* GPO, 1961.

113. ——. *Census of Governments, 1962.* GPO, 1963.

114. ——. *Census of Governments, 1957.* Vol. III, No. 5, *Compendium of
Government Finances.* GPO, 1959.

115. ——. *Census of Governments, 1962.* Vol. IV, No. 4, *Compendium of
Government Finances.* GPO, 1963.

116. ——. *Census of Governments, 1957.* Vol. II, *Governmental Employment.*
GPO, 1959.

117. ——. *Census of Governments, 1962.* Vol. III, *Governmental Finances.*
GPO, 1963.

118. ——. *Census of Governments, 1957.* Vol. V, *Taxable Property Values in
the United States.* GPO, 1959.

119. ——. *Census of Housing, 1950.* GPO, 1953.

120. U.S. Bureau of the Census. *Census of Housing, 1960.* GPO, 1960.
121. ——. *Census of Manufactures, 1947.* GPO, 1950.
122. ——. *Census of Manufactures, 1947.* Vol. III, *Statistics by Industry – Motion Pictures.* GPO, 1950. Special report.
123. ——. *Census of Manufactures, 1958.* GPO, 1961.
124. ——. *Census of Manufactures, 1963.* GPO, 1966.
125. ——. *1963 Census of Manufactures: Preliminary Reports.* GPO.
126. ——. *Census of Mineral Industries, 1954.* GPO, 1958.
127. ——. *Census of Mineral Industries, 1958.* GPO, 1961.
128. ——. *Census of Mineral Industries, 1963.* GPO, 1967.
129. ——. *Census of Population, 1950.* GPO, 1952.
130. ——. *Census of Population, 1960.* GPO, 1962.
131. ——. *Compendium of City Government Finances, 1947.* GPO, 1949.
132. ——. *Compendium of City Government Finances, 1948.* GPO, 1950.
133. ——. *Compendium of City Government Finances, 1958.* GPO, 1959.
134. ——. *Compendium of City Government Finances, 1963.* GPO, 1964.
135. ——. *Compendium of State Government Finances, 1947.* GPO, 1949.
136. ——. *Compendium of State Government Finances, 1948.* GPO, 1950.
137. ——. *Compendium of State Government Finances, 1958.* GPO, 1959.
138. ——. *Compendium of State Government Finances, 1963.* GPO, 1964.
139. ——. *Construction Reports: Value of New Construction Put in Place, 1946–1963.* GPO, 1964.
140. ——. *County Business Patterns, 1959.* GPO, 1961.
141. ——. *County Business Patterns, 1964.* GPO, 1965.
142. ——. *County and City Data Book, 1956.* GPO, 1957.
143. ——. *County and City Data Book, 1962.* GPO, 1962.
144. ——. *Enterprise Statistics, 1963.* GPO, 1968.
145. ——. *Governmental Finances in 1958.* GPO, 1959.
146. ——. *Governmental Finances in 1959.* GPO, 1960.
147. ——. "Housing Authorized in Permit-Issuing Places." *Construction Reports – Building Permits, 1964.* GPO, 1964.
148. ——. *Location of Manufacturing Plants, 1958.* GPO, 1961.
149. ——. *Location of Manufacturing Plants, 1963.* GPO, 1966.
150. ——. *Measures of Value Produced in and by Merchant Wholesaling Firms, 1963.* GPO, 1965.
151. ——. *Statistical Abstract of the United States, 1965.* GPO, 1965.
152. ——. "Valuation of Nonresident Building Permits, 1963." Unpublished tabulations.
153. ——. "Value of Manufacturing Industry Shipments: 1947, 1958, and 1963." Unpublished tabulations.
154. U.S. Department of Agriculture. *Agricultural Industrial Relations Study, 1955.* January, 1959.
155. ——. Statistical Reporting Service and Reporting Board. *Agricultural Prices – 1963 Annual Summary.* June 1964.
156. ——. *Agricultural Statistics, 1948.* GPO, 1948.
157. ——. *Agricultural Statistics, 1959.* GPO, 1959.
158. ——. *Agricultural Statistics, 1963.* GPO, 1963.

159. U.S. Department of Agriculture. *Agricultural Statistics, 1966*. GPO, 1966.
160. ——. "Charges for Ginning Cotton, Costs of Selected Services Incident to Marketing and Related Information, Season 1958–1959." GPO, May 1959.
161. ——. *Christmas Trees*. Agricultural Information Bulletin No. 94. GPO, 1957.
162. ——. Forest Service. *The Demand and Price Situation of Forest Products, 1963*. GPO, 1964.
163. ——. *The Economic Importance of Timber in the U.S*. GPO, July 1963.
164. ——. Economic Research Service. *The Farm Income Situation*. FIS 199, July 1965.
165. ——. *Farm Income State Estimates, 1949–1964*. FIS 199 Supplement, August 1965.
166. ——. *Farm Production and Efficiency, 1966*. Statistical Bulletin No. 233, June 1966.
167. ——. *Meat Animals – Farm Production Disposition and Income by States, 1955–1959*. Revised estimates. Statistical Bulletin No. 284, May 1961.
168. ——. Forest Service. *The Outlook for Naval Stores*. November 1962.
169. ——. *Rural Electrification Administration – 1964 Annual Statistical Report*. GPO, 1965.
170. ——. *Timber Resources for America's Future*. Forest Resources Report No. 14, January 1958.
171. ——. *Timber Trends in the U.S*. Forest Resources Report No. 17. GPO, 1965.
172. U.S. Department of the Army. Corps of Engineers. *Annual Report, Chief of Engineers, U.S. Army Civil Works Activities, 1965*. Washington, D.C., 1965.
173. ——. ——. "Civil Works Expenditures by State and Fiscal Year, 1958 and 1959." Unpublished tabulations.
174. U.S. Department of Commerce. *Business Establishments, Employment, and Taxable Payrolls, First Quarter, 1947*. GPO, December 1948.
175. ——. *Construction Statistics, 1915–1964*. GPO, 1966.
176. ——. *Highway Statistics – Summary to 1965*. GPO, 1967.
177. ——. "Maintenance and Repairs Expenditures Exceed $20 Billion." *Construction Review*. GPO, July 1965.
178. ——. "State Distribution of Construction Activity, 1939–1947." *Construction and Construction Materials*. Supplement. GPO, June 1948.
179. ——. Bureau of Public Roads. "State Highway Department Expenditures Within Counties Comprising Standard Metropolitan Statistical Areas." Unpublished.
180. ——. Office of Business Economics. "Gross Product Originating Deflators." Unpublished tabulations.
181. ——. ——. *Growth Patterns in Employment by County, 1905–1960*. GPO, 1965.
182. ——. ——. *Growth Patterns in Employment by County, 1940–1950*. GPO, 1965.
183. ——. ——. "Industry Description Appendix to Input-Output Study, 1958." Unpublished, November 1964.

184. U.S. Department of Commerce. Office of Business Economics. "Input-
     Output Structure of the U.S. Economy: 1963." *Survey of Current
     Business* 49 (November 1969): 16–47.
185. —. —. "Military Employment – Non-Civilian." Unpublished.
186. —. —. *National Income, 1954 Edition*. GPO, 1954.
187. —. —. *The National Income and Product Accounts of the U.S., 1929–
     1965: Statistical Tables*. GPO, 1966.
188. —. —. "Personal Consumption Expenditures by Type of Product."
     Survey of Current Business 45 (November 1965): 20–23.
189. —. —. "Personal Income by States, 1963." *Survey of Current Business*
     44 (April 1964): 12–32.
190. —. —. *Personal Income by States Since 1929*. GPO, 1956.
191. —. —. "Regional Markets in 1958." *Survey of Current Business* 39
     (August 1959): 9–24.
192. —. —. "State and Local Government Receipts and Expenditures:
     Annually 1929–1964." *Survey of Current Business* 45 (August 1965): 38–
     39.
193. —. —. *Survey of Current Business* 31 (July 1951).
194. —. —. "The Transactions Table of the 1958 Input-Output Study and
     Revised Direct and Total Requirements Data." *Survey of Current Business*
     45 (September 1965): 33–49.
195. —. —. "Wages and Salaries, Private Households, 1948–1958–1963."
     Computer printout.
196. —. —. Regional Economics Division. Unpublished data.
197. U.S. Department of Defense. "Funds Appropriated by the Congress for
     Military Construction, Fiscal 1962." Unpublished.
198. U.S. Department of Health, Education, and Welfare. *Bi-Annual Survey of
     Education in the U.S.* Chapters II and IV. GPO, 1950.
199. —. *Digest of Educational Statistics*. Bulletin No. 4. GPO, 1965.
200. —. *Financial Statistics of Instructions of Higher Education, 1959–1960*.
     GPO, 1964.
201. —. *1963 Report of Operations: Federal Credit Unions*. FCU561. GPO,
     1963.
202. —. *Projections of Educational Statistics to 1974–1975*. GPO, 1965.
203. —. *Statistics of State School Systems, 1965–1966*. GPO, 1968.
204. U.S. Department of the Interior. *Annual Report of the Secretary of the
     Interior for the Fiscal Year Ending June 30, 1948*. GPO, 1949.
205. —. *Annual Report of the Secretary of the Interior for the Fiscal Year
     Ending June 30, 1958*. GPO, 1959.
206. —. *Annual Report of the Secretary of the Interior for the Fiscal Year
     Ending June 30, 1959*. GPO, 1960.
207. —. *Annual Report of the Secretary of the Interior for the Fiscal Year
     Ending June 30, 1963*. GPO, 1964.
208. —. "Construction Schedule and Progress." Unpublished.
209. —. "Estimated Distribution of Annual Appropriations and Allotments to
     States, 1963–1968." Communication.
210. —. *Fishery Statistics of the United States, 1947*. GPO, 1950.

211. U.S. Department of the Interior. *Fishery Statistics of the United States, 1958.* GPO, 1960.

212. ——. *Fishery Statistics of the United States, 1965.* GPO, 1967.

213. ——. *The Interindustry Structure of the U.S. Mining Industries, 1958.* GPO, 1967.

214. ——. *1947 Minerals Yearbook.* GPO, 1948.

215. ——. *1963 Minerals Yearbook.* GPO, 1964.

216. U.S. Department of Labor. Bureau of Labor Statistics. *Employment and Earnings Statistics for States and Areas, 1939–1965.* Bulletin No. 1370-3. GPO, June 1966.

217. ——. ——. *Industry Classification Manual for the 1947 Interindustry Relations Study.* Revised, March 20, 1953.

218. ——. ——. *1947 Interindustry Relations Study.* December 1951.

219. ——. ——. "Notes for the 1947 Interindustry Relations Study." Unpublished.

220. ——. U.S. Department of Commerce. *Construction Volume and Costs, 1915–1964.* Supplement to *Construction Review.* GPO, January 1966.

221. U.S. Independent Telephone Association. *1959 Annual Statistical Volume 2 of the United States Independent Telephone Association, Statistical Reports of Class A, B, C, and D Independent Telephone Companies for the Year 1958.* Washington, D.C., 1959.

222. ——. *Annual Statistical Volume 2 of the United States Independent Telephone Association – Statistical Reports of Class A, B, C, and D Telephone Companies for the Year 1963.* Washington, D.C., July 1964.

223. ——. *Annual Statistical Volume 1 for the Year 1963.* Washington, D.C., 1964.

224. ——. *Statistics of Class A, B, and C Independent Telephone Companies, Year Ended December 31, 1948.* Washington, D.C., 1949.

225. U.S. Securities and Exchange Commission. *Private Uninsured Pension Plans.* GPO, 1964.

226. U.S. Treasury Department. Internal Revenue Service. *Statistics of Income, 1947.* Part 2, *Compiled from Corporation Income Tax Returns and Personal Holding Company Returns.* GPO, 1952.

227. ——. ——. *Statistics of Income, 1948.* Part 2, *Compiled from Corporation Income Tax Returns and Personal Holding Company Returns.* GPO, 1953.

228. ——. ——. *Statistics of Income, U.S. Business Tax Returns, 1957–1958.* GPO, 1960.

229. ——. ——. *Statistics of Income, U.S. Business Tax Returns, 1958–1959.* GPO, 1961.

230. ——. ——. *Statistics of Income, U.S. Business Tax Returns, 1961–1962.* GPO, 1964.

231. ——. ——. *Statistics of Income, U.S. Corporation Income Tax Returns, 1957–1958.* GPO, 1960.

232. ——. ——. *Statistics of Income, U.S. Corporation Income Tax Returns, 1958–1959.* GPO, 1961.

233. ——. ——. *Statistics of Income, U.S. Corporation Income Tax Returns, 1961–1962.* GPO, 1964.

234. ——. ——. *Statistics of Income, U.S. Individual Income Tax Returns, 1963.* GPO, 1966.

235. Veterans Administration. "Direct Loan Program, December 31, 1957."
     Unpublished.
236. ——. "Direct Loan Program, December 31,1958." Unpublished.
237. ——. "Selected VA Home Loan Activity." Unpublished.

About the Author

John M. Rodgers is an economist at Jack Faucett Associates, Inc., a private research company. He was awarded the degree of Bachelor of Science in Economics by the Wharton School, University of Pennsylvania, in 1962. During 1962 and 1963, Mr. Rodgers was employed as a market research analyst by the Black and Decker Manufacturing Company. Returning to the academic community in the closing months of 1963, he pursued graduate studies at Vanderbilt University until 1966. At that time, he joined the staff of Jack Faucett Associates. Mr. Rodgers has been associated, in either a supervisory or an advisory capacity, with several projects undertaken by his company in connection with the implementation of a multiregional input-output model by the Harvard Economic Research Project. In addition, Mr. Rodgers has conducted studies dealing with transportation, micro-economics, national economic impacts, and market research. He belongs to the American Economic Association and is a member of the panel of arbitrators, American Arbitration Association.